❖   THE SOCIOLOGY OF RELIGION

The Sociology of Religion

CLASSICAL AND CONTEMPORARY APPROACHES

Barbara Hargrove

Yale Divinity School

AHM Publishing Corporation

ARLINGTON HEIGHTS, ILLINOIS 60004

ISBN 0-88295-211-0, paper

Library of Congress Card Number:
79-50879

PRINTED IN THE UNITED STATES OF AMERICA
880
Second Printing

Contents

A Note to Instructors

This volume represents a considerable revision of my earlier text, *The Reformation of the Holy.* I hope it also reflects the changes in the field and in my knowledge of it that have occurred in the eight years since that book was written.

However, there are enough similarities to prompt me to issue a caveat based on the experience of colleagues with the last volume. People who teach the sociology of religion are a varied lot and have the habit of gathering up a number of books to be read by their classes that reflect their own particular emphasis in the field. If you have in mind adding this book to such a list to be read in one short portion of your course, my advice is, don't do it!

This book is more of a survey, to be sampled a little at a time, along with other sources which can bring out your focus in each of its sections. So parcel it out, use it in pieces, and read other things with it. For this purpose I have included at the end of each section a short list of those books I have found helpful to use in conjunction with this one in my courses. If they are useful to you, fine; if not, you will have others you favor that will make your course your own.

Incidentally, each of the four parts of this book stands pretty well by itself. I, of course, think they go together well the way they are placed, but you could probably put them in a different order or even omit a part or two without sowing confusion.

Finally, I would like to put it on the record that I make no claim to have covered all the significant theory and research in the sociology of religion. This book is intended as an introduction to the field, to stimulate thought and discussion. If it does that, the student can then move out into a field that is constantly developing new concepts and reaching new findings. I could not ask for more. Could you?

Acknowledgments

There is no way to thank all the people who have contributed to the writing of a book like this. Based as it is on my earlier work, *The Reformation of the Holy,* thanks must go to all who helped with that effort. The changes evident in *The Sociology of Religion* are only partly the result of changes in the society and its religious institutions. They mirror advances in the field of the sociology of religion made by many colleagues, to whom we are all indebted for new insights and greater sophistication in our work. They also are the result of my own growth in understanding of the field, and I owe that to many colleagues, particularly fellow members of the Religious Research Association, the Society for the Scientific Study of Religion, and the Association for the Sociology of Religion; members of the Religious Conscious team headed by Charles Glock and Robert Bellah; and my colleagues at Yale Divinity School. I have learned more from my students over the past decade than I could ever measure, and that is reflected here also.

I would particularly like to thank Jim Richardson for his editorial advice and Bee Hall for her critical and supportive reading of the manuscript. The response and suggestions of those who have used my earlier work have been invaluable.

So with gratitude I dedicate this book not to any particular individual, but to all those whose ideas it shares and all those who hope to use it to share some understanding of the field of the sociology of religion.

New Haven, Connecticut
January 1979

Part I

THE NATURE AND FUNCTION OF RELIGION

A few years ago the sociology of religion seemed a dying subject. It was taught mainly in those schools whose student bodies were expected to have a prior commitment to the religious institution, and it tended to be thought of only as a useful tool for church people who needed to know how to keep programs going in the face of the mounting secularism of the society. Sociologists have long felt most comfortable defining religion in terms of its functions. As they saw one function of religion after another being taken over by other social institutions, they assumed that it was only a question of time until religion per se would no longer be a vital part of modern society. They looked to other fields in which to concentrate their study, and they left the observation of the social organization of religion to the anthropologists, who after all were interested in primitive tribes where it still mattered. Individual religiosity was left to the psychologists who studied those who deviated from normal patterns of behavior.

But somewhere in the mid-sixties some strange phenomena began to appear. Within the churches a position of radical secularity was espoused, and theologians seemed to confirm the expectation that religion was on its way out by proclaiming the death of God. Yet instead of holding a proper funeral for the deity and closing down their churches they began to discuss "religionless Christianity" and to push for a greater voice for the church in the decision-making processes of the society. By itself, this phenomenon could be taken as proof of increasing secularization. The religious institutions were themselves abandoning religion for politics; how secular can you get?

However, two more movements must be noted along with these occurrences in the churches. The first is the tremendous gain in the membership and activities of more traditional religious bodies which offered the "old-time" gospel and a high degree of ritual participation.

1

The average sociologist might have shrugged this off as a predictable reaction of the blue-collar masses to their leaders' proclamations on the nature of change. But one who investigated would likely be shaken by the number of white-collar people in these congregations, and by the fervor with which a graduate engineer or physicist might be joining in the singing of the "good old gospel songs." Was this a small minority, or were there things about religion we had been ignoring when we made our predictions?

Even more startling were the trends and fads that began to appear in the movement that came to be labeled the "youth culture." Here, among the most privileged, most highly educated, and presumably most intelligent of the rising generation, could be found all sorts of mystical, cultic practices, ranging from witchcraft and astrology to the disciplined abstractions of Zen Buddhism and Yoga. While many of these proved to be passing fads, many others have shown a remarkable tenacity and seriousness. And even the fads posed the question: Why should this sort of activity have appeal for secular youth?

As these phenomena grew and changed and took on a life of their own, they raised other questions concerning their meaning and importance and their relation to more traditional religious forms. Sociology of religion, having fallen by the wayside in the academic pursuit of "relevance," was pulled back into respectability if not prominence by that same current. Then, just as sociologists began to get some grip on the "new religiosity" by viewing it as primarily a youth movement that might be only a temporary pause in processes of secularization, the world was stunned by the news from Jonestown, Guyana, of one religious congregation, composed of all ages, that had taken its commitment seriously enough to murder intruders and then commit mass suicide. Easy assumptions about the fading influence of religion in the face of overwhelming trends toward secularization were jolted by a demonstration of the raw power of religion over urban people who were not all poor or uneducated. Even more compelling questions were presented to sociological theory.

Since religion has so stubbornly refused to die, we find the need to check the methods of study that led us to predict its demise. Shaken into some amount of humility, we go back to the beginning, to see if we have even correctly defined this object of our study, this phenomenon known as "religion."

1

A Definition of Religion

The title of Part I may seem unduly ambitious; it is obvious that anyone undertaking a study of the *sociology* of religion will not be dealing with the full scope of what religion is and has been to people through the ages. And yet to speak of a "sociological definition of religion" is also to give a somewhat false impression, if not to fall into the kind of errors noted in the introduction. True, sociologists have their own particular focus: They are concerned with empirical data—that which can be verified by the senses; they are concerned with behavior, and particularly with socially structured or group behavior; they, as all scientists, attempt to categorize and generalize what they observe. But some of the most miserable failures in the attempt to understand sociologically that phenomenon we call "religion" have occurred through the literal and narrow application of those principles. To limit the study of the sociology of religion to the observation of behavior of organized groups labeled as religious and generalized into categories of faith, denomination, geographical area, or social class is to deal with so small a segment of the meaning of religion in human life as to be almost useless.

Human beings have their peculiarities, and among them is the ability to symbolize. We can never take for granted that the meaning of any human behavior is to its author what it seems to be to the observer. Because behavior, and perhaps most particularly religious behavior, is likely to have symbolic content, two very dissimilar actions may be classified by their originators as almost the same thing, or two similar actions as meaning nearly opposite things. For this reason the sociologist of religion is unable to create the categories or make the generalizations necessary to the discipline without at least rudimentary knowledge of the meaning systems behind the behavior of the persons observed. Hence one must become involved to some extent in the study of philosophy, theology, and mythology.

Talcott Parsons provides a framework for understanding other inter-disciplinary demands on the sociologist of religion when he speaks of religion's involvement in at least three of the four general systems that constitute human life. These four systems are the physiological system of the organism, the personality system of the individual, the social system of the group, and the system of culture. Religion, says Parsons, is the point of articulation between the cultural system and the social system, where values from the former are embodied in the latter.[1] It also is clear that religion is one of the vehicles through which those cultural values embodied in the society are internalized in the personality system. Taking these factors into account, it becomes obvious that the sociologist of religion must have contact with the disciplines of an-thropology and psychology.

Religion also involves traditions of the groups adhering to it. As a consequence, an appreciation of history is helpful to any student of religion. In addition, we find that the relationship between sacred myth and objective history is a close one.

Thus, when we attempt a sociological definition of religion, we can-not stay within the narrow confines of empirical observation of explicit group behavior. To understand the peculiarly sociological focus it may be helpful to visualize religion as a mountain at whose base are many observers who stand ranged about it in such a way that none sees exactly the same configurations. The sociologist must look at the whole mountain, as must the anthropologist or the psychologist or the theolo-gian. But the configuration that is described is dependent upon the angle of vision provided by the point of observation.

How, then, does one define religion when viewed from a sociological angle? We cannot beg the question. Whether stated or implicit, the definition we give to any phenomenon structures the questions we ask, the behavior we observe, and the type of analyses we make. We can ease pressures upon us in one way and not pretend that ours is an absolute definition; it is operational. What we are searching for is a definition of the concept that is adequate for the scope of this particular study, not for all time and all occasions, even within the discipline. It must, how-ever, be broadly based to encompass more than any one religion, regard-less of the universality that religion may claim for itself.

There are several methods of coming to a definition. The scientific approach dictates that we consider only those methods that begin induc-tively—that is, those that seek to define religion on the basis of that which can actually be found empirically, rather than developing an ideal of what religion should be and then looking for evidence of it. This inductive method seeks to distill from all behavior that has been called religious those factors that seem to form an irreducible core to which people generally apply the adjective "religious." Two general ways of going about this appear common: an historical or developmental approach and one that seeks elements of function and structure through comparative analysis.

The historical approach seeks to find this common core of characteristics by pursuing religion back to its sources, hoping to find there a pristine state free of the complicated excess baggage of tradition and elaboration. This approach may also be divided into two sections, one based on personal histories and one on the development of human cultures.

The approach based on personal histories is an attempt to go back to early stages in individual development to find sources and trace the development of religious behavior. The beginning is found in the peculiarly human condition of freedom of behavioral choice. If instincts are defined as genetically determined, complicated patterns of behavior, we are distinguished from other animals by our lack of instincts. Aside from the involuntary functions of internal organs and a few basic reflexes, our behavior is characterized by a potential malleability shaped by a culture that has itself been shaped by those who went before us. The survival value of such flexibility is enormous, but so is its destructive capability The infant is helpless. Unguided by instinct, the child must learn to control his or her body, to channel emotions and actions. This very helplessness has created the necessity for social order if the species is to survive. Children must be cared for, nourished, and taught behavior appropriate to their survival in the physical and social setting. Yet each new experience is the occasion for more choice, bringing with it the possibility of immobilizing indecision. Each of us lives, to this extent, on the verge of chaos. Guiding the behavior of the child, then, involves not only specific instruction for the immediate situation, but also guidance in the development of generalizations, in finding categories of situations to which the same behavior may be applied. This process of generalization, of abstraction, of patterning occurs throughout the human life span and becomes part of the culture that is shared as well as part of the continuing development of the individual. The patterns that are shared are those that have been worked out in the experience of the particular society. They provide the framework within which one comes to understand oneself as a person as well as one's relationship with the environment. These patterns hold back the chaos of unlimited choice by providing a setting in which meaning can be found and consequences of acts predicted. In other words, a person lives largely in a world of his or her own fabrication, maintained by continuing dialogue with those who share that world.[2]

Our ability to generalize does not end with the imposition of patterns upon the potential chaos of everyday existence. Generalization is by nature capable of infinite extension. If we can create patterns in our day-to-day existence, we can also conceive of larger frameworks within which individual histories have meaning for the whole of human life and that life has meaning for the universe. The search for meaning extends to infinity. As a result, we generally live in three worlds at once: the world of nature, which is always present and must be considered in any action; the everyday world made of the pattern in which we have come to understand our existence; and an ideal world created by our extension of that pattern beyond everyday reality.[3] Much of what we have called religion has been involved with the effort to keep these three worlds in meaningful relationship to one another.

Whether or not all efforts in this vein should be called religious is another problem. Glock and Stark, for example, discuss the human quest for meaning in terms of "value orientations," which are placed in two categories, the humanistic and the religious. They treat as religious only those value orientations that have a supernatural referent.[4] Yinger, in contrast, considers the possibility that an adequate definition of religion may have to include opportunity for forms in which a supernatural world view may or may not be necessary and in which religion may deal either with ultimate or immediate utilitarian concerns.[5]

Sources of religion in personal histories also may be traced to those areas of experience where the known patterns may not fit as well as could be expected. Not everything in human culture can be perceived by the individual as immediately and personally beneficial. In fact, society is maintained to some extent by the repression of personal desires and traits. Freud says that religion develops from the need to exorcise the terrors of nature, particularly the cruelty of death, and also to make amends for the deprivations that the culture imposes upon the individual.[6] Fromm goes even further, saying that religion functions to provide consolation for all the privations that life exacts, plus encouragement of persons to accept their station in life, either by providing emotional support for those in an inferior position or relief from guilt for those who impose that position upon them.[7] DeGrazia finds the sources of religion in the experience of the child, who, having felt the omnipotence of paternal figures in early years, projects the need for such powerful figures first to political rulers and finally to gods as the nearer figures prove fallible.[8]

Religion frequently attempts to account for those factors in human experience that fail to fit the frameworks provided by the belief systems of the culture. Much religious belief and practice involves dealing with the unknown or uncontrollable aspects of life. What cannot be explained or predicted may be dealt with religiously in order to provide psychological stability. In fact, many functional definitions of religion find this their focus, saying that religion applies to those areas of existence that have not yet been understood in or controlled by the culture. A natural corollary of this type of definition is that as the scope of scientific knowledge and control advances, that of religion is bound to decrease. While this may be a simplistic understanding of the nature of religion, much of it has involved dealings with forces beyond human control and with the attempt to explain phenomena that do not fit cultural generalizations. The experience of any individual transcends, at least in a few details, his or her ability to explain and control it, culminating for all in that most inexplicable and uncontrollable of human experiences, death. If we live on the verge of chaos through our ability to choose, we are also faced with the ultimate chaos of losing our ability to organize existence. This is one of the continuing sources of religion in human experience.

However, seeing the way in which religion functions in individual life can never be sufficient for the sociologist, even though it must never be forgotten. We know that religious practices and religious organizations have throughout human history exercised important influences in society at large. Thus, in addition to searching through individual life histories for the sources of religion, there has also been an effort to trace these sources back through history to their origins in the antiquity of human culture. Unfortunately, the evidence of beliefs and rites is not easily preserved, and the search tapers off into the silence of preliterate times. Efforts that have been made in this direction tend to have been undertaken at a time when it was assumed that modern primitives were models of early stages of human development. By far the most famous of these efforts was that of Emile Durkheim, who sought the origins of all religion in the primitive totemism of the Australian aborigines. He found that the object of worship in this primitive religion was symbolic of the society itself. His final definition of religion was "a unified system of beliefs and practices relative to sacred things, that is to say, things set apart and forbidden—beliefs and practices which unite into one single moral community called a Church, all those who adhere to them."[9] Since later anthropology has cast great doubt on the premise that primitive tribes in the modern world are living the same lives and making the same assumptions as our primitive ancestors,[10] we must treat Durkheim's conclusions with caution, but with consideration. What is the relationship between society and religion? If it is true that in undifferentiated primitive societies it constitutes, at least indirectly, the worship of the society itself, is this equally true in differentiated modern societies which contain separate institutions of church and state, family and school? One factor his work does point up is that in nearly all cases religion involves some kind of *community*—some group of people who share the activities and anticipations of the religion, even if they may not practice it together with any amount of frequency or regularity.

One of the important facets of Durkheim's definition comes in his description of the church as a moral community. Our exploration of the way religion works in individual life has shown how it can organize a person's experience into some kind of order which has ultimate meaning. Insofar as that is true, religious institutions may provide particularly strong sanctions for or against any type of social behavior that is deemed relevant to the religious world view. If behavior enhances or diminishes one's relationship to the ultimate meaning of existence, people are likely to accept moral and ethical guidance from an institution that defines that meaning, even when its message is applied not only to individuals but also to other institutions or to the society at large.

Those structures of meaning and the moral strictures they involve are not the same in all cultures. To derive a comprehensive definition many social scientists turn to a *comparative* method. This practice is most common to anthropologists, but it also attracts sociologists, psychologists, and others. It seeks the basic ingredients of religion in those overlapping areas that exist within the great variety of human religions. These areas may be treated in two ways, as areas of *function* or areas of *structure.*

Many sociologists of religion say that the only way we can avoid the ethnocentrism of our own religious view is to concentrate on a functional definition of religion. As we define the economic institution of any society by finding what functions to facilitate the distribution of shared goods and services, or the political institution in terms of the use of power, we should be able to define religion by functions it performs in all societies.[11] Of all the consequences of religion in human life, which ones are found in all societies? We might define religion as that which accomplishes those functions.

Most generally recognized is the integrative function, whether applied to the individual or to the society as a whole. We have already seen how this applies to the integration of meaning at the cultural level. We have also hinted at what form this integration takes at the societal and personality levels. If religion provides a unified system of meaning, it also provides the rationale for the structure of the society and the individual's place in it. It allows for the integration of the personality by organizing the chaos of existence and choice. These statements seem to hold up in cross-cultural comparisons. Though systems of meaning vary greatly, they all seem to have this relationship to the society and to the life of the individual in that society.

Religious practice is also integrative because in most cases it brings people together in ritual reenactment of their shared understanding of the structure of their world. One benefit from a comparative study of the world's religions is an understanding that religion is not concerned simply with ideas; it is basically a system of action.[12] Religion is more than a belief; it is a practice. It functions to integrate society in the shared behavior it involves, as well as the meanings that behavior symbolizes.

Further functions often include the reinforcement of social moral codes, either directly by positing such codes as of divine origin and deserving of divine judgment or indirectly by offering the mythic basis within which given normative expectations are rationalized or exemplified. Ritual awakens an appreciation of normative structures and maintains the equilibrium of a society. Commonly practiced during periods of crisis, whether for the individual or the society, ritual offers an emotional safety valve and a source of shared enthusiasm which can restore equilibrium.[13] It enforces acceptance of changing codes of behavior with changed status just as it recognizes the "new" person who achieves adulthood or marriage.

Functional definitions often suffer from misinterpretations by those who fail to make the distinction between *manifest* and *latent* functions, as first discussed by Robert Merton.[14] Manifest functions are those recognized and intended consequences of an institution that are often stated as goals or objectives. Latent functions are their unintended consequences. Latent functions of religion may include the maintenance of class distinctions, even when the manifest function is to break them down by acknowledging human equality before God. It is such consequences of religion which have inspired Marxian definitions of religion as "the opiate of the masses." When we view religion in terms of its functions, we must constantly beware of imputing motives for participation in a particular religious action or group in terms of its latent functions. People are often unaware of ways in which their religion functions for them. They may belong to a particular religious group because it offers them security and personal identity, yet once they gain that identity they may be able to move into very insecure activities if the religion encourages it. On the other hand, they may be motivated to involve themselves in some religion out of a desire for adventure, but once they take it up they may become so involved within its circle that they never perform another adventurous act.

The weakness of functional definitions lies in the contradictory nature of religion. We may define it as that which integrates or that which disturbs, that which preaches commonality or that which legitimates class or ethnic differences, that which prevents change or that which inspires change. Not only is defining an institution in such conflicting terms an exercise in nonlogic, but it also could be applied to the institutions of the state, education, or the family. Clearly, by itself the functional definition of religion is insufficient.

Another way of finding cultural universals in religion is to view it structurally, that is, in terms of elements and patterns. The most obvious structural element in religion is reflected in Durkheim's definition. All religions are composed socially of a group of adherents, a community of believers, whether or not they are formally organized or further differentiated. As we will see in Part II of this book, however, the extent to which there is conscious organization and role differentiation that provides leaders or religious specialists varies from one culture to another. More universal are components that can be defined as myth and ritual.

As a "narrative charter of religion," myth involves one or more stories that provide an understanding of the meaning of the society and its structure within a universal setting. Most religions offer mythic explanations of the origin of the universe and the human race—usually defined in terms of that society, which is seen as most truly human. Important forms of activity are related as first having been performed by dieties or original ancestors, thus stressing both the importance of these acts and the unity through time of those who perform them. Myths provide in story form the rationale for the particular world view constructed by a society, and they reinforce belief in it. They tend to stress common themes based on experiences universal to the human condition. They deal with birth and creation, success and failure, death and disintegration. Elements in myth transpose the experiences of individual life into an interpretation of the human story, thus creating within the listener a sense of assent and confirmation.

Ritual increases this sense of assent by providing ways in which the individual or group may participate in the myth through reenactment in one form or another. There is always disagreement as to the relative importance or historical precedence of myth and ritual. Discussion of the matter tends to be fruitless. As with most human phenomena, the effect of myth and ritual upon one another is circular, each maintaining the other. The important point is that repetitive activities that provide a sense of participation in the mythic framework are generally characteristic of religion. Ritual may be performed in groups or individually, but even individual ritual involves activities known to be shared by others in the group.

As the myth provides a framework for comprehension of phenomena outside ordinary experience, ritual provides a way of participating in it. It creates ways of acting out the fears and frustrations common to human experience, relating them to a unifying myth, and obtaining social support in the process.

Religion also can be defined in terms of the order of reality with which it deals. This approach conforms to the pattern of finding universal characteristics through cross-cultural comparisons. It is generally agreed that most societies distinguish between the "sacred" and the "profane" in one way or another. Certain times, places, people, objects, or activities are invested with special meaning that sets them apart from the ordinary. As religion provides a mythical network of meaning that extends into the unknown, it also of necessity involves a consideration of that unknown. As ritual provides social support for a belief in the cosmic order provided by the myth, it also provides the vehicles by which persons can participate in the experience of that which is beyond the day-to-day patterns of life. Consequently, religion concerns itself at least partially with that which elicits a sense of being outside ordinary experience. Involved in this is the idea of the "holy"—something that has elements of urgency, overpoweringness, awefulness—a fascinating quality that reaches out to something sensed as "other."[15] Though its definition is difficult—perhaps impossible—this quality is generally recognized as having to do with genuine religious feeling. Such feeling is aroused by the symbols of the religion, through its rituals, by the words and meanings of its myths, and by the persons who are set apart as religious functionaries.

A constant problem of defining religion in order to study it is the temptation to objectify it not only in terms of separating oneself from that which is studied, but also by treating the object of study as a static, fixed *thing*. Yet religion must always be seen as more than an object; it is also a *process*, involving personal development and action, interpersonal relations, and the ebb and flow of intra- and interinstitutional influences and actions. Even to attempt to define religion—or any social phenomenon, for that matter—as the *pattern* in which the processes of social and personal activity occur is to miss the point, for the pattern itself evolves, changes, moves. Yet patterns do exist, and institutions and movements have boundaries, form, and solidity. Any definition we use must be recognized as existing in that area of tension between the solidity of a thing and the fluidity of a process.

Elements of the discussion above will be expanded as we go further into the sociological study of religion. At present, only enough has been said to provide a framework for what we hope will be a useful definition of religion within which to pursue that study. It must be made clear, however, that such a definition is made for the purposes of study, rather than as any final assertion of the nature of religion. Assumptions made here concerning the logical or necessary relationships between factors have not been fully tested and could well be sources of hypotheses for further empirical study. With this in mind, and with the thought that at the end of our consideration we may want to alter our basic definition, let us posit a definition of religion based on the elements we have discussed. As an operational definition of religion for purposes of investigating a sociological understanding of it, let us use the following:

Religion is a human phenomenon that functions to unite cultural, social, and personality systems into a meaningful whole. Its components generally include (1) *a community of believers* who share (2) a common *myth* that interprets the abstractions of cultural values into historic reality through (3) *ritual behavior,* which makes possible personal participation in (4) a dimension of experience recognized as encompassing something more than everyday reality—*the holy.* These elements are united into recognizable *structures* that undergo *processes* of change, development, and deterioration.

Notes and References

1. This is perhaps best summarized in "An Outline of the Social System," in Talcott Parsons et al., eds., *Theories of Society* (New York: Free Press, 1961), particularly pp. 36–38 and 78–79.
2. This discussion is largely an interpretation of elements in Peter L. Berger, *The Sacred Canopy* (Garden City, N.Y.: Doubleday, 1960), particularly Chapter 1, "Religion and World Construction."
3. Julian Hartt, "Secularity and the Transcendence of God," in James F. Childress and David B. Harned, eds., *Secularization and the Protestant Prospect* (Philadelphia: Westminster, 1970), pp. 159–173.
4. Charles Y. Glock and Rodney Stark, *Religion and Society in Tension* (Chicago: Rand-McNally, 1965), pp. 11–12.
5. J. Milton Yinger, *The Scientific Study of Religion* (New York: Macmillan, 1970), p. 14.
6. Sigmund Freud, *The Future of an Illusion* (London: Hogarth, 1934), pp. 28–31.
7. Erich Fromm, *The Dogma of Christ* (New York: Holt, 1934), p. 20.

8. Sebastion de Grazia, *The Political Community* (Chicago: University of Chicago Press, 1963), pp. 3–26.

9. Emile Durkheim, *The Elementary Forms of the Religious Life*, trans. by Joseph Ward Swain (New York: Free Press, 1965), p. 62.

10. See, for example, Alexander Goldenweiser, "Religion and Society: A Critique of Emile Durkheim's Theory of the Origin and Nature of Religion," *Journal of Philosophy, Psychology, and Scientific Methods* (1917), pp. 113–124; A. R. Radcliffe-Browne, "The Sociological Theory of Totemism," *Proceedings of the Fourth Pacific Science Congress* (Java, 1929), Batavia, 1930; and Robert Lowie's discussion in *Primitive Religion*, enl. ed. (New York: Liveright, 1948).

11. Thomas Luckmann, *The Invisible Religion* (New York: Macmillan, 1967), pp. 22–26.

12. See, for example, Talcott Parsons, *The Social System* (New York: Free Press, 1951), pp. 367–368, where philosophy and religion are distinguished on the basis that religion is a commitment to action.

13. George Homans, *The Human Group* (New York: Harcourt, 1950), p. 310.

14. Robert Merton, *Social Theory and Social Structure*, rev. ed. (New York: Free Press, 1957), pp. 19–84.

15. Rudolph Otto, *The Idea of the Holy*, trans. by John W. Harvey (London: Oxford University Press, 1936), pp. 8–41.

2

The Holy

It is the element of the holy that has often been characterized as the most primitive aspect of religion, the one from which all other components have developed. What do we mean by the experience of the holy? In its most basic form it may simply be based on a fear of the unknown. Kroeber produced behavior that hints of this sort of awe in a group of chimpanzees. They were presented with an artificial donkey with button eyes, which could not be mistaken either for a real donkey or for any normal object in their environment. Their behavior lacked the usual curiosity and investigative activities in which chimpanzees ordinarily engage when presented with a new object of ordinary qualities. They remained wary, would not even take food placed near the "donkey" until it was the only possible choice. They appeared both attracted and repelled by this inexplicable object in their cage.[1]

Religious awe seems to have similar characteristics. It can be described as a feeling of being in the presence of the unknown and inexplicable. But it also appears to have to do with a particular class of unknowables, for, unlike other unfamiliar things in the environment, it does not invite further investigation and experimentation. It is from a recognition of this fact that we get the common distinction, most famously presented by Durkheim, between the *sacred* and the *profane*.

This distinction, which appears common to all cultures, expresses a recognition of two orders of existence. In that order called the profane we find all that is routine and taken for granted in the workaday world. Attitudes toward things in the profane world are casual; they are accepted on the basis of familiarity and commonness. Things and ideas that are classified as profane may be dealt with manipulatively; they are the stuff of which we create the day-to-day activities of our existence.

On the other hand, those things that are sacred are outside the sphere of everyday life. They dare not be taken for granted. They are approached with attitudes of awe and reverence, for there is an air of mystery about sacred things.

Durkheim held that the distinction between sacred and secular is not simply a classification of things within a single category, as good and evil are classes of morality. Sacred and profane are two entirely different orders, and there is no way to join the two in a single universe of meaning. He went on to say that the fundamental characteristic of all known religious beliefs is this classification into sacred or profane categories of everything that people think about, whether concretely or abstractly.[2] In recent years, this view has come under considerable criticism. Since it has broad implications in the field, we should examine this idea in depth before continuing our discussion of the relationship between religion and society.

Human ideas are based on two things—experience and the ability to generalize from it. Generalizations from past experience interpret present experiences and project future ones. The ability to generalize and project, as we have seen earlier, leads to the ability to posit a reality that is beyond present experience. To have lasting significance, however, such a reality would need at least occasional confirmation in experience.

This seems a contradiction in terms. How can one experience something that is beyond experience? That this can happen is well attested in countless biographies. The primary ingredients are subjectivity and a puzzling responsive character. It is puzzling because the experience is an emotional response under circumstances in which it is difficult to interpret just what the individual is responding to. It is not experienced as physiological; the subject does not classify this as a response to bodily states or needs, although one may cultivate a return of the feeling through the manipulation of bodily states. It is felt to be a response to something outside—or beyond—one's self, at least as that self is ordinarily understood. There is the feeling that whatever is being responded to has particular potency. More than anything else, this sense of power and of "otherness" seems common to the experience, although its range of intensity may be great.

In his book *The Idea of the Holy,* which has become a classic among scholarly attempts to deal with this phenomenon, Rudolph Otto coins the term "numinous" as a classificatory title for the experience. He includes in the concept an element of awefulness—that is, the ability to inspire awe. He also says that the experience of the holy has about it a sense of overpoweringness, and of energy or urgency. Otto's classification includes a sense of being in the presence of the "wholly other," which may be interpreted in terms of a person who is "wholly other" but which is more accurately classified as the feeling that one is faced with an entirely different order of existence.[3] The experience is occurring, the person recognizes it, but it does not fit into any of the experiential categories learned in the culture. One cannot fail to believe something has happened, but it seems impossible to find a way truly to interpret what it is. The only logical interpretation of such a happening lies in the world beyond actual experience which we have been able to posit through our ability to generalize and abstract. This is the experience that lends reality to the world that lies beyond reality.

Such an experience is not held lightly by the person who has participated in it. The fascination remains. Anything that was involved in the original experience may remind one of it, bringing back, if only briefly, that same element of power. Just as at a more shallow level a romantic may take great pleasure in seeing and touching the faded corsage from the "big night" or hearing "our song" or seeing spots in which cherished moments occurred, so the person who has had the experience of the holy cherishes objects and places that are reminders of the high moment and that reawaken the feeling experienced then.

To see how such experiences have been conceptualized we may begin with a concept developed from the religious practice of the Polynesians, that of *mana*. As explained to early researchers, the Polynesians defined mana as a force—not physical power per se—which works to affect everything beyond the common processes of nature or the ordinary powers of humankind. It can reside in anything, and it is possessed or controlled by certain people.[4] Because there is no word in most Western languages to denote the concept without invoking narrower definitions from specific religious traditions, the word has been retained and the concept made more abstract for purposes of study. It is generally used to refer to a sort of impersonal power which can reside in objects, places, persons, or times. Attempts to describe mana as an entity tend to fail. Perhaps the best way to conceive of it is as a sort of electricity, a power that may or may not be harnessed and may accomplish good or evil.

Closely allied with the concept of mana is that of *tabu*. Tabu refers to a restriction of behavior and can usually be traced to the possession of mana. That is, something that possesses mana should be approached or handled with great caution, or injury could result. Only the person who has the right—through position, knowledge, or condition—dare handle anything that is laden with mana. For others it is tabu.

Examples of this can be found in widely varying traditions. In Polynesian culture royalty held much mana, so much that on some of the islands royal personages had to be carried when they traveled lest the touch of their feet make the land tabu for their subjects. It is from this concept that the practice of royal incest developed. Who else dare touch a royal person? In the Judeo-Christian tradition we find evidence of the same sort of quality. Included in the story of the Hebrews is the incident when an unwary—and unauthorized—Israelite touched the sacred Ark of the Covenant and dropped dead.[5] The story of Samson reveals a belief found in many cultures that mana resides in the hair or the head. It also portrays a common linking between mana and physical force or strength.

In fact, the notion of mana provides some understanding of the nature of sacred objects, or acts, or times. Mana may reside in any of these things. If it does, the thing itself becomes mana in terms of the way it is treated. Some places contain mana and so are holy. Rituals consecrating churches or temples acknowledge this. This power may also reside in people, people who in some way display a particular potency. We have already seen that mana frequently is found in chiefs or royalty. The concept provides the basis for their ability and right to rule. Such power may reside in persons because of a particular position they occupy, or it may be an individual characteristic through which a person is particularly influential, whether that influence is exercised over people, evil spirits, or natural forces. Weber uses the term *charisma* in writing of this particular class of power, stating that by the term he means to include the concept of mana and other terms denoting a class of extraordinary powers inherent in objects or persons.[6] The term comes from the Greek *charis,* and denotes the gift or grace of God. Charismata are not to be understood as gifts emanating from a friendly, generous disposition on the part of the divine, but as consequences of divine power.[7] In common usage in the discipline the term charisma has come to be used most often in reference to power attributed to persons, while mana is used in a more general sense.

The concept of mana posits something that transcends the ordinary world. The concept of tabu sets the limits on ordinary experience, pointing out how far one may go with the casualness appropriate for the workaday world.[8] At some time, and in some way, this power has been authenticated by experience.[9] Firth makes it clear that in its original use in Oceania the concept of mana was always found in conjunction with some person or thing, not just an abstraction. It is the philosopher and the scientist who attempt to abstract the essence of what is much more concrete to common folk. The religious experience is something that happens to particular people under particular circumstances; powers outside the ordinary are made known through their consequences in the everyday world, or they are not recognized at all.[10]

Because an experience of any kind, even the confrontation with the holy, does occur at a particular time and place and in conjunction with certain objects in the environment, it becomes easy to assume that mana can reside in certain objects, places, times, or persons. If a person sitting on a rock in a circle of trees is visited by this awareness of a powerful presence, this experience of the holy, he or she may find that every trip back to that circle of trees reawakens at least some portion of the original experience. One returns again and again to renew this high moment in one's life, and the circle of trees becomes a sacred place. The rock on which one sat may become sacred also, as well as the attitude or posture taken when the great moment occurred. In all these things a special power resides, a power we may call mana. All these things are part of the world of the sacred rather than the profane.

Because these things symbolize something sacred to the individual, and perhaps because he or she fears that any change in them would destroy their power to reproduce the experience of the holy, the person may deliberately institute tabus to protect these things; he or she will certainly support any existing restrictions on changes in the sacred scene. For this reason there comes to be a connection in the minds of most people between the sacred and that which must not be changed. This process has been identified by Berger as one of alienation, out of which there is produced a "false consciousness." Patterns of behavior that are in reality human artifacts come to be treated as objective natural realities, and people forget that the social world and the socialized self are the products of human activity. When the process concerns patterns developed in relation to the holy it assumes an even greater separation between what was a human process and what is now defined as the sacred order. No longer can the process of development and adjustment of the social world continue; rather, patterns are fixed as eternal verities.[11]

Yet the beginning of this process is often rooted in an experience of the holy that wrenches a person out of customary patterns of behavior. This ambiguity concerning the holy as source both of radical change and of radical rigidity has been given conceptual solution by Hartt, who postulates a separation between the concepts of the "holy" and the "sacred." While he sees the holy as that which is elevated above random, coarse, or abusive treatment, he finds that the sacred is arbitrarily set aside for such use to protect a stake certain persons or groups have in it.[12] The link between the two, of course, is that the experience of the holy in sacred settings gives people that kind of stake in them.

So we reconstruct the idea of sacred objects and places in individual experience. But this idea assumes sociological significance only when it is shared by a group. This can occur in several ways. The experience may first have occurred to several people at once, particularly if it involved some unusual natural occurrence—a bolt of lightning, a sudden cessation of a storm or other danger, an eclipse. In this case they are likely to share mutual reconstruction of their great experience. If the experience is that of an individual, he or she is likely to want to communicate such a wonderful feeling to friends and to try to reconstruct the event so that they may share in the emotion. One takes friends to the sacred place, the sacred rock, has them assume the same position, duplicate the same thoughts. One tries to put them where he or she was, that they might feel what was felt at that time.

All this may sound like mere speculation about primitive origins of human religion. It is not. Modern observers have been able to witness the same process, particularly in the recent "drug culture." Individuals who experienced the "mind expansion" of a drug-induced "trip" evidenced a sense of mystery, fear, and fascination as well as the tendency to recreate the condition of a "good trip" in order to share the experience with friends.[13] A small circle of people sitting on the floor of a psychedelically decorated room passing around mutually shared "joints" of marijuana or joining in "dropping acid" was a prototype of primitive religion in this attempt to share that which is beyond ordinary experience, although the pervading secularity of modern culture seems now to have reduced such practices to secular pursuits of thrills or relaxation. Among earlier experimenters, even before many turned to the explicit use of religious language, it was evident that their drugs were sacred objects, believed capable of inducing awareness of another level of existence. The attitude of some young drug users toward their implements of mind expansion could be likened to the care and protection bestowed upon sacred stones by the Australian aborigine or upon holy relics by the medieval Christian. The human ability not only to conceive of other frameworks of existence than the one in which life is expected to be spent, but also to experience them, has been of particular fascination throughout the ages, and in many cases the drug-related experience has led contemporary young people into involvement in activities defined as religious by ancient tradition.[14]

This pursuit of some relation to powers outside the ordinary is closely allied to magic as well as religion. There has been considerable dispute among anthropologists as to the relation between these two practices, including their use of mana. Some say that magic and religion simply use the power of mana in different ways and for different purposes. Goode, for example, sees magic as the attempt to manipulate mana for specific, individually oriented goals. Dealing with mana becomes a means toward some end, where religion is an end in itself.[15] Malinowski counters that the power of magic is localized in persons and released by them through the performance of specific rites, while mana is not localized. One very important point that Malinowski makes is that magic is rigidly governed by tradition—the power is obtained through learning the exact ritual and using the exact equipment that has been effective before—while mana symbolizes a breakthrough from a form of existence not covered by given traditions.[16] We shall return to this idea later.

Other distinctions between magic and religion include the comparative complexity of religion as compared to magic; the involvement of all in religious rites, at least in primitive society, where magic is in the hands of specialists; and the fact that while magic can be "black" or "white," religion claims a deeper reality beyond performing or undoing human acts.

The more one looks into distinctions made between magic and religion, the more tenable becomes Marett's stand that the two are not mutually exclusive classes and that things can pass from one into the other. The two concepts may be seen as "ideal types" or end points on a continuum along which are ranged a great variety of actions that are best understood as mixtures of both. It is not hard to postulate this as a sort of division of labor developed out of a more formless unitary sort of earlier perception. The way in which the two concepts can be intertwined in a sort of formless response to the experience of the holy is expressed well in the words of the modern writer Leonard Cohen, which have been popularized as a song by Buffy Sainte Marie:

God Is Alive, Magic Is Afoot

God is alive. Magic is afoot.
God is alive. Magic is afoot.
God is afoot. Magic is alive.
Alive is afoot.
Magic never died. God never sickened.
Many poor men lied. Many sick men lied.
Magic never weakened. Magic never hid.
Magic always ruled.
God is afoot. God never died.
God was ruler though his funeral lengthened.
Though his mourners thickened Magic never fled.
Though his shrouds were hoisted the naked God did live.
Though his words were twisted the naked Magic thrived.
Though his death was published round and round the world
The heart did not believe.
Many hurt men wondered. Many struck men bled.
Magic never faltered. Magic always led.

Many stones were rolled but God would not lie down.
Many wild men lied. Many fat men listened.
Though they offered stones Magic still was fed.
Though they locked their coffers God was always served.
Magic is afoot, God rules.
Alive is afoot. Alive is in command.
Many weak men hungered. Many strong men thrived.
Though they boasted solitude God was at their side.
Nor the dreamer in his cell, nor the captain on the hill.
Magic is alive.
Though his death was pardoned round and round the world
The heart would not believe.
Though laws were carved in marble they could not shelter men.
Though altars built in parliaments they could not order men.
Police arrested Magic and Magic went with them
For Magic loves the hungry.
But Magic would not tarry.
It moves from arm to arm.
It would not stay with them;
Magic is afoot. It cannot come to harm.
It rests in an empty palm.
It spawns in an empty mind.
But Magic is no instrument. Magic is the end.
Many men drove Magic but Magic stayed behind.
Many strong men lied.
They came to God in secret and though they left him nourished
They would not tell who healed.
Though mountains danced before them they said that God was dead.
Though his shrouds were hoisted the naked God did live.
This I mean to whisper in my mind.
This I mean to laugh with in my mind.
This I mean my mind to serve
Till service is but Magic moving through the world,
And mind itself is Magic coursing through the flesh,
And flesh itself is Magic dancing on a clock,
And time itself the Magic Length of God.[17]

The tendency to confuse magic with religion has been a constant point of contention within religious bodies. Today we find ministers and theologians denouncing as sacrilege the use of religious talismans or prayers for what they deem magical ends—health, success, or winning a game. Others rely on such practices, healing the sick by "the laying on of hands," advertising religion as the key to success, blessing the handkerchiefs of the faithful to bring health, a whole range of practices that go from the fashionable to the ridiculed. However, there has been constant pressure from religious bodies and functionaries to reserve the encounter with the holy as an end in itself and to call it a perversion to use sacred things in the pursuit of one's own ends.

Also involved in this criticism is the awareness that the basic vague and formless response to a sensed power can be interpreted by the subject in terms of good or of evil. Some would divide magic and religion along this axis, saying that religion is the experience of good power, magic of evil. This is not too useful a distinction, since it does not allow for "white" magic—that is, magic used to accomplish good—nor for the common practice of conquering groups or successful movements for change to define the gods of the old order as the devils of the new. But even though definitions of good and evil may vary between individuals and cultures, it must be recognized that for some the experience of the "wholly other" has seemed diabolic rather than divine.

There are at least two possible sources of this variation of interpretation, beyond the sociologically unverifiable contention that there are objectively good and evil powers. First, a power may be defined as evil if for any reason the response is one of terror rather than inspiration or reassurance. This may be seen in modern form in the phenomenon of the "bad trip." Here we find a person seeking pleasurable experiences in a drug-induced reality, who instead is terrorized by a reality that is not in the least pleasurable. The quality of experience beyond the boundaries of the ordinary is apparently very difficult to control. The element of risk involved may be part of the fascination of this sort of experience, but the terrorizing reality remains a possibility to be feared.

Another source of differing interpretations of the experience may come from the religious tradition itself. One thing that must be noted is that while we may assume that some experience of the holy is basic to the formation of any religion, the ability of its sacred objects, rituals, and doctrines to communicate this experience is never total. Thus, regardless of the form in which a religion is institutionalized, not everyone who participates in it is likely to reproduce the original experience. Some may have no great emotional involvement at all. Others may have the sort of experience we have defined as religious under circumstances other than those provided for in the rites of the religion. They may interpret such experiences as visitations from a power antagonistic to the divinity revealed by the religion, and hence evil. They may even be encouraged in such an interpretation if their response to the experience of the holy becomes disruptive to the sacred order or the rituals practiced in the religious institution.

There is, of course, another and perhaps more political way of viewing this second interpretation of evil. Throughout history religious systems have regularly been replaced by other religious systems, either as the forms practiced by conquering groups are imposed upon certain societies or as cultural diffusion or reform have led to changes defined by those in power as improvements over the old ways. When such changes occur, old gods usually become the devils of the new religions. Experiences based on rituals used in the old tradition become, by the simple process of labeling, visitations of the demonic or the calling up of ancient evil powers. Practices that were religious rituals in the old days are defined as magic, in contrast to the rituals of the new religion. Most of our knowledge of magic, witchcraft, sorcery, and demonology in European culture, for example, has come from writings within the medieval church during the period when it was particularly concerned with weeding out the old ways.

Taking these distinctions into account, Glock and Stark[18] have constructed a useful paradigm for categorizing another important phenomenon that we must recognize: the different levels on which religious experience may occur. First, they divide religious experience into two roughly parallel classes, experiences of the divine and of the diabolic. These classes are based on the interpretation of the individual having the experience—that is, whether he or she feels the encounter to be with forces of good or evil. It is also clear that individual interpretation is guided by the social milieu, as may be seen in recent increases in experiences defined as demon possession, after the rise in popularity of a number of novels in which this was a central theme.

In either case, the most frequent kind of religious experience is what is known as the *confirming* experience. This simply involves an awareness that one is confronted by a situation or an object that arouses a sense of awe or sacredness. Depending upon cultural definitions as much as anything else, it may involve a sense of the presence of another person. This type of religious experience is not only the most likely to occur, but also—in the case of experience of the divine, if not the diabolic—the one most encouraged within the society and through its religious institutions. Most services of worship are structured with the intention of providing participants with a "sense of the presence of God." Yet it is also true that even this most elemental of religious experiences is not shared by all members of religious bodies. For example, in a survey of church members in the San Francisco area Glock and Stark found that slightly less than half their respondents felt that they were sure they had experienced a feeling of God's presence.

In order of frequency, the next type of religious experience is the *responsive* experience. This occurs when the individual who experiences the divine presence is also convinced that he or she is acknowledged by the divinity. Glock and Stark postulate three phases of this experience: the salvational, where the individual experiences a sense of confirmation of his or her status vis-à-vis the divinity; the miraculous, where the experience is that of the divine having created a change in the physical or environmental state of the subject; and the sanctioning, where one feels the divinity has intervened to prevent some intended action. There is somewhat less encouragement of these responsive experiences through the religious institutions than of the confirming experience. Those religious groups that encourage this type of experience most strongly generally tend not to be "establishment" bodies. In the case of responsive experiences of the diabolic, the three subcategories are temptational, that of being singled out to be tempted to sin; damnational, where supernatural forces reward evil; and the accursed, where intervention of the supernatural brings ill fortune. (It is perhaps in this area that the close connection is made between magic and such practices of witchcraft as hexing or cursing and the service of diabolical powers.)

The third level of religious experience is that of the *ecstatic* (or, in the case of diabolic experience, the *terrorizing*). Here there is a close personal relationship with the divinity, sometimes with sexual overtones. Many of the reported experiences of the great mystics of the Middle Ages, for example, reveal strong sexual themes; and the recent book and movie *Rosemary's Baby* recalls a common theme of sexual liaisons with diabolic entities. Sex is not the only kind of experience at this level, of course, and ecstasy is encouraged in some religious bodies, usually those criticized by more established groups for their emotionalism. On the whole, this level of experience is not only less common but also less encouraged in the mainstream of the society. Such experience is usually reserved for a limited number of people, who are then given particular religious status. Thus the shaman and the saint may be expected to have had ecstatic experiences.

The final level of religious experience, the one least likely to occur and least likely to be encouraged by religious institutions, is the *revelational* experience, in which the individual becomes the confidant or agent of the divine (or the diabolic). In this role one may function to confirm, alter, or deny present religious practice. Since the person speaks from a presumed knowledge of the mind of the divine, he or she is not likely to submit to the control of given religious institutions. This is one obvious reason for their lack of encouragement for this level of experience. It is at this level that true charisma may be developed in the sense that Weber used the term.[19] It is from this kind of experience that prophets come, able to speak with authority to society and religious bodies alike: "You say . . . but thus saith the Lord. . . ." It involves a kind of enlightenment that may be related by its possessor to specific or general situations.

Clearly this paradigm applies to a religious tradition in which the divinity has been personalized. It would be of interest to see whether it could be applied in the case of a more impersonalized belief. Can these levels of response occur without their subject having a personal conception of the divine? While considerable research has been done in recent years into various forms of mystic and meditational practices, there has been little testing of this particular paradigm of religious experience in that area.

The more intense levels of religious experience shade into characteristics of what is most often recognized as *mystical* experience. William James notes four characteristics common to this kind of occurrence. First is its *ineffability*. No matter what attempts are made to describe or communicate the mystical experience, it remains at its core inexpressible. He also speaks of the *noetic* quality of the experience. It is not only a feeling; even though it cannot be expressed in words, it imparts a state of knowledge previously unreached. It is an experience that adds to the framework that structures the individual's outlook and responses. It is not just an ephemeral feeling. At the same time, it is *transient.* Mystical states cannot be maintained indefinitely. It also is characterized by a sense of *passivity.* The subject feels more acted upon than acting.[20]

Mystical states have something in common with the kinds of altered states of consciousness or peak experiences that have become subjects of psychological study in recent years. A direct link between that area of psychology and work in religion based on James's concepts has been made, both theoretically and empirically. W. T. Stace has enlarged James's schema by noting eight factors in mystical experience: a loss of the sense of the self; a perception of a unity of all things, including the self; the experience of a subjective nature in parts of the environment ordinarily perceived as objects; a transcendence of time and space; a feeling of joy or blissfulness; and a religious quality; as well as James's categories of ineffability and noetic quality. Hood, using a mysticism scale designed to elicit these categories, has shown that there may be two factors involved, one generally mystical, the other explicitly religious.[21] Many similar studies are currently attempting to map the terrain of religious and mystical experience.

There are several cautions, however, about equating religious experience with mystical experience. The less intense levels of religious response may not share all the attributes of mysticism and still be recognized by the subject as religious experience. People who have mystical experiences may classify themselves as nonreligious.

Troeltsch has a further caution. To him, in religious experience of the sort we have been considering in our definition of religion, experience and expression are one. The religious ritual of the group is the direct embodiment of the experience. Mysticism, as the term is generally used, is a deliberate attempt to cultivate religious experience, made against the forms of institutional religion, even though those forms were first created to transmit and encourage religious experience.[22]

It is not necessary to resolve such distinctions to recognize that the primary point of religious experience is that it provides for the subject's actual entry into a frame of reference outside the empirical. It is a step into the world of the holy and out of the common routine of the profane.

There has been considerable criticism in recent years of definitions of religion centered in its tendency to divide the world into separate spheres of sacred and profane, at least by Christian theologians. Some agree that this is indeed a characteristic of religion, and on that basis speak of "religionless Christianity." While this is an unacceptable contradiction to the sociologist, it deserves our attention because it has important implications for the function of religion in societies whose central tradition has been Christian.

Tied into this discussion is the concept of *secularization,* to which we will return again and again as we examine various facets of the sociology of religion. The term came into common use in Western culture in the post-Renaissance period, where it was applied to the transfer of church holdings to the state or private owners. At a broader and deeper level, it is taken to mean the transfer of things or ideas from the sacred realm to the profane. That which was treated as holy now becomes commonplace. Much of the discussion of secularization focuses around the loss of functions of religious institutions within the society. We speak of secularization when we discuss the transfer of functions of welfare from the church to the state, of moral education from the church school to the public school, and so on. But more relevant to the present discussion is the categorizing of experience into sacred and profane. The oft-heard cry today, "Is *nothing* sacred?" is the prototype of secularization at this level.

It is generally assumed that in primitive cultures a large proportion of the world was sacred. The power apparent in the subjective experience of the holy was inherent in all the environment. One was constantly faced by that which could neither be explained nor controlled. One trembled in awe at most occurrences and objects in the environment. All were imbued with an immanent power. As people became more adept at dealing with these frightening forces, they were able to remove them from their perception of the locus of sacred power and conceive of the holy in ever more transcendent terms. The power applied most specifically to those areas of life beyond ordinary knowledge and control. If the sacred was the inexplicable, then the accretion of human knowledge has pushed back the frontiers of the sacred by granting increased ability to explain what was previously mysterious. We who earlier trembled before the powers of Nature have now come to understand and control those powers. As time has passed, we have come to understand the dynamics not only of natural forces in our environment, but many of those of our personal and social lives as well. In such a frame of reference it is easy to see why science should be taken as the enemy of religion, and it may be taken as evidence of highly advanced secularization that we attempt to use the techniques of social science to study religion. Truly, is *nothing* sacred?

A corollary of this is that if the main concern of religion is to deal with the sacred, it is losing ground at a rapid rate as the boundaries are pushed ever backward. If at the present time those boundaries are retreating to the ultimate mysteries of life and death, it may concern us to see in the background the shadow of the scientist almost able to create life in the test tube, or by techniques of transplantation and chemical renewal to push back the moment of death indefinitely. Where in this projection is the role of religion and its concern with a sacred universe?

The secular theologians have replied that, at least in the Christian tradition, that is not what religion is about, but rather is a perversion of the tradition. In essence, they argue that the Christian doctrine of the Incarnation is a symbolic presentation of an understanding that the holy is found within the profane. It is not the unknown, but the common, which reveals the power of the holy. The Jewish tradition allowed for the conception of a transcendent God, and the experience of the holy was a confrontation with this Supreme Being. But in the incarnation as symbolized by Jesus Christ, they say, the transcendent became immanent in human life. This theological perspective must be dealt with again when we take up the study of myth. For the present let it suffice that there is some official support from the Christian tradition for those moderns who seek the experience of the holy within rather than outside themselves, as there has always been in Buddhist and Hindu traditions.

It is a mistaken assumption that secular theologians have had no appreciation of the emotional experience of religion. For example, some of the writings of Dietrich Bonhoeffer, whose work influenced much of the work of secular theology, shows a deep appreciation of the emotional aspects of religious experience. In fact, Bonhoeffer often sounds a strong strain of pietism that is akin to mysticism. Harvey Cox, who in the early 1960s celebrated the secular city, turned later to prescribe festival and fantasy as important dimensions of religious practice. His description of fantasy involves the ability to conceive of and experience a world beyond ordinary experience.[23] There are many indications that the final result of the secularization of Christianity may be a resacralization of secular life. Parallel trends appear in the scientific world, where scientists on the frontiers of knowledge find themselves not so much expanding the realm of profane manipulation, perception, and control as entering into new worlds of unpredictability and wonder. Not only through a counterculture reacting against the strictures of a desacralized world, but through institutional structures within that world, the holy seems to be coming into a more central place in modern culture than would have been expected. This trend is, again, a thread we must pick up later, for it runs counter to most of the predictions of sociologists of the past several generations.

Notes and References

1. A. L. Kroeber, *Anthropology,* new ed. (New York: Harcourt, 1948), pp. 66–67.
2. Emile Durkheim, *The Elementary Forms of the Religious Life,* trans. by Joseph Ward Swain (New York: Free Press, 1965), pp. 52–57.
3. Rudolf Otto, *The Idea of the Holy,* trans. by John W. Harvey (London: Oxford University Press, 1936), pp. 8–41.
4. R. R. Marett, *The Threshold of Religion,* 4th ed. (London: Methuen, 1929), pp. 104–105. Marett credits R. H. Codrington with originating the idea.
5. II Samuel 6:3–10.
6. Max Weber, *The Sociology of Religion,* trans. by Ephraim Fischoff (Boston: Beacon, 1963), p. 2.
7. G. van der Leuew, *Religion in Essence and Manifestation,* trans. by J. E. Turner (London: Allen & Unwin, 1938), pp. 33–35.
8. Marett, op. cit., p. xxvii.
9. van der Leuew, op. cit., pp. 25–28.
10. Raymond Firth, *Tikopia Ritual and Belief* (Boston: Beacon, 1967), pp. 174–194.
11. Peter L. Berger, *The Sacred Canopy* (Garden City, N.Y.: Doubleday, 1967), Chapter 4.
12. Julian Hartt, "Secularity and the Transcendence of God," in James F. Childress and David B. Harned, *Secularization and the Protestant Prospect* (Philadelphia: Westminster, 1970), pp. 157–158.
13. Harvey Cox has also discussed the importance of the setting in drug-related experiences in his *Turning East* (New York: Simon & Schuster, 1977), pp. 35–51.
14. Further discussion of this issue may be found in Walter H. Clark, *Chemical Ecstasy* (Mission, Kans.: Sheed, Andrews & McMeel, 1962).
15. William J. Goode, *Religion Among the Primitives* (New York: Free Press, 1951), pp. 50–54.
16. Bronislaw Malinowski, *Magic, Science, and Religion* (Garden City, N.Y.: Doubleday, 1948), pp. 76–79, 88–89.

17. Leonard Cohen, *Beautiful Losers* (New York: Bantam, 1969), pp. 197–199. Music may be found on Vanguard Record VSD 79300, *Illuminations*. Division into poetic lines is suggested by the music.

18. Charles Y. Glock and Rodney Stark, *Religion and Society in Tension* (Chicago: Rand McNally, 1965), pp. 39–66.

19. See, for example, Weber, op. cit., pp. 46–49.

20. William James, *Varieties of Religious Experience* (New York: Modern Library, 1902), pp. 370–372.

21. More will be said later in this volume about current history and research in the area of peak experiences, mediatation, and modern mysticism. For the theory involved in this particular example, see W. T. Stace, *Mysticism and Philosophy* (Philadelphia: Lippincott, 1960). Specific empirical references are to R. W. Hood, Jr., "The Construction and Preliminary Validation of a Measure of Reported Mystical Experience," *Journal for the Scientific Study of Religion* 14, no. 1 (March 1975): 20–41.

22. Ernst Troeltsch, *The Social Teachings of the Christian Churches,* trans. by Olive Wyon (New York: Harper, 1960), pp. 730–731.

23. Harvey Cox, *Feast of Fools* (Cambridge: Harvard University Press, 1969), pp. 59–97.

3

Myth and Ritual

The close relationship between myth and ritual makes it pointless to consider them separately. There has been much argument as to which of the two is more basic, but little enlightenment as a result of it. It will benefit us to consider some of these arguments, but only to find in them some of the basic characteristics of these deeply interrelated concepts.

All societies appear to have some forms of repeated symbolic behavior that is tied by explanatory verbalization to their basic way of understanding human existence. The repeated symbolic behavior we call *ritual;* the explanatory verbalization is *myth.* When seeking reasons for the universality of myth and ritual, some scholars have found it in individual psychological needs, others in the needs of society. Reality probably lies somewhere between, since individuals are born and live in social milieus.

Those who seek the source of myth and ritual in individual experience trace it to the observable fact that much of the behavior we term religious occurs in relation to events that are on the borderline of the uncontrollable, the threatening, the unknown. One common factor in ritual in particular, but also present in myth, is a certain rigidity of form. That is, there is a specific way in which it is gone about, and to be effective it must be done that way. This is particularly observable in the rituals of preliterate or semiliterate peoples, where the tradition is carefully handed on and each specific word and motion carefully taught and imitated. The knowledge of the correct details of a particular dance often constitutes the credentials of a leader. To do something wrong is to lose the effectiveness of the whole ceremony. This seems less true of literate people, who can, after all, go back to a book of instructions to check out the proper ceremonial behavior. Yet anyone who has dealt at length with the religious activities of any group becomes aware of the

power of repetition. A group of "low church" American Christians—
Baptists, for example—may spend considerable time decrying the formal liturgies of Catholic or Episcopal "high church" practices, strong in
their belief that you cannot imprison the Spirit of God within rigid
ceremonies. Yet if a new minister comes to their church and changes the
order of service or attempts to use new phraseology to present the
ancient truths, their reaction is often immediate and hostile. There is a
universal tendency for religion to become ritualized, to involve highly
predictable patterns of behavior and words.

From the standpoint of the individual, one reason for this tendency
toward rigidity of form may be found in the concept of "reaction formation," rigid formal behavior in situations of uncertainty or ambiguity.
In those areas of life where it is most difficult to predict what is going
to happen next or what can be done about it, we can in reaction so
rigidly structure our behavior that every detail is predictable. And we
do tend to do this whether or not it has been set forth in tradition. In
the face of an impending death in the family, for example, modern
secularists often find themselves at a loss as to what to do once the
doctor turns to them and says, "I've done all I can." The response,
generally, is to insist that the doctor never reach that point, but continue
"doing something" (ritual?) until, or beyond, the actual moment of
death. In less secular surroundings the individual may find a good deal
of gratification in repeating a set of fixed ritual prayers prescribed for
the occasion, lighting incense, preparing for later funerary rituals, and
the like, all of which reinforce the particular religion's interpretation of
the meaning of death—and of life.

At points where an individual is faced with a change of status, again
the provision of a particular ceremony with appropriate explanations
facilitates stepping over the boundary of the old position into the new.
The prescribed behavior of the ritual provides a pattern which carries
the initiate far enough into the new role to be able to go on meeting its
expectations.

Reaction formation is only one of the defense mechanisms myth and
ritual may provide. Introjection, for example, may be accomplished
through identification with mythic heroes, sometimes to the extent of
providing ritual opportunities to reenact their deeds and postures. To
meet the unknown in the person of the mythic hero is much less threatening than facing it as one's own inept self. Again, this mechanism can
be found in the myths and rituals of a wide variety of religions, from
the primitive who gains strength from the tribal totem to the Christian
who repeats with St. Paul, "It is no longer I who live, but Christ who
lives in me."[1]

Projection is another defense mechanism provided by myth and ritual, particularly the portion that concerns witchcraft. To be able to pinpoint sources of evil and to have at hand rituals appropriate to their exorcism provides comfort in the face of threat. Ritual activity may often provide for individuals the opportunity to take some action in the face of the unknown. The activities of ritual sublimate aggressive tendencies which are released by an anxiety-producing situation. If nothing else, ritual provides an anxious person with something to do, which in itself relieves some anxiety.

Basically, then, myth and ritual reduce anxiety, or the anticipation of disaster. Kluckhohn says that everyone has some kinds of private rituals and compensatory fantasies. Under changing conditions some persons' obsessive behavior or fantasy becomes congenial to others and is socialized into ritual and myth.[2] There are incidences of this in anthropological research, some of which will be considered when the subject of religion in social change is discussed.

Wallace sees some forms of ritual as a natural reaction to danger or injury to one's self-identity. Strenuous efforts are often undertaken to understand and repair the injury to the self, to resynthesize the identity, which include actions with no other practical result. Usually if such actions are guided and supported by others and provide models for the process, success in identity restoration can be achieved. The combination of myth and ritual provides an image of an orderly world system in which the individual has a place, along with activities by which that person can assume the role he or she needs to occupy that position.[3]

If myth and ritual provide a universal function of relieving anxiety in the individual, the nature of the anxiety is usually formed by the society. This is what Kluckhohn refers to as "type anxiety." Each culture, he says, has a particular area that makes it most anxious; it is around this area that myth and ritual concentrate their efforts. In cultures where physical well-being is tenuous, a high proportion of the myth and ritual is concerned with preventing or healing disease or with fertility and food getting. In our culture, at least among those who have a reasonable amount of physical and economic security, sex seems to be the greatest source of anxiety. Sexual morality is consequently the focus of much religious attention.[4] A proposition that seems to be gaining credibility, at least in implicit usage, is that changes in our society are beginning to cause sex to be replaced with another, more general area of "interpersonal relations" as the most anxiety producing—our "type anxiety." The combination of a particular geographical environment, a specific group history, and the distribution of personality types produced by a society's peculiar genetic pool and socialization patterns create the framework in which individual needs are felt. The particular culture also develops its own way of meeting those needs. So while needs are made concrete in individuals, we must look to their societies for both their sources and their gratifications.

The structures of myth and ritual reflect the structures of the society, as the way people perceive the world generally is based on categories provided by their particular culture and its language. Victor Turner has observed that ritual symbolism is bound to involve the nature and relationship of groups within the society.[5] This includes the relative amount of power within the society wielded by those who participate in the ritual as well as the place where they perceive the boundaries to be between themselves and their environments.[6]

Individual needs are met through the strengthening of a dependable social structure in which the individual has a secure place. There is biological value in beliefs that reinforce mental attitudes of reverence for a tradition that keeps the social structure predictable, maintains harmony with the environment, and provides confidence in the face of difficulty or death. These are preserved through ceremony and cult, and they have reality in their effectiveness.[7]

Kluckhohn divides the consequences of myth and ritual into *adaptive* and *adjustive* functions: By adaptation he means behavior that results in survival; adjustment is behavior that removes the stimulus that has motivated the individual to action. Most of the adaptive uses of myth and ritual seem to fall into the category of social benefits. They include the promotion of social solidarity and the enhancement of the integration of the society. This, of course, is of value to the individual because it provides for the continuation of a group which can offer support when a person most needs it. Another adaptive function of myth and ritual is the accurate transmission of the culture. This provides for the retention of knowledge gained in the past by the society, and it is particularly important in cultures where literacy does not aid greatly in maintaining the fund of experience.

The adjustive functions, in large part, are those we have already discussed. Myth and ritual provide the security of the familiar in the face of the potential chaos of the unknown. Myth structures the unknown; ritual assures that even in the most insecure areas of life behavior will be predictable. In such a way the motivating anxiety is lessened, if not totally removed.[8] The close connection of the social and personal can be seen in the fact that through having performed a ritual duty an individual often gains assurance of having made a contribution to the maintenance of the social and natural universe of which he or she is a part. This assurance reduces one's anxiety and strengthens one's identity as a member of the group to which such a duty is owed.[9]

Homans shows how the personal and social elements in ritual and myth are interwoven as he sets out seven basic elements of ritual, beginning with universal sources of anxiety in the inability to master every situation life may offer:

1. Primary anxiety—a recognition of one's inability to achieve certain ends through ordinary knowledge and skills
2. Primary ritual—the performance of actions which, though they have no direct effect in achieving the end, do relieve the anxiety
3. Secondary anxiety—the fear that primary ritual was not done correctly, nor the tradition properly followed
4. Secondary ritual—ceremonies of purification or expiation to compensate for possible errors in primary ritual
5. Rationalization—reasons given for the specific form of primary and secondary ritual
6. Symbolization—reference to the connection between the rituals and primary myths of the society
7. Function—incorporating all these consequences of myth and ritual we have been discussing[10]

For example, in primitive agricultural societies there was no assurance that crops planted in the spring would survive the vicissitudes of weather, disease, and predators until they could be harvested. This could reasonably be expected to induce primary anxiety. Rituals that would relieve that anxiety might involve offering some sort of sacrifice to an agricultural diety believed to have power to protect the crop. However, there is always room for doubt about the consequences of the sacrifice. How can one be sure that the god wanted what was given? Was it perhaps presented in a way that would insult rather than placate the god? This secondary anxiety might be dealt with by going to a diviner who through the practice of certain rituals could ascertain the response of the deity—secondary ritual. Rationalization in this case would involve tales about the agricultural deity, his or her tastes and favorite ways of communicating with mortals, so that the rituals chosen would seem appropriate. Symbolization would set those tales in a broader mythology by which the particular deity is put in the context of a family of gods, whose story includes the founding of the particular tribe and whose relationship mirrors that of the different activities identified with each god. Function, then, would deal with the kind of social solidarity reinforced by this web of divine relationships and human responses, as well as the psychological assistance given people in coping with their environment. It may also include particularly practical consequences such as would ensue if the sacrifice to the agricultural deity were a dead fish buried near the seed, whose decaying body would provide needed fertilizer for the crop. Thus we see that the social tradition incorporates the forms of relief of anxiety in appropriate ritual, while at the same time it furnishes cause for some of the anxiety it would relieve.

Wallace,[11] who sees the chief concern of religious ritual as the achievement or prevention of "transformations of state," finds five areas of transformation in persons and in nature which become the focus of specific ritual. The first of these areas is the focus of ritual as *technology* and involves divination, the various rites of intensification connected with hunting and agricultural activities, and protective rituals. Such rites run the gamut from the observation of the entrails of a chicken or goat in the attempt to predict the future, to the pious farmer's prayer for rain. Much technological ritual is present in modern society in forms recognized as superstition. When we knock on wood as we boast of good fortune, we are participating in an ancient rite for fending off the jealousy of unfriendly spirits. When we say it is likely to rain if we wash the car or water the flower beds, we are indulging lightly in a world view which says that ritual action can control nature. Current interest in astrology and horoscopes shows that this dimension of myth and ritual is with us in forms similar to those common in less scientifically oriented cultures. It is also quite probable that the faith we place in scientists and their inventions is often more ritualistic than practical.

Closely related is Wallace's second area, that of ritual as *therapy* and *antitherapy*. Antitherapy here refers most directly to witchcraft. One of the constant concerns of myth is that of theodicy—the consideration of sources of evil and the imperfect linkage between suffering and rightness or wrongness of behavior. It is the ancient question, "Why do the righteous suffer?" One answer is that persons who have ritual control over evil forces are using those forces to create suffering in persons against whom they have some grievance. If this is given as the reason for illness or misfortune, then the way to counter it is through stronger, more effective ritual. In many folk cultures on the edge of or within modern industrial societies, many of the brief, unexplained illnesses of children are attributed to the evil eye and treated by antiwitchcraft rituals. Since many children's fevers are of short duration, ritual treatment for evil eye often works. It eases the mind of parent and child, and health returns. Because witchcraft is the ascribed source, antitherapy has been involved. The effects, however, are not unlike those achieved by the modern suburban mother who takes her feverish child to a pediatrician for an examination and the prescription of aspirin. She, too, feels relief that she has done something about it, and the child's fever goes away. Our former concentration on the germ theory of disease made all treatment for illness comply with antiseptic medical models. Our present understanding of psychosomatic illness and the stress theory of disease makes us far more willing to recognize the effectiveness of the cures of the witch doctor—and perhaps also the evangelistic faith healer. Under some circumstances ritual can provide the confidence and sense of well-being necessary to maintain physical health.

A third area finds ritual used as *ideology*. Here myth and ritual combine to control moods, values, sentiments, and behavior for the good of the group. The first type of ideological ritual is the rite of passage, in which persons undergo changes of status ritually recognized. These include all manner of initiatory rites and those connected with birth, puberty, marriage, and death. They involve group confirmation of the new status and the mythic and ritual presentation of new rights and responsibilities. The most common forms of this ritual provide some symbolic enactment of the death of the old self and the birth of the new. This involves in some way separation from the old group, transition, and incorporation into the new relationship. The institutionalization of these rites is important in all societies, as we shall see. The power of such ceremonies to reinforce group solidarity and shared values is particularly high. Those who weep at weddings are pledging allegiance to romantic love—and to their spouses. Ceremonies of baptism, confirmation, bar mitzvah, and the like affirm not only the individual but also the group.

The group is renewed and reaffirmed also in that type of ideological ritual found in social rites of intensification. The most common form of these in the Western world are the regularly recurring worship services provided by church, mosque, or synagogue. Such services recall with predictable regularity the relationship between the individual and the social unit and between individuals in that unit. There is good reason, for example, for using the term "revival" to refer to special religious services of high intensity and occasional occurrence. They call the group together in moments of high emotional content, reestablishing commitment and unity.

The effectiveness of ideological ritual comes not only through explicit interpretations and psychologically therapeutic activities, but also in the very way space is used, the positions taken by various actors, and the like. Here the very structure of ritual practice reinforces taken-for-granted structures at the unconscious level.[12]

Mary Douglas has also shown the relation of particular ritual acts to symbolic meanings of different parts of the human body emphasized in the action.[13] This understanding of symbolism in ritual helps us to recognize the close ties between ritual and religiously prescribed behavior. Wallace discusses as one form of ideological ritual the kinds of day-to-day behavior involved in ceremonial obligations and tabus, the structure of behaviors enjoined or forbidden. The performance of specific acts as part of a particular group reinforces identification with the group. One complaint against the removal of the restriction against eating meat on Friday has to do with ritual reinforcement of Roman Catholic identity. The giving of the Ten Commandments in Exodus, as well as the more detailed spelling out of Hebrew law, is preceded by a statement that this behavior is to be performed because of the peculiar nature, call, and history of the people of Israel. Working in counterpoint with the structure of ritual obligations is that of the ritual of rebellion, during which ordinary obligations need not apply. Many societies have ritual periods during which tabus against certain foods, drink, or sexual practices are relaxed or reversed. In American society secular examples of this include New Year's Eve, Halloween, and Mardi Gras, though the last two at least have direct religious origins. In some religious groups, emotional levels of behavior are allowed to rise much higher during services than would be tolerated at any other time. Such rituals provide relief from the rigidity of restrictions on behavior imposed by other ritual requirements.

A fourth class of religious activity involves religion as *salvation*. In this context, "salvation" is taken to mean the restoration of self-identity at times when it is damaged or seems inadequate. This kind of ritual can involve "possession" by a spirit—good or evil—the mystical experience, or that which Glock and Stark termed revelational. In this kind of ritual, the individual becomes a new person, in a new relationship to the cosmic universe that also affects his or her relationship to the profane world.

Wallace's final category considers ritual as *revitalization*. It is similar in some ways to salvational ritual, except that its focus is on the society rather than the individual. Such a function usually requires a restatement of the myth and a reordering of ritual in order to establish a new identity for the society. It is the result of social change, but it is also a way of creating, guiding, and incorporating social change. The ability of the group or society to develop "relevant" myths and appropriate ritual ways of reinforcing them may be the ability of that group or society to survive under changed external (or internal) conditions. In some way new relationships to the environment must be fitted into the cultural conception of the larger cosmos, and the individual's place must be affirmed in the ordered picture. Otherwise, individual and group identity is likely to be lost in the chaos of change.

A tension between continuity and change is always potential in religious myth and ritual. On the one hand, it is concerned with maintaining contact with the beginnings of things, the roots of meaning; and frequently this contact is maintained by rigidly prescribed forms which preserve the original. On the other hand, it is is called into play to validate immediate experience. In fast-changing times this may be a difficult task. Changing rituals may cause some people to feel they have lost their moorings. Slowness of change may prompt some people to feel they have no part in the sacred cosmos portrayed by the myth and ritual. Yet because these are problems of identity and consequently are of deep importance to the individual, each will have difficulty understanding the point of view of the other.

Ritual behavior provides experience that crosses the threshold of the sacred cosmos. It often provides symbolic gestures through which people imitate the behavior of divine models. This allows both the feeling of participating in the reality of the sacred world and a sanctification of the empirical world in which the participant acts.[14] Day-to-day experience is given broader and deeper meaning by this union of it with the sacred universe. In such behavior, lives circumscribed by time and mortality participate in the immortality of the timeless. In fact, one reason for the appeal of rigidity and repetitiveness in ritual behavior is the reassuring knowledge that these same words were sung and actions taken down through the generations, so that here, at least, is visible proof of the continuation of human culture through time and beyond mortality. The continuity of the sacred universe is not only reiterated but experienced.

The element of timelessness is important to myth and ritual. This is difficult for moderns to recognize, particularly in a culture based on the Judeo-Christian tradition. The concept of "sacred time" is perhaps best expressed in what the Australian aborigines called "the Dreaming." It is not historical past, or present, or future, but "everywhen." Its myth provides a narrative of what has happened as a sort of chart for what is happening or may happen. It is, if you will, Universal Time, which is all time.[15] The repetitiveness of sacred ritual provides a return to the sacred world in order to transfigure ordinary existence. In the world of the profane, such repetitiveness provides a pessimistic world view, indicating that nothing changes or can be influenced. It is important to our understanding of the subject of religion in general to note that this is not necessarily true in the sacred world, where repetition may lead to renewal.[16]

One reason for our difficulty in understanding this is the peculiarity of the basic Judeo-Christian myth, which offers the possibility of the sanctification of historic time. The Judeo-Christian myth stresses the importance of its events having taken place in history rather than in the nonhistoric sacred universe. This does not mean that traditional historic mythology has not collected around the central structure, but the antagonism of the basic orientation of the tradition makes it hard for such variations to survive. Consequently, narratives of the days in the Garden of Eden, complex angelologies, and the like, which have been formed in the tradition, are relegated to obscure sources and subgroup traditions.[17] The potential historicism of Christianity and Judaism provides a basis for much misunderstanding of the meaning of myth in religion.

Littleton has given us a helpful model for interpretation of the relationship of myth to history. He classifies the narratives common to a group or society on two axes, the first extending from the "factual" at one end to the "fabulous" at the other. The second goes from the "secular" to the "sacred." Narratives may fit anywhere in the space of the two-dimensional model enclosed by these axes, as may be seen in Figure 1. A story may be treated as within one of the categories for a time, then be moved to another, depending upon circumstances. For example, the rise of a great historical leader may, over time, become material for a hero saga or myth, in which actual events of history are interwoven with mythic factors pointing up other kinds of basic truths.

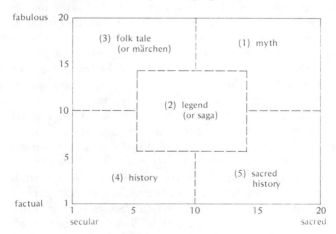

FIGURE 1   Two-dimensional Scheme for the Classification of Narratives.

From C. Scott Littleton: "A Two Dimensional Scheme for the Classification of narratives, in *Journal of American Folklore* 78:26 (Jan–Mar, 1965), p. 307. Reproduced by permission of the American Folklore Society from *Journal of American Folklore*, 78:26, 1965.

A secular example from American history and legend would be the story of George Washington and the cherry tree, in which the historical person became a mythic symbol of the values of honesty and forthright- ness in American culture.

Given the historical claims of the Judeo-Christian tradition, it becomes unusually important there to establish the boundaries between sacred and secular history as well as between myth and sacred history. It is a task that has caused much religious conflict in Christian history. The attempt to bring such conflict to resolution has created in Christian cultures a strong emphasis on the belief aspects of religion, making it difficult to understand the importance of ritual in most religions, includ- ing our own. In order to present a more balanced view of the religious dimension of society, we shall try to remain uninvolved in the contro- versy over the historicity of basic myths. They are important to us because they are the sources of particular religious phenomena in soci- ety, and they have historic reality in that they are related to the rise of particular religious expressions. Their relationship to history beyond that is irrelevant to our discussion. The consequences of specific reli- gious beliefs within a society are of great importance to sociologists; their relation to ultimate historic truth is beyond the scope of sociology. Let it suffice that when we speak of any myth we do not mean to denigrate the possibility of historic truth within it any more than we mean to posit such truth.

The importance of myth is not so much that it explains given phe- nomena or behavior, but that it vouches for it. Myths do not merely satisfy curiosity, they give confidence that situations can be met. They establish a continuity of belief through day-to-day occurrences.[18]

A way in which myths vouch for things or persons is to speak, in one form or another, of the beginnings of things. For most humans there is at least in some degree the feeling that things are what they are and we are what we are because of what has gone before. Myths tell what went before and so why things are the way they are now. The relation of myth to history is made apparent when we come to understand history as the effort of a people to understand themselves in the context of both past and present. This was made clear during the rewriting of history undertaken in this century by such nations as Germany under Hitler and Russia under different Communist regimes, each accusing the other of "revisionism." Controversies over textbooks in the United States show that this application of a point of view is common in all "objec- tive" history and that the complaints of those who want black history or who object to the assumptions about the place of the United States in the world prevalent in American histories indicate a growing realization of how important it is for individuals and groups to find their roots in history. Thus, history, though it claims to be objective and impartial, is used the way myth is used. It could be described as the myth of a culture whose ethos is framed by a secular scientific world view.

In many cases, as we have seen, myth is based on historic figures, particularly leaders. In these cases, a development may be traced from history to myth, and the incorporation of some sort of ritual by which the mythic events are reenacted can be seen as growing out of the myth. Two elements can be found specific to this sort of development. First, in the mythic telling and ritual reenactment of the deeds of heroic leaders the society celebrates its origins and meaning. Its people are drawn together in mutual affirmation of their common heritage and purpose. They are social rites of intensification. Second, such occasions provide reinforcement of basic values and behavior patterns important to the society. The heroes are models of identity and behavior.

It is in this context that we may note the recent movement among women in Western society aimed at seeking out not only neglected stories of influential women for inclusion in standard works of history, but also those to be found in sacred history that could offer models of female involvement legitimated by the religious tradition. Richardson has traced influences in church history that have relegated women to a limited number of roles. Women are found positively portrayed in the myth in roles of the mother or the sacred virgin. Negative roles with mythic reinforcement have been those of the witch and the prostitute.[19] In a society that asks women to assume positive roles outside the home or the cloister, there is a need for mythic support for such action. Consequently, biblical scholars are searching through the scriptures for stories of women in positive leadership roles, and theologians are dealing with both the content and the language of explanations of the faith so that women are no longer ignored or denied full partnership in a religion that has at some times affirmed their right to it. This may be one of the clearest examples in contemporary society of the strains involved when the need for constancy in myth is faced with the need for its applicability to actual experience, a process particularly interesting to the sociologist of religion.[20] We will see later in this work the importance of such restructuring of the myth for movements among blacks and those in former missionary countries.

While in many cases it is clear that ritual is used to make the myth more real, it is also true that many myths seem to have been developed to explain, justify, or reinforce extant rituals. Comparative anthropological studies show that neighboring tribes may have identical rituals interpreted by highly varied myths. The logical interpretation of this phenomenon is that they have borrowed particularly pleasing or satisfying ritual behavior from one another, then developed myths appropriate to their own culture to explain and reinforce the ritual.[21]

Many myths are concerned with specific actions to be taken in particular ceremonies, their sources, and their performance. Myths justify ritual by giving fixity to ideal patterns that are acted out and so become the basis for ideals of behavior and attitude in society. It is a mistake to divide too rigidly ceremonial behavior and practical or profane behavior. Much myth and ritual are pointed toward the fixing of specific patterns of behavior outside the ceremonial occasion. The way a man treats his wife or mother-in-law or the stranger in his village may be ritual behavior, reinforced during occasional formal ceremonies, lodged in a set of reciprocal behaviors demanded of them. The habits and sets of mind reinforced by myth and ritual may be found in rich variation in the many ethnographic studies that describe specific myths and ceremonies and the patterns of daily life among their participants. They may also be found in the variety of emphases given basic myths in a heterogeneous society. As a familiar example, it is quite instructive to go through commentaries and novels of different periods and different groups within Western society and see the many interpretations given of the Christian gospel. Christ may be portrayed as a gentle friend, an angry revolutionary, a successful public relations man, a rock star, or a host of other model personalities. The relevance of the model to the specific group from which and for which it is developed is clear. The Hero is the ideal toward which we are expected to strive, and the basic Christian myth allows variations on the theme that range from "gentle Jesus, meek and mild" to the all-conquering Son of God.

Ritual celebrations of these models also vary widely. Since singing is a good example of participatory ritual, it is of interest to compare the words of the hymn

> And He walks with me
> And He talks with me
> And He tells me I am His own;
> And the joy we share as we tarry there
> None other has ever known.[22]

With Martin Luther's

> Let goods and kindred go
> This mortal life also
> The body they may kill
> God's truth abideth still
> His kingdom is forever.[23]

Certainly different attitudes toward life can be noted here, each supported by Christian teachings. Attitudes toward the self expressed in Christian hymnody also show a wide range, as indicated in the following:

> Alas! and did my Saviour bleed,
> And did my Sovereign die
> Would He devote that sacred head
> For such a worm as I![24]

> Rise up, O men of God!
> The Church for you doth wait,
> Her strength unequal to her task;
> Rise up and make her great![25]

Newer hymnals of liberal denominations delete the phrase "for such a worm as I!" in Watts's hymn, substituting for it "for sinners such as I!" Thus the self-image reinforced by the singing of the hymn is more acceptable to the values of modern psychology. Similarly, the second hymn has now been removed from many hymnals because of its sexist language. The church today—or at least some branches of it—acknowledges that it depends upon its women as well as its men.

The wording of hymns may seem a minor point, but again the particular emphasis of the American outlook may blind us to its importance. Particularly in the Protestant tradition, it has been assumed that the sacred history is carried in (for some, exclusively in) the Bible. Sermons and songs are minor variations of that theme, unimportant in themselves. Yet studies have shown that words of frequently sung hymns are memorized and confused with memorized scripture. The ritual presentation of the myth through music makes the more lasting impression.

This variation of mythic emphasis points up a phenomenon of modern industrial society: while primitive myth and ritual give identity to and bind together all the people in their homogenous society, in highly differentiated societies the myths either proliferate or recede into abstractions. To the extent that they are different from one subgroup to another, they may encourage divisive tendencies in the larger whole, while providing useful feelings of identity for the smaller group. To the extent that all can be fitted together as variations on a single theme, they may support a larger unity. We shall see an example of this later when we consider the phenomenon tagged "American civil religion" in the context of what Bellah has termed the "multiplex symbol system" of modern religion. The admixture of secular and sacred mythology in modern society is also a peculiar phenomenon and will require specific study. We will have to consider in concrete form the relationship between religion as it is usually defined, in terms of concern with the supernatural, and secular ritual, which seems more political or social than religious.

First, however, we must consider the implications of these more general concepts for the ethos of a society and for the range of personality types and behavior patterns expected within it.

Notes and References

1. Galatians 2:20, Revised Standard Version (Division of Christian Education, National Council of Churches of Christ in the U.S.A., 1946).
2. Clyde Kluckhohn, "Myths and Rituals: A General Theory," *Harvard Theological Review* 35 (January 1942): 68–71, 52–53.
3. Anthony F. C. Wallace, *Religion: An Anthropological View* (New York: Random House, 1966), pp. 140–142.
4. Kluckhohn, op. cit., pp. 71–72.
5. Victor W. Turner, *The Forest of Symbols: Aspects of Ndembu Ritual* (Ithaca: Cornell University Press, 1967), p. 37.
6. On this subject, see Phillip E. Slater, *Microcosm: Structural, Functional, and Religious Evolution in Groups* (New York: Wiley, 1966).
7. Bronislaw Malinowski, *Magic, Science, and Religion* (Garden City, N.Y.: Doubleday, 1948), pp. 89–90.
8. Kluckhohn, op. cit., pp. 65–68.
9. A. R. Radcliffe-Brown, *Taboo: The Frasier Lecture, 1939* (London: Cambridge University Press, 1939), pp. 31–32.
10. Adapted from George Homans, *The Human Group* (New York: Harcourt, 1950), pp. 171–172.
11. This dicussion is based primarily on Wallace, op. cit., Chapter 3, "The Goals of Religion: Ritual, Myth, and the Transformations of State," pp. 102–166.
12. For a further development of this idea of three levels of meaning in ritual, see Turner, op. cit., also his *Drums of Affliction* (Oxford: At the Clarendon Press, 1968).
13. Mary Douglas, *Purity and Danger: An Analysis of Concepts of Pollution and Taboo* (London: Routledge & Kegan Paul, 1966).
14. Mircea Eliade, *The Sacred and the Profane,* trans. by Willard R. Trask (New York: Harcourt, 1959), p. 99.
15. W. E. H. Stanner, "The Dreaming" in A. G. Hunderford, ed., *Australian Signposts* (Melbourne: Cheshire, 1956), p. 52.
16. Eliade, op. cit., pp. 104–113.
17. A fascinating survey of the rich mythological structures of the Judeo-Christian tradition may be found in Alan Watts, *Myth and Ritual in Christianity* (Boston: Beacon, 1968).
18. Malinowski, op. cit., p. 84.
19. Herbert Richardson, *Nun, Witch, and Playmate* (New York: Harper & Row, 1971).
20. This is attested to by the theme of the 1978 combined meetings of the Society for the Scientific Study of Religion and the Religious Research Association, "Religion and Sex Roles."

21. See, for example, Franz Boaz et al., *General Anthropology* (Washington, D.C.: U.S. War Department, 1944), p. 617.
22. Words by C. Austin Miles, 1912.
23. Words by Martin Luther, 1529.
24. Words by Isaac Watts, 1707.
25. Words by William Peirson Merrill, 1911.

4

Beliefs and Community

The other component of religion listed in our definition is a community of believers. Where it seemed best to combine the two components of myth and ritual, with this element we need to begin with the opposite —discussing separately what we mean by belief and then its relevance to community. Thus we will be able to see the peculiar significance of the concept "community of believers."

When we use the term "belief," and particularly in the case of religious belief, we may be speaking of a wide range of human responses. Anthropology, sociology, psychology, and philosophy have each struggled to define the concept of belief in such a way as to deal with it in a consistent manner. Closely related to it are concepts of values, attitudes, ideologies, value orientations, and sometimes even world views. It is necessary for us to distinguish between these terms if at all possible, though their overlapping meaning may make the task quite difficult.

Probably the most useful scheme for the consideration of these matters has been advanced by Rokeach in his work *Beliefs, Attitudes, and Values.* He first says that beliefs may not always be those things a person claims to believe, but rather are inferred by an observer from the responses, verbal and otherwise, that the person makes to particular objects or situations. Beliefs, according to Rokeach, are "underlying states of expectancy."[1] That is, they are basic assumptions about what is real or possible and what is not.[2]

Rokeach sets up a model of types of belief based on the assumption that not all beliefs are equally important to the person holding them. His way of handling them can be seen as a series of concentric circles, with the most central beliefs most basic to the maintenance of the individual's understanding of personal identity and one's place in the world. Peripheral beliefs, though they may be held with considerable intensity, will not greatly affect the concept of self or the rest of the belief system if they are changed. However, a change in a central belief may require extensive changes in the whole system. Such beliefs, because of the great number of contingent factors that involve them with other beliefs in the system, are much less likely to change than peripheral beliefs, which being further from the center are most likely to come into contact with other factors and be least tied into the system.

Since religion has been defined by numerous scholars as involving matters of "ultimate concern," we have reason to suspect that religious beliefs would by their very nature be in or near the center of an individual's structure of beliefs—of great consequence, and very difficult to change. The truth of this hypothesis requires further consideration.

For example, we may return to Rokeach, who has created and to some extent empirically verified a typology of beliefs. His five types are

Type A: Primitive beliefs supported by a full concensus. These are basic truths shared by everyone, about which there is no occasion to doubt. They are often not even thought of as beliefs but are taken-for-granted assumptions upon which the interpretation of experience is based.

Type B: Primitive beliefs with no consensual support. These are the beliefs one holds *in spite of* the opinions of others. They are "primitive," as Type A beliefs are primitive, in that they are points of departure for further belief and action. Often they include self-concepts, positive or negative. They are the products of individual life experiences, hence held to be irrefutable.

Type C: Authority beliefs. These are beliefs that do not have the taken-for-granted quality of Type A beliefs but are held because of trust in the reference group or person that is their source. It becomes a matter of "we believe" or "he says" and involves a person's understanding of self in relationship to certain groups or persons.

Type D: Derived beliefs. These beliefs are held because of their association with Type C beliefs. They are natural outgrowths of Type C beliefs or of the character of the groups or persons that are their sources. These include everything from institutional ideologies to beliefs based on recommended sources such as encyclopedias.

Type E: Inconsequential beliefs. These beliefs are not called "inconsequential" because they do not matter to the person holding them. Often they are vehemently held and defended. But they have little consequence for other beliefs and are largely matters of taste.[3]

Sometimes beliefs are distinguished from attitudes and values by defining beliefs as purely cognitive phenomena, attitudes as affective or emotional, and values as concerned with behavioral or moral aspects. Rokeach, however, finds all these dimensions within beliefs. He says that, cognitively, beliefs represent knowledge of what is true or false, good or bad. Affectively, beliefs can arouse emotions about the object of the belief or about people or groups who take positions for or against it. Behaviorally, a belief, by definition a predisposition to act, can be triggered into action by an appropriate stimulus. The specific belief may be more strongly oriented toward one or another of these dimensions, but there is no direct relationship between such orientation and the degree of centrality of the belief.

All a person's beliefs are organized into an interlocking system. Within this general belief system there are groupings of beliefs organized around particular objects or situations. These groupings are what Rokeach defines as *attitudes,* when they represent a relatively enduring organization that inclines a person to act in a preferential way.

Rokeach considers his definition of attitudes somewhat unique because it incorporates both objects and situations as targets of attitude. However, he is not alone in this way of looking at it, since, among others, Allport cites situations as well as objects in his definition[4] and Sherif and Sherif discuss the target of an attitude as a "stimulus domain," which could be interpreted quite broadly.[5] Rokeach is correct, however, in claiming particular importance for this concept because it allows the consideration of two variables when interpreting behavior: the person's attitude toward the object involved, and the person's attitude toward the situation in which one is to act. As we shall see, this distinction becomes particularly important as we consider religious attitudes and behavior.

When we consider attitudes as a cluster of beliefs we are in a position to assess the relationship of religious beliefs to behavior with perhaps a little more clarity than is sometimes found in this area. At the present time we find that some of the "best sources" report that religious beliefs appear to be the bedrock upon which all other belief and attitudinal systems are founded, and "best sources" contrarily report that there is no observable linkage between religious beliefs and attitudes and behavior. What are we to think? Can both be right? It is possible that under certain circumstances they are.

A careful examination of Rokeach's five types of belief will show that in many cases religious beliefs may be found in any one of these types. For example, those who have done research in primitive societies are most likely to have found a high percentage of religious beliefs in Type

A. The cosmology of the society is recognized by everyone as the one way in which life and the world may be experienced and explained. That is simply the way things are.

At this point it is advantageous to consider the idea of community in connection with beliefs. As long as the community and the society are one homogeneous entity most beliefs are likely to be of Type A and to be related to a religious cosmology. As long as conditions do not change there is little reason for questioning or doubt. The world is as it is, and the given explanations of it are taken for granted. There can be little doubt that in a heterogeneous society there is a much smaller area of a person's belief system that can be of Type A. There are groups of people and life experiences that may put any number of basic beliefs into question and thus either change them or move them from Type A to Type C or E. Yet it would be a mistake to say that heterogeneity leads to the eradication of this type of belief. Some of the profound differences in modern society are founded upon beliefs of Type A, in which persons assume such a consensus that they cannot understand one another's questions. Stark and Glock, for example, have found age relevant to the degree of religious orthodoxy only in terms of a sort of "watershed" division between those who had reached maturity (defined as age 25) before World War II and those who were younger. World War II was a period of massive change, which hurled a large proportion of the American people from rural or stable town life into the highly mobile urban mass society of the present era.[6] An interpretation of this phenomenon in relation to religious beliefs involves the experience of those generations. The world view of most older people was developed during a stable and ordered era. They understand from early experience and confirm among themselves a world view of stable fixed categories and definitions. This includes the various beliefs of their religion. It is quite appropriate to them that religious doctrines and social distinctions should be fixed and immutable. An older person, though castigated by younger coreligionists as a hypocrite and a racist, may really mean the statement "I just don't think God intended black folk and white folk to mix, or He wouldn't have made them so different." For that person order exists in maintaining given categories.

By contrast, those whose formative years have been spent in a fluid, changing environment reinforce one another's experiential perception of a world in which no categories are fixed, but all things flow and coalesce along continua. They can accept no categories as given, but rather see them imposed for particular and often transient reasons. So they of course assume such statements as the above to be based in a conscious desire to continue a practice of racial discrimination which is to one's personal advantage. Neither group understands that some of their basic assumptions about the nature of life and its categories are not shared by the other. The presuppositions of both groups are based on Type A beliefs about the way the world is ordered. Since they do not recognize the lack of consensus about this basic model, they are unable to enter fully into the same universe of discourse. What the older people call a lack of standards among the young causes the young to accuse their elders of hypocrisy and arbitrariness. Such primitive beliefs likewise color their expectations as to the nature and permanence of specific religious doctrines or total religious viewpoints.

In a 1973 survey, Robert Wuthnow was able to refine the idea of the "watershed" around World War II, finding instead four different "meaning systems" that appear close to Type A beliefs. Over half the thousand San Francisco Bay Area respondents gave answers that consistently placed them in one or another of these meaning systems, to the exclusion of the other three. The primariness of the systems could be seen by the fact that they structured everything from definitions of the meaning of one's life to attitudes toward social legislation around these basic motifs. The two meaning systems that appear to be founded in the earlier side of Stark and Glock's watershed were those Wuthnow has termed the "theistic," who define things as being either the will of God or subject to some capricious fate, and the "individualistic," who put individual free will at the center of their explanatory modes. A large percentage of those who had reached maturity after World War II subscribed to what Wuthnow called the "social scientific" meaning system, where the central motif was that of an infinitely malleable human nature given shape by social forces and institutions. The fourth type, the "mystical," tended to base their view of the world on inner subjective experience, understanding all reality structures as creations of the human mind rather than fixed in the nature of things, and it was found most often among those under age 30.[7]

This last category may be more within the domain of Type B beliefs, which include religious beliefs arising out of individual experience, particularly at the mystical or revelational level. No one could doubt the centrality or the surety of Joan of Arc's belief in her "voices," or of Paul's conversion, or of the call of many of the prophets. Indeed, one strength of the more evangelical sects is their emphasis on the personal experience of conversion, which becomes the sort of Type B primitive belief from which all other action and thought are structured. Since these experiences are defined as completely subjective, there is no reason to expect confirmation of them from others, but neither is there any need for such confirmation. The vastly differing life-styles based on different understandings of the self that William James has named the "healthy-minded," the "sick souls," and the "twice born" are centered in Type B beliefs.[8]

For most moderns, however, the greatest proportion of their recognized religious beliefs would be considered Types C or D. People admit that not everyone adheres to the same set of religious beliefs. This opinion is reinforced frequently by religious groups themselves, who often claim uniqueness in their possession of ultimate truth, in contrast to the error of heathen or rival groups. In fact, much of the controversy within and between religions has arisen over this point of authority. It was authority that was called into question by the early Hebrew prophets as they thundered against tradition saying, "Thus saith the Lord. . . ." It was authority that was questioned by Jesus when he said, "It is written . . . but I say unto you. . . ." It was problems of authority that caused Paul to write critical letters to early Christians engaged in disputes between the followers of Peter, of Paul, and of Apollos. What more direct appeal for authority could be found than the Moslems' cry of "There is no God but Allah, and Mohammed is his prophet!" or the Calvinists' creed which defines the Scriptures as "the only right rule of faith and practice"? And in modern controversies over whether converts to new religious groups have properly converted or been brainwashed we find two authorities in conflict—that of religious groups and that of some psychiatrists called in as experts.

Again, it is the group—the community of believers—that provides the authority. Either the group itself is the authority, as in traditional Roman Catholicism, or it has authorities that it recognizes as appropriate for defense and for argument. The problem in a heterogenous society is that people are seldom members of a single community but may share communal assumptions with several fairly diverse groups. So we see that if we follow Rokeach's definition of an attitude as a cluster of beliefs, it is quite possible that in any specific situation the attitude motivating a person's behavior may be composed of beliefs emanating from two or more dissimilar groups. An example may be taken from early days in the civil rights struggle, where a Louisiana housewife was excommunicated from the Roman Catholic church because of her refusal to obey her bishop's order to desegregate parochial schools in her parish. She was a member of the Roman Catholic church, and she identified with that community of believers; but she was also a Southern white and shared basic beliefs from that community. Her behavior showed the interaction of at least three beliefs coming from these two sources. Probably the most central one—most nearly Type A—was based on the seldom questioned assumption of racial differentiation and inequality which was endemic in the culture of the area. It was probably less open to question than any of her religious beliefs, so it might be expected to exhibit greater potency. Alongside it were two beliefs about religious authority—one from her own church, the other from the more generalized Southern culture. Although she recognized that according to her Catholic faith she owed obedience to the bishop's decree, she instead confronted him with scriptural evidence that he was wrong, appealing to the authority of the Bible in a manner more customary for her Southern Baptist neighbors than for a person acting within the Roman Catholic tradition. Such behavior indicates that when beliefs more nearly Type A are challenged we may search out alternate authorities to support them in the Type C or D range.

If attitudes may be held concerning either objects (including persons) or situations, it is worth considering whether one of these concerns may be more peripheral than the other. The concern of religion with ultimates might indicate that many times religious beliefs gather their power by defining situations in terms of their relationship to ultimate concerns. For example, some church people have been condemned as hypocritical for doing "good deeds" for the poor in the context of their church, while doing things that continue oppressive conditions among the poverty-stricken in the conduct of their businesses. Since this behavior logically would be based on attitudinal definitions of the two situations which do not place the objects (in this case, the poor) in the same light, it would seem that religious teachings might profitably be aimed at helping people redefine their secular settings in line with religious definitions. However, the structural differentiation that has occurred in modern society makes this task extremely difficult. We frequently hear churchly polemics against this kind of compartmentalization, but their effectiveness has not been particularly noticeable.

Type E beliefs may seem unimportant in religious matters, these inconsequential beliefs that are simply matters of taste. Yet no one who has done any amount of work within institutional religion would say this. Many local congregations have foundered and sunk over such peripheral matters as the choice of choir robes or styles of music, pictures hung in the sanctuary, styles of preaching, and a host of other details that seem petty to everyone except those involved. The problem here is one of symbolism. Each word, each action, each article of dress, picture, or object used in religious services stands for far more than its own form or nature. This is a factor recognized in ancient tribal rituals, where exact motions must be copied, and which is still basic to highly liturgical churches. It is less often realized by Protestants who pride themselves on their freedom from idolatry of objects and forms. Yet the universal human reaction to symbolic objects wins out over the antisymbolic ideology, even though what is symbolized varies with the individual. While symbols evoke a shared response in a homogeneous community, in heterogeneous situations the opposite can occur. Thus the picture of the fair-haired, blue-eyed Jesus in the sanctuary is to the avid civil rights advocate a symbol of institutional racism and a perversion of the Christian Gospel, while to the traditionalist it is a symbol of all the warmth and love and inspiration experienced in the religion —a picture of the Lord. To the sentimentalist it may be the lovely picture given to the church by a grandparent, and to move it would defile the memory of that saintly ancestor. And so it goes. Religion, concerned as it is with much that is abstract and subjective, must deal heavily in symbolism. Symbols recall important verities of their faith to the minds of the faithful and unite them in a common response. Such shared response, says Parsons, is an elementary form of culture.[9] But what is it when the response is neither similar nor complementary, but antagonistic; do these responses share a culture? Obviously they do, but one of the problems faced by students of religion in a secular age is that it may not be recognized religious symbols that bind people together in their responses, even within the same church congregation.

Symbols tie together belief systems that structure our response to other persons, the group, nature, and the cultural system itself. They involve cognitive, expressive, and evaluative factors. In other words, symbols help us respond in an organized manner to objects and situations in terms of what we think they are, how we feel about them, and how much value we place on them. They mobilize beliefs, attitudes, and values.

The relation of beliefs and belief systems to values has been defined in so many ways in so many studies that the concept of values seems almost worthless. Yet somehow values seem to be the strongest of these concepts to study. Rokeach, who makes beliefs the most specific of the concepts, the building blocks of belief systems from which come attitudes and so on, defines values as beliefs of a very general sort, much fewer in number than other kinds of beliefs or attitudes, and hence more appropriate objects of study.[10] This seems something of a contradiction. How can they be the most general when placed in the class of the most specific? Where does this place them in relation to attitudes? Thomas and Znaniecki distinguish values from attitudes by their social, rather than individual, content.[11] Kluckhohn strikes a note echoed by perhaps the largest number of students of the subject when he discusses values as conceptions of the desirable and the undesirable, which influence the choice of ways of acting, their modes, and their goals.[12] Valuing seems always to involve the hierarchical ranking of objects, situations, or actions on the basis of what is good, right, or desirable. It may be that the difficulty in defining values is mainly due to a tendency to seek that definition in terms of structure rather than in terms of process. Yet values imply action; they are the process of ranking. They are based on beliefs, but the ranking of beliefs from Type A to Type E may be seen itself as a process of valuing. Values both grow out of and control attitudes.

Values, attitudes, and beliefs are social products; they are also personal characteristics of individuals. They develop out of actual experiences of an individual and the way he or she has learned to interpret those experiences. Where everyone's experiences are very similar and one interpretation is generally offered to all, the systems of values, attitudes, and beliefs held by all will be nearly identical. This, as we have noted, has been the experience in primitive tribes, and it is only slightly eroded in peasant societies. In such circumstances the religion of the people expresses these shared assumptions and extends them to include the sacred cosmos.

In this context we must again take up the subject of secularization, for the society we have just pictured is the kind described by Becker as "sacred."[13] At this point we need not consider "sacred" in exactly the same way we have used the term "holy." It is not so much that all life is infused with mystery as it is that practically all beliefs are Type A. They assume a taken-for-grantedness that militates against change, since any change would shake a pattern that extends into the sacred cosmos. Sacred societies, as Becker defines them, are those least likely to change. In terms of religion we can see that such societies assume the nature of divinely ordained social arrangements. A particularly telling demonstration of this has been provided by Swanson in *Birth of the Gods,* in which he uses statistical methods to compare cosmologies and social structures of fifty societies. His work indicates a close relationship between the structure of the society and the number and type of gods acknowledged in its religion.[14] It is not within the province of sociology to say whether the gods of a people are simply their own creation or do not really exist. We can, however, note that the way in which people perceive the divine is based on their experience, and in simple societies the structure of the divine realm has close ties to the nature of the only social arrangement the people have experienced. How true this may be as well for more complex cultures will be a subject of consideration throughout this work.

It is not only in the cognitive elements of belief structures that sacred societies may be distinguished from secular ones. There is a strong affective component as well. Such societies often resemble large families, holding close primary ties, shared associations, and a sense of belonging to one another. Their religious practice expresses this, providing ritual celebration of their shared lives and values.[15]

This picture changes as a society becomes more heterogeneous through the introduction of higher levels of technology or warfare requiring greater division of labor, or through contact with other cultures and the diffusion of their ideas. The experience of every member of the society is no longer nearly the same, and given interpretations no longer fit all groups equally. One religious answer to this, well marked in Swanson's survey, is to recognize different divinities as concerned with different groups and to symbolize the unity of the various groups into one society through a belief system that puts all the gods into relationship with one another in some kind of pantheon. Thus there are certain central beliefs and rituals that apply to the whole group, others that are the special concern of particular groups within it. The closeness of fellowship is likely to be greater in the smaller groups who share a specific interest rather than in the larger, more loosely knit totality. Between groups, ties are more likely to be rational and based on need, rather than emotional and based on identity. Yet the central rituals maintain a certain amount of identity and affectual response.

In Parsons's comprehensive systematization of the study of social action,[16] he delineates five continua, known as "pattern variables," within which action takes place. These are as follows:

Universalism————particularism
Performance————quality
Affective neutrality—affectivity
Specificity————diffuseness
Self-orientation————collectivity orientation

These are particularly relevant to the analysis of the process of secularization in society and its relationship to religious beliefs and values. In general, the process of differentiation and specialization that leads to secularization within a society increases the proportion of demands for action of the type represented by the left side of the listing. That is, we become more likely, as society grows more complex, to emphasize role definitions that apply universally rather than treating each individual in terms of his or her unique characteristics. We value specific performance at a particular task more than general craftsmanship, and so we treat all action in terms of specific components rather than wholes and tend more toward objective, affectively neutral evaluations of these specifics, rather than emotional involvement with the person. Since the complexity of life is too great for us to encompass all of it, we tend to take from it what we most desire, making the self rather than the group the focus of our orientation.

Religion traditionally has been more concerned with qualities represented by the right side of the list. It aims at individuals as particular persons rather than replaceable entities. It is concerned with the quality of life, including emotional involvement in the life process, and sees this as part of a total cosmology rather than breaking it down into specific parts. It is a group-oriented activity, expressing common sentiments and beliefs. The trend of society, then, seems to be away from all that religion has stood for, and the behavior of church members caught in this dilemma indicates some of the consequences.

In terms of belief systems, it means that for many church members it seems proper that dealing with these weighty matters is the specialized job of the minister and the theologian, and that all the person in the pew need do is assent to what is, after all, the product of specialized scholarship. Of particular importance is the movement from collectivity to a self-orientation, a movement frequently referred to as the "privatization" of religion. As in the rest of life, so in religion the individual picks those elements that fit into his or her particular life-style, with little consciousness of the fact that the tradition may demand total commitment to the religious body or its teachings. In truth, there are many who would take issue with the assertion that religion is geared to a collectivity orientation, because in their secular world they have never experienced much of this kind of expectation. Where else but in a fully secularized society would we find no fault with the phrase "the church of your choice"?

In order to supply symbols at all useful to the society at large, this form of secularization necessitates increasing abstraction in the interpretation of religion. It is left for the subgroups to provide concrete interpretations in the light of their own experiences. In terms of beliefs, then, there appears to be a withdrawal of much religious belief from the area of Type A, where full consensus supports religious assumptions, to Type C, where each group develops its own appropriate authorities upon which to base religious interpretation. While the manifest function of such a process is obvious and necessary—the provision of societal unity while legitimating a needed diversity of life-styles—it has the latent consequence of removing many specific beliefs from the central identity-fixing part of the belief system to a more peripheral position. In terms of beliefs, this is the nature of secularization.

The consequences may be seen in studies of religious belief done in modern societies as well as in various forms of religious performance. For example, in recent polls a very high percentage of Americans responded that they believe in God. This seems to be one of those core, Type A beliefs that provides common assumptions in American culture, although it has shown some erosion. Although it may be diminishing, there is still a connection in the minds of most Americans between belief in God and social and moral responsibility. But when Glock and Stark questioned the meaning of that response and queried a group of church members on just what or who they believed God to be, they found a decided variation between the anthropomorphic and the abstract, with a small percentage of church members claiming no belief in God at all.[17] In Wuthnow's later study of a more general population, a significant portion of the respondents—particularly the younger ones—chose a statement phrased, "I am uncomfortable about the word 'God' but I do believe in something 'more' or 'beyond.' "[18] With so great a variation, it would seem inevitable that beliefs in God would lead to disunity rather than unity—if they were ever discussed or were treated as very important. The price of unity has been the trivialization of religious belief.

Wilson points this out in *Religion in Secular Society,* particularly in comparing responses to secularization in England and the United States.[19] In England, he says, the existence of an established church has provided Nonconformists with a focus, both religious and social, against which they can mobilize beliefs. Hence, within the churches, beliefs have not been as trivialized as they have in the United States. As beliefs become less important to members of the English churches, as they are likely to do in a secularized society, the members simply quit attending the churches that hold them as important. Secularization of beliefs is accompanied by a significant reduction in ritual participation. In the United States, on the other hand, trivialization of beliefs has occurred at a more central point—within the churches themselves—and is accompanied by an increase of organizational activity. Higher percentages of persons join churches, and they provide a proliferating number of activities, from study groups and worship through Boy Scout troops and bowling teams. One of Kelley's points in *Why Conservative Churches Are Growing,* however, is that this process is no longer producing involvement, and the English model seems more nearly to hold in the 1970s than previously.[20]

Wilson's model is based on the historic position of the United States as a new nation and a nation of immigrants. Since a high proportion of these immigrants came from peasant societies, they were accustomed to finding their community symbolized in its church, and they acted upon this custom. In later generations the diversity of ethnic churches has been replaced by the more unifying, more bland denominationalism now offered in main-line churches. But the expectation of community reinforcement is still tied to the church. Since beliefs may not be unifying if they are expressed very concretely, church organization and activity have taken the place of beliefs as the expression of the sense of community. Wilson reports that the sense of community purveyed by such arrangements seems false and uncomfortable to the European who still has some contact with traditional communities where people have a good deal more in common than do the members of the average American suburban congregation. For the American congregation religion becomes a way of seeking rather than expressing community, and beliefs are not allowed to endanger its fragile existence. The success of the conservatives noted by Kelley is based on a much more explicit belief system, but one very much privatized. And there is little doubt that organizational activity is a central concern in these churches as well.

However, considerable argument could be given as to the importance of particular, concrete religious views, as opposed to the abstract orientations we have mentioned, remaining at the core. These alternative ways of dealing with the world and ultimate goals may provide the basis for the value ranking of beliefs and attitudes. In fact, the American example may be taken as the extreme result of one of four such religious world views posited by Weber—the one he applied to Calvinist Christianity—and hence considered significant for American culture. Weber's two-dimensional typology of general religious orientations involves goals on the one hand and means on the other. He finds that goals or ends may chiefly be conceived in terms of those in the present world (inner-worldly) or the sacred cosmos (otherworldly). The means for reaching such ends through religion may lean toward the ascetic or the mystic. Asceticism here is concerned with control—control of self or environment or both. Mysticism involves a certain loss of selfhood, a submission to the experience of the Other. The dominant orientation of Calvinist Protestantism, said Weber, is one of ascetic inner-worldliness. Calvin's teaching that one's vocation in the workaday world could be treated as a religious calling, that the God of history is served through work in this world, led to a religious affirmation of scientific investigation and technological progress.[21] If control of self and nature can be better accomplished through science and technology than through religion, then it is the religion itself that legitimates the value process that rates science and technology more important than religious belief or practice. This, of course, is not the way Calvin taught about belief and practice, but it is a logical consequence of the religious perspective of inner-worldly asceticism.

Such considerations of the relationship of religion to general value orientations lead us once again into a discussion of a tension within religion which Weber has demonstrated to be extremely widespread if not universal. This is the tension based on the common tendency, in dealing with matters of ultimate concern and sacred character, to want to preserve them in their exact form because they are too holy to manipulate. This is contrasted with an appreciation of the sacred cosmos as the repository of unreached ideals and untapped power, out of which may come at any time the impetus for major change leading to a better realization of those ideals. Many sociological studies of religion concentrate on the former manifestation of the religious consciousness, since it is out of this orientation that religious experiences and beliefs become social institutions. This sort of "sacred" orientation (in Becker's treatment of the term) is similar to what Rokeach has termed "closed mindedness." In a closed system of beliefs, he says, the Type C and D (authority and authority-derived) beliefs are seen as coming from absolute authority; the acceptance or rejection of other people is based on their agreement or disagreement with that authority. This factor has led to many social psychological studies of the relation of religion to the "authoritarian personality," and much of the history of religious conflict can be traced to this orientation to authority. What we have not dealt with is the opposite pole of the model, which Rokeach calls the "open system." In the open type of belief system, he says, authorities are held as less absolute, and agreement or disagreement with them is not a vital criterion for ranking other people. The closed system involves Type A beliefs that the world or the present situation or both are threatening, while behind the open system is a much more positive view of life.[22] This theoretical perspective has been supported in recent empirical work by Dean Hoge, who found a strong tie between the more explicit and boundary-maintaining beliefs of conservative Presbyterians and a sense of "social threat" when comparing them with more liberal coreligionists.[23]

While much religious effort is expended in the construction of closed systems of belief that can provide salvation from a threatening world, there are always some religionists who say it is only through religious faith that we can transcend the world enough to be open. For example, Leslie Newbigin, one of the founders of the ecumenical United Church of South India, has written that Christians can claim absoluteness only for Christ and so must reject claims of absoluteness of their understanding of the faith.[24] While discussing the thought of the German theologian Friederich Gogarten, Shiner says:

> Therefore, only when the church ceases to treat the claim of the crucified and risen Christ as a religious message and begins to see that it concerns the being of man before the mystery of the future will its preaching become authentic. This is why Gogarten says in *The Preaching of Jesus Christ* that wherever we are pushed out of our self-evident truths and securities and experience the uncanny power of the oncoming future, there Jesus Christ is nearest.[25]

So we see that religion—even the same religion—may be used as the basis of general orientations that become open or closed systems. The combination of religious and other beliefs shared by particular communities comes into play as we look at value systems based on open and closed patterns. In general, it is the experience of high mobility, rapid change, and relative success that provides experiential support for open systems. So while Christian theologians may find their support in a religious belief system, Orr and Nichelson see values of openness as a natural orientation for modern suburbanites. It is not faith that allows one to affirm openness in the face of potential threat of change, but experience in finding change no threat that allows openness. If, as Orr and Nichelson say, modern suburban people's openness to change causes them to hold all things lightly, we may find them happily subscribing to the theology of men like Gogarten or less ponderous celebrators of secularity such as Harvey Cox, without deep levels of commitment. It may be only a Type D or E belief, enriching more firmly held beliefs in the goodness of life, change, and progress.[26] The relevance of specific religious beliefs to such modern people is no more deep than that of traditional theology to William James's "healthy-minded" of a couple of generations past.[27]

However, such experientially based optimism is open only to those who are successful in modern life. For many, modernity compounds anxiety rather than relieving it. And even here the problem may take two different forms. The problem of the "expansive" type described by Orr and Nichelson may be found in areas of cultural lag, where institutions prove too slow to expand and are felt to be constricting, alien forces to the individual. In this case, rather than optimistic and expansive, a person may become *alienated.* The experience of the alienated, as Berger has described it, is the consequence of too much objectification of the social world. Although in reality there is a kind of dialectic always going on, where people shape their perceptions of reality and their social institutions and are in turn shaped by them, the alienated only perceive the second half of that process. They experience social institutions as objective forces completely outside their power, forcing them into unwanted conformity, distorting what they understand to be their true selves. They become prone to paranoia and/or revolutionary ideologies.[28]

On the other hand, the person who has been unable to master expansion that fits into change, who may actually be losing status, employment, or a sense of identity in the process, is likely to experience a lack of normative structure in the society. The person who cannot find the rules of the game of life in order to play it may frantically seek to recapture or recreate some meaningful structure. Such people suffer from *anomie*.[29] For them Type A beliefs are no longer possible, since their taken-for-granted world has been shattered. But they may seek a "secondary naiveté" either through experiences leading to Type B beliefs or through allegiance to some group with a strong form of authority in its Type C beliefs. The relevance of this type of reaction occurring in the same society as the expansive development will become apparent as we later consider the various religious movements of the past two decades.

In summary, in modern society the place of religious beliefs in the total spectrum of beliefs, attitudes, and values is ambiguous, particularly because they no longer are the expression of a shared community life. Their symbolic nature allows them to be retained in form while changing greatly in the content of what they symbolize to individual believers. As a result, they tend to become more abstract, so that they involve the basic process of valuing without direct recognition as religious beliefs; or in their concrete forms they are pushed to more peripheral positions in the belief system. If they remain explicit, it is in groups with separatist tendencies, likely either to withdraw from the society or to experience its institutions as negative forces to be opposed rather than deserving their positive participation.

For many Americans, few specific religious beliefs carry the symbolic weight they once did. The police officer on the corner is for them a more potent symbol of negative social control than a devil, and for many the *Encyclopaedia Britannica* a far more reliable authority than the Bible.

Yet the abstract, value-oriented form of religious belief may hold some power in the society. A greater question may be whether at this level of abstraction these really are *religious* beliefs or whether they may be philosophical world views developed from the interplay of religious and secular beliefs. If they are philosophical world views, what will happen to them if the society becomes so secularized that there are no central religious beliefs with which secular ones can be intertwined? If explicit religious beliefs are maintained under such circumstances, must they become so peculiar to certain subgroups that the society becomes polytheistic? And if this becomes the case, can social unity be maintained without an overarching "civil religion" that affirms that polytheism in the face of historic attachments to monotheistic creeds? These are some of the questions arising out of a study of beliefs that must be addressed as we study the actual practice and institution of religion.

Notes and References

1. Milton Rokeach, *Beliefs, Attitudes, and Values* (San Francisco: Jossey-Bass 1968), p. 2.
2. A similar definition is advanced in Clyde Kluckhohn, "Values and Value Orientations," in Parsons and Shils, eds., *Toward a General Theory of Action* (Cambridge: Harvard University Press, 1951), p. 432.
3. Rokeach, op. cit., pp. 3, 6–11, 113–114, 112.
4. As quoted by Kluckhohn, op. cit., p. 432.
5. Carolyn W. Sherif and Muzafer Sherif, *Attitude, Ego-Involvement, and Change* (New York: Wiley, 1967), p. 115.
6. For further discussion of the "watershed" phenomenon in American religious belief, see Rodney Stark and Charles Y. Glock. *American Piety: The Nature of Religious Commitment* (Berkeley: University of California Press, 1968), pp. 2–7 ff.
7. Robert Wuthnow, *The Consciousness Reformation* (Berkeley: University of California Press, 1976).
8. See William James, *Varieties of Religious Experience* (New York: Modern Library, 1902), Chapters 4 through 7.
9. Parsons and Shils, op. cit., pp. 16, 165–166.
10. Rokeach, op. cit., pp. 159–160.
11. W. I. Thomas and Florian Znaniecki, *The Polish Peasant in Europe and America* (New York: Knopf, 1927), pp. 27–29.
12. Kluckhohn, op. cit., p. 395.
13. Howard Becker, "Current Sacred-Secular Theory," in Howard Becker and Alvin Boskoff, eds., *Modern Social Theory in Continuity and Change* (New York: Dryden, 1957), pp. 140–144.
14. Guy Swanson, *The Birth of the Gods* (Ann Arbor: University of Michigan Press, 1960).
15. Full discussions of this type of society may be found in Emile Durkheim, *The Division of Labor in Society*, trans. by George Simpson (New York: Free Press, 1947), where he discusses it as a type of society characterized by "mechanical solidarity"; in Ferdinand Tonnies, *Gemeinschaft und Gesellschaft*, trans. and ed. by Charles Loomis (Lansing: Michigan State University Press, 1957), in which it is called the "Gemeinschaft"; and in Robert Redfield, *The Primitive World and Its Transformations* (Ithaca: Cornell University Press, 1953), as the "folk society."
16. These concepts run through all Parsons's works, and may be found clearly developed in *The Social System* (New York: Free Press, 1951), among others.
17. Charles Y. Glock and Rodney Stark, *Religion and Society in Tension* (Chicago: Rand McNally, 1965), pp. 70–92. See also Stark and Glock, *American Piety*, op. cit., pp. 25–32.
18. Charles Y. Glock and Robert Wuthnow, "The Religious Dimension," presented at the Second International Symposium on Belief, Vienna, Austria, January 8–11, 1975.

19. Brian Wilson, *Religion in Secular Society* (Baltimore: Penguin, 1969), pp. 109–149. See also Will Herberg, *Protestant Catholic Jew* (Garden City, N.Y.: Doubleday, 1955), which Wilson uses as much of his background.
20. Dean Kelley, *Why Conservative Churches Are Growing* (New York: Harper & Row, 1972).
21. Max Weber, *The Sociology of Religion,* trans. by Ephraim Fischoff (Boston: Beacon, 1963), especially Chapters 11 and 15.
22. Rokeach, op. cit., pp. 55–56.
23. Dean Hoge, *Division in the Protestant House* (Philadelphia: Westminister, 1977).
24. Leslie Newbigin, "The Quest for Unity through Religion," in *Journal of Religion* 35 (1955): 17–35.
25. Larry Shiner, *The Secularization of History: An Introduction to the Theology of Friederich Gogarten* (Nashville: Abingdon, 1966), p. 78.
26. John B. Orr and Patrick R. Nichelson, *The Radical Suburb* (Philadelphia: Westminister, 1970), pp. 16–62.
27. James, op. cit., pp. 77–121.
28. See Peter L. Berger, *The Sacred Canopy* (Garden City, NY.: Doubleday, 1967), Chapter 4.
29. Ibid., Chapter 1.

Berger, Peter L. *The Sacred Canopy*. Garden City, N.Y.: Doubleday, 1967.

Glock, Charles Y., and Hammond, Phillip, eds. *Beyond the Classics?* New York: Harper & Row, 1973.

James, William. *The Varieties of Religious Experience*. New York: Modern Library, 1902.

Kluckhohn, Clyde. "Myths and Rituals: A General Theory." *Harvard Theological Review* 35 (January, 1942): 45–79.

Malinowski, Bronislaw. *Magic, Science, and Religion and Other Essays*. Garden City, N.Y.: Doubleday, 1948.

Wallace, Anthony F. C. *Religion: An Anthropological View*. New York: Random House, 1966.

Part II

THE CULTURAL BASIS OF RELIGIOUS ORGANIZATION

The chief concerns of the sociology of religion have to do with the social manifestations of religion—the way in which religion in any society is structured into patterns of action and role expectations, and the relationship of this structure to the society at large. In this section we will consider the first of these two areas, the internal structure of the religious institution.

Obviously there is great variation among religions in institutional structure, and many attempts have been made to provide meaningful classification of these variations. The classificatory scheme that will be presented in the next few chapters is based mainly on the evolutionary stages set forth by Robert Bellah in "Religious Evolution."[1] Though he calls it a typology of evolutionary stages, Bellah clearly denies that this is a unilateral development that must occur, that later stages are in any way "higher" than earlier ones, or that earlier ones, indeed, are no longer present in modern society. It is a pattern of growing complexity in the religion and in the society, and in each more complex form the simpler forms may yet be found. Sometimes these simpler forms are present mainly in the history of the group, but they are found more often within some groups or in certain practices currently exercised. In many cases it would be hard to understand the development of one of the stages had it not had the previous stage upon which to build, or against which to react. It is in these ways that it may seem an evolutionary pattern. For our purposes, however, since we have postulated that many of the forms are extant in modern society, it becomes the basis for classifying observable religious organization more than a developmental sequence.

Bellah's first category is that of *primitive* religion, a type similar to what has been called folk religion, where the religious consciousness is diffused throughout the whole life of the group, and the group itself is the religious organization. This is followed by *archaic* religion, in which the mythology has become more explicit and a diversity of cults has developed as an expression of the growing heterogeneity of the society. In *historic* religion, symbol systems become more transcendent—the religion is applied more universally than just to the "folk" or group. Religious organization becomes differentiated from the group or society, with an identifiably separate group of specialist leaders whose position is part of the hierarchical order of the society. The hierarchy collapses in *early modern* religion, and religion comes to be more an individual orientation to the sacred cosmos. The various religious institutions serve to equip persons with a sacred interpretation of their secular calling. The *modern* form, which may be difficult to define as religion at all, appears to be an extension of the early modern emphasis on the individual to the assumption of full responsibility of secular persons for the control of symbol systems and their own lives.

This basic outline can better serve our purposes of interpreting the social organization of religion if it is overlaid with several other typologies. Thus, at the primitive end of the spectrum, it will be useful to consider three types delineated by Wallace.[2] These are the *individualistic,* the *shamanic,* and the *communal* cult institutions. His

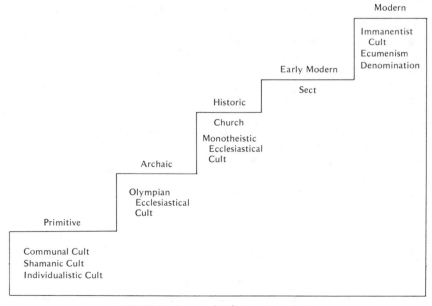

FIGURE 2 Forms of Religious Organization.

fourth category of such institutions, the *ecclesiastical*—which is divided into the Olympian and the monotheistic—extends through the later categories of Bellah's evolutionary scheme. The finer distinctions he makes within the primitive type are useful not only for understanding primitive tribes, but also for those "survivals" extant in modern society.

Bellah's categories of historic and early modern cover the periods and the organizational types usually denoted by the concepts of *church* and *sect* as developed by Troeltsch. Somewhere near the end of the early modern and the beginning of the modern types we encounter the *denomination,* in the sense in which it is used by Niebuhr and others.[3] More nearly within the boundaries of the modern type may be found that form of recombination known as ecumenism, particularly as this phenomenon is treated by Wilson.[4] Current observation leads to the tentative statement that modern religion also is characterized by the development of cult groups based on mystical experience, or at least a theology that defines the divine as present within the individual. These may be called "immanentist cults." While other subtypes may appear, the essential framework within which we shall view the social organization of religion is delineated in Figure 2.

Notes and References

1. First published in *American Sociological Review* 29 (June 1964): 348–374, this paper has appeared in several anthologies and has now been incorporated by Bellah into his book *Beyond Belief: Essays on Religion in a Post-Traditional World* (New York: Harper & Row, 1970).

2. Anthony F. C. Wallace, *Religion: An Anthropological View* (New York: Random House, 1966), pp. 84–88.

3. For further explication of these concepts, see Ernst Troeltsch, *The Social Teaching of the Christian Churches,* trans. by Olive Wyon (New York: Harper, 1960) and H. Richard Niebuhr, *The Social Sources of Denominationalism* (New York: Meridian Age, 1957).

4. Bryan Wilson, *Religion in Secular Society* (Baltimore: Penguin, 1969).

5

Primitive and Civil Religion

The social manifestation of religion known as "primitive" is not given that name because it applies only to preliterate societies, but rather because it appears to be present to some degree in all religious behavior. It may be understood as the basic structure from which all religious phenomena have developed. Durkheim, for example, felt that he found in the primitive religion of the Australian aborigines the germ of all higher religions—the division of things into sacred and profane; notions of the soul, of spirits, and of mythic personalities; ascetic cults; incipient high gods; and rites of communion, imitation, commemoration, and expiation.[1] While he may have overstated his case to some extent, it is certainly true that elements of primitive religion are ubiquitous.

Included in the category of primitive religion are the three subtypes delineated by Wallace: the individualistic cult, the shamanic cult, and the communal cult.[2] The entire category shares the qualities often attributed to "folk" religion because it involves religious expressions that are closely tied to the daily life of the people. It belongs to what Redfield has termed the "little tradition," rather than the "great tradition" celebrated by most high religions.[3]

The peculiar nature of primitive or folk religion is wrapped up in the identity of the religious organization with the society itself. The religious tradition is intertwined with the total tradition of the society, and special religious lore or skills are passed down from generation to generation along with the other cultural traits of the group. Religious identity is one's identity as a member of the group.[4]

Primitive religion is based on visions and a belief in spirits—evil spirits, which are involved in witchcraft; good or neutral spirits, which are the basis of magic; and personal spirits or souls. It is these beliefs that prompt the organization of primitive religion into its three basic forms.

The first of these subtypes, the individualistic cult institution, is nearly magical in some of its manifestations. Persuasive arguments have been made that religion and magic are not opposite, mutually exclusive categories, but rather are two ends of a continuum upon which all human behavior in regard to the supernatural or ultimate may be placed.[5] Radin defines magic as the attempt to coerce forces to meet personal needs, and he notes that religion is full of this element. Religion, however, tends to reinterpret the symbols and to mitigate the coercive aspects in comparison with unadulterated magic.[6] The line of demarcation between the two, however, is indistinct.

Wallace includes in individualistic cult institutions all those ritual acts that in our culture are connected with "luck." To knock on wood or cross one's fingers is to participate in individualistic ritual. It is part of the social structure because the behavior is given common symbolic meaning that is taught and understood in the society. Such rituals also include the individual quest for a guardian spirit as undertaken by such groups as the Plains Indians. Various hunting, sailing, and other technological rituals performed by individuals also fall into this category. The basic characteristic of this form of religion is that it requires neither group participation nor any specialist. It is open to all members of the group according to their individual tendencies or needs.

As we have said, there is a close relationship between this form of religion and magic, which is often defined as that having to do with the attainment of one's own specific ends. And yet such rituals can also be particularly religious, in that they are aimed at providing an identity or character traits most desired in the religious value structure. So the young Plains Indian sets out on a quest for his vision, and in so doing is much like the Protestant Christian engaging in regular Bible reading to learn the meaning of faith for one's own life. Both are doing privately what is expected of them religiously, not as an unusual exercise but as a common practice.

Not all cases of individual cult practice are encouraged by the official religion, yet they persist. Their function appears to lie in the realm of individual psychology. In a discussion of the social organization of religion they are of relatively little importance, but they do need to be noted. Such individual practices affect the forms that more organized religion may take; they also reflect the influence of the organized religion on the individual's private behavior. It is one small thread which will be picked up again as we examine other types of religious organization, for it is present in all societies, regardless of the relative sophistication of their religion. In fact, Durkheim asserts that the role of individualistic practices is less important in primitive than in more

differentiated societies because the individual is much less clearly defined as a separate entity in primitive society. In complex societies the
value of the individual is greater and the individualistic cult is more
important and less open to influence from the outside.[7]

The first form of specialization in the religious organization of human
society may be found in the shamanic cult institution. Although a
shaman need not be a full-time practitioner, he or she is a specialist in
the religious role and has clients who exercise a lay role in the ritual.[8]
As with individualistic cult institutions, the border line between this
cult and the practice of magic is extremely unclear. The role of shaman
can be considered an intermediate one between that of the magician as
a private practitioner and that of the priest as a public official.[9] The term
"shaman" comes to us from northern Asiatic tribes, but the type of role
played by the shaman is found in most societies. In general a shaman
is an individual practitioner who performs rituals for individuals or
groups, usually for some sort of payment. The shaman does not demand
of clients that they share in the fullness of his or her religious experience.[10] Yet even this statement is subject to question. For example,
Lowie finds that the Crow shaman often did not just perform rites for
clients, but might also share some particular power with them.[11]

We generalize, however, that the shaman is a person usually considered to be possessed of power or spirits, who performs helpful rites,
usually for individuals or for families. He or she—and there are many
societies in which female shamans outnumber the males—is expected
to have undergone a comparatively rigorous initiation which has resulted in possession by or at least close contact with one or more spirits.
This possession is recognized in the behavior of the shaman, who often
acts in an unusual manner and is expected to have extraordinary powers. These powers, which may have come from outside but which are
understood to reside in the individual, are the basis of Weber's concept
of charisma. In the case of the shaman they are often induced by special
rites. The role of shaman is one in which ecstatic states are expected to
prevail. The ordinary lay person can afford ecstasy only occasionally,
perhaps at times when one courts intoxication or participates in an orgy,
but one cannot maintain such a state for long. Shamans can.[12] Often
they exercise ascetic rituals, inducing ecstasy through exposure, hunger,
or lack of sleep. In their attempt to participate in the sacred world
shamans may attempt to suppress ordinary consciousness or to heighten
it, sometimes with the use of drugs.[13] Often the call to be a shaman
originates in the personality type of the subject. Shamanism calls for a
particular sort of person, more excitable, less stable, more sensitive than
the average, but also with intelligence and a certain amount of

"drive."[14] The role of shaman comes very close to our description of a schizoid or schizophrenic personality. The shaman is expected to be detached, at least at times, from his or her normal personality and surroundings.[15] Wach hints that in many primitive societies any emotionally unstable person is likely to be honored as a shaman; in higher cultures people become a little more discriminating about who will mediate sacred power to them.[16] Wallace adds that the role of shaman provides a functional spot for personality types our society often shunts off into custodial institutions.[17] It may be the shamanic role within more institutional priestly or ministerial roles of modern society that induces some relatively negative scores of seminarians on standard psychological tests.

Yet there is much more to the role than real or simulated madness. The initiatory process, almost without exception, is rigorous. To attain this position a person must have suffered,[18] and that suffering tends to continue, since a shaman is seldom able to live a normal life or to enjoy the ordinary comforts and friendships of common folk. He or she is a person set apart.

A high proportion of shamanic cult practice centers around sickness and death. In most tribes the shaman is the "medicine man" or the "curer," called in to perform the proper rituals to exorcise evil spirits or bless the sufferer. The treatment, of course, is dependent upon the cultural definition of the illness, but it may include the "laying on of hands," the manipulation of the affected parts of the body (often to remove foreign objects believed implanted there through witchcraft), and, of course, ritual singing and dancing. There is an ambiguity in the role of shaman that is recognized generally, even among shamans themselves and their clients. On the one hand, many of their practices are closely related to the magical sleight of hand of the modern carnival performer. The "foreign object" induced from the sufferer's body may have been up the sleeve of the shaman all along. On the other hand, many shamans appear to have genuine gifts of healing, whether through the confidence they invoke or other means. The function of "faking" is often found in the psychological comfort it provides, even as the modern doctor has found the value of the placebo scientifically valid.[19] Things we are learning about the relationship between body chemistry and psychological states make the shamanic "song and dance" appear more functional to the scientific mind than it did a few years ago.

The shaman is often expected to perform certain funeral rites as well. Since the primitive attitude toward relations with the dead is that there should not be any, the shaman frequently is expected to provide a proper exit for the spirit of the dead person so that it will remain in the spirit world and not continue to bother the living. Certainly any rites at the time of death provide mourners with the satisfaction of having done something at a time when little can be done. And to have the ritual performed by one who has already demonstrated a contact with the spirit world would be comforting indeed.

Wallace points out another consideration concerning the function of shamans. Often, he says, the shaman serves as a sort of psychological lightning rod who displaces some of the ambivalent feelings of the group. At various times he or she may play the role of savior or of scapegoat and in so doing take pressures off the public.[20]

There is little or no formal organization around the shaman in most primitive cultures. One is there when needed; one serves but is seldom served. Sometimes there will be a small group of faithful followers, or if the culture calls for that sort of thing, a few apprentice shamans around the shamanic leader. If there are several shamans in the community this may lead to rivalry and feuds, as it did, for example, among the Crow Indians.[21] The shaman is not expected to represent or lead the tribe, although some powerful personalities have been able to combine this role with that of chief, and the charisma of the chief's office may impose upon its incumbent duties similar to those of a shaman.

Shamans exist in modern society, usually on those fringes of the social order where institutionalized religion does not meet the needs of the people. In many areas of the Third World the influence of Western industrialization has penetrated formal religious structures, influencing the practices of the more affluent classes. Often, however, the poor and those in rural areas or unskilled occupations are unable to understand the new practices and turn to informal sources of religious leadership. The process may be seen, for example, in many African nations, and it continues to be a factor in Japan, where industrialization seems to have become the dominant pattern. In that nation, shamans remain an important part of the religious life of the people and serve as attendants at local shrines or as mediums or leaders of local rituals. As in most other societies, these religious leaders fall into three classes: the hereditary shamans, whose office is based on some kind of formal initiation; the spontaneous shamans, whose work is based on personal visions or trances; and the pseudo-shamans, who operate strictly from economic motives.[22]

It takes no great flight of imagination to find parallels for these practitioners in American society. Certainly we do not use the word "shaman" in ordinary conversation about such people, but the role seems fairly clear. These individuals, usually working on the border lines of the Christian church, specialize in curing illnesses and in contacting spirits in much the same style as the primitive shaman. Many of these persons profess a direct tie to spiritual beings, often God or Christ, sometimes specific angels, saints, or other spirits. Like shamans in simpler societies, they may have groups of followers, but these are usually personal followers rather than continuing groups. The groups tend to disintegrate when the leader dies or leaves the area. Most but not all of their clientele comes from sections of the society left out of the rationalizing process of modern industrialization—isolated rural people, the poor, urban isolates who have few ties to any specific group, or in some cases ethnic enclaves still bound by old and less secular patterns.

As in other societies, American shamanic practitioners may be healers, magicians, diviners, mediums, or ritual performers. As in other societies, an ambiguity exists concerning the genuineness of their motives because there is usually a direct reward for their services.

While the practice is making a comeback in some main-line churches, faith healing is usually somewhat outside the institutional structure of modern religion and in the hands of practitioners whose methods appear shamanic. The rapidity of change in the society appears to have resulted in an increase in both numbers of faith healers and the segments of the society in which their practices are accepted. One of the aspects of the charismatic movement has been that of healing, and in many small prayer groups shamanic healing is practiced in middle-class homes as well as in marginal areas. Full-time faith healers tend to depend on donations of the faithful for sustenance, and some seem to make a good living at it. Some of these healers have achieved considerable prominence through radio and television. Others are unknown except to a close group of followers. Many travel around the country, often making "one-night stands" and moving on the next day. The level of acceptance of faith healers varies greatly. Such well-known healers as the late Kathryn Kuhlman and Ruth Carter Stapleton have raised the level of acceptance, and the growth in understanding in the society at large of mental and psychosomatic illness has helped build the bridge to acceptability for some faith healing. Much of the rationale expressed by Mrs. Stapleton, for example in her "healing of memories," sounds like a combination of religious language with a sort of lay psychiatry.[23] Other healers whose style and motivation are more suspect are frequently subject to ridicule or abuse.

There are times when the shamanistic role may become the entry point into more institutionalized religious positions. One of several cases of people whose first claim to fame came through faith healing but who have now moved on to a broader ministry is Oral Roberts. Beginning as a faith healer within the pentecostal tradition of the Church of

God, he built a nationwide reputation through televised broadcasts of his healing services. As acclaim and affluence mounted, he changed his allegiance to the United Methodist Church and founded Oral Roberts University in Tulsa, which has been gaining academic acceptance as well as basketball fame. Television programs sponsored by Roberts in recent years have frequently not been religious services as such, but rather variety shows with a religious message centered on Christianity and Americanism. He has moved out of the shamanic role in the usual sense, yet, as we shall see shortly, his version of American civil religion may exhibit some of the characteristics and functions of primitive religion in the nature of the communal cult.

To many modern people, shamanic practitioners are frauds of the worst kind, making a living from donations of those who can least afford to give, offering false hopes of betterment. They must, however, be providing some functional service needed by those to whom they minister, or they would not be followed. They appear to be an anachronism in modern society, with all the scientific medical technology available to it. And yet they flourish. It is possible they treat illnesses caused rather than relieved by industrial society. It is also true that the society's emphases militate against continuing shamanic practices. Roberts's success, for example, has resulted in his adoption of a much more conventional style, with less emphasis on the miraculous and more on the evangelical facets of Christianity. One could venture the hypothesis that in many ways he has been "co-opted" by modern society. It is also reasonable to assume, however, that as he has moved away from shamanistic practice, others will move in to take his place. This has clearly been true of such movements in the past.

Also part of the modern American version of shamanic cult institutions are the "spiritualists." Some of these have formed organized groups identified as churches within the American denominational system, but their organization tends to be tenuous and loose because they seem dependent upon the shamanic gifts of leaders. Spiritualists range from the out-and-out commercial fakers to those with a genuine belief in spirit possession. They are not totally separated from the faith healers; often they also are known to have healing powers.[24] A good example of the spiritualist leader was Guy Ballard, who gathered a fairly wide following for his "I Am" movement in the 1930s, although it did not really survive his death. And while suit was brought against Ballard for obtaining money by fraud, the usual ambiguity applies. He appears to have been a fraud, yet he also appears to have been sincere. Could he have been both?

Where faith healers bring hope that illness can be overcome, the main contribution of the spiritualists is hope against the finality of death. Unlike shamans of primitive tribes, they are more interested in encouraging communication with the dead than cutting it off. Their contact with the spirit world reassures their clientele of the existence of a life beyond death and often of the continued existence of those whom they have loved. Both these assurances are institutionalized to some degree in the religious structure of the churches, but in secular society they are not emphasized by the established religion to the extent that they are by the spiritualists.

The role of shaman often shades into the more fully institutionalized role of priest. In primitive societies the two tend to be closely intertwined, with the shaman in some cases officiating at community rituals.[25] As society becomes more complex the roles are differentiated more sharply, and the shaman usually loses status in comparison to the functionary who deals with regularized community ritual and other priestly functions.[26] Certainly the shamanistic role does not carry high status in the mainstream of modern society, although it may be a position of great power vis-à-vis the clientele of the practitioner.

The third subtype of primitive religion, and the one apparently most in the mainstream of the development of organized religion, is the communal cult. Unlike the shamanistic cult, the communal cult is not led by specialists as such. Specialized roles in communal religion are performed in fulfillment of more generalized roles in the community. The two most common forms of such cult activities are those crisis rituals, or rites of passage, which involve change of status of the individual in the community; and cyclical or calendrical rituals, involving the changing needs and activities of the community through the seasons.[27] Three sorts of natural groups form the basis of such religious practice—the family, kinship or locality groups, and groups based on natural affinity such as age and sex.[28]

Family cults provide activities that symbolize the shared background and activities of the family group. In some cases, all participate similarly. For example, the placing of offerings at ancestral shrines in some societies is done at appropriate occasions by each member of the family, or it may be done by a particular representative. A similar ritual for some American families may be seen in the placing of flowers on graves of family members on Memorial Day or at other appropriate times. Other family rituals may be led by father, mother, or any particular member. Ceremonies involving the shared food of the family, institutionalized in American society in the diminishing practice of prayer at the table, may be led by the head of the household or any other member or shared in unison, and are often carried on in a tradition peculiar to that family, becoming symbols of its individual nature. At the same time, they may be highly ritualized and the same in all families of the larger group. For example, in Jewish ritual the youngest member of the family is expected to ask the traditional questions at the Seder meal. The child's questions and the answers of the adults together retell the history of the Passover, that great basic tradition of Judaism.

The unity of the primitive family as a work group was expressed in shared rituals aimed at the blessing of the task and its performers. Other rites centering in the family include those accompanying birth, puberty, marriage, and death. Sometimes these rituals involve other members of the community; sometimes they require the services of the shaman or the priest; sometimes they are performed by the family alone. The leader of such rituals may be the father or mother, someone who holds a specific relationship in which this role is institutionalized, or a hereditary family priest. Even when the larger community is involved, there are often further rites carried on within the family circle alone. Modern survivals of this ritual activity may be found in such practices as the family dinner following a christening, confirmation, or funeral, the wedding breakfast, and the like. All are occasions for the family to get together and reaffirm its identity and unity.

This mutual affirmation and sense of identity is the chief focus of communal cult institutions, whether of the family or a larger group. In Wallace's terms, they are rituals of intensification. They are the religious form most clearly represented in Durkheim's studies, which led him to the conclusion that the society itself is both subject and object of religious worship.

In groups larger than the family, based on kinship or shared locality, extensions of many family rituals take place. Birth is celebrated not only as an extension of the family but also as a welcome for the newborn to the community at large. Marriage automatically involves two families, regardless of the final family membership granted the marrying couple. Funerary rites unite the whole community in mutual loss—and in mutual renewal of the awareness of human mortality. Puberty rites most often involve the wider community, since they signify the entrance of the young into full adult roles in the community as well as the family. Such ceremonies remind all community members of the meaning of their membership and of the responsibilities it entails. Ceremonials of this wider type often show considerable variation due to particular traditions developed in specific families or localities. These innovations were probably begun by some charismatic individual and are the most primitive evidence of a function we shall later differentiate as that of the prophet.

Sex and age groups also relate the individual to the community by binding him or her to those within the larger whole who share common interests. In many societies there are specific religious practices that apply to women or to men, to the young or to the old. Early *kachina* societies of the Hopi Indians were ritual groups open only to adult males. A great amount of the initiation of boys in the tribe was initiation into such identification. Such practices are mirrored in modern society in lodges and other secret societies, although in most places such groups no longer have sufficient standing to provide community identity along with membership. Particularly in small towns, however, identification with at least a certain broad segment of the community may be conferred with membership in the Masons, the Knights of Columbus, the Odd Fellows, or even the Ku Klux Klan; and that kind of small-town effect also occurs among the "urban villagers" of ethnic city areas. All these groups preserve secret rituals disclosed only to members and use religious symbolism and ritual.

In modern society, women's groups may have been even more communally oriented than men's. Certainly membership in the Junior League or the Women's Club may provide specific community status, even though ritual is at a minimum and religious definitions muted. The explicitly female identification of many such clubs is obvious to anyone who has been—or been with—a male attending such a function. Perhaps the greatest regular ordeal of the traditional pastor's role has come through demands that he attend meetings of the women's organization of his church. In few places in American society is the narrowness of definition of sexual (or gender) role more obvious, and that narrowness has created problems in the contemporary women's movement, both inside the church and outside it. Women struggling for a broader definition of the female role in society frequently find themselves in conflict with those whose primary social focus outside the family is in such groups. Women's group members are often threatened at the thought of the loss of such traditional structures of support, just as those who would expand their horizons are threatened by the narrow role definitions they institutionalize. Much of the success or failure of contemporary women's movements may be determined by the confrontation in this area, where patterns based on primitive traditions are challenged. And if male pastors have felt uncomfortable with their women's groups, the relation of the rising number of female pastors to those groups is far more problematic.

In primitive tribes a distinct but usually short-lived function is performed by associations of pubescent youth. Usually these are groups of apprentice adults, sometimes living in communal huts of their own, awaiting or participating in initiatory rites. The temptation is great and probably correct to equate such a society with the modern school system. Education in modern society can be seen as an initiatory rite of excessive length. The individuation of the youth society from that of adults has grown as the length of time—whether it is considered as hours of the day, weeks of the year, or number of years—has grown. As a consequence, the importance of the association has grown. In our secular society we do not find many rituals in the youth subgroup that we would ordinarily call religious, but certainly the mass hysteria of a pep rally or an important game has long been a focus of community loyalty and identification. During the 1960s the importance of this type of rite seemed to diminish. The football game, the school itself, became less central to the institutional structure of a more highly self-conscious society of the young. As their separation from adult society grew, other institutions evolved, supported by new forms of ritual and new sets of values. The customary function of youth associations in providing an intermediate binding force between the individual and the larger society diminished as their loyalty centered more exclusively on their own group rather than on the culture of the adults. We shall see later some of the dynamics of that process. At the moment, let it suffice to note that young people appeared to be developing their own communal and shamanic cults based on their own community. Institutionalized activities sponsored by the adult society were suspect because the youth saw that they did not serve to fit them into that society, which to them was also suspect. It may be hypothesized that more recent movements back into closer ties to the institution are reactions to a sense of anomie among those who found too little structure within the youth culture of the 1960s.

This leads to another trend that we must pursue through our consideration of all types of religious organization. While Durkheim's definition of religion in terms of social identification and integration is important, we cannot accept it as the totality of religious expression even in the kind of community in which he found it. Communal religion is a vital social institution, and it seems to be the religious form most open to secularization. That is, ritual that binds the individual to the community may lose all supernatural or ultimate orientation. It may knowingly focus on the community as its goal and its object. Ritual is perhaps the strongest nonbiological bond that unites people into a functioning social unit.[28] Since such unity is often necessary for survival, it may become the acknowledged end of the ritual. However, it is questionable whether such an end can indeed provide the unity it seeks unless it has some referent beyond itself. Does the family that prays together stay together if the only reason they pray is that they may stay together?

Given the focus on bonds of likeness, the outgrowth of communal religion can be racial and national cults. There is little doubt that the consciousness of *folk,* the ritual of the mass meetings, and the many other facets of German Nazism bore the stamp of primitive or folk religion. It may be found more subtly in most societies, regardless of the form of religion recognized in their culture. Folk religions have a tremendous vitality. They can digest all sorts of religious expressions, even those of high religions, into variations of familiar themes from the life experience and sense of identity of a people.[29] The question arises: Is this true of American society? Let us examine the record.

A review of the nature of primitive religion provides the following characteristics: Primitive religion is based on a near fusion of the religion and the rest of life. The individual performs certain religious acts because of the role he or she plays in the group. Primitive religion is not concerned with a clearly defined mythology or theology; instead it is an expression of corporate values, desires, and emotions. It makes little use of specialized functionaries, with the exception of the shaman, who tends to provide in his or her person a center for the emotional content of crisis occasions. It is in such crisis situations that primitive religion is expected to operate, whether they be the crises of individual life—birth, death, changes of status—or those of the group—war, the cycles of production, problems of order. Primitive religion serves to bind the society together in affirmation of a common purpose, giving individuals the sense of participating in such purpose and finding identity in it.

Bellah captures the essence of this religious expression of American life.[30] He discusses the way in which Americans treat religion in public occasion and community life. For example, in America there are religious obligations attached to roles played in the community. Political addresses, particularly solemn ones such as inaugural speeches and the like, generally give reference to God and in one way or another to the concept of "one nation under God." In fact, God is mentioned directly or indirectly in all inaugural addresses of American presidents except Washington's brief Second Inaugural. It is not only leaders who are expected to provide a verbal framework for this public religion; a religious side is defined for all communal roles. It is assumed, for example, that a good, moral, upstanding citizen will be a member in good standing of "the church of one's choice"—regardless of what church that is. While membership in church is assumed to be voluntary, affiliation with one is interpreted as an act of allegiance to the society. Not joining becomes suspect, as if the individual were rejecting the American Way of Life.[31]

That phrase, "the American Way of Life," names the focus of belief and loyalty, and its low level of articulation fits into the pattern of mythological vagueness expected of primitive religion. The historical sources of this phenomenon have been traced to several main developments. The base of American civil religion is Protestant, but it represents a peculiar compromise between the "right wing" Protestantism of the churches of Calvin and Luther, which assumed the need for a state church, and the "left wing" dissenters who stressed individual freedom of conscience and the separation of church and state. Also present at the beginning was the Enlightenment concept of "natural religion." This laid the foundation for the voluntarism of American religion and also the expectation that some religion would be chosen voluntarily. Later immigrants to America found their identity in ethnic churches brought with them from the homeland. Their children tended to reject these churches in their desire to become true Americans rather than "hyphenated-Americans." Herberg records that at least in the 1950s the third generation felt the pressure to belong to a church as part of their American identity and returned to the major faith of their grandparents, purged of its ethnic specificity. As Protestants, Catholics, or Jews, their identification was with the American Way of Life first, the specific religious variation of it second.[32] Current movements toward a "new ethnicity" often continue to see the religious expression of that as important and demand that it be treated as part of the American Way of Life, which remains the ultimate legitimation.

The chief values of the American Way of Life include individualism and pragmatism, a thrust that is dynamic and materialistic yet insists that materialistic gains be used for humanitarian ends. It is based on democracy, which is interpreted to mean constitutional government, free-enterprise economics, social equality, and spiritual idealism. Religion is judged, and churches tend to judge themselves, more on the basis of the services they are able to perform than on the truths they affirm.[33] Form and dogma are not important in maintaining American values. In fact, in a pluralistic situation such as is assumed in the American Way of Life, too much emphasis upon such things could be divisive rather than integrative. As a consequence, these points are downgraded, and activity in the field of social service is stressed.[34]

Children are trained in the public schools to participate in the rituals and dogma of the civil religion. This has been made clear in some of the controversy over state support of parochial schools, when Catholics contend that the schools do teach religion, but not Catholic religion. They assume it is Protestantism. In actuality, it is not that either, but the religiopolitical value orientation of the nation. The Jehovah's Witnesses recognize that the salute to the flag is a religious ritual and so refuse to participate on the grounds that it would violate their religious faith. Many other churches in the country incorporate the flag salute into some of their ceremonies. Many rites of passage are school related and semireligious, even though there have been major changes in the blatancy of the religious element. Few public schools go through the school year without some religious references at Thanksgiving (a national religious holiday), Christmas (a school holiday for a Christian celebration), Easter, and the like, although they tend to stress secular symbols of Pilgrims, Santa Claus, and the Easter bunny. It is a clear indication of the support given to civil religion by the churches that Santa Claus and Easter bunnies tend to share the stage with Jesus in their holiday celebrations as well.

Since America has no officially established religion, it has no organized priestly class entrusted with articulating its religious dogma. Religion is kept simple so that the individual who cannot spend full time studying it can choose his or her affiliation, or at least this is how it seems. Consequently, as in primitive religion, the civil religion has no experts, just participants.

While shamanistic tendencies in American life have been discussed primarily in relation to religious expressions at the fringes of the society, Berger makes a good case for at least one evidence of the shamanic role in civil religion, that of the military chaplain. These ministers are expected to keep up the morale of the troops. The function here has a clear relation to the role of the primitive shaman called in to whip up enthusiasm and commitment before the battle or the hunt.[35] Again, it is the effect of religion, not its content, that is of prime concern.

Warner, in many of his works and particularly in *The Family of God,* gives direct parallels between modern American religious expressions and those of primitive societies as well as the later types we shall examine. He discusses the celebration of holidays like Memorial Day in terms of communal religion, where people participate in ceremonies that remind them of their roots in the society. The Christian framework given many rites of passage does not obscure their identity of function with such rites in primitive tribes.

When we examine the structure of organized religion in America in more detail, we will find many examples of the way in which religious groups serve as communal religions to bind persons to subgroups that are parts of the larger society, and hence to its totality. At its broadest level, this sort of phenomenon is found in what Lenski has called socioreligious groups. These are subsections of the community whose understanding of themselves is reinforced by the particular religious expression appropriate to each. Lenski found four such major groups— Jewish, Catholic, white Protestant, and negro Protestant—whose people recognized boundaries between the groups in their behavior. While theoretically Americans are tied to their churches by voluntary, associational ties, many also respond to communal links as bases of identification and boundary maintenance. Interaction within each of the groups was much higher than between members of different socioreligious groups. Each group maintained its own variation on the theme of the American Way of Life, giving its people a self-concept in terms of their identity as Catholic Americans, white Protestant Americans, Jewish Americans, or black Protestant Americans.[36]

The relationship between certain denominations and local congregations on the one hand and social classes or local cliques on the other can also be seen in terms of the exercise of communal religion. And within the churches, the various age-sex organizations provide subgroup identification within the larger structure. All are expected to build communal appreciation, attachment to the values of the American Way of Life as they apply to the specific social role around which each organization is centered. The individual is reinforced in being a good Christian (or Jewish) woman (man, young person) citizen of a nation whose destiny is a special concern of the God of the Judeo-Christian tradition.

The vague theology of American civil religion comes from that tradition. America is seen as the Promised Land in much the same light as Canaan was portrayed in Jewish tradition, and Americans somehow feel kin to the ancient Hebrews as the Chosen People, who are to bring salvation to the rest of the nations through the conduct of their society under the guiding hand of God. How this is to be done, or how the nature of that God is to be defined, is not the concern of civil religion. It exists simply to reinforce the "obvious." That the obvious may be becoming somewhat less than that is indicated by disagreement over the ways in which the civil religion should be exercised and the accompanying cry for some sort of formal statement of national purpose to which we could all subscribe. During the Bicentennial year of 1976 the nature and function of civil religion became a focus of study and discussion. It was raised by some as a potential source of renewal, in that a sense of responsibility to a transcendent God could provide a sense of meaning and a moral base currently found wanting in the society. Others have castigated civil religion as nationalistic narcissism, a form of idolatry inimical to the idea of a transcendent God. Regardless of the valuation given it, few observers deny the existence of some form of civil religion in America.[37] However, the assumptions of the civil religion seem still solid and not suspect to a majority of Americans, who continue to send their children to Sunday school so that they will not become juvenile delinquents and through the years have subscribed to the belief that Jesus (or perhaps Moses or David) was the prototype of the ideal American.

Notes and References

1. These concepts are summarized in Emile Durkheim, *The Elementary Forms of the Religious Life,* trans. by Joseph Ward Swain (New York: Free Press, 1965), p. 462.
2. Anthony F. C. Wallace, *Religion: An Anthropological View* (New York: Random House, 1966), pp. 86–87.
3. See Robert Redfield, *Primitive World and Its Transformations* (Ithaca: Cornell University Press, 1957) and also his *The Little Community* (Chicago: University of Chicago Press, 1960).
4. Robert N. Bellah, "Religious Evolution," *American Sociological Review* 29 (June 1964): 363.
5. See, for example, William J. Goode, *Religion Among the Primitives* (New York: Free Press, 1951), pp. 50–52.
6. Paul Radin, *Primitive Religion: Its Nature and Origin* (New York: Dover, 1957), pp. 60–65.
7. Durkheim, op. cit., p. 472.
8. Wallace, op. cit., p. 86.
9. E. O. James, *The Nature and Function of the Priesthood* (London: Thames & Hudson, 1955), p. 33.
10. Wallace, op. cit., pp. 125–126.
11. Robert H. Lowie, *Primitive Religion* (New York: Grossett & Dunlap, 1952), p. 16.
12. Max Weber, *The Sociology of Religion,* trans. by Ephraim Fischoff (Boston: Beacon, 1963), pp. 3–4.
13. G. van der Leeuw, *Religion in Essence and Manifestation,* trans. by J. E. Turner (London: Allen & Unwin, 1938), p. 487.
14. William Howells, *The Heathens: Primitive Man and His Religions* (Garden City, N.Y.: Doubleday, 1962), p. 136.
15. Wallace, op. cit., pp. 140–150.
16. Joachim Wach, *The Sociology of Religion* (Chicago: University of Chicago Press, 1944), pp. 334–336.
17. Wallace, op. cit., pp. 150–152.
18. Radin, op. cit., p. 107.
19. For a review of recent studies of this phenomenon, see Norman Cousins, "The Mysterious Placebo: How the Mind Helps Medicine Work," *Saturday Review* 5 (October 1, 1977): 8–12+.
20. Wallace, op. cit., p. 209.
21. Lowie, op. cit., pp. 17–18.
22. Ichuo Hori, *Folk Religion in Japan* (Chicago: University of Chicago Press, 1964), pp. 185–186.

23. See Ruth Carter Stapleton, *The Gift of Inner Healing* and *The Experience of Inner Healing,* both published in Waco, Texas, by Word, Inc., 1977.
24. Charles S. Braden, *These Also Believe: A Study of Modern American Cults and Minority Religious Movements* (New York: Macmillan, 1944), Chapter 9, pp. 257–307.
25. William A. Lessa and Evon Z. Vogt, eds., *Reader in Comparative Religion: An Anthropologocal Approach,* 2nd ed. (New York: Harper & Row, 1965), p. 452.
26. S. F. Nadel, "A Study of Shamanism in the Nuba Mountains," *Journal of the Royal Anthropological Institute* 76 (1946), reprinted in Lessa and Vogt, op. cit., p. 472.
27. Edward Norbeck, *Religion in Primitive Society* (New York: Harper & Row, 1961), pp. 138–168.
28. Wach, op. cit., pp. 56–88.
29. Hori, op. cit., pp. 13–29.
30. First published in *Daedalus,* Winter 1967, pp. 1–21, this paper has been encorporated by Bellah in his *Beyond Belief: Essays on Religion in a Post-Traditional World* (New York: Harper & Row, 1970). Page references here are from the *Daedalus* publication.
31. Peter L. Berger, *The Noise of Solemn Assemblies* (Garden City, N.Y.: Doubleday, 1961), p. 63.
32. This is the main thesis expressed by Will Herberg in *Protestant-Catholic-Jew* (Garden City, N.Y.: Doubleday, 1953).
33. Daniel Boorstin, *The Genius of American Politics* (Chicago: University of Chicago Press, 1953), p. 141.
34. Herberg, op. cit., pp. 82–83.
35. Berger, op. cit., p. 67.
36. Gerhardt Lenski, *The Religious Factor* (Garden City, N.Y.: Doubleday, 1961), particularly Chapter 9.
37. For some examples of this discussion, see Robert Bellah, *The Broken Covenant* (New York: Seabury, 1975), and Russell E. Richey and Donald G. Jones, eds., *American Civil Religion* (New York: Harper & Row, 1974).

6

The Specialization of Religion: Priesthood and Sacraments

The two forms of religious organization Bellah has called "archaic" and "historic" are part of a larger pattern of social diversification, particularly the rise of occupational specialties and the social classes that have been their consequence. Primitive religion can and does appear in all cultures, but its diffused and general character tends to make it inadequate in societies where different groups, in order to function within the social system, must emphasize different aspects of the moral order and have different experiences upon which to build a world view. In fact, the very existence of such social differentiation affects the world view of all who experience it.

The basic symbolism by which archaic religion is distinguished from primitive religion involves greater differentiation of the human from the divine. Where in primitive religious rituals humans had the opportunity to participate in divine feeling and action, in archaic religion the ritual recognizes a gulf between god and worshipper which cannot be bridged completely by the believer. The fluidity of myth and the relative indistinctness of boundaries between the sacred and the profane have been replaced by a more ordered and well-defined understanding of the cosmos. An immediate consequence of such a change in the symbol system is the creation of religious rituals aimed at lessening the gap between people and their deities. Sacrifice and, in some of its manifestations, sacramental action are provided by an order of specialists who stand in the place of the worshippers in contacting their god. These specialists form what is best known as a priesthood.[1]

The movement from primitive to archaic religion was not instantaneous but was an adjustment to different social conditions. Murray's theory is that archaic forms were developed out of primitive ones. For example, early ritual, as we have seen, often focused on yearly cycles and was connected with the experiences and needs of agriculture, war, and the hunt. As Murray sees it, the participatory rituals honoring the principles of fertility, strength, or courage easily became identified in the popular mind with the totemic or other symbolic representations of those principles and with the leader of the ritual. So the tribe that traditionally feasted on the meat and blood of the bear in order to share in its courage and ferocity began to make the symbols more explicit by dressing the participants—or at least the shaman leading the ceremony —in the head and hide of the bear. Early drawings and carvings of gods show them as humans in such animal garb. But powerful gods should not be subject to the weaknesses evident in their local representatives, so their form was projected outward to a more idealized sphere and they became anthropomorphic, situation-specific gods.[2]

The explicit form of the gods of archaic religion required more than this circumstance for their creation and maintenance. Swanson has shown statistically that the presence of a pantheon of gods such as is most characteristic of archaic religion is closely linked to the presence of a number of groups of specialists within the society.[3] Both the cross-cultural comparison used by Swanson and the historical-archeological approach of Murray and others point to a pattern of development of superior gods within territorial consolidation and social and occupational differentiation of a society. The pattern begins with the family as the ultimate sovereign group, and the religious practice is directed toward ancestral spirits and family gods who oversee the affairs of that particular family or clan. The particular interest of such gods is the particular interest or specialty of the family, which of course differentiates more clearly as the society becomes more complex. In this way the god of one family may become linked with a particular occupational specialty. At the same time, the local gods are expected to be concerned only with that group, and even if a neighboring group or society has a god of the same name, it will be considered an entirely different god.[4] As larger social groups appear some local gods may be merged to form the single god of some occupational specialty or particular season, but the very process of merging may require a sufficiently clear definition of the final entity to prevent further mergers. Where this does not appear, and the gods are merged into a smaller and smaller number, archaic religion may be treated as a passing phase of religious development. In many cases, however, circumstances have militated against total merger, and the political and social differentiation has made it more natural for religious expression to take the form of a pantheon of gods. This was clearly the case in ancient Greece and Rome.

In the city-states of Greece and later in Rome, religious practice centered first in the home and the city government. Each family of citizens had its sacred fire and the appropriate rituals for maintaining, using, honoring, and renewing it. This ritual activity is, of course, the sort of communal religion we discussed as primitive religion. So also were the basic rituals of the state, but in Greek and Roman cities only the patrician families who claimed full citizenship had a share in either of these ceremonies. The plebians and strangers were outside the body politic precisely because they had no part in the civic religion. If they came under the protection of a patrician family in a client relationship they then shared in the worship at that family's hearth. Otherwise, they had no part in the recognized religion of their society.[5]

As time went on and the need for plebian labor and particularly military manpower forced the patricians to allow citizenship of sorts to plebians, there still remained the strong two-class system which Bellah makes one of the characteristics of archaic religion. The religions of the two classes are not the same; the higher class claims to have the higher religious expression also. So in ancient Greek mythology we have a dual system of gods. First there are the gods who have obviously developed from the primitive ritual divinities—the earth mother and the corn goddess of an agricultural people, and gods seemingly related to totemic or magical animal symbols. While they are part of the pantheon, they are popularly honored more in the rural areas and among the lower class. Imposed over them are the Olympian gods of classical Greece and their counterparts in Roman mythology. The nature of these gods points to their source in the Aryan conquerors who invaded ancient Greece from the north. Many characteristics of the Indo-Germanic gods may be found in these Olympian dieties, who exist more as conquerors of the land than as providers of crops and hunting success.[6] This gives another clue to the continued existence of numerous superior gods in a society—they are likely to accompany a history of successive settlement, where conquerors and conquered remain to form a single society.

The religion of the lower classes in this case was centered more on the primitive type of gods or on gods specific to their occupation and station. They also retained rituals of witchcraft, sorcery, and the celebration of ancient mysteries. The higher gods in the pantheon were more closely allied with the "established religion" of the patricians.

Yet, at the level of archaic religion, in neither case do we find the establishment of a separate body of adherents such as we would define as a church. There is differentiation at the level of the specialist, and it is here that we first encounter the priest as a full-time role. But in archaic religion the priest does not have a congregation as we would understand the term.

The existence of the priest is necessitated by the differentiation between persons as subjects and gods as objects of worship. When the gap is conceived as so wide that it would be impossible to provide the sort of participatory rituals characteristic of primitive religion, new ways must be devised for establishing and maintaining communication between people in the profane world and their gods in the sacred order. The gap, which admits a greater amount of intentionality and will on the side of both god and people, also increases the level of anxiety.[7] One of the problems of dealing with forces of the divine realm as anthropomorphic gods has to do with this assumption of intent. Given a situation such as the biblical one discussed in our treatment of mana and tabu, where a concerned and faithful follower was "zapped" for touching the sacred Ark, how does one deal with this incident if it is defined as an intentional act of an anthropomorphic god? The interpretation of natural events as the conscious acts of gods may lead to the conclusion that the gods are cruel, capricious, or fickle.[8] This may lead eventually to the replacement of this type of religion by another, but in the meantime it has important consequences in the level of personal anxiety at the base of religious practice.

Such anxiety accounts for the centrality of sacrifice in archaic religion. In general, sacrifice may be defined as the destruction of a victim or the personal renunciation of a possession in order to restore or maintain a good relationship with the divinity. It may be done with the idea of creating or strengthening a bond of union with the deity, in which case the sacramental nature of the activity becomes important. It may be done as an expiation of guilt for wrongs wittingly or unwittingly done. Often there are elements of magic in sacrificial action, for it is also possible to interpret it as a bribe offered to the gods for some favor or desired action.[9] For sacrificial ritual to be effective it must be done exactly, for to offer the gods a gift in an improper manner would be to cause offense and to widen rather than bridge the gap between the worshipper and the diety.[10] This secondary anxiety leads naturally to a dependence on a specialist who is free to devote full time to making sure every detail of the ritual is correct. It is the specialist, and the specialist only, who has the expertise to address the god directly. Thus it is the duty of the priest to perform sacrifices and to maintain the bond between people and their gods.[11]

In archaic religion we find local cults and a reasonably organized priesthood. The relationship of the priest to the followers of the god is not a permanent, pastoral one. Rather, the priest is attached to the local temple, to which worshippers come at times when ritual sacrifice is deemed necessary. This may include personally determined times, as when a person is passing from one status to another and needs ritual protection during the change or when one has particular need of favors from the god. Sacrifice also is offered at special communal times, as on holy days or important points of the calendrical cycle. In this event, the priest acts as mediator for the whole community at once. Yet the people are not bound to the priest in any continuing organization other than that of the community or the society as a whole. One priest may, in fact, officiate at some ceremonies but be supplanted by the priest of another god on other occasions. An individual may go to the particular god who is most applicable to the immediate situation, never claiming just one priest to be one's representative at all times. Yet the representativeness and the intermediary role of the priest range from this occasional service all the way to the example of the divine ruler who directly links a people with their god. The primary characteristic, then, is that the believers are not separated out into a distinct group within the society, with the priest as their leader.

Archaic religion is by no means confined to classic cultures. In fact, a good deal of the religion defined as primitive in the literature would be better classified as archaic because of the social structure in which it is found and the formation of a priestly class. Such cases include many of the religious systems of Africa and Polynesia, as well as those of ancient New World, Middle Eastern, Indian, and Chinese civilizations.[12]

In his *Religion of China,* Weber portrayed Confucian China in terms similar to descriptions of archaic religion. The Confucian emphasis on propriety reflects archaic attitudes toward sacrifice and ritual: By specific correct behavior the gods could be placated and misfortune avoided. In China, as elsewhere, archaic religion was mixed with primitive cult. The state cult was in the hands of the officials, but everyone they included was expected to participate in communal cults of ancestor worship. The division between the more rational beliefs of the educated minority and the popular cults was similar to that which developed between the ancient Greek philosophers and followers of Greek popular religion.[13]

Weber's discussion of India's religions shows much of the same pattern but also involves more clearly the transition into historic religion. Early religious practices in India, based on the family and transferred to the caste, bear the usual marks of primitive-moved-toward-archaic religion. The dominance of Brahmans through the religious organization parallels the rise of Confucian literati to some extent. The difference lies in the individual merit expected of the Confucians and established through testing, as opposed to what Weber interpreted as "gentilial," or familial charisma, in which the special power is attributed to kinship.[14]

Though we are unaccustomed to think of ancient Judaism in terms of archaic religion because of its strong monotheistic tendencies, much of the temple worship of the Hebrews fits the archaic pattern, and the treatment of the gods of neighboring peoples as well as the mythology of the common people refute the idea that their monotheism at that time would fit our definitions.

It is also possible to consider archaic religion the appropriate definition of religious practice in some Christian countries, perhaps particularly those of Latin America, where the social order still often is primarily a two-class one. Here priests have tended to be functionaries of the ruling class, performing special rites for the common people only on special occasions, since the size and population of their parishes has prevented closer contact. In many cases local saints may be only peripherally related to the Christian tradition and their feast days only perfunctorily blessed by the priests. So, as Nilsson's description depicted the Greeks, in these modern societies also the high gods are honored by patricians but seem distant to the masses, so that the ceremonies in their honor are essentially secularized celebrations of groups or of seasons.[15]

Vallier's study of Latin American Catholicism confirms this view. He found the primary loyalties of the people tied up in "extrasacramental, communal units." Ritual participation in the church was frequently based on a need to placate or manipulate the diety, resulting in "naive expectations and petitionary prayers," with a high level of devotion to and worship of the saints. Says Vallier, these emphases are

central to "folk Catholicism," which is strongest among the peasants and urban poor. God and the saints, as well as the priest, are approached for help in meeting the exigencies of daily life. The supernatural is accessible and subject to manipulation. Religio-magical beliefs pervade all sectors of social life and affect deeply the ways in which men approach problems, make plans, and explain misfortune. This instrumentalism is accompanied by a generalized dependency on God and his helpers: People conceive a sense of immutability. Things are as they are and little can be done to alter the over-all pattern. The most that is possible is to petition for special favors in relation to immediate problems. The tension between these two levels—the underlying deterministic nature of the world and the possibilities for securing particularistic favors—is fundamental, and produces a series of broad orientational postures: resignation, and also naive hope.

The priest is typically inaccessible to the rural poor and the lower classes in the city, except for periodic visits to celebrate the mass before a *fiesta* celebration, or at points throughout the year when the priest's blessing of the land, domestic animals, and newly planted crops is needed. He is viewed as a quasi-magician—someone who can help to structure the universe in ways that will favor material outcomes.[16]

As we shall see in later chapters, this pattern has been changing in some areas in recent years, sometimes under the leadership of the priests. At this stage, however, practices and world views clearly echo those of archaic religion and are reinforced by a stress on the sacrificial nature of the mass, as over against its use as a sacrament.

Similar patterns have been traced on the Philippine Islands by Manglapus, who has pointed out the economic consequences of some of the religious activities. *Fiestas* there, he says, are not only archaic celebrations only tangentially related to Christianity; they also involve such high levels of expense that they prevent investment that could lead to economic development and social mobility, thus contributing to the two-class system upon which archaic religion is built.[17]

The relationship between archaic types of religious organization and the underdevelopment of nations involves many factors. One is the world view encouraged by archaic religion, which is a more rigid cosmology than is found in most other types. Archaic religion defines the world—sacred and profane—in a way that has a place for everything and everything in its place.[18] Such a view is not likely to support much social change, although it can incorporate small changes by simply adding to its pantheon. The consequences of this depend upon the addition that is made. For example, when the inhabitants of the ancient New World sought to place the invading Spaniards in their cosmology, it could have eased many adjustments. What could not be handled was the religious exclusiveness of the Christian conquerors, who were horrified at the prospect of becoming in any way pagan deities or their representatives. Yet in the long run Catholic saints have been treated as local gods in much of the territory they conquered, and the religio-political power of Catholic priests in isolated areas of Latin America has been not unlike that of the priest-kings of some traditional archaic religions. This world view, in itself not supportive of economic development, has in recent years been challenged most effectively by those priests, particularly those who have come from Europe or North America instead of Italy or Spain as was the earlier custom. However, the strain between the sources of their authority and the content of their message has created no little anxiety. Interestingly enough, much of Latin American Protestantism has also exhibited archaic tendencies toward specificity of myth and group exclusivism which have also led to conflict within Protestant ranks over the value of economic development and social change.[19]

In Japan, archaic and primitive forms of religion appear to have assisted the process of modernization. The Meiji reforms in Japan were based on the family system and the existing structure of loyalty to the emperor, who occupied the position of the priest-king. Economic reform, decreed from above, was effective at least partially because of this chain of obedience and loyalty.[20] We will see more later of the lasting effects of such social reform from within an archaic religious structure.

Sometimes reaction to pressures toward modernization may take the form of archaic religion as a kind of nativistic movement.[21] Bellah makes a good case for this interpretation of some of the cultural-religious phenomena of the Hitler period in Germany. Given the faster rate of both economic and political modernization in France and England as compared with Germany, he sees Germany as one of the first underdeveloped nations to experience outside pressures toward modernization. Bellah finds that where great religious differences exist between the underdeveloped nation and nations that are the source of pressure to modernize, reaction to the pressure is likely to be nationalistic and often secular. When great religious differences are internal, as was the case of Germany with its unresolved conflict between Catholicism, Lutheranism, and other Protestantism, the reaction may reach back into primitive and archaic sources of national unity. Thus Nazi Germany revived the old Teutonic myths, celebrated in the music of Wagner, as a basis for a form of romantic nationalism.[22]

Former colonial states have been sources of emerging nationalism based on archaic tribal religions, particularly in Africa. We also find here new mythic emphases arising out of particular situations. For example, in South Africa, where the system of apartheid maintains a firm boundary between blacks and whites, "Ethiopian" versions of Christianity have developed which bear many marks of archaic religion. South African territorial apartheid has been sanctioned by Boer churches as a way of preserving the missionary principle or establishing indigenous churches. If the parish system is considered normal, then to have an indigenous church in metropolitan areas of mixed population it is best if the natives all live in one neighborhood. Hoekendijk finds that missionary attitudes toward natives in South Africa have taken three forms: to treat natives as *heathens,* who need only to be baptized to become part of the fellowship of believers; to treat them as *pagans* or barbarians, who need both to be baptized and to be civilized; and to treat them ethnocentrically, as a *different* order of humanity, and hence never really able to be fully part of the missionizing fellowship. The movement has been from the first of these types toward the last. Black Africans who have received both Christianity and education now find themselves thwarted by the third attitude and so have come to reinterpret Christianity to apply to their group rather than universally, or to the whole society. Noting all biblical references to "Cush" or "Ethiopia" and tracing African church history to the visit of the Queen of Sheba to Solomon, they have pulled together a bibliomythic basis for claiming special significance for the black African in the Judeo-Christian tradition. Insofar as they remain a specialized group with its own mythology, they exhibit some of the elements of archaic religion.[23]

Racism in any society reinforces this sort of reaction, though, as we shall see, it is also possible to trace here a sectarian response more in the realm of the early modern than archaic forms in some cases.

There are a number of areas where elements of archaic religion can be found in American Christianity, often similarly rooted in reactions against modernization. Exclusiveness of mythic interpretation and group identity, and stress on the distance between sacred and profane and the need of sacrifice to bridge it are applied to Christian doctrine and are evidence of a certain archaism of approach. They often are found in groups that are isolated from or adversely affected by the form or pace of economic development. As we have seen, romantic nationalism is one manifestation of this phenomenon.

One important characteristic of archaic religion is that in spite of its many divinities and mythologies, it retains much of the monism of primitive religion. That is, while the sacred and profane are understood to be widely separated realms, both are present in this world. The divine infuses all of life rather than existing in a separate realm. Modern survivals of archaic religion may use the language of transcendence, but the sphere of divine action is much more this-worldly than otherworldly. The gods are immanent in one's life and surroundings and must be dealt with there. Secularization under such circumstances is the loss of the mythic dimension, rather than a denial of transcendence.

From this point of reference there are close affinities between archaic religion and the so-called new ethnicity, even when that is expressed entirely in secular terms. If one's god is, as H. R. Niebuhr has said, one's "center of value," then the conflicting interests and values of various ethnic groups may mirror the polytheism of archaic societies. One of the sources of debate over civil religion then becomes whether this form of primitive religion has the power to unite the various gods of the interest groups or whether there is need here, as in prototypical archaic religions, for a pantheon that unites those gods into some kind of social system to provide symbolic support for mutual interdependence of groups in the society.[24]

The solution to finding unity in diversity provided in the type of religion Bellah termed "historic" has been the development of a symbol system in which the divine is much more transcendent, usually involving a single high god who either rules the plural lesser deities or has replaced them. Both primitive and archaic religion find their center in the world and the life of their adherents, even though in archaic religion the gods may be thought of as existing outside the realm of everyday life. The distinction between sacred and profane is a distinction between objects or actions of different types, but not between worlds. In archaic society the gods are tied to and act out their desires in this world and are to be used to attain goals within temporal existence. Historic religion projects beyond this; here it is possible that a transcendent world has priority over present experience.

As a result of this, religious action becomes involved with more than the direct sacrificial behavior aimed at righting a specific wrong or gaining a particular favor. In transcendental religions it becomes possible for people to conceive of themselves as totally unworthy of a place in the transcendent realm. Religion becomes an antidote to guilt rather than just to error. It is less involved with facilitating participation in the sacred, as it does in primitive types, or setting right particular circumstances, as is the case in archaic types. In historic religion the quest is for salvation, enlightenment, or release; and basic changes occur in the state and the nature of the participant. The risks and possibilities for the individual are much greater in historic religion, and activities of the religion must be of a nature designed to provide broad support in anxiety-producing situations.

Out of this need and focus religious organization may become for the first time that which can be identified with the sociological concept of the *church*. Religion becomes a separate institution distinguished from the society as a whole. Not only is the priesthood a recognizable order in the society, but the association of priest and followers is also an identifiable entity. Within this association the individual recognizes a role that is at least somewhat different from roles played in other institutions.[25]

The classic definition of the church identified with Weber[26] and refined by Troeltsch[27] is that of a religious organization that is an institution of the society, supporting and supported by its other institutions. It is expected to be coextensive with the society; that is, to be born into the society is to be born into its church. Yet as an institution it is differentiated from such institutions as the family, the economy, and the government. It has its own focus, its own role relationships, its own normative emphasis. With the church, these emphases are not antithetical to the expectations of other social institutions but rather enrich and reinforce them. Historic religions, having a transcendent focus, interpret the normative patterns of family life, economic exchange, political power, and the like in terms of transcendental goals, thus giving ultimate meaning to proximate practice. The particular way in which the religion of a society makes these interpretations has considerable effect upon the direction of growth and development of the society.

Bellah states that historic religion accompanies a greater social differentiation than the two-level society found in archaic religion. In societies evidencing historic religion, he says, there tend to be four main social groupings: a political-military elite; a cultural-religious elite; a lower-status group which is mainly urban and includes merchants and artisans; and a rural group of low-status peasants.[28] This clearly indicates a differentiation between governmental, religious, and economic institutions, at least.

Historic religions, of course, carry with them the baggage of past religious forms developed in their societies. We have already seen how the mythology and orientations of primitive and archaic types linger in modern religious institutions. Bellah states that all religious forms we know today as major religions have had, and have current histories of, historic stages. That is, we can look to history, if not to the present, to find details within the major faiths of their appearance as the historic type of religion. Although the particular form in which it was worked out varies, we can find examples of historic religion in the development of Hinduism, Buddhism, Islam, and the Judeo-Christian tradition.

In all these forms we find that distinguishing the religion as a recognizable social institution affects the role of the religious leader in rather predictable ways. As in primitive and archaic religion, these specialists still perform particular functions in the society as a whole. They are expected to be bearers of charisma or mana and to perform those rituals which can renew contact with the divine. Now, however, they have added to these the whole dimension of leadership within a recognized religious organization. The priest of historic religion is not only the charismatic shaman and the intermediary, he or she now is expected to take on a pastoral role, leading and counseling a congregation, directing them toward the goal of salvation, however it may be defined in the particular religion. One is still expected to be in contact with mana, whether it is defined as the Holy Spirit or enlightenment, or institutionalized in the chain of apostolic succession. One still must be trained in the specific liturgical skills through which mediation between the people and the divine can occur. But now the training must include the interpretations which the religion has developed as to the proper path to salvation.

The road to salvation may be defined primarily in terms of proper behavior. In this case, the pastor-priest may need to be trained in legal aspects of the identification of correct and incorrect behavior. He or she then must serve as teacher for the congregation, instructing them in the moral and ethical aspects of their faith. If the emphasis is on right belief, the priest must become an expert in the dogma so as to teach the people to refrain from error. In any case, the amount of specialized training for the religious leader grows, as does the amount of learning that is expected to be transmitted to the people. The proportion of religious specialists in the society is also likely to grow under these circumstances. Also, differentiation is likely to occur within their ranks. If their role requires a large body of specialized knowledge, then there must be distinct provision made for acquiring that knowledge. Some of the specialists must become teachers within the ranks, and as the body of knowledge grows, considerable division of labor may develop among these religious teachers. Those with the greatest amount of knowledge or in the most responsible positions will come to outrank less skilled and responsible priests. And what is true of specialized learning is also true of the administration of order within the religious association. The priests, in turn, will stand above the less specialized laity. Consequently, it is not difficult to see why Bellah should say that historic religion is characterized by a hierarchical form of organization.

It is the dynamic of history that seems most responsible for the development of a recognizable form of historic religion. That is, the clearest examples of the historic type are self-conscious movements within a society which developed at least to some extent in contrast or even in conflict with that society's earlier, archaic religion. Historic religions developed from sectarian movements within their societies. Their distinction lies first in the fact that they posited a new object— a transcendental aim—not central to the older religion, and second in that in most cases they were successful enough to become the official religion of the society in place of the older religion. This second, more political, aspect is less clear in the case of Eastern religions. In both India and China Buddhism cannot be said to have become the official religion, though it occupied that position for a brief period in India before the resurgence of Hinduism. The clearest contrast between archaic and historic types among well-known religions can be found in Islam and Christianity.

Islamic faith, which claimed exclusiveness, swept over a fair share of the known world in the centuries immediately following its founding in the seventh century. Its form included the organization of community and state into a pattern that would reflect the divine will. The organization of society and the mutual obligations it entailed were affected through religious prescription. In those countries where Islam became and remained the dominant religion, it fit both the concept of historic religion and of the church as a social institution. Family life, education, politics, the economic order, social stratification, social welfare—all contributed to and were supported by the Islamic faith.[29]

The form of historic religion that has received the most attention from sociologists is that of medieval Christianity. It was on this religious form that the concept of the church was based, to be adjusted later to fit other religions and to be contrasted with the concept of the sect. Some of the most valuable and certainly the classic work in the sociology of religion has been done on the basis of Christian religious development.

Ignoring for the present the early, primitive days of the Christian church, when it could best be described as a sectarian development out of Judaean and Roman societies, we can find much of the richness of the meaning of historic religion in the study of Christianity after it became the state religion of Rome, and later of the emerging European nations.

The framers of Christian doctrine by this time had spelled out in fairly clear terms the relationship of life to salvation. Augustinian thought colored many of the assumptions of religion and society at that time. It was taken for granted that there were two interlocking planes on which human existence was involved—the City of God, transcendent and pure, to which all aspired and owed allegiance, and the City of Man, in which mortals lived out their imperfect lives in obedience to the God who created and governed both. It was the church that held the keys to the City of God, and all of life in the City of Man was brought under the influence of the church so that it might apply to the world of that other, heavenly City. The church took charge of people from birth to death, and the rites of passage which had always been part of the religion of human society now became sacraments. Their meaning was double: they not only provided identifiable moments of role changes in earthly society; they also indicated new levels of integration into the world beyond. Baptism welcomed the child to the community; it also marked his or her inclusion into the community of the faithful. The funeral not only marked the loss of an individual to the community and the change of state of his or her next of kin; it also was the celebration of final entry into the heavenly City. Other high points of secular life, as well as the regular celebration of the mass, spoke not only of their immediate social meaning but also of the ultimate relationship of life in this world to salvation in the next.

The church exercised discipline over marriage, education, commercial relations, property, and the relations between social classes. It held the ultimate sanctions, the keys of St. Peter, the power to grant or deny salvation to the individual. At the same time, its very ability to stand in judgment over other institutions in the society bespoke its greater separation from them in comparison with primitive and archaic religious forms. This was brought about primarily through the salvational emphasis of this religious expression. Other social institutions regulated the life of the City of Man; the church applied their functions to the City of God.

The great synthesis between this sort of social arrangement and the classical understanding of human endeavor came through the work of Thomas Aquinas. Given the society in which he lived, he was able to interrelate the salvational aims of the Christian religion with the philosophical, natural, and social knowledge of his day. The supramundane aims of the religion were used to interpret earthly phenomena in terms of natural law, attributing to the Divine Creator a framework of existence in the given structures of nature and society.

In western Europe the separation of the church as an institution accompanied the development of the feudal organization of society. It comes as no surprise, then, that this separation was expressed in the gaining of feudal powers by the church. It became one of several temporal powers, holding vast domains of property, exercising direct political strength. This, however, was not a necessary condition to the development of historic religion, or even of the characteristics of the sociological concept of the church.

In eastern Europe the Christian church never gained the sort of political power it did further west. Several factors were involved in this difference, most of them directly or indirectly due to the greater identification of Eastern churches with the specific nations in which they developed. One continuing difference between Roman Catholic and Eastern Orthodox churches has been the insistence of the Roman church until quite recently that the mass be conducted in a uniform and universal language—Latin. Eastern churches have always been more oriented toward the vernacular. The use of local languages, in fact, was deliberately cultivated as a symbol of the continuing manifestation of the power of the Holy Spirit to speak to each believer in his or her own tongue, as an extension of the miracle of Pentecost through which the church was founded.[30]

The growth of the Western church within the context of the Roman Empire gave rise to a legalistic bent in the churchly organization and in the development of dogma as well. The whole emphasis of Western Christianity on "justification" is legalistic. In a legalistic order the priest is the representative of divine law and judgment and bears the power to absolve the sinner. Legalism can also be seen in doctrines of good works, particularly in the effectiveness of "supererogatory works," by which particularly saintly individuals can amass extra credit for the sake of others. In summary, the form in which the Western church held the keys to the City of God was a legal one.

This was not the case with the Eastern church. Here the key to the City of God was mystical rather than legal. The believer could participate in the experience of the City of God through the liturgical practices of the church. Disciplinary powers were used to assist the believer in attaining sufficient spiritual maturity to be able to participate fully in the liturgical life of the gathered community. It is not surprising that a church with this sort of definition of itself would not become the same sort of political power the more legalistic Western church became. Instead, the Eastern church in general has allowed the political realm to be dominated by secular rulers. Since it is, as in the classic definition of a church, coextensive with the society, the Eastern Orthodox church has become in most cases an arm of the secular government, serving to create and preserve conditions favorable to the continued dominance of that government.

There are consequences of this difference other than political ones. Foremost among these, perhaps, is the role of education in the society as a whole, and in regard to the priestly role in particular. In a society dominated by a legalistic understanding of religion, and particularly one which developed that understanding into an inclusive doctrine of natural law, it becomes necessary for the church to sponsor a great amount of scholarship among its priests. The fine points of dogma in a legalistic framework require the application of well-trained logical minds. Also, all of knowledge can be subsumed under the religious categories of natural law, so that all education can be taken to be the realm of the church.

By contrast, the proper conduct of the liturgy through which believers can experience the divine mystery requires much less formal education. This tendency in the Eastern Orthodox church was aggravated by their different attitude toward celibacy. Unlike the Roman Catholic church, the Eastern Orthodox church has allowed priests to marry. However, they must marry before they take their orders and must not remarry if they lose their wives. More important, bishops must be celibate. This has had the effect of establishing two orders of Orthodox priesthood—the married parish priests who have received only enough education to be able to conduct services properly, and the monastic orders of priests educated to be leaders.

Another important consequence of this different attitude has to do with the position of the church regarding general learning. Where in the Western church the schools and universities grew out of the church's concern with knowledge, the Orthodox emphasis on mysticism made secular learning suspect. Thus, monastic academies remained more concerned with devotional meditation and liturgy rather than theology, philosophy, and—as eventually happened in the West—science. This does not mean that these subjects were never undertaken, only that they suffered from a comparative lack of emphasis.

Yet both these forms of Christianity can be defined as forms of historic religion, and both were part of what came to be known as Christendom. This understanding of religion as applying to a specific geographical area is not peculiar to Christianity; it is obviously important to Islam and can be found in the orientation of many other religions. It is, however, a particularly strong characteristic of historic religion to understand that the particular religion is the religion of the society, its government reflects that religion, and its people are members of the church. Within Christendom, for example, the Christian interpretation of life was taken for granted, although there may have been many disputes over the details of that interpretation. The concept is of importance to us now in that for the Western world the development of religion through the historic and early modern stages has taken place in the context of Christendom. As we will see later, one of the distinguishing characteristics of the transition from early modern to modern religion lies in the loss of this assumption.

Concurrent with the idea of Christendom, and with both the historic and early modern stages of religion that it encompasses in Western culture, is the development of *missions.* One essential characteristic of Christian missions has been the expansion of the boundaries of Christendom. Again, there are differences between the Eastern Orthodox and Roman Catholic conceptions of missions. In the case of the Roman church, Christendom was expanded as priests moved out into new territory and converted pagans to a loyalty to the Church of Rome and a participation in sacraments and ceremonies standardized in Rome. It was easy to recognize the expansion of Roman Christendon: One could walk into a church anywhere in the area where it had reached and find the essentials of the familiar services. This was somewhat less true in regard to Eastern Orthodox churches because their emphasis on the vernacular led to the establishment of somewhat varied national churches, only loosely tied to the "sending" or home churches. The very fact that these were national churches allowed a greater amount of conversion by government fiat. The result was an extension of Christendom that did indeed spread similar ceremonies, art, and beliefs but did not extend as fully into the rest of the society—especially its political structure.

In these cases, and with Buddhist missionary efforts and the expansion of Islam as well, an important consequence of missions was the spread of the cultural base along with the religion it claimed. No matter how otherworldly their emphasis or how divine the origin or universality they claim, all religions are interpretations channeled through specific people who share a specific culture. Certain frameworks of culture are taken for granted and woven into the interpretations of the religion.

In many instances Buddhism, cradled in Hindu India, carried with it castelike organizations of society, even while Buddhist doctrine undermined the caste system by de-emphasizing *dharma*.[31] The close tie between social organization and Islam made a particularly strong imprint in the spread of Islamic culture through the Near and Middle East and beyond. Eastern Orthodoxy brought a degree of cultural similarity to the areas over which it spread. Roman Catholicism spread Western civilization first to the outer edges of western Europe and then to the newly opened lands of the Western Hemisphere and parts of Africa. The full effects of this religious and cultural enterprise would be felt in the areas of early modern and modern religion.

During the time of the dominance of historic forms of Christianity, a picture of local congregations developed in which participation at least at an occasional level was expected of all local residents. Here the sacraments were dispensed, without which salvation was impossible. Here also the priest exercised a pastoral role of counseling and guiding the people, interpreting the roles and sanctions of the church to them. Ties extended from the local congregation to bishops and archbishops who held authority over specific areas, usually coinciding with political boundaries, so that the identity of the church with the secular unit was recognized. However, the ties continued back to the papacy in Rome and, through the belief in apostolic succession, back through history to all the saints and martyrs and the early apostles to, finally, Christ himself. This interlocking organization, involving great cultural variety and yet encompassing a number of cultural uniformities, was Western Christendom. It formed the context of the world in which the Christian was born, lived, died, and hoped for eternal life. Yet the religious organization was not the only organization of the society. Economic activity, though regulated by the church through ethical teachings and definitions of natural law, was not the exclusive concern of the church, but rather was recognized as a separate sphere. While family life fell under the guidance and instruction of the church, the family and the congregation were not one and the same, nor was the head of the family its priest. The religious framework was present but not fully inclusive of other social institutions. It provided the ultimate basis for them. Thus it may be seen as the most well developed example of the concept of the church, as well as of historic religion.

The historic stage of Judaism is a somewhat more complicated case. For one thing, it did not develop as a self-conscious movement over against archaic religion—at least not at one identifiable time and place. It grew out of earlier forms. Perhaps the chief way in which it differs from other developments of historic religion lies in the nature of its transcendent focus.

Although there are many indications that ancient Judaism involved a plurality of cults and a general orientation like that of other archaic religions and that its god, Yahweh, was understood to be a pan-tribal war god not unlike others at this stage, the tradition seems to have held a unique element. Alongside the customary understanding of Yahweh as a national diety was the tradition of the covenant—the belief that Yahweh was not only the god of the Hebrews, but that they were in some special way his people, bound to him by a contract executed by both parties. Involved in this covenant relationship was the idea that this particular nation was to be used by their god in the execution of history, in ways that would be of concern to all humankind.[32] This notion is carried from the most ancient tradition; for example, it appears in the story of the call of Abraham, whose promise included that his descendents would prove a blessing to all people.[33] Here, then, mingled with the notions and rites of primitive and archaic religion, is an element of universalistic transcendental faith. It carries through the tradition and is basic to the story of the joining of the covenant on Mount Sinai during the Exodus. It seems to carry less weight through the history of the conquest of Canaan, where the war-god image of Yahweh predominates and the society is ruled as a loose confederation judged by military heroes and strong leaders.

The tradition, however, was never lost, and it figured strongly in the pronouncements of the prophets, whose influence moved Judaism into what could be interpreted as its historic stage. The ambiguity of its relationship to historic religion, as we have mentioned, lies in its definition of transcendence and salvation. The preaching of the prophets was not couched in terms of some ethereal world and in individual's chances of belonging to it. It vas very "inner-worldly," to use Weber's term. Their concern was m. inly with the establishment of a just society, free of entangling alliances with pagan neighbors. But the interpretive framework in which they spoke was that of the ancient covenant tradition: The people of the covenant owed it to their god to create and maintain the sort of society he had decreed as the sign of their fulfillment of the covenant. When evil befell the society, it was not because their tribal god had failed them or was weaker than the gods of their enemies. Rather, such events were interpreted as the judgment of Yahweh upon a faithless people. In this way the transcendence of the god became more apparent, and salvation had to do with the entire nation rather than the individual. When the "day of the Lord" came, his people would be vindicated or rejected according to their faithfulness. And if they were faithful and were vindicated the consequences would affect all humankind, over whom they would rule in a righteous kingdom.

Early prophets shared many of the characteristics of primitive shamans. They tended to reach their prophetic heights through ecstasy. Early rulers, including the famous kings David and Saul, were also shamanistic prophets at times. But this tradition was denigrated. The classical prophets minimized customary ecstatic behavior and made their claim not so much on emotional states or on visions but on having had their god speak to them, giving them messages for the people and their rulers.[34] They did not build up permanent followings. They did not form churches.

The religion of their day was perhaps less differentiated from other social institutions than in most cases of historic religion. But the prophets were distinct from all the institutions, including the official state religion.[35] They spoke in the name of their god to abuses they saw in family life, foreign policy, trade, religious observance, and the relationship between social classes. In this way they led the national religion into a relationship with other institutions of the society which interpreted them in the context of a transcendent, salvational ethic.

The Hebrew prophets are important not only in having achieved an approximation of historic religion, but far more because of their influence on the development of early modern and modern religion in the West.

In summary, then, historic religion can be understood as the stage of development of any religion when it becomes the "established" religion of a society, if it also sets up transcendent, salvational goals for that society. Establishment presupposes other institutional structures which recognize the legitimacy of the religion and also assumes that it will be largely supportive of those structures. Yet, because historic religion posits some transcendental realm or set of ideal values, there is always the possibility that resistance to some of the institutions of the society may arise from it. No longer is the present society taken as an unquestioned given, since there is a more important realm it serves. The development of the congregation as a social unit can serve as a supportive base for new movements aimed at more nearly approximating the ideal structure, and it is possible for these movements to focus on any of the institutions of the society, including religion itself.

Although historic religion shows a strong tendency toward conservative support of the status quo, both its symbolic content and its organizational structure are more likely to admit social change than are archaic forms of religion. It is not too difficult to understand, then, why most of the world religions are no longer in the dominant position they once held throughout the society, but rather exhibit a more pluralistic outlook. Even if they remain "established," they may recognize the fact that no one form is exclusively the religious expression of the society. Part of the pluralism, of course, comes from increasing contact with other cultures whose religious expression is different, but the recognition of diversity does not automatically imply its acceptance. We have only to look at history, at wars and inquisitions, burnings of heretics and witches, to know that historic religion is not predisposed to new interpretations. It is a type from which prophets may arise; it is also the type of institution that stones its prophets and disposes of their followers. Development out of historic types is more likely to be lasting if it is based upon their symbol systems—that is, if it comes from within— and is likely to be accomplished slowly rather than by violent or political means.

The total dominance expected of historic religion exists in modern society only in those areas where communication is cut off by geography, political pressure, poverty, or ignorance. A broad view shows that while the pure type is seldom found, elements of historic religion are everywhere, coloring the thinking of people whose allegiance is assumed to be to another type. Much of what we have identified as civil religion combines the function of primitive religion with some of the assumptions of historic religion, especially the assumption that the church will be coterminous with the society and the various forms of salvational ethic attached to such assumptions. Bellah himself, in some of his more recent work, appears to urge a kind of civil religion like that of the covenantal style of ancient Judaism rather than the unexamined forms it seems more likely to take. In other words, his prescriptive treatment of American religion posits a development from the primitive to the historic stage.[36]

The nature of such versions of historic religion may become more clear as they are contrasted with those later forms he describes, the early modern and the modern, which have arisen out of this stage.

Notes and References

1. Robert Bellah, "Religious Evolution," *American Sociological Review* 23 (June 1964): 365.
2. Gilbert Murray, *Five Stages of Greek Religion* (New York: Columbia University Press, 1925), pp. 38–44.
3. Guy Swanson, *The Birth of the Gods* (Ann Arbor: University of Michigan Press, 1960), pp. 82–96.
4. Max Weber, *The Sociology of Religion*, trans. by Ephraim Fischoff (Boston: Beacon, 1963), p. 17.
5. Numa Denis Fustel de Coulanges, *The Ancient City* (Garden City, N.Y.: Doubleday, 1956), pp. 231–234.
6. Murray, op. cit., pp. 59–79.
7. Bellah, op. cit., p. 365. See also the discussion of secondary anxiety in Chapter 3 of this work.
8. Murray, op. cit., pp. 80–95.
9. E. O. James, *Sacrifice and Sacrament* (London: Thames & Hudson, 1962), pp. 13–14.
10. Fustel de Coulanges, op. cit., p. 160.
11. James, op. cit., p. 36.
12. Bellah, op. cit., p. 364.
13. Max Weber, *The Religion of China*, trans. by Hans Gerth (New York: Free Press, 1951), pp. 199–201. A good discussion of Weber's views on these matters may also be found in Reinhold Bendix, *Max Weber: An Intellectual Portrait* (Garden City, N.Y.: Doubleday, 1960), pp. 117–151.
14. Max Weber, *The Religion of India*, trans. and ed. by Hans Gerth and Don Martindale (New York: Free Press, 1958), pp. 49–50.
15. Martin P. Nilsson, *Greek Popular Religion* (New York: Columbia University Press, 1940), pp. 86–87.
16. Ivan Vallier, *Catholicism, Social Control, and Modernization in Latin America* (Englewood Cliffs, N.J.: Prentice-Hall, 1970), pp. 23–32; quotation from p. 31.
17. Raul S. Manglapus, "Philippine Culture and Modernization," in *Religion and Progress in Modern Asia*, ed. by Robert N. Bellah (New York: Free Press, 1965), pp. 30–42.
18. Bellah, "Religious Evolution," op. cit., p. 364.
19. José Miguez Bonino, "Catholic-Protestant Relations in Latin America," in *The Religious Situation, 1969*, ed. by Donald Cutler (Boston: Beacon, 1969), pp. 138–139.
20. Josepha M. Saniel, "The Mobilization of Traditional Values in the Modernization of Japan," in *Religion and Progress in Modern Asia*, op. cit., pp. 124–149.
21. For a more complete discussion of nativistic movements, see Ralph Linton, "Nativistic Movements," *American Anthropologist* 45 (1943): 230–240.
22. Robert N. Bellah, *Beyond Belief: Essays on Religion in a Post-Traditional World* (New York: Harper & Row, 1970), pp. 70–71.
23. J. C. Hoekendijk, *The Church Inside Out*, ed. by L. A. Hoedmaker and Peter Tjimes, trans. by Isaac C. Rotenburg (Philadelphia: Westminster, 1966), pp. 128–142.
24. While such an idea may seem ridiculous in a modern secular society, it has its proponents. See, for example, David L. Miller, *The New Polytheism: Rebirth of the Gods and Goddesses* (New York: Harper & Row, 1974). Some also see similar trends in the renewal of interest in myth through the writings of C. S. Lewis, J. R. R. Tolkien, and Charles Williams, though the basic Christian themes of their work raise questions of such an interpretation.

25. Bellah, "Religious Evolution," op. cit., pp. 366–368.
26. Weber, *The Sociology of Religion,* op. cit. See also Talcott Parsons's introduction to that volume for an interpretation of it in these terms.
27. Ernst Troeltsch, *The Social Teachings of the Christian Churches,* trans. by Olive Wyon (New York: Harper & Row, 1960), summarized on p. 993 ff.
28. Bellah, "Religious Evolution," op. cit., 367.
29. William H. McNeill, *The Rise of the West: A History of the Human Community* (Chicago: University of Chicago Press, 1963), pp. 420–422, 434–436.
30. Ernst Benz, *The Eastern Orthodox Church: Its Thought and Life,* trans. by Richard Winston and Clara Winston (Chicago: Aldine, 1963). Further discussion of the Eastern Orthodox church in this chapter is also based upon this work.
31. Weber, *The Religion of India,* op. cit., pp. 257–264.
32. For further discussion of the relationship between Yahweh and his people, see Max Weber, *Ancient Judaism,* trans. and ed. by Hans Gerth and Don Martindale (New York: Free Press, 1952), Chapter 5.
33. See, for example, Genesis 12:2–3.
34. Weber, *Ancient Judaism,* op. cit., pp. 289–292.
35. A good example of this may be found in the Biblical record of the confrontation between the prophet Amos and Amaziah, the priest at Bethel, in Amos 7:10–17.
36. See in particular Robert N. Bellah, *The Broken Covenant* (New York: Seabury, 1975).

7

The Move to Modernity: Individuation and Pluralism

Bellah finds the only fully developed example of early modern religion in the Protestant Reformation, though he sees partial evidence of it in reform movements within Islam, Buddhism, Taoism, and Confucianism. The distinguishing characteristic of this stage is "the collapse of the hierarchical structuring of both this and the other world."[1] This does not mean that the distinction between the transcendent and present worlds has diminished, but rather that the structure of mediation between the two has broken down. In historic religion salvation was available to the individual only through institutionalized channels: obedience to a set of laws, performance of mystical or liturgical rites, participation in a system of sacraments, or the like. Mediation also existed through religious elites, who in many traditions were able to amass a fund of grace in the name of the less worthy. In early modern religion all this was dropped, and the individual faced direct contact with the transcendental world.

Christendom's debt to the prophets of ancient Judaism is most noticeable in this stage. Two specific elements of their approach stand out. The first is the direct confrontation with the divine which they claimed and which became in early modern religion an expectation of all committed believers. The second element was their "inner-worldly asceticism," as Weber called it. The prophets applied the insight gained from their confrontation with the divine to the patterns and practices of the temporal world. Far from denying the transcendental world, they chose not to escape into it but to apply its standards to the everyday world in which they lived. The sacred was less a separate order from the profane than the source of meaning and evaluation for it.

This stance was adopted in the religious action of the Protestant Reformation. While direct contact with the divine was seen as an act of grace on the part of God, its fruits were sought in the conduct of the daily life of the believer. This implied several departures from earlier types of religion. Rather than seeing the sacred realm as a feature of the profane world which could be used for secular ends, the Protestant emphasis reversed the accent and found the profane world a feature of a transcendent order. This is not to say that historic Christianity did not contain elements of this type of thought. Rather, it became a pivotal part of the Protestant orientation, instead of peripheral as it had been. Christianity has to deal with this aspect of religious thought somewhere along the line insofar as it accepts the basic myth of a transcendent god having entered into human life in the person of Jesus. This mythic statement is probably the clearest example of the reversal of emphasis from primitive religion. Now the central thrust is on the participation of the holy—the god—in human affairs, rather than human participation in the holy. Early modern or Reformation thought also retains the reversal of archaic thought present in historic religion. The focus and meaning are in the transcendental realm rather than the ordinary. The change from the historic involves the tremendous growth of a basic lay ethic. To a certain extent the laity now have an advantage over religious specialists. They have a real field of action in which to apply their religious calling. With the service of this world being the fruit of religious vocation, service in the church is no more worthy than more practical vocations; it may even be suspect.

This sort of thought leads to religious organization of a type we have waited until now to discuss at length—the *sect*. In sociological theory this concept has been paired with that of the church in a structure of "ideal types." That is, they are conceived as opposite ends of a continuum, between which all empirical examples may be ranged according to how nearly they approximate the type. We have noted that the church was defined as a social institution, supported by and supporting other institutions in its society, coextensive with the society in its membership. The sect, by contrast, is an exclusive association of those committed to its ideals and beliefs, which is usually critical of or antithetical to at least some of the institutions of the society.

Early modern religion is a religion of sects, even though the early thrust of the Protestant Reformation which it describes assumed a churchlike organization. The breakdown of the hierarchical dispensation of salvation and the emphasis upon individual access to it and the "priesthood of all believers" led to making distinctions between those who had had the experience of salvation and those who had not. This, in turn, encouraged a definition of the church as a voluntary association of the saved. Since the fruits of salvation were to be found not so much in religious observance as in secular behavior, normative patterns for members' daily lives became tests of their worthiness to be part of the fellowship. The greatest effect of the sect upon other social institutions, then, became its influence upon the activity of its members in those institutions. At the same time, since the fruits of salvation were found in the wider society, such activity was likely to be high and to be exercised with a fierce determination to create within the imperfect institutions of the society conditions under which sectarian members could live up to the moral and ethical prescriptions of their faith.

This, of course, creates a paradox. If a sect is defined as an organization antithetical to at least some of the given institutions of the society, how can its members find ways to exercise the norms of their faith within those institutions? It is this peculiar paradox that gave rise to the form of early modern religion. Not all sects have had or retained the "inner-worldly asceticism" of the prophetic strain of the Judeo-Christian religious tradition. Sects antithetical to given institutions in a society, including its religious institution, may take the route of "otherworldliness" and simply withdraw from a society they consider wicked into a religiously oriented one of their own. In this case they may have no effect on the society that surrounds them, or they may have an eventual effect as they provide a living example of a radical alternative to the present social order. They may be ascetic while otherworldly, practicing a personal asceticism that works toward their own salvation. They may be mystics, focusing their mystical experience within this world or a transcendent one. If their break with other institutions is not focused on the religious institution, they may be subsumed under its organization as special orders, often even those orders whose special good works may assist the less strenuous adherents of the faith in their quest for salvation. This was the way in which sectarian impulses were kept within the bounds of historic religion; sectarians became monks, or nuns, or other types of religious votaries. None of these forms is likely to develop into early modern religion as defined by Bellah. This is much more the province of sects built upon inner-worldly asceticism.

At the same time, the pull of inner-worldly asceticism is toward the establishment of a churchlike organization. If believers are to work out their salvation in the everyday world, then it behooves them to try to put that world under the domination of their religion in order to provide appropriate structures for religiously motivated secular action. Inner-worldly sectarians, then, have tendencies toward being agents of social change. Their religion is transcendental, so that they do not regard the present order as divine in itself. At the same time, they claim temporal history as the stage upon which the divine will is enacted and in which they are expected to exert influence as instruments of that divine will.

The affinity for change engendered by this type of sectarianism can be traced to the social dynamic through which sects normally develop. We have seen that sects tend to be in opposition to at least some of the social institutions of their time. It comes as no surprise, then, that sectarian members are seldom recruited from among the comfortable, established sectors of a society. In Niebuhr's term, sects are the "churches of the disinherited."[2]

The type of "disinheritance" may vary considerably and may have a good deal of influence on the nature of the sect that arises—or whether a sect will arise at all. Various sects in the Western world have come from situations of economic underprivilege, lack of access to the political process, social cleavages that allow only low status to the groups involved, changes in the social order that result in loss of status for particular groups, and similar problems. Glock has found five types of deprivation associated with this process, defining deprivation as any way in which an individual or a group may feel disadvantaged in comparison with others, or with some external set of standards. To first of these forms of deprivation is *economic,* and he notes that the important factor here is a subjective appraisal of one's relative economic status rather than any objective criterion. The second, *social* deprivation, includes all assessments of relative advantage in regard to power, prestige, status, and opportunity. The third, *organismic* deprivation, concerns relative states of health and well-being. The fourth, and one that is receiving more study in recent years, is what he calls *ethical* deprivation. This can occur in groups that appear far from deprived; in fact it is quite likely to occur at fairly high status levels. Ethical deprivation involves perceived discrepancies between the objective reality of a culture with which one identifies and its goals and values. A final form of deprivation is that which Glock calls *psychic,* a product not of conflicting values as in the previous type, but of a lack of clear values or norms—of *anomie.*[3]

Some of these conditions seem quite personal and can be traced more often to the individual's motivation for joining a religious sect than to its formation in the first place. Yet there are times when social definition may cause them to apply to a group or a stratum in the society. Other conditions may influence the outcome—whether a religious sect or some other kind of social movement arises. Werner Stark finds that, in general, where the situation of deprivation appears to be hopeless, religious sects are formed. Where hope of ending the deprivation is present, political solutions may often be chosen. The choice between political and religious solutions may also depend on the relationship between the church and the state in the society. For example, since the Reformation, political movements have been favored over sectarian development in predominantly Roman Catholic countries, while in Russia and England, where the political ruler was also head of the church, religious sects have appeared in significantly greater proportion. Stark traces this difference to the fact that in Roman Catholic countries, where the hierarchy of church and state are separate, the church concentrates more on keeping its dogma pure, allowing less opportunity for the development of doctrinal deviation, while in caesaropapist societies a wide latitude of religious practice and interpretation is allowed, so long as it does not undermine the political structure.[4] It is also true that the particular emphasis of the culture predisposes groups toward secular or religious solutions for their problems. In an era when religious interpretation of problems is common, religious solutions will be the first tried. In a secular age, religious solutions often are adopted as a desperate last resort.

On the other hand, societies with an established religion often provide a setting where religious disaffection results in anticlerical rebellion against religion as a whole, while in cultures such as the American, where religious groups are treated as voluntary associations, social movements may be defined as religious sects with considerable ease. More than one American denomination might well have been a secular reform organization under less voluntaristic definitions of religion or in a society where religious groups are less likely to receive uncritical toleration from the political system.

There are patterned ways in which a sect may function to provide solutions for problems of deprivation. First of all, we must remember that the sect is an exclusive community of the committed. It is also nearly always a fairly small group. This means that it affords a closed situation in which the individual may function relatively free of the pressures from the outside society that have created the feeling of deprivation. The sect has its own values and norms; here, one's deprivations may be turned into blessings, or at least virtues. As St. Paul wrote in the days when Christianity as a whole was sectarian, "In our sorrows we have always cause for joy; poor ourselves, we bring wealth to many; penniless, we own the world."[5] What is cause for a sense of deprivation in this world becomes entirely the opposite when viewed from the transcendental plane. The individual's sense of worth is renewed. And within the closed system of the sect that renewal is confirmed in social interaction. In this small group one's status is assured; one's opinions have influence. Here a person's talents are needed, and he or she has opportunity to develop and strengthen them. The intensity of the social bond strengthens the individual, and a sense of the distinctiveness of the group and one's commitment to it provide further reinforcement. Thus, on the level of social psychology, the sect relieves individual feelings of deprivation.[6]

At the same time, these interior group dynamics often result in changed external conditions for the group as a whole. The self-confidence, self-discipline, and practice in social interaction within the shelter and normative redefinition of the sectarian group may change a mass of demoralized outcasts into a unified group capable of exercising individual or collective influence on the society. Miyakawa traces this process in the American frontier experience. Here, sectarian groups formed among the displaced who moved to the frontier for many reasons, often involving failure of one kind or another in the society "back home." As in most sects, moral discipline was very strict but social support was strong. The sect-group took the place of the family from which the pioneers had been uprooted, offering them not only transcendental hope but also practice in social and political skills. As they learned to organize their church groups they came to organize their community, and skills gained in these small associations were later practiced in regional meetings and eventually in political representation and the like.[7]

While the frontier situation is not always present to stimulate this process in its entirety, portions of it have been observed in many times and places. The original Protestant Reformation combined several elements of deprived groups, which is one of the reasons it did not remain a monolithic religious organization. Their motivations and needs were not always very similar. Many of the leaders of the Reformation can be numbered among the ethically deprived.[8] The society, and particularly its religious institution, with which men like Luther identified strongly, did not live up to their values and ideals. The princes who supported Luther felt politically deprived; the capitalist class that became the carrier of the Calvinistic wing of the Reformation comprised social outcasts in feudal society.[9]

The dynamics of the sect in this instance are carefully delineated by Weber in *The Protestant Ethic and the Spirit of Capitalism.* The reassessment of roles found in the Reformation came as a reaction to medieval Catholicism's definition of religious vocations as of a higher order than secular work, as well as feudal society's lack of place for the merchant and incipient capitalist. The Protestant ethic, particularly as developed in Calvinism, declared all of secular life the domain of God, who is Lord of history, and made each person's daily work a religious vocation. This is the ideological statement of the breakdown of the hierarchical structure mentioned by Bellah as central to early modern religion. The gap now was not within the inclusive church, between the religious and the laity, but at the boundaries of the sect, between the saved and the damned. Calvinism emphasized the sovereignty of God: Salvation was the work of God, not humankind. Yet the fruits of salvation could be found in the way in which a person responded to the call of God—that is, in his or her vocation. If one worked hard in one's job, lived soberly and uprightly, it was clear one was a member of the elect: "By their fruits shall you know them."

Weber finds in this process the mechanism by which capitalism was joined to newly developed technology to provide the Industrial Revolution. The Christian who worked hard and lived modestly made and saved money; this in turn was expected to be used in a productive way if one was a good steward of God's gifts. Consequently, the good Calvinist found investment in capital stocks—the means of production—as well as direct production, a worthy choice. This, says Weber, provided the dynamic for the rise of capitalism in the West. It also was the force behind the rise of the capitalist, who not only gained economic and political power but also became the possessor of high status as a fine example of the proper pursuit of a Christian vocation.

As this occurred, the sect of the capitalist Protestant began to resemble the church of earlier society. It supported a social order in which capitalist entrepreneurs were honored, and in its assumption of their superior morality it accorded the base for their gaining and retaining political power as well.

Within the framework of the Protestant ethic this same dynamic has worked to provide social mobility for new groups through time. The very process just described set up conditions of deprivation for persons entering the industrial culture at lower levels, and new sects developed to meet the needs of these groups. Stark traces the rise of new sects in England, pointing out a new one for each century since the Reformation. In the sixteenth century he finds the Baptists rising from among the weavers, who were economically deprived and socially isolated in cottage industry. In the seventeenth century the Quakers came to the fore, also out of the lower classes but taking much of their motivation from a sense of political deprivation. The Methodists can trace their founding from the artisans and skilled workers of the eighteenth century, whose skills had still not afforded them any difference in status from the lowliest of unskilled workers. In turn, it was from the unskilled workers and lowly classes that the Salvation Army was formed in the nineteenth century, and in the twentieth the Jehovah's Witnesses have been picking up the pieces discarded by the other groups.[9]

In most of these cases, sectarian membership has been accompanied by social mobility—often a mobility of the sect itself. The process is similar to that traced in the rise of early Protestantism. The sect provides a sense of identity and purpose and enforces a moral code that results in increased respectability as well as financial stability because of its emphasis on work and thrift. Because of its strictly enforced and often slightly old-fashioned morality, the sect's members become noted for their respectability and dependability. For example, Weber found in a tour of the American frontier that membership in a sect often served in the place of a letter of credit for people of that time and place.[10] This still tends to happen. The result, of course, is that members of the sect become more affluent. Their children are afforded a better education. The sect continues to recruit, but has as its nucleus these children of earlier members, whose sense of deprivation is not so great and whose commitment is not as total as that of first-generation converts. They tend to lead the sect into practices, teachings, and forms of organization more consistent with the larger society in which they feel much more comfortable than their parents could have. The sect begins to resemble a church. Eventually the organization no longer has the appeal to the disinherited, and recruitment from this segment of the society falls off. A new sect must be formed to take them in.[11]

As Niebuhr traced this process, he assumed that sects begin their transformation within a single generation as they seek to deal with problems of training their children to become members, and these new members take over the reins. Wilson disagrees on two counts. In the first place, he says, most sects continue to recruit, and strongly evangelical sects may continue indefinitely to have newly converted recruits as a majority of their members. In many cases of this sort, there may be fairly high attrition among the more affluent second-generation members who confirm their social mobility by leaving to join more congenial denominations. This, of course, allows the sect to continue largely as a first-generation group. The second reason for objecting to this deterministic view of the development of the sect is that it applies to some kinds of sects but not to all.[12]

Wilson has developed a typology of sects particularly applicable to Christendom which illustrates the latter objection. There are, he says, four major sectarian forms, along with several more minor types. Sects may be *conversionist,* the sort of evangelical type to which Niebuhr's expectation is most applicable. They may also be *revolutionist,* engrossed in the anticipation of an overthrow of the present social order through the second coming of Christ, the final judgment, or similar exchanges of secular for spiritual power. These groups are less likely to stress behavior deemed responsible in an ongoing society; they may, indeed, widen the economic and social breach between their members and their neighbors. A third type is *introversionist,* which seeks withdrawal from the evils of society and the cultivation of inner holiness within the sheltered confines of the sect. Again, this type of sect seldom grows to become part of the religious establishment, except in the very limited way by which monastic orders were made part of the larger church structure. The fourth type, the *manipulationist,* tends to concentrate on religious methodology for the manipulation of social and psychic forces through gaining some new form of knowledge. It generally remains more at the cultic level, without requiring the all-encompassing commitment characteristic of most sects. Minor types, which can be noted as a mixture or approximation of the major types, include the *thaumaturgical* (or spiritualist), *reformist, Utopian,* and *ritualist.* [12] The sort of movement characteristic of early modern religion centers around conversionist sects; yet all these may participate in the breakdown of the dual hierarchical system—earthly and transcendent—which was characteristic of historic religion.

An important characteristic of early modern religion is its emphasis on individualism. The breakdown of hierarchical structures is evidenced in the common phrase "the priesthood of all believers." At various times this has been taken to mean that no person needs an intermediary to reach "the throne of grace," that each believer provides priestly offices to fellow believers, or that the divine charisma, the Holy Spirit, is resident and active in each believer, guiding thoughts and actions. All these interpretations militate against any emphasis on the corporate life of the church other than as a voluntary association. Yet sects tend to claim that membership in them is the mark of the redeemed. An important consequence of this rather paradoxical combination of beliefs is the nature of evangelism and missionary work conducted by such sects. On the one hand, sects tend to reinforce their distinctiveness from other religious groups by proselyting among members of those groups. Convinced that theirs is the only religious body that can assure salvation, they have no hesitation about engaging in what more settled churches call "sheep stealing." On the other hand, their evangelistic fervor has made them strong supporters of missions, where they may join with other Christian groups in the effort to convert pagan peoples. Mehl suggests that this may be a first step to departure from the sectarian position in the direction of becoming a church. [13] This is a debatable point, however, for many foreign workers of established denominations report that one of the greatest problems they have to deal with is the undercutting competition of the fundamentalist sects.

The methodology of the conversionist sect is to construct circumstances in which the individual is confronted with the divine presence and the demands of the divine order. Such a confrontation is expected to result in individuals' realization of their unworthiness and the sinfulness of the life they have been leading and to a consequent resolution to repent and change themselves and their style of life. They are offered the power of divine grace to accomplish this feat and the social support of those who have faith that it can be—indeed, that it has been—accomplished. Services generally involve a good deal of singing and prayer—often spontaneous—which sets the mood of participation and expectancy. Great emphasis is placed on preaching that tends to make frequent reference to biblical passages, which are taken as God's direct and personal word to the individual. These are intended to show (1) the poverty of a person's attempts to work out his or her own salvation, (2) the sad fate awaiting those who depend upon such inadequate justification, (3) the free grace of God offering true salvation, and (4) a call to sinners to repent and accept this freely offered grace. In full sectarian situations, the sinner who becomes a convert is immediately taken into the fellowship of the sect for further training and the support that can be given by that community. Over time, however, the individualistic emphasis of the religious form has led to revivalism, where the kind of service described above is provided in mass meetings, and the converts are left to find their own supportive group or attempt to work out their response to salvation on their own. This phenomenon frequently results in what could be interpreted as a regression to something approaching primitive rather than early modern religion, with people gaining an emotional sense of participation through attendance at periodic revivals, and generally evidencing little change in their life-style between them.

When true to form, the early modern type of religion brings back into view a consideration of the process of secularization. A good case can be made for the thesis that the evolutionary progression of religious types from primitive to modern is a constant process of secularization, in which the sacred realm is progressively removed from secular life. At the same time, the specific differentiation of the religious institution which occurred in historic religion seemed to be a concentration and focusing of the sacred in a powerful position in the society. Early modern religion both changes and extends this pattern. Sectarian religious experience tends toward a concentration of participation unequaled since primitive types. The breakdown in the hierarchy puts each believer in direct contact with the divine, so the experience of the holy is the expectation of all, not just the shaman or the priest or the cloistered religious. At the same time, such religious experience is not sought as an end in itself. It may be this factor that causes Bellah to find early modern religion only in Western Protestantism. In Eastern religions, new input of religious ideas may come from those who could be called prophets, most likely those Weber has termed exemplary rather than ethical prophets. While exemplary prophets empty themselves of all desire and all contact with the secular world in order to become vessels which contain their god, ethical prophets keep in touch with the secular world in which they can be used as instruments of their god.[14] The experience of the immanence of the divine is an end in itself for the exemplary prophet. Early modern religion concentrates more on ethical prophecy. The Calivinistic doctrine of the Christian vocation in the world is a clear example of this orientation. For all its emphasis on the importance of action in the secular world, early modern religion at its core is transcendental. The meaning of secular action is found in the sacred realm. The real rewards of righteous living are to be found in Heaven, and any incidental benefits to be reaped along the way are at best ephemeral and at worst satanic temptations to turn away from the pure goals of salvation toward earthly satisfactions. The established churches are seen as living proof that the temptations of this world can lead to apostasy in this way. The sects, unlike the churches, are poor and humble, not trusting in earthly riches or power or prestige.

For most churches were once lowly sects, but now they have changed. In societies dominated by early modern religion, there is seldom an established church as such. The sectarian pull of early modern religion results in a kind of pluralism in which former sects, now more affluent and socially acceptable, become less closed as units and begin to cooperate with one another, depending on rational forms of organization rather than the unpredictable leadership of the Holy Spirit. Since early modern religion developed concomitantly with modern bureaucractic forms, the rational type of organization it took up was that of bureaucracy. While no hierarchy was needed in the dispensation of salvation, the specialized expert could certainly assist in the propagation of the faith. Thus sects grew into denominations, which developed specialized boards and agencies guiding cooperative ventures of the various congregations. This process is one Weber speaks of under the rubric of the "rationalization of charisma," and it was one of the steps that led to the establishment of modern religion. At the same time, it served to separate the denominations from the sects, who could see in the whole process a growing apostasy of the successful church, which was now putting all its efforts into controlling its possessions and making distinctions between fellow members which should not be made.

In true sectarian organization there is no professional ministry. The Word is spoken by the faithful as a sharing of their experiences and the insights given them from the scripture through the Holy Spirit. Even when a particular person is chosen to be the full-time minister, there is little emphasis on theological education. The Christian is to depend on the Spirit, not others who consider themselves experts, to lead him or her into a true interpretation of the Word of God. Religious organizations that make no formal demands of their ministers concerning education or other training perpetuate the sectarian form, as do societal circumstances under which such training is difficult to obtain.

Circumstances of this sort encouraged sectarian development in the American West and South, and the Civil War and its aftermath prolonged this condition for the South. Here the sectarian emphasis of early modern religion remained ascendent in a broad segment of the society for a sufficient length of time to delay, if not prevent, the rise of modern religion. The breaking of denominational ties during the Civil War cut off religious contact with the more urban sections of the country and emphasized even further the differences in religious organization between this and other areas. The South had developed along more agrarian lines than the industrial North and East and had always carried a strain of anti-intellectualism which made the rationalization of church organization less acceptable. Even those denominations most characterized by high educational standards and rational organization, such as the Presbyterians and the Episcopalians, retained in the South many of the less rational elements introduced by the Great Awakenings, such as the revivalistic method of evangelism. The dominant religious groups were more sectarian in tradition. The cultural climate and lack of an educational base worked in favor of the development of Baptist and Methodist churches, where lay ministers were more acceptable and enthusiastic, conversionary religion a more common form. The influence of these sectarian groups, where emphasis was on the local congregation, made it possible to allow schism from the Northern churches to occur at the time of the Civil War. It also made it less of a scandal that black and white churches of the same denomination should exist side by side with no real contact between them. The South suffered a state of relative deprivation vis-à-vis the North and East in regard to economic and political power after the Civil War which carried into the twentieth century. We have already mentioned that such conditions tend to produce sectarian religion; it is not surprising that sects should be a persistent form of religious organization in that region.[15]

The American South, then, is an excellent example of the sectarian paradox of religion being divorced from other social institutions yet seeking to influence them. The solution in the South, as in many other areas where sectarian styles have dominated, has tended toward a form of pietistic individualism, in which the church is expected to deal only in the personal salvation of individuals but the society is expected to reflect the values of the redeemed. Corporate social action by Southern churches has not been strongly encouraged, except in those areas that deal with individual morality. It is expected that the church will exert all its power to prevent such sinful behavior as the drinking of intoxicating beverages (at least in public), gambling, sexual promiscuity, and keeping businesses open on Sunday. The churches have shown themselves quite powerful in maintaining these sorts of mores in the South. They also can be noted for maintaining high rates of participation in church activities, which become another public expression of morality. Southern churches are attended by a far higher proportion of the populace than those in any other large section of the country, and adult participation in Sunday schools is far greater than in other regions.

In recent years the dominance of the churches has led to some activity on the part of church leaders in attempting to extend their moral leadership into areas of social problems and concern. In most cases, however, such activity has been almost directly accompanied by a decrease in lay participation in those churches. The individual evangelical approach is statistically far more popular.

The influence of Southern culture may be one of the factors giving rise to the apparent growth of popularity of evangelical religion in the country at large during the latter part of the 1970s. The election to the presidency of Jimmy Carter, an active evangelical layman from the South, has given that style of religiosity greater public exposure and respectability. At the same time, migration to the "sun belt" has introduced many more Americans to a culture based on an evangelical world view. And the experience of moving to an area that is undergoing rapid economic expansion creates the kind of setting that has historically been most conducive to the growth of early modern types of religion.

The emphasis on lay participation, practical consequences, and voluntarism found in early modern religion has been particularly congruent with the American experience as the continent has been settled and developed. The development of bureaucratic structures as part of the movement toward urban forms and away from expansionist development is a trend still not fully accepted in the religious institution. In a recent study of Presbyterians, Dean Hoge has documented a division in the denomination between those who support the policies and views of the denominational hierarchy and those whose orientation is much more within the world view of early modern religion. He assumes, probably rightly, that similar divisions exist in all the major Protestant denominations, cutting across traditional differences of class, race, and religious tradition.[16]

Similar divisions appear to have emerged in Roman Catholicism as well, with a strong movement of the early modern type emphasizing lay participation, individual responsibility in religious matters, and voluntarism. As will be seen later, this has had particularly interesting consequences in areas of the so-called Third World traditionally dominated by Roman Catholicism and now undergoing economic development.

It is in such areas of economic development that other types of early modern religion may be found. For example, the Japanese movement known as Sokka Gakkai—and brought to America as Nicheren Shoshu Buddhism—seems to fall into this category, although the transcendence of its focus is sometimes muted. Many of the new native religions of Africa appear also to be sects that are both transcendent and inner-worldly in the style of the early modern. Groups claiming an international focus, such as Sun Myung Moon's Unification Church, also appear to fit into this category.

However, there is much more resemblance to Bellah's concept of modern religion in the very multiplicity of these new movements, as well as explicitly in the ideology of some of them. Modern religion, says Bellah, has as its central feature the breakdown of the dualism that has developed in religious symbolism. This does not mean that there is a return to primitive monism; rather, existence has come to be seen as a multiplex phenomenon. All of life is regarded as infinitely revisable, containing within it not just the sort of "either-or" possibilities suggested by the concepts of "sacred/profane," "worldly/otherworldly," or "heaven/hell." The possibilities are infinite, and an openness exists as to how they may be used and combined.[17]

This orientation of modern religion can be thought of as an end-product of secularization, particularly when viewed in terms of Becker's "sacred-secular continuum,"[18] as diagrammed in Figure 3. The sacred, says Becker, is that which is least ready to change; the secular is most open to change. The sacred society is dominated by primitive religion, is isolated territorially, and maintains its isolation through rigid social and mental structures. The unity of the society rests in the shared behavior of its members; as a consequence nearly all behavior attains the status of ritual. The religious symbols are concrete objects and actions, and the social organization of the tribe is the chief symbol of its ultimate meaning. The relationship of this sort of symbol system to reluctance to change is clear. Any change in the daily routine or the social order threatens the visible representations of ultimate meaning. The society itself is holy, or at least demanding of ultimate loyalty, and its main form of reinforcement of this feeling is through ritual.

As one moves along Becker's continuum from the "sacred" to the "secular," the emphasis seems to reflect the sort of growing dualism that Bellah traces through archaic to historic religion. The focus moves toward a more abstract frame of reference, one more general than the specific ritualistic behavior of the sacred "proverbial" society. Under the "sanctioned rationality" of the "prescriptive" society, the orientation seems to move from identification with the society to the guidance of an identifiable self that is seeking to develop within the framework of the society. Instead of seeing society as holy, or deserving of ultimate loyalty, participants in the prescriptive society think in terms of the intimacy it provides them, of their relations with their peers in social groups. Or the orientation becomes moralistic, so that behavior is seen as a changeable characteristic of the self rather than an integral part of the nature of the individual. It seems that somewhere in this area could be found the transition between historic and early modern religion. The crucial actions in regard to salvation in historic religion involved participation in sacraments of one sort or another. In early modern religion it came to deal with daily behavior. It may be an oversimplification to discuss the change from the intimate sharing of the means of grace to the moralistic structure of the everyday world, but the prime emphasis does seem to fit this designation. Two other ways of valuing are mentioned in Becker's prescriptive society—the "fitting" and the "appropri-

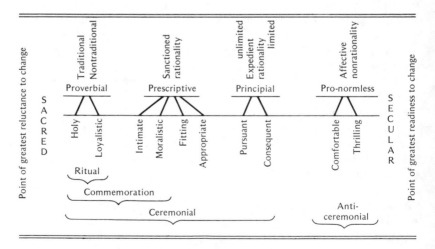

FIGURE 3   Becker's Sacred-Secular Continuum.

As depicted by Charles P. and Zona K. Loomis, *Modern Social Theories: Selected American Writers*, 2nd edition. Princeton: D. van Nostrand, 1965, p. 48.

ate." These are clearly less stringent than the moralistic orientation, but at the same time are also concerned with specific behavior patterns.

The next major societal type on Becker's continuum is the "principial." Here normative patterns are based not on concrete behavior so much as on the consequences or goals of such behavior. Valuing occurs in accordance with an understanding of the whole web of relationships that may be affected by certain behavior. The value base is in more abstract principles. Individual behavior is not judged according to a preset pattern. This can be compared with Bellah's discussion of modern religion, where he says he sees in some of the present trends "the increasing acceptance of the notion that each individual must work out his own ultimate solutions and that the most the church can do is provide him a favorable environment for doing so, without imposing on him a prefabricated set of answers."[19]

Mehl discusses religious symbolism in much the same way when he speaks of the break between Catholicism and Protestantism in terms of a mutation of the religious object. That is, in medieval historic Christianity the mass was an objective reality around which the devotion of the faithful and the hierarchy of the organization both were centered. Statues and images also contributed to the concreteness of the religious object. This concreteness led to specificity in regard to rules for dealing with the object of worship, as well as relationships among those who were concerned with it. The objectivity of the focus of worship led to institutionalization, to unchangeable definitions and well-defined dogma and authority. Mehl found the Protestant Reformation truly iconoclastic because it made a change in the religious object. Instead of the concreteness of the mass, or of images and symbols that pointed to it, Protestant theology pointed to a process—the revelation of the Word, which is seen as "act and event." While there has been continual pressure to reintroduce the objective view of the focus of worship by taking the Bible as the objective Word, or some particular dogma in the same way, there are counterpressures within Protestantism pushing to remain open to the more process-oriented view. Institutionalization, in such a case, rather than being the welcome outcome and strengthening force behind the religious object, threatens it. In Protestantism, religious organization is not central but peripheral and sometimes even suspect. So although Protestantism has its institution, its cult, its social aspect, it is always struggling to avoid becoming a prisoner of these elements. The proliferation of sects under the Protestant banner is one indication of this struggle. There are other ways, too, in which the process of moving from "event" to "institution" is always threatened by a return to the "event" in institutionalized processes of worship.[20] Catholic scholars have agreed with this point of view. For example, Weigel identifies as the "Protestant principle" this event of the immediate knowing of God through an awareness that is largely nonconceptual, and which requires building lives faithful to the experience.[21] Many of the changes introduced into Catholicism since Vatican II have been termed processes of "protestantization," and none are more clearly so than those that have occurred in this area of diminishing concreteness in symbols and organization.

Thus Protestantism, or cultures largely influenced by Protestantism, might seem the basis for the development of modern religion. However, Bellah finds it not confined, as he feels early modern religion is confined, to Protestant Christianity. He finds strong indications of the rise of modern religion in Japan in recent years, and he states that there may be factors that encourage the development of modern religion in several strains of Mahayana Buddhism and several of the other great traditions as well.[6] Insofar as religion develops out of an interpretation of our understanding of ourselves and our relationship to a broader framework of meaning, it may be assumed that any given religion is the product of the interaction between the inherited tradition of the group and the objective reality of the situation in which it lives. The situation for many people living in highly urbanized, technologically based societies seems very like that which Becker described as the secular society, where isolation has been changed to accessibility and change and movement are virtually unrestricted. It would seem logical that any religious tradition that could be interpreted in a "principial" manner, giving opportunity for change and growth, would be so interpreted in modern industrial society.

The stages of religious evolution postulated by Bellah reflect to a large measure changes in our understanding of human nature; they are involved with a growing differentiation of the self from the group and from the blind forces of fate. As Bellah puts it:

> The historic religions discovered the self; the early modern religion found a doctrinal basis on which to accept the self in all of its empirical ambiguity; modern religion is beginning to understand the self's own existence and so to help man take responsibility for his own fate.[22]

While this world view is now articulated mainly in intellectual and philosophical circles, Bellah finds evidence that many modern people are living within it without bothering to spell it out. He cites the casualness about dogma, the appreciation of writers like Tillich and Bonhoeffer who do state it, and an almost cavalier attitude toward institutions as part of this. Orr and Nichelson seem to find the same phenomena in the lives of their "expansive men" of *The Radical Suburb.* Speaking of older symbols as blueprints or laws, they say these no longer appeal because the chief end has become openness rather than institutional rigidity. Surely the following speaks of the problem of institutionalized Protestantism noted by Mehl:

> The radical believes that when symbols are taken too seriously, they cease to be pointers to realities beyond themselves and become barriers—idols that foreclose further insight. Playfulness and eclecticism express his unashamed acceptance of man's location in history, with all that this location means by way of depriving him of omniscience. Caught in history, radical man celebrates the lack of connectedness of his religious experiences and symbols, because this very absence of order reminds him that he cannot readily put his finger on the universal pulse. Paradoxically, dividedness can become for him the vehicle by which he points to the God of the Judeo-Christian faith, whose oneness and whose sovereignty stand in contrast to man's eclectic attempts to penetrate mystery symbolically.[23]

Orr and Nichelson compare this perspective with two other lifestyles they find in the suburb: the "conscientious," which appears to be a moral emphasis based on early modern religion; and what they term "savage," a life-style based on the kind of group loyalties institutionalized in historic as well as archaic and primitive religion. For modern people, they say, conscientiousness becomes too restrictive, and savage styles are idolatry.

Modern religion allows us to treat all our assumptions as tentative, including those of our religion. Another way in which this has been interpreted can be found in the work of Harvey Cox, who in *The Secular City* discussed the process of secularization as an extension of individual freedom and responsibility. Falling in with Bellah's expectation that modern religion will be developed primarily from an extension and reinterpretation of extant religious myth and symbol,[24] Cox finds the basis of the process in some of the earliest events celebrated in the Judeo-Christian tradition. The Genesis story of creation, he says, divorces the creator from his creation, thus freeing humankind to manipulate nature, and in fact contains the demand that they exercise dominion over it. The story of the Exodus is, among other things, a legitimation of rebellion against a divine-right king, thus laying the groundwork for a desacralization of politics. Finally, and more directly pertinent to the problems of religious symbolization in modern religion, is the giving of the Ten Commandments, the first of which demands worship of God alone, not anything made by humankind. Cox extends the traditional interpretation of idols beyond images to ideologies and institutions. So in the ancient tradition he finds justification for the modern approach.[25]

The fundamental symbol system of modern religion, says Bellah, is that in which one understands oneself to be a "dynamic, multidimensional self capable, within limits, of continual self-transformation, and capable, within limits, of remaking the world including the very symbolic forms with which he deals with it, even with the forms that state the unalterable conditions of his own existence."[26]

In the case of modern Christian religion, the symbolization and the social organization are predicated also on the recognition that Christendom has come to an end. Symbolically, this phenomenon is treated in a number of ways, ranging from discussions of ours as a "post-Christian era" to the declaration of "the death of God." The situation out of which this orientation arises is that of modern life-styles and worldwide communication. As the media have made it customary to conceive as neighbors people dwelling on other continents, over time they have brought the realization that fewer of those neighbors are Christian than are not. The growing freedom of choice in life-styles and values afforded by an urban society opened up the possibility—and the actuality—that one's immediate neighbors might not be Christian either. Yet the necessity of dealing with those neighbors, near and far, has grown as human society has become more specialized and interdependent. The rules for dealing with one's neighbor could no longer be assumed to coincide with assumptions about how one deals with fellow Christians; a framework of rights and responsibilities had to be developed which took precedence over the rules of any religious in-group. That framework had already begun to take shape through the exercise of early modern religion, for the pluralism of Protestantism demonstrated that the rules were not always the same within Christendom. However, until recently there have been a number of assumptions about agreement on the divine lordship of Christ or at least of the God of the Judeo-Christian heritage. The salvational aims of all the churches could be interpreted as fairly similar, as they were "all trying to get to the same place." These assumptions can no longer be made. The picture of Christendom has shattered into a vast, ever-changing kaleidoscope.

The immediate organizational response to this condition is that which developed early on the mission field where it was obvious that Christendom did not yet prevail: the churches began to coalesce into larger organizations. Two factors are involved in such action. First, when faced by a massive non-Christian situation, individual denominations have found that the fine points of dogma and organization that separate them are totally irrelevant to the situation. Besides, they are downright embarrassing to explain to non-Christians while at the same time teaching them about Christian love and community. The second factor in denominational reunion has to do with organizational strength and efficiency. Churches threatened with being unheard and impotent need a focal point from which to speak and an efficient way to spread out their personnel to the best advantage. As a result, one of the first responses to the loss of Christendom was the ecumenical movement.

We have said that doctrinal differences did not matter greatly in the face of a non-Christian milieu. It is also true that the growth of the conditions of modern religion lessened the relevance of such differences for persons who still participated in church structures. Two forms of ecumenism grew at nearly the same time. In the mission field and at the upper levels of denominational bureaucracies, cooperation grew into combination and often into merger. In the parishes of urbanizing society also, cooperative and joint ventures were undertaken in the inner city from which the churches had fled and in the rural areas from which the people had fled. Amid the concentrating masses of suburbia, denominations faced with overextended budgets for new church buildings were led to reinforce the nonchalance of the suburbanites toward denominational differences by affecting comity agreements: they parceled out particular areas to one denomination or another, according to projections based on denominational preferences of people who could afford the price range of housing in that development and, to some degree, on which denomination had a turn coming. Suburbanites who found a reasonably congenial church with a church school within walking distance for their children did not insist on staying within particular denominational boundaries. The mobility of modern society being what it is, many middle-class young people have had the experience of learning Christianity at the hands of three or four denominations, as their parents' jobs moved them from the neighborhood of the Shady Glen Methodist Church to the Rolling Hills Presbyterian to the Mountain View Congregational, or whatever. Those who have remained involved in the structure of the church have little at stake in denominational identity and tend to support upper-level bureaucrats who seek denominational unity.

At the same time, the conditions of modern religion tend to make the whole problem irrelevant, in that the church as an institution may be largely irrelevant. The open, ever-changing, growing attitude toward the ultimate militates against institutionalization. A common definition of institutions states that they are frozen answers to basic questions. The kinds of questions asked in modern religion cannot tolerate "frozen answers." The church, for many moderns who are involved in it at all, is rather more like a service station than an institution. It provides celebrations for special events—christenings, marriages, funerals, and the like. It provides a brief and cheap education in moral values for the children. It is a good place to get together with people who share similar interests and points of view. And through short-term study groups or the like it can be a useful tool in the modern religious quest.

When religious groups begin to function in this way, it becomes problematic whether they can be classified as either "churches," as the concept was defined in our discussion of historic religion, or "sects," such as those that developed with early modern religion. In those cases the religious organization has tended to take precedence over the individual. The church of historic religion held and dispensed the "means of grace" through which the individual might attain salvation and without which that salvation was in jeopardy. The sect of early modern religion had the power to certify one's status as a member of the elect and exercised the power of moral sanctions over its members. In modern religion, however, the individual is the focus and the exerciser of power. Salvation is likely to be defined in terms of "self-actualization" and religion treated as a useful tool in achieving that end.

Under these circumstances, religious organization tends toward a type most commonly identified with the sociological concept of the *cult*. This type of religious organization is defined by Eister as

a loosely organized, generally impermanent group of adults who seek to realize, through their association with some leader or leaders and with each other, satisfactions including some sort of religious "thrill" or exaltation. . . . Other tendencies may be present, such as a noticeable disregard for strict or narrow theological definitions, a common preference for eclectic universalist patterns of belief and practice, and a commitment to the group which, in contrast to the kind of commitment demanded of sect members, appears partial, segmented, "faddist" rather than unequivocating, complete, and final.[27]

Here we find the logical movement along Becker's continuum toward the "secular," where the basis of valuing is the "thrilling." It is also the end point of the process noted by Bellah of the development and growth in centrality of the sense of the "self" as we move from primitive to modern religion. Again, Eister writes:

Although religious thrill, as we have seen, may be experienced in many forms and under a variety of circumstances, it is invariably a personal affair, an experience which, in the cult, heightens or plays on the interest of persons in their "selves" and in what they conceive to be their relations both to God and to other people. . . . To the extent that the thrill response is by its nature inward and personal the cult will underscore to some extent what we may call an egoistic or person-centered outlook.

At the same time, it should be noted that the thrill which the cult participant enjoys need not be confined to satisfactions in his own personal salvation (or in some other purely individual gain) but may include satisfaction
in achieving new kinds of personal relationships with intimate friends and
strangers alike.[28]

There is some relationship between this idea of religious "thrill" and
the experience of the holy, perhaps including genuine mysticism. Troeltsch, in discussing mysticism, warns against mere "enthusiasm,"
which he finds leading to involvement in the sect. And there are those
who have found that the cult as defined here may be an early stage in
the development of a sect, which may later become more established
and eventually find its place as a denomination.

But what of "real" mysticism? Troeltsch has said that in its widest
sense it is "simply the insistence upon direct inward and present religious experience."[29] The focus then becomes the type of society in
which there is support for religious structures that make this experience
their primary focus, and which may be relatively enduring.

In trying to locate "mysticism" as a type like church or sect, Troeltsch
makes an interesting comment that "the modern educated classes
understand nothing but mysticism."[30] If we return to Becker's continuum, we find that his "ideal type" of secular society is one in which
there is universal literacy and access to knowledge and—again—one
characterized by the pursuit of the "thrilling" in a style he terms "anti-
ceremonial"—the seeking of nonrational experience in inward, subjective, unique ways rather than through traditional communal rites.

The symbolic foundation for such religious forms comes out of the
cultural relativity fostered by high levels of accessibility and education.
Experiences in societies that contain these factors lead persons to a
realization of the symbolic nature of all language and concepts.

In a recent article Eister has noted that

exceptional individuals throughout history, including philosophers, theologians, and others, have as individuals entertained serious doubts about the
adequacy and reliability of concepts, the possibility of rational communication, and so on, but there seems to be something "new" and perhaps unique
about the extent to which these understandings have spread among intellec-
tuals and those who in various ways rely on them.[31]

Such a view of modern religion is supported by Glock and Wuthnow's
recent research. One clear example of the loss of confidence in traditional symbols may be seen in responses to a question about belief in
God, where 8 percent of those over age 30 and 19 percent of their

younger respondents passed over the usual choices of belief, doubt, or unbelief to say that they were uncomfortable about the word "God" but did believe in something "more" or "beyond."[32]

Similarly, Wuthnow found that a significant proportion of the respondents whose answers consistently fell into a world view he termed "mystical" appeared to order all their perceptions around inner, subjective experience. His final chapter, titled "The Politics of Diversification," describes the way in which a culture characterized by the cult as a primary religious form may operate. Although people may hold widely varying world views, he says, the society manages to hold together through a number of processes by which those world views do not interfere with interaction between those who hold them.

One such process is *commercialization,* where religions and values are essentially packaged and sold in a marketplace of ideas. As we have seen in our definition of the cult, individuals are expected to "buy" as much of any of these "packages" as they wish, with no sense of permanent commitment to them or the world views they represent. Competition among them is not destructive because of the trivial nature of religious choice.

A second process he notes is that of *privatization,* where the choices are understood to take place in the private realm, as matters of personal taste and preference. Again, the public consequences of such choices are trivial. Similar are his processes of *ritualization,* the relegation of religious activities to particular times when they will not interfere with the ongoing life of the society, and *isolation,* their confinement to particular places outside the stream of public activity.[33]

Under such circumstances, as Eister has said, the cult "is no challenger of the social order."[34] Here we find the opposite of the sacred society, where all of life is permeated by primitive religion. In the fully secular society, modern religion becomes a personal, idiosyncratic pursuit which provides certain emotional gratifications considered enriching to the individual.

In the process it becomes clear that the religious experience sought has little reference to an objective or transcendent deity. Rather, the divine impulse is found within the depths of the self and its relations with other selves. Thus the cult form of modern religion may best be described as "immanentist." Troeltsch noted this early in the twentieth century when he distinguished the sect from the church by its insistence on a subjective form of attaining grace as opposed to the church's objective attainment, but he said that both viewed God as transcendent. By contrast, he went on, mysticism is differentiated from both those types by its understanding of God as immanent.[35]

There is some indication in Troeltsch's work that he sees the three types of church, sect, and mysticism in process terms, so that mysticism is a later development depending on the existence of church and sect for institutional frames against which it may react. This leaves, then, the question of whether the cult, as a form of organization, can provide sufficient grounding for the immanent religiosity for which it seems to have a natural affinity.

In the minds of most people, the term "cult" is taken to be pejorative and is usually applied to alien, bizarre, or potentially dangerous religious groups. Yet there are many parallels between this religious type, as defined here, and the ways in which familiar religious organizations are functioning in our society. From the "church-hopping" of the "expansive" suburbanite to the experiential activities of church-sponsored encounter groups or charismatic services to the periodic "highs" of revivalist crusades, religion in the service of the self is endemic. In addition, there appears to be less and less support for public aspects or influences of religious institutions.

The proliferation of new religious groups whose roots may be in Eastern mysticism, primitive nature religions, secular psychology, or millenarian prophecies only bears witness to a process already evident in more familiar religious groups. The multiplex world of modern religion appears to have relevance for the current situation.

Becker's concepts of the sacred and the secular society are, of course, "ideal types," extremes which are not reached in real situations. It will, however, be one of the tasks of the following chapters, as they survey more specific aspects of the relation of religion to modern society, to explore the existence and possible rates of movement in the direction of the forms of modern religion in a secular society.

Notes and References

1. Robert N. Bellah, "Religious Evolution," *American Sociological Review* 23 (June 1964): 368–369.
2. H. Richard Niebuhr, *The Social Sources of Denominationalism* (New York: Meridian Age, 1957), Chapters 2 and 3.
3. Charles Y. Glock, "The Role of Deprivation in the Origin and Evolution of Religious Groups," in Charles Y. Glock and Rodney Stark, *Religion and Society in Tension* (Chicago: Rand McNally, 1965), pp. 246–250.
4. Werner Stark, *The Sociology of Religion: A Study of Christendom* (New York: Fordham University Press, 1967), vol. 2, pp. 51–83.
5. II Corinthians 6: 9–10, *The New English Bible* (Delegates of the Oxford University Press and the Syndics of the Cambridge University Press, 1961).

6. Bryan Wilson, *Religion in Secular Society* (Baltimore: Penguin, 1969), pp. 210–211.
7. T. Scott Miyakawa, *Protestants and Pioneers* (Chicago: University of Chicago Press, 1964), summarized on pp. 213–215.
8. Glock, op. cit., p. 248.
9. Werner Stark, op. cit., pp. 6–36.
10. Max Weber, *From Max Weber: Essays in Sociology*, trans. and ed. by Hans H. Gerth and C. Wright Mills (New York: Oxford University Press, 1946), pp. 302–322.
11. See Niebuhr, loc. cit.
12. Wilson, op. cit., pp. 224–240.
13. Roger Mehl, *The Sociology of Protestantism*, trans. by James H. Farley (Philadelphia: Westminster, 1970), p. 231.
14. Max Weber, *The Sociology of Religion*, trans. by Ephraim Fischoff (Boston: Beacon, 1963), pp. 55–57. See also Talcott Parsons's introduction to that volume, pp. 36–37.
15. See Samuel Hill, *Southern Churches in Crisis* (Boston: Beacon, 1968) for a good account of this phenomenon.
16. Dean Hoge, *Division in the Protestant House* (Philadelphia: Westminster, 1977).
17. Bellah, op. cit., p. 371.
18. Howard Becker, "Current Sacred-Secular Theory," in *Modern Sociological Theory in Continuity and Change*, ed. by Howard Becker and Alvin Boskoff (New York: Dryden, 1957), pp. 133–185.
19. Bellah, op. cit., p. 373.
20. Mehl, op. cit., pp. 313–317.
21. Robert McAfee Brown and Gustave Weigel, *An American Dialogue* (Garden City, N.Y.: Doubleday, 1960), pp. 193–203.
22. Bellah, op. cit., pp. 371–373.
23. John B. Orr and Patrick Nichelson, *The Radical Suburb* (Philadelphia: Westminster, 1972), p. 141.
24. Bellah, op. cit., p. 372.
25. Harvey Cox, *The Secular City* (New York: Macmillan, 1965), pp. 21–37.
26. Bellah, op. cit., p. 372.
27. Allan W. Eister, *Drawing Room Conversion: A Sociological Account of the Oxford Group Movement* (Durham, N.C.: Duke University Press, 1950), p. 82.
28. Ibid., p. 213.
29. Ernst Troeltsch, *The Social Teaching of the Christian Churches*, trans. by Olive Wyon (New York: Harper, 1960), p. 741.
30. Ibid., p. 798.
31. Allan W. Eister, "An Outline of a Structural Theory of Cults," *Journal for the Scientific Study of Religion* 11 (December 1972): 325.
32. Charles Y. Glock and Robert Wuthnow, "The Religious Dimension: A Report on Its Status in a Cosmopolitan American Community," paper presented at the International Symposium on Belief, Baden bei/Wein, Austria, January 8–10, 1975.
33. Robert Wuthnow, *The Consciousness Reformation* (Berkeley: University of California Press, 1976).
34. Eister, *Drawing Room Conversion*, op. cit., p. 214.
35. Ernst Troeltsch, "The Stoic Christian Natural Law and the Modern Secular Natural Law," mimeo quoted by Paul Gustafson in "The Missing Member of Troeltsch's Trinity: Thoughts Generated by Weber's Comments," *Sociological Analysis* 36 (Fall 1975): 225.

Bellah, Robert N. *The Broken Covenant.* New York: Seabury, 1975.

Durkheim, Emile. *The Elementary Forms of the Religious Life.* Trans. by Joesph Ward Swain. New York: Free Press, 1965.

Herberg, Will. *Protestant-Catholic-Jew.* Garden City, N.Y.: Doubleday, 1955.

Lenski, Gerhardt. *The Religious Factor.* Garden City, N.Y.: Doubleday, 1961.

Miyakawa, T. Scott. *Protestants and Pioneers.* Chicago: University of Chicago Press, 1964.

Orr, John B., and Nichelson, F. Patrick. *The Radical Suburb.* Philadelphia: Westminster, 1970.

Redfield, Robert. *The Primitive World and Its Transformations.* Ithaca, N.Y.: Cornell University Press, 1957.

Swanson, Guy E.. *The Birth of the Gods.* Ann Arbor: University of Michigan Press, 1960.

Troeltsch, Ernst. *The Social Teaching of the Christian Churches.* Trans. by Olive Wyon. New York: Harper, 1960.

Weber, Max. *The Sociology of Religion.* Trans. by Ephraim Fischoff. Boston: Beacon, 1963.

Part III

FUNCTION AND PROCESS IN INSTITUTIONALIZED RELIGION

While in the preceding chapters religion has been treated as the expression of an entire culture, we find in modern society a diversification great enough that we must speak of subcultures with differing religious characteristics. These may be based on such ineradicable differences as race or sex, or more arbitrary categories of ethnic group or economic class, but in each case they reflect a different life experience which requires some uniqueness of religious expression. Also, as we have traced the development of human society into more and more complex organization, it is apparent that religion is not the only aspect of society that has developed its own institutional framework, organization, and personnel. Education, the family, the economic system, and government have each become identifiable systems rather than overlapping activities of an undifferentiated tribe. Each of these is related to the other in patterns of influence and interdependence, and to understand the sociology of religion it is necessary to trace the ways in which it interacts with these other social realities.

In this section some of the broad relations of religion to institutions and processes of the society will be traced. Because there are notable differences among various societies in the way institutions are defined and related, the primary focus of this section will be on American society, though in a world as closely connected as ours the discussion cannot be totally limited to that focus. It is important to remember, however, that generalizations from one society or culture to another need always to be undertaken with caution, while at the same time applications to some concrete society are necessary for meaningful content. The American focus, then, should not be taken as a model for other societies, but as a single case that can illustrate the dynamics of interinstitutional relations. Similarly, while there is an attempt to present some of the historical development of current patterns, it should not be assumed that the configuration noted here will hold over time. In many ways a sociological analysis of modern American society is a snapshot, both true and distorted, because it must represent the peculiar focus of a specific time and point of observation. Only time will tell whether patterns noted here will continue to develop in directions now observed or swerve in unexpected new directions. Yet there is enough continuity in human culture to make it worthwhile to trace underlying factors and to generalize—with caution—from them.

8

Religious Aspects of Class, Race, and Ethnicity

One of the inescapable elements of modern industrial society is that of social class. Both religion and political ideology may posit a norm of human equality, but the specialized roles of a technological society require a range of levels of skill and responsibility that inevitably lead some people into positions of power and others into more subservient roles. Even if economic rewards were equal—and there is no modern society in which that can be proven to be the case—such differences in access to power create different perceptions of human life, as do the activities and milieus of the many specialized roles required for the functioning of the society. Since religion, like all other human phenomena, rises out of the life experiences of its participants, it must be expected that it will vary with the social position of those who are involved.

According to Marx, the religious institutions of a society are created and dominated by the ruling class of that society, and the chief function of religion is to provide moral pressures and psychological outlets which preserve the class structure. Yet even as he terms religion an "opiate" he notes that it helps make life tolerable for the oppressed. Durkheim also sees religion as the foundations of the social order, but Weber finds within religion the potential for creating movements that may change that order. Given such divergent points of view, it is not surprising that a large proportion of the empirical work in the sociology of religion has been in some way connected to the problem of the relation of religion to social class.

In order to deal competently with this subject, one must recognize that religion is a complex phenomenon, which may fulfill many functions at the same time. Thus Glock and Stark's delineation of the dimensions of religion provides a good way to begin to come to terms with this issue.[1]

137

The first dimension of religiosity that they consider is religious *belief* (or as they termed it earlier, the *ideological* dimension). For some church members this dimension is the crucial factor, and an individual's religiosity is graded on a scale of nearness to or distance from a particular orthodox doctrine. Such a dimension is not easy to judge in the context of scientific objectivity because definition of the orthodox position varies not only between but also within specific religions. Yet if it is considered crucial by many people in the religious institution, it must be dealt with. We shall see later some of the ways, successful and unsuccessful, in which it has been approached.

Another dimension of religiosity is religious *practice* (earlier termed the *ritual* dimension). This involves participation in ritual activities of the group as well as private devotional behavior. Group participation has long been a standard measure of religiosity in the sociology of religion. It is easy to remain objective while counting memberships or taking records on the frequency of church attendance. Private devotional life is less easily observed and hence less frequently used by sociologists as a measure of religious commitment. Yet we shall find that in the study of the religiosity of various social classes one may be led to spurious conclusions by concentrating on one facet of religious practice and ignoring the other.

A third dimension, religious *experience,* is also difficult to deal with in the context of sociology, because it involves subjective states rather than observable behavior. Yet we have taken as one of the defining characteristics of religion this experience of the "holy." Its importance in various church bodies and to individuals is germane to a consideration of religion and social class, as well as other social functions of religion.

The *knowledge* dimension has to do with the possession of facts about the religion and must be seen as somewhat separate from the belief dimension. To know about a religion does not necessarily lead to conviction about its correctness, and belief in its effectiveness may be based on a minimum of knowledge about it. Yet it must be assumed that a person committed to a particular religion will strive to know more about it—one more indication that these dimensions, though conceptually separate, are closely interrelated.

The final dimension that Glock and Stark have traced is the *consequences* of religion. Surely the highly religious person should show in attitude and conduct some effect of religious commitment. Yet behavior is also affected by other factors of life, including the life-style and the vested interests of one's social class. The use of this dimension to measure religious commitment has proved particularly difficult, although it is also a matter of particular interest.

Some findings in studies of the belief dimension show that it does have certain specific relationships to social class. It is generally understood that people of low educational attainment tend to be more concrete in their thinking and to notice fewer fine shades of distinction between apparently opposing viewpoints than those who are more highly educated. At first glance the concreteness of their thinking should lead us to expect lower-class people to have little belief in supernatural aspects of religion. Yet exactly the opposite holds true. The need for a clear differentiation between conceptual opposites seems to lead the uneducated, on the whole, to require a clear recognition of the division between the sacred and the profane. If everyday life involves the natural, then religion involves the supernatural. They have not been indoctrinated deeply with a faith in reason and the scientific method, so they are willing to accept as proper the supernatural aspects of religion. The need for concreteness is met through a specifically defined orthodoxy.

Stark and Glock constructed tests to determine the degree of supernaturalism in the belief systems of members of various church bodies. They ranked denominations according to the percentage of members in their sample who agreed with the following statements:

I know God really exists and I have no doubts about it.
Jesus is the Divine Son of God and I have no doubts about it.
Jesus was born of a virgin. (Completely true.)
Do you believe Jesus will actually return to earth some day? (Definitely.)
Miracles actually happened just as the Bible says they did.
There is a life beyond death.
The devil actually exists.[2]

They also compared denominations from a national sample on a similarly constructed orthodoxy index. The rank order of denominations on their orthodoxy index shows a clear similarity to rankings of denominations according to the percentage of lower-class people in their membership. Those containing the greatest percentage of persons from the lower social ranks show highest rates of orthodoxy. Such studies reinforce the observation that the churches of the affluent and well educated exhibit less acceptance of the literalistic, supernatural interpretation of the basic myth of a religion than those whose members have less wealth and education.

As we come to the dimension of ritual practice, we find in general that there is a direct positive relationship between religious membership and social class. In countries with an established religion, where membership is taken for granted, it is something of a fact of life that those out of the mainstream of the life of the nation are more likely not to participate in its churches. In America, where the church is taken to be a voluntary association, special consideration is required to understand the relationship between social class and church membership. One clear point is that church membership is part of a consistent pattern of membership in voluntary associations. Demerath[3] adds a caveat by noting that for many people of lower social class, church membership and participation may be the only or one of very few associational connections, whereas it may involve a smaller proportion of the memberships of those of higher class. Thus the question of intensity of concentration intrudes even into the simple task of computing the percentage of church memberships by class.

Participation in ritual activities becomes somewhat more complicated as a measure of religiosity. In general, we find that people of higher social classes attend church services more regularly than those in lower classes. However, these generalizations must be controlled for church type. As a whole, regular participation in worship is stressed more by liturgical types of denominations than by the less liturgical. At the same time, nonliturgical sects often demand more frequent participation than either "high church" liturgical bodies or the moderate Protestant denominations. Much of the confusion in assessing frequency of attendance comes from attempting to equate participation in the single weekly worship services expected in some denominations with the plethora of Sunday school classes, Bible study groups, prayer meetings, hymn sings, and special interest groups offered by others. Not enough work has been done in comparisons of this sort to substantiate the assumption that participation of those higher in class standing may involve a greater proportion of activities in leadership groups—vestries, sessions, trustees, deacons, councils, special committees—in comparison to lower-status members. At the same time, comparison of attendance at regular Sunday worship services shows that there is a direct relationship between status and attendance, or in some cases a curvilinear relationship, with those of highest status less frequent in attendance than the middle classes, but the poor much lower than either.[4]

In America, particularly outside highly urbanized areas, participation in church activities is part of the expected behavior of the middle class. It may also be a method of status striving by those aspiring to middle class or above. Membership in the "right" church can help to establish one's credentials as a good, solid citizen, providing associations for the family with the "right" people. A common complaint of many lower-class people is that the clothes worn to church often exclude them from comfortable membership, as the strivers attempt to be seen in the "right" thing by the "right" people. Such attitudes clearly tend to reinforce middle-class attendance at the expense of that of the lower-class members who neither desire nor can afford this kind of activity. Also related to this is the tendency in middle-class churches to choose and retain ministers on the basis of their education and social graces rather than doctrinal orthodoxy. We have already seen that this probably would be less acceptable to lower-class persons on the basis of their values; it also often results in a level of intellectuality in the services which they complain is "over their heads."

The pattern in Europe, where churches are less often considered voluntary associations, is even clearer. Mehl cites a number of studies that show that laborers are vastly underrepresented in attendance statistics of both Protestant and Catholic parishes. This is true in spite of efforts by the Catholic church to organize workers' groups such as the French Confederation of Christian Workers and Christian Worker Youth.[5] Wilson sees church membership in England to be more reflective of than productive of characteristics of social classes as compared to America. Since other evidences of social class and ascriptive status are still present in England, if in somewhat attenuated form, religious membership and participation do not have much importance as status symbols. As a consequence, increasing secularization of the society has led to a reduction in church participation at all levels. The phenomenon of participation in a specific denomination as evidence of social status, and of high participation in public religious activities as an indication of middle-class rank, is strongest in the United States.[6]

In the devotional aspects of religious practice, however, religious participation has been found to be higher in the lower classes. Studies of private devotional behavior, prayer, and Bible reading, of course, are dependent upon self-reporting by respondents rather than direct observation. But low reliability of such reports may be balanced by a consideration of the context of such practice. The lower-class person who engages in regular reading of the Bible or other devotional literature often reads little else; middle- or upper-class persons, if they read such material, are likely to do so as a fairly small portion of their total reading time.

This impression is reinforced by studies of the knowledge dimension of religiosity, where in spite of expectations based on educational and IQ levels, lower-class persons have been found to have more knowledge of the details of their faith than persons of higher class and rank.[7] Lower-class persons also have been found to score higher on a more general index of "intellectual involvement," which includes reading of religious magazines and books and looking to the church for information and advice.[8] The inverse relationship between social class and religious belief may be treated as a combination of greater stress on concreteness and specificity as well as orthodoxy, lack of confusing input from other more secular sources, and perhaps a greater saliency of religion for personal identity and adjustment for lower-class persons. It may also be treated as a type of substitute for ritual involvement, where they are more likely to run into problems of status or relationships that make it difficult for them to participate.

However, recent studies indicate that this phenomenon may be more one of denomination than of social class. We have already noted that conservative church bodies have a higher proportion of lower-class members than do liberal ones. It is also clear that conservative churches stress specific religious knowledge and provide training in it to a greater extent than most liberal churches. So it should not be too surprising that Stark has found that when he controlled the data from the California studies for type of denomination (liberal, moderate, conservative), lower-class members were lower in their knowledge of the religion than were their higher-status coreligionists.[9]

This leaves unsolved the question of voluntarism in religion and whether lower-class persons who opt for religious involvement seek out those churches that do provide concrete religious knowledge. However, as we shall see later, the assumption of voluntarism in religion is not on too solid ground. The effects of socialization are marked in any consideration of religious choice.

Religious experience seems to be more valued and more actively sought by members of the lower class. In modern society, high levels of education tend to militate against belief in the mystic or the nonempirical. Emphasis on religious experience also tends to decrease with the growth of a sense of mastery over the exigencies of life. Given the assumption that social status is closely related to power and economic stability, it is logical to expect that, in general, higher-status people need less reassurance from religious experience, since they receive more than other sources. Generally churches of the poor reinforce the expectations of religious experience far more than those of the well-to-do.

It is in the consequential dimension of religion, however, that the greatest amount of information may be applied concerning religion and social class. In our consideration of religious types, we found that from primitive religion on there is an expectation that the moral values of the society will be upheld and reinforced by its religious institution. Part of the moral structure of any society is concerned with the reinforcement of those characteristics and behaviors most needed by the society. In a society whose existence depends largely on the products of the hunt, religious myth usually glorifies the hunter and ritual reinforces the skills and attitudes appropriate to the hunt. The successful hunter wins not only the approval of the tribe but also the blessing of the gods. In the long struggle of the more nomadic Hebrews with the agricultural peoples of Canaan, the ancient myth was preserved that told of the killing of Abel by his brother Cain because Cain's sacrifice of agricultural products was less pleasing to God than Abel's sheep. Similar reinforcement of the kind of social behavior deemed most needed for continuing the society is expected—and provided—by religious institutions in modern society.

The rise of early modern religion and its relationship to industrialization has already been discussed. Whether one does or does not accept Weber's assumption of a direct causal relationship between the rise of Protestantism and the capitalist organization of industrial society, there are clear ties between the two. In Protestantism the treatment of economic activity as part of a total picture of religious vocation provides a moral basis for investment and profit making. Human institutions tend toward a certain amount of logical consistency. Therefore it is natural to expect that if God could be served by successful enterprise leading to riches, poverty might well be interpreted as slothfulness or disobedience to the divine call. As the successful hunter of the hunting society was seen as the favorite of the gods, so in capitalist society the successful entrepreneur was treated as the exemplary Christian. This, of course, was particularly true of those who lived simply in spite of all their wealth, plowing back profits into the expansion of their enterprises, with a sizable chunk set aside to the service of God through the church. Churches hastened to do honor to members who could plead their pet causes with power in the community and the nation, as well as provide financial support for programs they considered important to their ministries. Generations of American Sunday school children have grown up on stories of the exemplary life of Charles LeTourneau, who in building his mammoth and highly successful heavy-equipment firm gradually increased the share of his profits dedicated to the work of God from 10 to 90 percent and was blessed by further millions in profit. (An interesting contrast to the lives of the saints studied during that same period by Catholic youngsters!)

One of the most popular preachers on the lecture circuit in America was Russell Conway, whose talk "Acres of Diamonds" was delivered over six thousand times between 1877 and 1925. A sample of the inspirational word this Baptist minister had to give can be found in the following:

Money is power, and you should be reasonably ambitious to have it. You should because you can do more good with it than you can without it! Money prints your Bible, money builds your churches, money sends your missionaries, and money pays your preachers, and you would not have many of them either, if you did not pay them.

I say, then, you should have money. If you can honestly attain riches, it is your Christian and godly duty to do so.[10]

Yet the very process of sectarian development that created a Protestantism that so wholeheartedly endorsed the capitalistic enterprise also provided religious legitimation for counterarguments. As we have seen, sects tend to develop among those whom Niebuhr has termed the "disinherited." At the beginning of the Industrial Revolution it was the rising class of capitalists who had no real place in feudal society, but as the Protestant ethic has institutionalized and celebrated their activities and attitudes, it is mainly those who lost the economic race who have taken over the development of new sects.

Existing denominations have been subject to pressures from status-striving members which have made lower-class attendance somewhat uncomfortable, as we have seen. In reaction against church services that require more education and better dress than they could afford, as well as against policies designed to avoid alienating affluent supporters of the congregation, lower-class people may choose several responses. One, of course, is alienation from the organized church, such as is evidenced in the low participation rates we have noted and the behavior of European lower classes. Another is the creation of sects that are also based on the ascetic inner-worldly ethic that Weber took to be the basis of the Protestant faith. These groups criticize wealthier churches for their ostentation and celebrate their own simplicity and purity. They encourage hard work and law-abiding behavior, often condemning social activities such as card playing, dancing, and the use of alcohol. The net result of such moral strictures tends to be the development of middle-class values and behavior on the part of their lower-class adherents, even though the rhetoric may be strongly favorable to poor-but-honest people as opposed to the more affluent. Over time, a number of such sects have gradually moved toward becoming middle-class denominations as their members have become more affluent, and new generations are better educated as well.[11]

A type of sect with similar origins in the lower classes but somewhat different consequences stems from chiliastic or millenarian movements, which anticipate divine intervention in the present social scene, with a consequent overturning of the scales of justice and status and with the saints being made rulers over the world. Rather than providing motivation for supporting or tolerating the present system, this kind of orientation often fosters resistance against at least some portions of it. As a consequence, groups such as the Jehovah's Witnesses have run afoul of the law rather than pledge allegiance to the flag of the nation, since they feel they owe allegiance only to God. In recent publications of the group, Jehovah's Witnesses have joined liberal groups in reaction against government suppression of dissent, knowing that they as well as political radicals are likely to be affected if there is a diminution of toleration.[12] Free of the belief that the society has the right to exercise ultimate sanctions over them, such groups can be sources of potent social criticism.

Dissenting sects need not come from the lower classes alone. As we have seen earlier, they also may come from the "ethically deprived" of the more privileged classes. On the whole, however, their dissent is more likely to be kept within the bounds of an organized church or turn secular, while lower-class chiliasm usually requires its own religious organization.

In many cases, lower-class members may find expression for their disillusionment with the present state of affairs in religious groups that concentrate on otherworldly rewards and sanctions. In most cases these sects offer two kinds of relief from the lack of success and low prestige given the poor. First, they offer them the rewards of Heaven and the promise that in the final order the poor will be exalted and those in mourning comforted. At the same time, they offer in this world the close supportive fellowship of their membership. Rejected by the outside world, they find their worth affirmed in the religious fellowship and the assurance of acceptance by a loving God at the end of this vale of tears. This type of sectarian religion seldom leads to social mobility but rather makes tolerable the present state of its adherents. It is this type of religion that most nearly deserves Marx's definition as an "opiate of the people." In America, the black church traditionally has been of this type. It has provided comfort and hope to a people whose opportunities for social recognition have been minimal if not nonexistent. Its function in improving the life of its people has been psychological rather than social.

Not all black religion is otherworldly, but in America all its forms have come out of the experience of slavery. Unlike European ethnic groups whose religion is supported by a long history and mythology, blacks in America were deliberately deprived of their tribal religions, partly because they were considered pagan, partly because they could provide a focus for identity which could lead to rebellion. As a consequence, the religion of the American black is a fully American product, created by people of a tribally diverse background out of forms of Christianity taught by white masters and the experience of slavery and segregation in the society. The black church occupies the peculiar position of being an institution forced upon the population it serves and at the same time the only social institution that for many generations they could call their own.

Slavery and segregation have always been somewhat tender subjects in American society, with its tradition of belief in open institutions and equality for all. The Christian church has also had to deal with a conscience developed in a religious tradition which declares that in Christ there is neither Jew nor Greek, neither slave nor free, neither male nor female. Yet it has managed to deal with these issues in such a way as to permit slavery and the growth of segregated institutions. Early slave owners were a bit uneasy about any attempt to Christianize their slaves, since there was a sort of tacit assumption that no Christian should hold a fellow Christian in bondage. Yet many took seriously the evangelical call to convert all heathen peoples. The Anglican church, as the established church of the colonies, soothed their fears by pronouncing that a Christian could indeed continue to hold slaves who had been baptized, and from then on the black church began to come into being.[13]

The considerable variability that black churches were allowed to develop by a generation concerned with liberty began to diminish by the second decade of the nineteenth century, when in the North separate black congregations began to seem more appropriate than integrated ones. In the South the opposite was true, and during the first of many "backlash" periods it was made illegal for slaves to gather outside the presence of their masters or other "reliable white men," for fear of their plotting a rebellion. Here slaves attended the churches of their masters. When they were relatively few in number, they sat in balconies or special "Negro pews." If they represented a large proportion of the congregation, they met in buildings especially provided them, or in the same building as their masters but at different hours. Their worship was directed by the white minister or someone handpicked for the job.[14] Even so, in some areas these laws were ignored, and in the South as well as the North the black church was concerned with freedom, both here and now and in the world to come. The message could be found both in the preaching and in the words of the spirituals that were sung, that religion had a this-worldly function of joining with God in fighting life's evils.[15]

Slaves taken along to camp meetings and converted there would slip off to other meetings for reinforcement of their new religious perspectives. Sometimes when they "got religion" they found themselves unable to keep quiet about it and confronted their masters with a call for repentance and rebirth. They were usually punished for such behavior, sometimes to the point of martyrdom in the name of Christ.[16] In the pre-Civil War South the church of the slaves was a captive institution, yet within it there developed clandestinely a religion of the captives that was based on freedom and equality. The idea of a transcendent God not only made slavery more tolerable by offering meaning outside it, but also made rebellion more possible by providing it with meaning beyond the immediate act.

In the decades before the Civil War the foundations of organized black religion were laid in the North as specifically black denominations began to develop. The largest of these were the African Methodist Episcopal Church and the African Methodist Episcopal Zion Church. These are still important denominations. A large number of Baptist churches were also formed, but their looser, more congregational structure did not allow for the sort of denomination building practiced by the Methodists. Most blacks joined one of these two denominations. While the Presbyterians and Congregationalists made declarations of openness, their comparatively high level of intellectualism did not have great appeal for many of the illiterate slaves or former slaves. The formal liturgies of the Catholic, Lutheran, and Episcopal churches did not appeal to most either, and their foundations as state churches gave them an ethnic identity either meaningless to blacks or too closely related to that of their masters. The Quakers showed a great amount of solicitude for black people, but they made little attempt to evangelize them, and the structure of their church organization provided few guidelines for blacks to follow in building their own denominations. The Methodists, at least at times, were also highly solicitous of blacks, and they did offer the necessary structural models. Baptist congregational autonomy also proved an appealing form to emulate. Over time, black Methodist churches grew stronger and Baptist churches, more given to schism, more numerous.[17]

The black church began as a protest movement against the racism and discrimination of the white church. As a consequence it has consistently identified itself with the black community, taking on its own relationship of "civil religion" to this segment of the population. This left the white church in the position of a counter-institution, identified with white America as the black church was with black America.[18] This racial schism in American Christianity made a considerable contribution to the close identification of the white church with white, middle-class values as it removed one whole segment of potential blue-collar members from its purview.

The nature of the black church changed after the end of the Civil War. During the years of slavery the churches had fanned the hope of freedom, and Northern black churches had taken action for freedom by providing important links in the Underground Railway through which slaves escaped the South. After the issue was no longer slavery per se, but rather the more subtle and pervasive racism of white opinions and institutions, the churches became less focal points for protest and more places of refuge. Their emphasis became less reformist and more escapist.[19]

It was this period in the history of the black church that gave rise to the stereotype of black religion—the emotional, otherworldly, spiritual-singing black congregation led by a subservient "Uncle Tom" who taught his flock to turn the other cheek against oppression and concentrate on the sort of virtuous life that would deserve Heaven (and prevent trouble here on earth). Much criticism has been leveled at this form of black religion, but its function as an institution of survival was great. Surrounded by a society so hostile that the Chief Justice of the Supreme Court could say (in the Dred Scott decision) that a black man has no rights that a white man is bound to respect, black people were hard put to maintain human dignity and self-respect. A religion focused on another world where the first would be last and the last first, and the just would be rewarded, became an important factor in psychological survival. An accent on moral behavior served to counteract white charges of the "bestiality" of black nature and also to offer some security against white repression. The black church offered the basis upon which other black social institutions could grow—institutions made necessary by white exclusiveness and segregation. Denied access to the structures of white society, blacks began to develop alternate structures, and their churches were the base for all of them.[20] Black churches functioned as centers for fraternal organizations which provided fellowship and mutual aid and served as allies in business and professional enterprises undertaken in the black community. Often the churches were the only places for group recreation open to blacks. They served as communications centers where people could keep up on the news of the neighborhood and wider areas. The church was the place where people could meet and visit with friends; where young people could meet, impress one another with their virtue, and lay the ground for courtship. Sunday schools of black churches often taught basic reading skills to a membership largely ignored or excluded in the public-school system; literacy was cherished as a basic tool in understanding the Bible. The local church became an important forum for the development and expression of opinion in the black community, and it offered a place to practice leadership and show authority seldom allowed elsewhere. The black church served as a welfare agency, providing as much as it could for the support of the poor, the sick, the disabled. It provided a continuing basis for cooperative effort.[21] In many communities this is still evident, with the black churches providing both leadership and housing for community organization, antipoverty projects, and other service activities.[22]

To speak of the black church in this fashion, however, may give a false impression of the unity of black Christianity. In reality, nowhere is the sectarian divisiveness of American culture more evident than in black religion. While the Christianity into which American blacks were initiated was sectarian from the beginning, their appropriation of it has been in no way homogenized by their common roots in the experience of slavery or their common relegation to an implicit caste system in this country based on race. The reasons for the continuing divisions have been given by C. Eric Lincoln[23] as (1) a confusion of values coming out of the loss of tribal cultures, and the consequent desire to emulate white culture in this way as in others; (2) a rejection of the leveling or homogenization implicit in the caste system, with a desire to show that not all blacks are alike; (3) the dearth of leadership positions available to blacks in the society at large, so that religious roles have often been the only option as an arena for action; (4) an overabundance of black leadership potential, requiring a large number of organizations to lead; (5) problems of personal identity best met by affiliation with organizations that have distinctive characteristics and personal interaction; and (6) a kind of exotic identity which could be reinforced by membership in what he terms "exotic cults."

Differences among the various forms of black religion are primarily sociological rather than doctrinal, organizational, or ritualistic, with the possible exception of those groups Lincoln termed "exotic cults." Distinctions of social class within the caste system began in slavery with differences in work assignments and are still reinforced by the evaluation of economic roles by the white community. Within the black community, in spite of lack of confirmation by whites, social class differences until the rise of black consciousness in the 1960s were also often predicated on lightness or darkness of the skin, in the notion that an infusion of "white blood" led to superior status. Some black churches literally banned particularly dark-skinned blacks from their membership. Often class differences were based on what appears a more logical referent of the level of one's education. As in white denominations, styles of worship and organization often reflect exposure to higher education.

In many cases the black church has become the bulwark of black respectability and status striving. In this process it has not been unlike other churches of the lower classes which have contributed to the social mobility of their members. The difference lies in the castelike position of blacks in American society, a position still not erased by recent gains in civil rights. The church has provided the usual values and skills for mobility, but the society has refused to accept blacks at the level to which they aspire. Consequently, the process has at times turned in on itself and become arid, an exercise in futility. The education of most blacks has not provided access to the broad humanistic forms of theology prevalent in leading white seminaries; Negro colleges have been theologically conservative and academically practical, with a few notable exceptions. As a result, when the black church abandons its transcendental, otherworldly orientation it seems to have no alternative except the status-mobility emphasis. With that cut off, the church becomes an empty shell of posing people playing games of make-believe—the sort of sham described as a way of life by Frazier in *Black Bourgeosie.* [24]

One response to this situation is the development of various cults, which provide a sort of bridge between the old order and the new, the past and the present. Cults tend to take up religious practices discarded by mainstream churches and combine them with spectacular and novel elements to meet religious needs that are not being met in the present system. The cult retains values that are important to some people and puts them in forms that appear relevant to the current situation. By so doing they often assist in adjustment to social change. [25]

A good example of such a cult in the black community has been the Black Muslims. Reversing prevalent themes of racism in the society, they have enforced many traditional moral codes through an ideology that is a counter-religion to traditional Christianity. That their appeal is to the disaffected from the black church is quite evident when we see that Black Muslims are primarily American, are ex-Christian, and are also young and predominately male. This contrast with a female-dominated, aging black church cannot be ignored. [26] At first the Black Muslims were treated as just another offbeat Christian sect, and their ministers were invited to the Christian churches as guest speakers. Often they were allowed to use the Christian churches as meeting places. However, other churches came to realize that the Muslims con-sidered themselves opposed to Christianity, and a strain has grown in the relationship. Black Muslims have attacked the black churches for having done less than nothing for their people, and some of the impetus in the movement toward black power came from this group. [27] However, after the split between Elijah Mohammed and Malcolm X, the two chief leaders of the Muslims, and with the assassination of Malcolm X, the Muslims retreated into the background of the black power struggle in many instances, and black power became more secularized. This loss of religious justification of the black power movement weakened its influence with more conservative black people while allowing the growth of black-white cooperation in secular political movements based on a Marxist analysis of the situation.

By constract, the importance of the black churches in the civil rights movement of the early 1960s, under the leadership of such ministers as Martin Luther King, Ralph Abernathy, and Andrew Young, led to a reappraisal of the relationship between white churches and black Christians. Within main-line denominations that are mainly white, black constituencies have become organized and visible, often nurtured by denominational staff who feel keenly the charges of hypocrisy leveled against a church that shows racial separation and discrimination. Various kinds of "black caucuses" have come on the scene within some denominations and as ecumenical organizations. In the Catholic church a Black Caucus has come to speak out on matters of relevance to the black community and has been active in protesting the assignment of all-white staff to black parishes. There is also a lay group within the Catholic church known as United Black Catholics, which is concerned with similar issues. The Black Sisters' Conference has been more involved with education than with politics within the denomination, but the rising awareness such a group embodies is in itself a political phenomenon. There are black caucuses in most predominantly white Protestant denominations, and the organization of the National Committee of Black Churchmen (NCBC) provided a focus that could unite them with leaders of all-black denominations as well. It was a subsidiary of the NCBC, the Black Economic Development Council, which made one of the more daring political moves in issuing a "Black Manifesto" demanding that white churches pay reparations for past economic exploitation of blacks. It is a measure of the moral power of such intrachurch groups that those demands were not summarily dismissed as unreasonable but rather were the occasion for considerable internal conflict in churches that struggled with the justice of such an idea.

One of the things that black church leaders have done in recent years is to address themselves to the creation of a theological interpretation of Christianity appropriate to their time and place. Recalling Christianity's theme of being good news to the poor and the oppressed, they find that the gospel has more relevance in the black ghetto than the white suburb. One of the spokesmen for this point of view, James Cone, has said that the church must attempt to recover the man Jesus by totally identifying itself with the poor and the suffering, which is to identify itself with black power. Otherwise, he says, "the Church will become exactly what Christ is not."[28] To him the black church is not much better, for it is simply a response to the white church at the level of survival, and that response has been made at the cost of freedom and human dignity. The white and black churches are similar, he says, because

> both have marked out their places as havens of retreat, the one to cover the guilt of the oppressors, the other to daub the wounds of the oppressed. Neither is notably identified with the tearing healing power of Christ. Neither is a fit instrument of revolution.[29]

One main thrust of black theology is found in its understanding of the gospel as the word that humanity is justified as it is, that people are free to affirm their own humanity and that of others. The emphasis on rewards in heaven are inappropriate. Cone's words once again:

> There is no place here for a reward. In fact, man is now made free for obedience without worrying about a pat on the back from God. He knows he is right with God because God has put him in the right. This new gift of freedom means that he can be all for his neighbor. To allow one's concern to be directed toward heaven is to deny freedom.[30]

This type of black theology involves a great deal of what Weber called "inner-worldly asceticism," just as Reformation theology did. It also is concerned with what Weber termed "ethical prophecy." The theme of being an instrument in the hand of a God who is active in history is strong in the preaching and writing of leaders of the movement. Just as white Americans have considered themselves God's chosen people, identified with ancient Israel, so the new black theology builds on early black identification with Hebrews as slaves in Egypt who were led by God to freedom. American blacks are seen as chosen to be an instrument of revolution and liberation in the world.[31]

One may also find themes more closely aligned with what Weber has called "exemplary prophecy," particularly in the work of such scholars as Deotis Roberts. Roberts equates the black experience with that of the "suffering servant" of the prophecies of Isaiah, thus giving to the black church a messianic role.[32]

In recent years there has been a coming together of black theology with a number of theologies of "liberation" and of "hope" coming out of South America and Europe. While there are disagreements among the various strains of theology in those categories, as well as within each of them, all appear to concern themselves in one way or another with teachings about the Kingdom of God and the place in it of the poor and the oppressed. As Jürgen Moltmann has put it, "The hidden presence of the coming Christ in the poor therefore belongs to ecclesiology first of all, and only after that to ethics."[33] That is, the poor by right constitute the church, rather than simply serving as its clients. Or, as William Jones has put it in applying that concept to the racial situation, we must be able to answer in the negative the question "Is God a white racist?"[34]

Much of the rhetoric of black theology is reminiscent of the theology of the early days of the Reformation, with its accent on justification and freedom from given social structures. This type of religious philosophy has proved supportive of massive social change in the past, offering as it does divine sanction for open structures and innovative behavior. The theology of the Reformation allowed the opening of the structures of society to new economic groups. The new black theology is intended to provide justification for the opening of structures to new racial groups. It can provide reinforcement for a positive sense of black identity. In this way it can form a base for a self-conscious black culture.[35]

As theology has contributed to a separate black culture, it has also articulated other aspects of the pluralism of American society. Sectarian groups have, as we have noted, provided cultural expression for non-dominant social classes, but now particular organizations within major denominations and specific theological statements have come to characterize various racial and cultural groups. Black caucuses have been joined by those of Native Americans, Hispanics, and Asians. New theologies have emerged in particular out of the Native American tradition, seeking to combine aspects of traditional tribal religion with Christianity in the context of an experience of economic and social oppression.[36]

All this has been accompanied by a revitalization of European ethnic traditions, once thought to be disappearing. In the 1950s Will Herberg traced the pattern of their disappearance into a "triple melting pot," through a three-generational process. He saw new immigrants settling in close proximity to others with similar language and cultural characteristics, making the ethnic church a center of interaction and identity in a relatively alien environment. Generally intentional immigrants, they encouraged their children to become enculturated. The young people, seeking to be accepted in the wider society and feeling restricted by ethnic ties, rejected their parents' church along with other aspects of ethnicity and became secular Americans. By the third generation, however, they found that American identity required some religious identification and so came back, not to the ethnic church, but to the major faith of which it was a part—Protestant, Catholic, or Jewish.[37] That pattern, however, proved much more relevant to the 1950s than the 1960s, when religious affiliation became less popular, or the 1970s, when people seem much more concerned about celebrating their ethnic roots.

The faith of the "melting pot," triple or not, tended to be that of American civil religion. In a number of ways, particularly through the ideological trauma of the Viet Nam war and its aftermath, Americans appear to have lost faith in that expression of cultural identity. Yet the chaos of the period has called for some expression of a center of meaning, and for many that has come to be their ethnic heritage.

There were particular circumstances that make this evident among those whose heritage was Jewish. With the exception of fairly isolated groups of Sephardic Jews of high social standing, Orthodox Judaism in America has been based on forms developed in the towns of Eastern Europe from which a majority of its adherents migrated. Jews as a group have been highly mobile socially, and the old peasant forms did not change fast enough to accommodate the new life-styles of many. At the same time, the radically assimilationist developments of Reform Judaism were often too great a jump for descendants of this group, although they had long provided a form of religion compatible with those whose background was that of German or other more urban and intellectual milieus. The result was the development of Conservative Judaism, which came to fit the needs of a fair proportion of middle-class American Jews.[38] "Church-hopping," as practiced by mobile Christians, then, was somewhat paralleled by Jews as they moved from Orthodox to Conservative congregations and sometimes on to Reform. However, two factors interrupted this process, which was generally one of secularization. The first was the experience of the Holocaust of the World War II period, with the wholesale massacre of European Jews and a consequent rise in ethnic identity through suffering. Second, the establishment of the state of Israel, and in particular the several wars and threats of war around that entity, have raised ethnic identity and stimulated a number of movements toward more orthodox, ethnic expressions of the Jewish faith among those whose social class is relatively high. The revival of Hasidism among young college students and the Havurah movement among young business and professional people are prime examples.

Most ethnic religion in America is the product of an established or state religion in the country of origin of the group—different types of Lutheranism from Germany or Scandinavia, Eastern Orthodoxy of various kinds, and Roman Catholicism. Lutherans have in recent years dissolved many of the distinctive ethnic denominations into larger, pan-Lutheran bodies. Eastern Orthodoxy has profited from the increased interest in ethnicity but has also come to find less ethnic emphasis in its increased acceptability in American society. Usually when ethnic religion is discussed, it seems to be in terms of the Catholicism of the Irish, Germans, Poles, Italians, and perhaps French Canadian and Spanish-speaking groups.[39]

Frequently the peculiar ethnic style of the Irish is taken as the "real" American Catholicism, since the Irish tend to dominate leadership positions in the American church. They arrived earlier than many groups and had the advantages of speaking the language and of a politically oriented culture. Germans, who immigrated at least as early in most cases, were less likely to cluster in the cities where they could develop a political base in the church. Also, they suffered severely from anti-German sentiment during World War I and to some extent World War II, so they tended to keep a low profile in political activity in church and society. The Irish tended to dominate parochial education, giving it a conservative tone and one less theologically progressive than would have been the case had German influence been greater.

Polish Catholicism has been less highly placed in American society, partly because of the relative lateness of major Polish immigration and the language barrier they faced. Economically, Poles tend to be a step or two behind in the mobility pattern of European immigrants. In addition, Polish Catholics have been less political in their participation in the church, though their loyalty to it has remained high. They have been more likely to form fraternal organizations than to become involved in the institutional hierarchy.

By contrast, Italians have had less difficulty adjusting to an Irish-dominated church but have also shown less loyalty to it. The institutional loyalty of Spanish-speaking groups is generally so low that students of American Catholicism such as Andrew Greeley frequently ignore them altogether. These include those whose roots are in the American West and the contact of early conquistadors with the native population, Mexican immigrants, and Puerto Ricans. Generally, their religion is more strongly related to a folk culture than to the organizational hierarchy. Yet new trends in the religiosity of these groups can be seen, particularly in the rise of such leaders as Cesar Chavez, who has combined a pervasive religiosity with social protest in a manner reminiscent of Martin Luther King and who has enlisted the aid of a wide spectrum of change-oriented Catholics and Protestants.

Roman Catholic ethnicity has also been affected by organizational and liturgical changes that have come into being since the second Vatican Council. Where before the ethnic parish was the only alternative to a strict membership by geographic location, there is now an increasing amount of movement across parish lines in search of a more satisfying liturgy or community. In the long run this may lead to a Catholicism divided more clearly along social class lines than those of ethnicity, although such class lines have never been absent from Catholicism. However, trends in the 1970s appear to run in the direction of reviving, maintaining, or even creating a sense of ethnic identity cemented by religion, as a counterbalance to what many people perceive as an increasingly meaningless mass society.

This interest and acceptance has extended beyond the historic Judeo-Christian framework of American religion to the many religious practices of the Near and Far East. As we shall see later, the ethnicity of these religions has become somewhat blurred by the rise of new groups that incorporate some of the ritual and symbol systems of such "exotic" religions but are basically American products appealing to the American public. Even in these cases, however, the basic thrust of ethnic religion as a source of identity and belonging appears to hold.

Notes and References

1. The most fully developed discussion of these dimensions of religiosity may be found in Rodney Stark and Charles Y. Glock, *American Piety* (Berkeley: University of California Press, 1968), pp. 28–39.
2. Ibid., p. 62.
3. N. J. Demerath III, *Social Class in American Protestantism* (Chicago: Rand McNally, 1965), p. 17.
4. Examples of this may be found in such community studies as Robert Lynd and Helen Lynd, *Middletown* (New York: Harcourt, 1929); A. B. Hollingshead, *Elmtown's Youth* (New Haven: Yale University Press, 1949); and A. B. Hollingshead, "Selected Characteristics of Classes in a Middle Western Community," in Reinhard Bendix and S. M. Lipset, eds., *Class, Status, and Power* (New York: Free Press, 1953).
5. Roger Mehl, *The Sociology of Protestantism,* trans. by James H. Farley (Philadelphia: Westminster, 1970), pp. 122–127.
6. Bryan Wilson, *Religion in Secular Society* (Baltimore: Penguin, 1969), pp. 138–143.
7. Yoshio Fukuyama, "The Major Dimensions of Church Membership," *Review of Religious Research* 2 (1961): 159.
8. Charles Y. Glock, Benjamin Ringer, and Earl Babbie, *To Comfort and to Challenge* (Berkeley: University of California Press, 1967), pp. 24–95.
9. Rodney Stark, "The Economics of Piety: Religion and Social Class," in Gerald W. Thielbar and Saul D. Feldman, *Issues in Social Inequality* (Boston: Little, Brown, 1971), Table 9.
10. Russell Conway, *Acres of Diamonds,* ed. by William R. Webb (Kansas City, Mo.: Hallmark Cards, 1968), pp. 25–26.

11. Benton Johnson, "Do Holiness Sects Socialize in Dominant Values?" *Social Forces* 29 (1961): 309–316.
12. For example, see "The Demand for Law and Order: Where Can It Lead?" *Awake!*, August 8, 1970, pp. 5–8.
13. Lawrence Jones, "Black Churches in Historical Perspective," *Christianity and Crisis* 30 (November 2 & 16, 1970): 227.
14. Carter Godwin Woodson, *The History of the Negro Church* (Washington, D.C.: Associated Publishers, 1921), pp. 130–133.
15. James H. Cone, *Black Theology and Black Power* (New York: Seabury, 1969), pp. 93–94.
16. Woodson, op. cit., pp. 146–147.
17. Ibid., pp. 91–99.
18. Rueben A. Sheares II, "Beyond White Theology," *Christianity and Crisis* 30 (November 2 & 16, 1970): 229–230.
19. Cone, op. cit., pp. 103–105.
20. Sheares, op. cit., pp. 231–232.
21. Woodson, op. cit., pp. 266–285.
22. Another excellent source on the black church is Joseph Washington, *Black Religion* (Boston: Beacon, 1964).
23. In a public address titled "The Social Cosmos of Black Ecumenism," presented at a conference on Black Ecumenism and the Liberation Struggle, sponsored by the Yale Black Seminarians at Yale Divinity School, February 17, 1978.
24. E. Franklin Frazier, *Black Bourgoisie* (New York: Free Press, 1957).
25. Ruby Funchess Johnston, *The Religion of Negro Protestants* (New York: Philosophy Library, 1956), p. 175.
26. C. Eric Lincoln, *The Black Muslims in America* (Boston: Beacon, 1961), pp. 22–26.
27. Robert S. Lecky and H. Elliott Wright, *Can These Bones Live?* (New York: Sheed & Ward, 1969), pp. 145–151.
28. Cone, op. cit., p. 3.
29. Cone, op. cit., p. 115.
30. Cone, op. cit., p. 125.
31. Cone, op. cit., pp. 130–131.
32. J. Deotis Roberts, *A Black Political Theology* (Philadelphia: Westminster, 1974).
33. Jürgen Moltmann, *The Church in the Power of the Spirit,* trans. by Margaret Kohl (New York: Harper & Row, 1977), p. 127.
34. William Jones, *Is God a White Racist?* (Garden City, N.Y.: Doubleday, 1973).
35. Cone, op. cit., p. 113.
36. See, for example, Vine DeLoria, *God Is Red* (New York: Grosset & Dunlap, 1973) and Benjamin A. Reist, *Theology in Red, White, and Black* (Philadelphia: Westminster, 1975).
37. Will Herberg, *Protestant-Catholic-Jew* (Garden City, N.Y.: Doubleday, 1955), Chapters 2 and 3.
38. Marshall Sklare, *Conservative Judaism: An American Religious Movement* (New York: Free Press, 1955), pp. 25–32.
39. The material on ethnic Catholicism in the ensuing paragraphs is largely taken from Andrew Greeley, William McCready, and Kathleen McCourt, *Catholic Schools in a Declining Church* (Kansas City, Mo.: Sheed & Ward, 1976), Chapter 3.

9

Sex, Gender, and the Family

The rise of interest in ethnicity, as we have seen, is often assumed to be part of a search for identity in mass society. The trend in American society, as in most cultures heavily influenced by modern industrialization, has been to expect personal development and identity formation to originate in the family and for that institution to be more and more narrowly defined. That is, the need for both social and geographic mobility to allow persons to fit into the structure of a technological society has resulted in tendencies to find one's base not in the clan or in the extended family of distantly related people, nor yet in an intergenerational family, but in a nuclear family composed of parents and minor children. It has been assumed that by the time one reaches adulthood the personality will be sufficiently grounded that later loyalties, associations, and relationships will be matters of personal choice, guided by circumstances surrounding one's choice of career, mate, and voluntary associations. To revert to such ascribed characteristics as ethnicity would seem to indicate that this grounding had not occurred, and for societal trends to be in that direction would indicate that the nuclear family as an institution has failed in this function.

Common assumptions and practices locate the family and religion in close proximity to one another in the society, each supporting the other in a number of ways, including the establishment of personal identity and moral development of the individual. If the family is having trouble fulfilling such functions, the possibility must be considered that religion is weak in support of that institution. Some exploration of their relation to one another in modern society is clearly indicated.

As human society has developed and become more differentiated, its institutional areas have separated into the private and the public spheres. Today the family is seen much less as the public organization it once was, and more as a private arrangement. The process of differentiation which Bellah traced in his model of religious evolution, and which others have noted as part of the process of secularization, has led to a similar "privatization" of religion. Religious belief and practice are considered personal affairs in modern society. It comes as no surprise, then, that the two institutions of religion and the family have maintained strong ties, each often claiming to be based upon the other.

Much of this can be seen in the practices of communal religion which are, as they have been through time, tied to important transitional stages in the life cycle—and by definition the life cycle of families as well. Nearly all religious groups have ceremonies marking entrance into the group through birth, baptism or other means as well as those marking puberty, marriage, and death. The particular emphasis given each of these ceremonies varies from group to group, as does their importance in relationship to secular rituals which also mark the high points in one's life history.

A good example of the variation among Christian groups may be found in the uses of the rite of baptism. In churchlike denominations baptism is provided for children of members as a symbol of their acceptance into the religious community. The vows taken by parents in the name of the children are later confirmed by them when they reach an age the church defines as sufficient to be held accountable for their own actions. In most churches this age coincides roughly with the time of puberty, so that the second ceremony usually granting full church membership can be seen as a continuation of ancient puberty rites. As in primitive tribes, this ritual marks for individuals the time when they are expected to assume adult roles in the group.

In churches with a more sectlike background, infant baptism may not be practiced, and the baptismal rite itself may become the puberty ritual. In actual fact, in either type of church such rites performed in the early teen years in modern society seldom do grant full privileges. The extension of dependency through a prolonged period of adolescence has given little expectation in the society at large that adult roles will be taken at this age, and the churches tend to reflect the social milieu in this matter. Most families do not take puberty rituals such as this seriously in terms of granting their children adult privileges at the time they are performed.

The Jewish parallels to Christian ceremonies of infant baptism and confirmation are circumcision and the bar mitzvah, and they tend to be treated in somewhat the same way as the Christian rituals by the families involved. Another effect of the social surroundings on such religious rites can be seen in the Jewish community. While the original rituals were concerned with males only, in more liberal Jewish communities there is a growing interest in similar rites for girls.[1]

Generally in modern society the ceremony of marriage may be a truer mark of entry into adult status than those based on puberty rites of an earlier day. Since Western society tends to demand of adults that they establish their own home separate from that of their fathers and mothers, and marriage is seen as the normative way of doing that, marriage is of considerable significance in the society at large. It also tends to be the most elaborate and newsworthy of special rituals provided by religious groups and may be one of the closest points of contact that peripheral members have with their religious group.

The other time they are most likely to desire or attend religious ceremonies is for funeral rites. In America, as in many parts of the world, funerals have become mainly the business of specialists whose function is not specifically religious. Clergy serve as something like adjuncts to the morticians. Some religious groups have resisted this tendency, and during the past generation or so there has been a small trend in denominations formerly accustomed to services in the "funeral parlor" to stress once again the use of the church and a regular service of worship at such a time. Funerary specialists have countered by building "chapels" that look like churches, but which are devoted exclusively to the holding of funeral services. In some cases they even have been expanded in use so that other quasi-religious ceremonies may be held there. Many advertise their facilities for weddings.

On the whole, civil marriages performed outside the church and without a clerical blessing have steadily increased in frequency. Yet, while funerals are usually conducted by clergy, a higher proportion of people are probably married in the church than have their funeral there.

When ceremonies of this type are held in the church, they are usually focal points for gatherings of the extended family, who may seldom get together at other times. When they are civil ceremonies, often there are fewer family members involved. In general, religious organizations do support the family by providing rituals that reinforce family roles and obligations as well as providing a framework of meaning for them. The ancient model of the family as a religious body and the head of the family as its priest remains an ideal for some, but on the whole a division of labor between the two institutions has developed. Their close interconnection, however, is frequently noted, often in language such as this excerpt from a working paper of the United Church of Christ:

> The family keeps its own distinctive character as a family as it nurtures its members in the Christian faith. The essential character of the parent-child

relationship, for example, becomes a means by which the love of God becomes available to the child. Parents are the chief interpreters of experiences to young children and, as such, they can be "teachers" of a Christian view of life.[2]

Jewish emphasis on the home and family is no less clear, as expressed for example in this statement by a member of the Central Conference of American Rabbis:

> Long ago, the Jewish people intuited the fundamental place of the family constellation in society as the necessary social vehicle for stability and growth. For us, the home has been the core and bulwark of the group and nation. We have regarded the family as a living, organic structure in which the major activities of life take place. Religion for us has been home-centered. Our ceremonies, symbols, and holidays all revolve in and about the home.[3]

For Catholics marriage is a sacrament, and the home and family founded through this holy act are a part of the divine order for humankind. The hopeful adage, first taken up by a Catholic group, that "the family that prays together stays together" is balanced by the expectation that the church is supported and sustained by these stable family units.

Yet there are indications that this close connection between family unity and religious activity is not always the proven fact, particularly in the case of Protestantism. There is no doubt that ideologically the various religious groups offer great support to the nuclear family. Support for the extended family is less clear. Among Catholics in Detroit, Lenski[4] found a positive relation between religious involvement and kin-group involvement. But this was true only for Catholics. Visiting patterns of Protestants showed a much greater tendency to spend time with neighbors than relatives in comparison with Catholics and Jews. This was further pointed up by Lenski's observation that he found Protestants at least twice as likely to have no relatives beyond the nuclear family in the city, in comparison with the other groups. This obviously has a good deal to do with their probability of spending time visiting relatives, but it also speaks to their willingness to move to a city as a nuclear group without further social support from relatives. Social class differences between major faiths could be taken as the explanatory variable, but Lenski found that the differences held when social class was held constant. Greatest differences between religious groups were found among middle-class people, with 20 percent of the white Protestants claiming no kin in Detroit except the nuclear family, as compared with 9 percent of the Catholics and none of the Jews.

Lenski explained these findings by noting the different emphases of churchlike and sectlike religious organizations. The churchlike, he said, will normally see the kin group as an ally and support it for that reason. Sectlike groups, however, with their emphasis on conversion and a break with past relationships, may see the kin group more as a competitor.

While this emphasis holds true for some of the religious groups included in Lenski's survey, it would not seem to be applicable to Protestant denominations that are essentially churchlike in their membership practices, unless one finds that the power of traditional ideological or theological positions holds in spite of the structure. Perhaps a more logical assumption might be that the congregational structures as they have developed have provided a substitute for the larger kin groups which have been difficult to maintain in a highly mobile society. Miyakawa has shown that Protestant congregations on the American frontier developed as surrogates for the families the pioneers left behind, offering emotional support, identity, and discipline for their members.[5] Glock, Ringer, and Babbie, in their study of Episcopalians, show that church involvement is higher among those who deviate from expected family situations than among those who do not. Widows, the childless, and unmarried adults seem to find in church activity some of the satisfactions not present in their home life.[6] Lenski also found that, among white Protestants, those who were more active in the church were more attached to friendship groups and voluntary associations than kin groups.[7]

Trends in Judaism indicate that the growth of Conservative Judaism has included replacing some of the emphasis on family ritual with a congregational base similar to that of Protestantism. Whether ideological differences between Protestantism and Judaism will prevent the same consequences has not yet been shown.[8]

Part of the problem, certainly, is time. For most people, there is a limited amount of time that may be spent in the private sphere of their lives. This is divided between time spent with the family, in private voluntary associations including religious groups, and often in increasing proportion on the maintenance of various forms of consumer goods purchased for private use and enjoyment.[9] Often it seems that the time taken by church groups to reinforce ideals of family life and unity may be a large proportion of the time available for the practice of that family life and unity.

An indication of the interaction of these two factors of ideology and the allotment of time may be found in Glock, Ringer, and Babbie's tracing of church involvement patterns through the family life cycle.

They found that in their Episcopal sample involvement in church activities was quite high before marriage and the birth of children, then diminished until the children reached school age. After that, the involvement of women in church activities continued to rise, while that of men leveled off.[10] Changes of this kind may be interpreted as responses to various kinds of competition for time, particularly between the church and the home. Yet the increased activity as children reached school age probably also points to the fact that the parents looked to the church for help in the socialization of their children, and high activity rates before marriage may reveal some dependency on the church for social activities and contacts that could lead to an approved marriage choice.

Certainly one of the ways in which religion has traditionally related to the family has been the provision for moral and ethical guidelines for family life. We hear frequent debate on the right of religious groups to speak with authority in the realm of public morality—on questions of poverty or civil rights, racial discrimination or war—but seldom do people question the appropriateness of church pronouncements on private morality. They may question the content of such statements, but it is taken for granted that religious views should be expressed concerning the regulation of sexual activity and the quality of family life.

In the past, the word "regulation" in the preceding sentence was nearly always interpreted "restriction," and most people assumed that Christianity at least was against participation in any more sexual activity than necessary for the propagation of the species within an ordered family structure. While this has never been a universal attitude, it has been reinforced in the public mind by observation of the higher status in the Roman Catholic church given celibate priests and members of religious orders, by religious campaigns against prostitution and extramarital sex, pornography, and the like. In some traditions there has been explicit teaching linking sex with original sin or "the Fall," and in many others that interpretation has been implicit. Religious training of the young has nearly always enjoined sexual continence until marriage, and the effectiveness of such training continues to be evident. Cardwell, for example, found significant negative correlation between premarital sexual permissiveness and religious commitment in each of the five dimensions of religiosity set out by Glock and Stark.[11]

Religious regulation of sex within marriage has most often been found in the context of varying attitudes on the regulation of family size through birth control or abortion. While Catholic doctrine has the reputation for being most rigid on this matter, some other religious groups voice similar opinions, and Catholic teachings have not remained static through time. A particularly interesting study of Catholic attitudes toward birth control was made several years ago, tracing the subject through fifty-five years of articles in the Jesuit weekly *America*. An excerpt quoted from an early article offers a point of departure for the discussion:

> To be born, even with a strong probability of future infirmity, is better than not to be born, and the hope of giving a human soul the chance to attain the endless beatitude of the Beatific Vision, might well outweigh even strong reluctance to bring a child into the world predisposed to disease.[12]

The author traces changes from this position through a gradual softening toward family limitation (discussed as "responsible parenthood") that found, in the 1930s, considerable knowledge of and acceptance of the rhythm method of confining intercourse to "safe periods" when the woman was probably not fertile. He followed the trend through to the 1960s when, without specific approval but also with no explicit prohibition, Catholic women were availing themselves of oral contraceptives as another "natural" method of controlling pregnancies. However, Catholic training was still shown to have an effect on the use of such contraceptives. In a 1965 study, Catholic women were found to use them only after they had given birth to as many children as they felt they should have. Women of other religious faiths were much more likely to use oral contraception for the spacing of children as well as for the termination of fertility.[13]

At that time Reiterman saw the gradual softening of the Catholic position on birth control as a result not of the interaction of the Catholic church with outside groups opposed to high fertility levels so much as an internal struggle between a rather inflexible hierarchy and lay Catholics supported by sympathetic priests. He stated that the rigidity of the Catholic position had spurred the defection of a sizeable number of members who felt they could not accept it.[14] Osborne also agreed that differences between lay and hierarchical attitudes toward birth control were important factors in a growing rift within the church.[15] The papal encyclical *Humanœ Vitae* made that division more rigid, with the result that Greeley, at least, claims this issue to be the single most important cause of Catholic defections in the 1970s. While he has been much criticized for possibly overemphasizing the point, it is difficult to ignore the statistical evidence he has amassed to prove it. In his view, the encyclical was not only a failure but a disaster, both organizational and religious. It did not end the trend to ignore the church's teaching on this matter nor improve the authority of the church's teachings. Rather, in

Greeley's eyes, at least, the encyclical resulted in more people leaving the church, and in a lowering of religious devotion and belief.[16]

The responses of other denominational groups to this issue have been different in many cases, but often equally controversial among their members. Most of the so-called liberal denominations and their primary organization, the National Council of Churches, have made pronouncements supporting in one way or another the concepts of family planning and population control as an exercise of Christian social responsibility. Just as statistical reports have shown a consistent tendency for better educated, middle-class or above Catholics to have smaller families regardless of the official position on birth control, so the statistical reports of family size among members of denominations favoring family planning show that their lower-class members tend not to practice birth control to the extent that middle-class members do. The regulation of births within the family depends on interaction of religious ideals with social class and regional expectations.

In recent years birth control has been replaced by abortion as an issue in many churches. The legalization of abortion has forced consideration of its moral status, with such ethical concerns raised as the relation of the practice to the taking of human life, issues concerning the rights of women to be free of bearing the consequences of rape, questions about the rights of male judges and doctors to decide whether a woman's body must be devoted to a pregnancy, and the like. The society currently is being treated to the sight of pickets, many of them women, parading in front of an agency where people, many of them women, are counseling women having abortions, both sides claiming Christian values as their motivation. Clearly this is not a time when all Christian values are evident to the casual observer.

In recent years, as the society has grown more permissive about sexual practices once considered deviant, liberal Protestant churches have tended to reflect that permissiveness. Pronouncements tend to try to balance a strong support of marital fidelity and extramarital chastity with a call for understanding those who do not fit that mold. Some of the ethical appeal for such a trend has come through the language of civil rights, defining homosexuals, for example, as a group in the society who are politically, economically, and socially oppressed. Religious claims of liberation are applied to the support of persons' rights to choose their own life-style in contradistinction from standard patterns of family life—to choose to live alone but not in chastity, to form lasting liaisons with people of the same sex, to serve as single parents in a home not defined as "broken," or to live in communal arrangements which may or may not honor permanent heterosexual coupling. There are movements within liberal church bodies seeking to provide the kind of support and moral guidance traditionally offered the family for persons who have chosen these other styles of life.

The motives behind such movements in the churches are mixed. Some supporters find nothing to condemn in such life-styles and seek religious grounding for that attitude. Others are less certain of the morality of some of the practices, but claim that the church has a duty to minister to people where they are and is being false to its purpose when it excludes people on the basis of their moral weaknesses. Others take a more pragmatic attitude, noting such things as the relationship of the *Humanae Vitae* encyclical to Catholic defections, and raise the question of whether the churches can afford to alienate a growing segment of the society by casting judgment on their sexual practices.

For some church members the opposite is true. They have depended upon the church for firm moral guidelines, particularly in areas of sex and family life, and they find these disappearing. Some of the defection from liberal Protestantism and the growth of conservative churches has been laid to that cause. Conservative religious groups have provided the focus for campaigns against Gay rights in many areas and have lobbied hard for local laws and ordinances restricting the hiring and/or housing of people whose life-styles they consider immoral and a threat to the order of their communities. The consequences of church involvement in sexual issues, then, have been mixed, with membership decline a possible threat if churches take either a negative or a positive stance toward changing practices, and yet with a demand that they take some stance on such issues.

The conflict over sexual issues has become internal to the professional leadership of the churches as well, as controversy has arisen over the issue of the ordination of avowed homosexuals to the professional ministry. Some critics are horrified, seeing a reversal of the role of the church from maintaining a barrier against non-normative life-styles to actively promoting them. Supporters either claim that responsible homosexual alliances are as moral as traditional family groups, or that if they are moral lapses they are no more serious than the greed, envy, covetousness, etc., which plague all imperfect humanity, including the clergy.

An issue involved in this controversy, though less openly acknowledged, concerns the sexual identification of the clergy role and consequent identity problems of males in that role. In modern Western society, though technological advances no longer require occupational differentiation on the basis of such sexual characteristics as strength, the tendency toward specialization has tended to harden some of the contrast in definition between masculinity and femininity. It may be that the lowering of *need* for such contrast has increased the level of intensity by which people cling to them in their desire for a firm personal identity. At least it seems clear that for many Americans it is important to fit the model of one's sex role. In simple outline, men are expected to be forceful, competitive, rational, and strong. Women are, by contrast, expected to be nurturant, supportive, emotional, and to have inner psychological strength rather than the physical kind. Yet clergy—traditionally male—are expected to play a nurturant, supportive role as pastors, to preside at ritual occasions that touch the emotions, and to exhibit inner, spiritual strength. While they are also expected in most instances to be rational and "good organizers," it is often seen as a failing if these traits dominate too much the other more "religious" aspects of their personalities. Thus the clergy role has been ambivalent in terms of its maleness, and it has been hypothesized that one defense against identity-confusion because of that ambivalence has been to maintain an exclusively male membership in the profession.

This exclusiveness has never been total but has tended to be correlated (with allowances of cultural differences in different regions or ethnic groups) with the distance between the priestly and lay roles in the particular tradition. Thus women have been more acceptable in sectarian or more "low church" traditions as clergy than in such highly liturgical churches as the Lutheran, Episcopal, Eastern Orthodox, and Roman Catholic. For barriers to women clergy in most of these traditions to have been broken down has been hard enough for some clergy —and some laity—to bear, but for openly homosexual persons to seek ordination threatens the masculinity of the role even more, in the view of many. There are fears that the entire church will be discredited as effeminate, which might become another factor in the defection from liberal denominations toward a more athletic evangelical style.

In the meantime, the number of women ordained to clergy positions in many denominations is increasing rapidly. Major theological centers serving liberal denominations now have a student body nearly half female. Many of the women in the field are the product of a 1960s adolescence and mirror the greater role flexibility celebrated during that period. They do not define ministry in terms of masculine or feminine characteristics until forced to do so by recalcitrant males in their chosen denomination. Others are older women, some who have married and raised families and are entering second careers. They often feel particularly qualified for the pastoral role because of their long training in the skills of nurturance, though others seek escape from a mother-image in the only institution in which they have found a public role during their childbearing years. Some have entered seminary through the trauma of divorce and are seeking to become independent professionals. The variety of backgrounds makes it clear that women seeking to enter the ministry, like their male colleagues, do not fit a single mold or offer a specific kind of alternative. Churches in which women clergy are new phenomena may force a certain conformity to their image of the woman priest, if only by requiring opposition to it; but over time it will become apparent that this role, like most others in the society, can be shaped to some extent by its occupant. The amount of that flexibility will be tested in the coming years as more and more women enter pulpits of Protestant churches and the Jewish rabbinate and continue to knock on the door of the Catholic priesthood.

The primary problem facing clergy in the late 1970s is not so much how to fit their gender into the role, but to find a stage on which that role may be played out. Recent studies have pointed up that if current trends in church membership and clergy training continue, the laity may within a generation or two be outnumbered by clergy in the liberal denominations. Those trends will inevitably shift, but at present one of the social realities is that just those churches that are opening clergy positions to women—and to homosexuals—are the ones in which there is least need for more clergy.

Another type of adjustment forced upon the churches by the ordination of women comes from a growing number of "clergy couples"— husbands and wives, both ordained, seeking a team ministry where each has professional status and professional pay. Many churches are still adjusting to changes over the past generation in the status of clergy wives. In denominations with married clergy it has long been the custom to assume that one salary hired two people and that while the minister led the congregation his wife would "help out" with women's groups, calling, church hospitality, and probably the education program as well. Ministers and their families were usually housed in homes owned by the church and immediately adjacent to it, so that they could be on call when needed. Often part of the work of the pastor's wife was to serve as hostess for meetings held in the manse. Except in small towns and rural areas or in very small churches, this pattern has generally changed. Ministers have taken housing allowances instead of church housing, to live in neighborhoods of their choice in homes of appropriate size for their families and with some measure of privacy. Their wives have not automatically filled positions in the church, and many have taken employment elsewhere. With the rise of the clergy couple, the woman has returned seeking not volunteer servitude but professional employment in the church, and her training is equal to that of her husband. They may alternate in the pulpit or each pursue specialized roles for which they are specifically trained or gifted.

For some churches the primary problem may be providing dual placements at the same time. They may also be forced to deal with questions about definitions of "senior" and "associate" pastors with those who would share the ministry equally. Denominations have had to reexamine minimum salary standards on the basis of a sense of fairness when faced with one couple seeking a housing allowance, family health insurance, or pensions which support both parties. Congregations at times are faced with dealing with their relation to other church-related agencies in the community through having the leaders of each married to one another. However, the primary issue at stake is that of church support for changing roles for women and the importance of acknowledging within their own structure the meaning of that change. Women in professional leadership in the church make a difference in the perception of the role of lay women in that institution as well.

In the past, one of the ways in which the church has supported traditional family structure has been to provide a channel for meaningful volunteer activity by women whose primary occupation was that of housewife. For those whose only training was in domestic skills and who had no money of their own, the bazaars, church suppers, and ice cream socials provided a way in which their sewing and cooking could be transformed into monetary contributions to the church. Money they made in this way or saved out of household budgets was sent to support missionaries at home and abroad. They contributed gallons of coffee and punch, tons of cookies and cakes, to the activities that maintained the fellowship of the church. They wrapped bandages for the sick, made clothes for the poor, visited the isolated, decorated the altar, and in general kept up many of the less noticed and less popular activities that allowed the church to function.

Many of these activities still go on in church women's groups, but the society has come to devalue voluntarism, and many of the women now are employed outside the home and the church. Traditional women's activities seem to them a waste of time. They would rather contribute money than handicrafts; they have more money than spare time. They have many more sources of contact with the outside world than missionary letters and community service projects, and in many cases they have the experience and the skill to occupy the same leadership roles in the congregation that men have traditionally filled. In many churches subtle or even overt conflict has arisen among women who represent these two styles of participation. One of the challenges of the clergy-woman is to be able to offer support and leadership for both factions when by her very existence she represents the second.

One of the challenges of the church at large is to reevaluate the place of voluntarism and the nature of lay participation in its life. Professional leadership by a married couple can be seen as a family function, thus raising the issue as to how other families might participate. Another form of this sort of question may be found in the Roman Catholic church, where a celibate priesthood is being challenged by married people, male and female, who seek lay ministry roles in the church—many of them ex-priests who now have families. In other traditions also a more educated laity has come to challenge the leadership of the clergy. The lines between church and family are changing, including the direction of authority.

However, there are constant functions that churches continue to take seriously in their relation to the family, and one of the primary ones is the nurture of children. While new ways are being devised to affirm and guide the more public roles of the laity in the church or outside it, a major focus remains the partnership of church and home in the private task of shaping the next generation. As developmental psychology has evolved, it has been expanded to provide new insights into the development of moral and religious character, insights that many churches are attempting to apply within their own programs and also to share with parents.

Except in sectarian groups with an emphasis almost entirely on conversion as a life-changing event, religious groups have come to recognize that mature exercise of the faith must be built on a foundation that ideally is begun in the earliest years of a child's existence. Religious teachings that assume this in situations where it may not exist have been discovered to have severe weaknesses. For example, to teach people that God is like a father is common, but it communicates something very different from what is intended if the hearer has never known a father or has had a brutal or uncaring one.

Most developmental psychologies posit a basic need for a sense of order and dependability in a person's world, without which further development will be stunted. Religious systems, as we have seen, are order-creating activities. They reflect a confidence in the ultimate meaning of things, allowing the believer to find patterns in human existence and to hope that even when those patterns are not evident there is someone in charge who can be trusted. This is made available to the child experientially if there is regularity and predictability in the home environment, and if parents are available to take charge when chaos threatens. As a child grows and his or her world expands, the parental role may be taken by other mentors, by community or national leaders, eventually by God. The assumption, then, is that for a person to have any positive idea of God there must have been this kind of development of a sense of trust in the universe in the family setting.

Where childhood has been chaotic, the introduction of the idea of God as an orderer of that chaos may be the trigger of conversion to a religious group. One young man, for example, who was very involved in a sectlike group, gave the following response to a question about significant events in his life:

When my father and mother were divorced.
When my father married my stepmother.
When my father divorced my stepmother.
When my father married my next stepmother I felt nothing.
When my brother left home I felt angry.
When I found Jesus I felt relieved.

Conversionist sects frequently assume this kind of history for their converts and are organized to act as surrogate families, providing a very predictable, if somewhat restricted, social world in which the individual may begin to trust the universe. Main-line churches work with families to prevent the experiences that lead to the need for such a conversion, aiming toward a more orderly and less traumatic development of the faith.

Yet changes in the culture constantly require new expressions of the religious universe if indeed the experience of the child is to be orderly and not problematic. In medieval times religion affirmed the worth of the individual in his or her own station in the feudal system and became oppressive to persons who were assuming roles not legitimated by that system, such as the petite bourgeoisie. The Protestant Reformation not only legitimated roles for them in the society, but also introduced an emphasis on individual responsibility that tended to be mirrored in— or to mirror—bourgeois family life.

Probably one of the most noticeable strains in present religious forms relating to the worth of the person is found in the wide if not exclusive use of masculine pronouns and terminology in religious language. As the family has become less a permanent unity, it is only in such non-main-line religions as the Mormons that the religious worth of the woman is tied to her role as wife and mother. In Mormon theology salvation is a family affair, not to be fully achieved by the unmarried, so that sexist terms in religious language do not in themselves make women feel excluded. But in most churches, as we have seen, there is some recognition that women are individuals in their own right, responsible for their own destinies. Yet most religions language spoken in those churches refers to God only in masculine terms and defines human affairs in such phrases as the "fall of man," "man in the image of God," and the like. Women have become uneasy singing "Rise Up O Men of God" or referring to the church as the fellowship of the sons of God, and they point to the fact that in its nurture of children a church using such language is implicitly telling girls that they have no place in it. In some churches the response to such criticisms has been to harden the distinction, as in the Roman Catholic pronouncement that women cannot be allowed to be priests because the priest serves as a representative of Christ, who was male. Many of the liberal churches, however, are responding to such criticism with attempts to expunge from prayers and hymns, and sometimes from scripture, language now labeled sexist. They also are beginning to examine some of their mythology to find neglected sources for a more equal inclusion of women.[17]

Meanwhile, as religious institutions try to deal with sexist traditions, many of the new religious movements appear to be reversing the trend. This is particularly true in the Jesus movement, where ties to fundamentalism and biblical literalism reinforce the older traditions—traditions not only of the subservience of women to men, but also of their inherent capacity to be for men "an occasion of sin."[18] In the neo-pentecostal or charismatic movement, the original freedom of expression by anyone touched by the Holy Spirit—male or female, young or old—appears to be following older patterns of giving way to a male-dominated structure.[19] Even some of the Eastern religions have moved from an earlier concentration on spiritual exercises open to all to a mirroring of more of the oriental cultures from which they have sprung, with a consequent reduction in the role of women in decision-making activities.[20]

While sex roles in many of the new movements are only partially spelled out because so many of them are associations of a single generation, there are few religions whose traditions are not closely tied to those of families. As religious norms help to shape family structure, so, too, the experience of growing up in a family helps shape the world view out of which religious activity and symbolism are born. In families where a democratic structure is the norm, where mothers may have valued roles outside the home and outside stereotypical female occupations, where it is assumed that the daughters will be as free as the sons in their career choices, a nonsexist religion is natural and desired. It usually accompanies a religious tradition in which church governance is relatively democratic and the theology liberal. But in families where it is understood that the meaningful structure that children need comes from the authority of parents, where it is necessary that there be an identifiable head of the household just as there is an identifiable God and that authority is by nature hierarchical, such changes are not only unnecessary, they are destructive of the family order.

It is in such taken-for-granted patterns of relationship between the divine order and that of the family that problems often arise concerning interfaith marriages. While patterns of mate selection have expanded far beyond the bounds of specific groups, and their ability to regulate such choices has almost disappeared, it has been found that persons tend to revert to early examples of familial roles when they marry and start families of their own. Patterns practiced in the home and legitimated by the church often become the point of reference, even when new families are begun with the intention of rebelling from those patterns. So a couple whose familial and religious backgrounds are significantly different may find themselves unable to understand the implicit expectations of one another that they carry into their relationship. Most studies show that marriages within the major socioreligious groups or major faiths have a better record of endurance and reported happiness than those between members of different groups. Interfaith marriages must deal with lack of social support as well as with problems of different norms about the nature of marriage.

One of the greatest points of contention in interfaith marriages is in the training of children. The obvious problem is the choice of which socioreligious group the children should be trained to feel a part of—the father's or the mother's. While even in American society there is considerable inclination to see the family as patriarchal, and hence to expect the child to follow the father's faith, we also have the opinion that mothers are in charge of the private sphere of the family's life, including religion. So no clear guidelines exist in the society as a whole. In a secular society such as this one, the solution often is to ignore both religious groups and assume the child will choose a religious identity when old enough to do so. However, direct affiliation with a religious group may be of considerably less importance than some of the expectations of the parents' different socioreligious communities regarding norms of child rearing. For example, Lenski found that even when social class is held constant, white Protestants and Jews tended to value training for autonomy more than Catholics and black Protestants. The latter groups were more likely to limit freedom and attempt to increase authority. The fact that white and black Protestants were on opposite sides of this distinction point up the complex interrelation between religious faith and other elements of the social order. Protestants whose beliefs were somewhat unorthodox but who were regular churchgoers gave greatest support to autonomous (some might say "permissive") child rearing. This pattern did not fit the Catholic respondents.[21] Belief and ritual dimensions seem not always mutually reinforcing.

One of the costs to the children of an interfaith marriage—or one in which one partner has a significant religious involvement not shared by the other—is the loss of consistency in the way in which their lives are ordered. In terms of Rokeach's typology as discussed in Chapter 4, small children need a considerable proportion of Type A primitive beliefs—unchallenged assumptions about the nature of things. This occurs when parents are in agreement in their own world views and where they also participate, with their children, in larger social groups such as extended families or church congregations where those views are shared.

Part of the necessary structure of a child's world is experience with and observation of a wide age range of people. Some questions about the nature of the future for themselves as persons are best answered simply by getting to know others whose lives are at various points along the scale of maturation. In a society in which there is considerable residential and social segregation by age, and where the family itself is generally composed of a few minor children and their parents alone, this is not as easy to do as it has been in the past. Even if older people come into the range of the child's experience they may be so culturally different that they can hardly be claimed as models for their future. Insofar as churches tend to be one of the few remaining organizations in which both young and old participate and in which there is the assumption of a shared culture, they might be expected to serve such a communal function. Few, however, take advantage of their unique composition in this way. Rather, they reflect the age segregation of the society by providing different programs for each age group, leaving children insecure as to the nature of their future development and older people frightened at the thought of having to turn over their world to the incomprehensible, barbaric young. Some recognition of both the need and the opportunity for the church to serve in this way has begun to emerge, particularly among religious educators, so it may be that programs designed to exploit the intergenerational composition of religious congregations will be an aspect of future development in American religion.

In summary, then, religious institutions in American society relate to the family by providing support and guidance for family relationships, legitimation for various role definitions based on early experience such as those surrounding one's sex or gender, and social support which may strengthen family ties or be a substitute for them. The two institutions of religion and family compose the private sector of the society and together shape and support personal identity and intimate relationships by providing an experiential base for a world view that is anchored both in some expression of the ultimate meaning of existence and in the nature of everyday life.

Notes and References

1. This began in Reform Judaism during the nineteenth century in Germany. See Nathan Glazer, *American Judaism* (Chicago: University of Chicago Press, 1957), pp. 27–28.
2. From "Christian Nurture in the Family and the Relation of the Church to the Family: A Working Paper for Curriculum Writers and Editors," copyright by the Board of Christian Education and Publication of the Evangelical and Reformed Church and the Division of Christian Education, Board of Home Mission of the Congregational Christian Churches.
3. Alfred Goldmann, *The Common Ground in Family Life Education* (American Social Health Association, 1950), p. 9.
4. Gerhardt Lenski, *The Religious Factor* (Garden City, N.Y.: Doubleday, 1961).
5. T. Scott Miyakawa, *Protestants and Pioneers* (Chicago: University of Chicago Press, 1964), pp. 130–131.
6. Charles Y. Glock, Benjamin Ringer, and Earl Babbie, *To Comfort and to Challenge* (Berkeley: University of California Press, 1967), pp. 63–74.
7. Lenski, op. cit., pp. 219–223.
8. Marshall Sklare, *Conservative Judaism* (New York: Free Press, 1955), pp. 40–42.
9. A good treatment of this last factor and of the increasing problem of time as a scarce commodity may be found in Staffan B. Linder, *The Harried Leisure Class* (New York: Columbia University Press, 1970).
10. Glock, Ringer, and Babbie, op. cit., pp. 45–59.
11. Jerry Cardwell, "The Relationship between Religious Commitment and Premarital Permissiveness: A Five-Dimensional Analysis," *Sociological Analysis* 30 (Summer 1969): 72–80.
12. From the October 21, 1916, edition of *America,* as quoted in Carl Reiterman, "Birth Control and Catholics," *Journal for the Scientific Study of Religion* 4 (Spring 1965): 213–233, quotation from p. 216.
13. Norman B. Ryder and Charles F. Westoff, "Use of Oral Contraception in the United States, 1965," *Science* 153 (September 1966): 1203.
14. Reiterman, op. cit., p. 214.
15. William Osborne, "Religious and Ecclesiastical Reform," *Journal for the Scientific Study of Religion* 7 (Spring 1968): 78–86.
16. Andrew Greeley, William McCready, and Kathleen McCourt, *Catholic Schools in a Declining Church* (Kansas City, Mo.: Sheed & Ward, 1976), Chapter 5.
17. For a sample of some of the literature of this movement, see Letty Mandeville Russell, ed., *The Liberating Word: A Guide to a Nonsexist Interpretation of the Bible* (Philadelphia: Westminster, 1976); Mary Daly, *The Church and the Second Sex* (New York: Harper & Row, 1968); Mary Daly, *After God the Father* (Boston: Beacon, 1973); and

Elizabeth Howell Verdesi, *In But Still Out: Women in the Church* (Philadelphia: Westminster, 1976).

18. See, for example, Mary Harder, "Sex Roles in the Jesus Movement," *Social Compass* 21 (1974): 345–353.

19. See J. Massyngberde Ford, *Which Way for Catholic Pentecostals?* (New York: Harper & Row, 1976); Richard Quebedeaux, *The New Charistmatics* (Garden City, N.Y: Doubleday, 1976), p. 110; Charles Barfoot, "Prophesying Daughters," *Review of Religious Research,* forthcoming.

20. See Stillson Judah, *Hare Krishna and the Counterculture* (New York: Wiley, 1974). I also have had personal communications concerning this process among the 3HO, the followers of Yogi Bajan.

21. Lenski, op. cit., pp. 230–297.

10

Education and Moral Development

Patterns of moral and faith development have been identified that reach far beyond the early nurture of the preschool child and have implications for the relation of religion not only to the family but to the educational institution as well. Perhaps the most seminal research in this area has been done by James Fowler, who has identified six levels of faith development built upon a beginning condition of "undifferentiated faith," the basic trust referred to in the preceding chapter.[1] Stage 1, *intuitive-projective faith,* says Fowler, is imitative and filled with fantasy, based on the example of important adults. Symbols at this stage are magical, and moral judgment is based on reward or punishment. Stage 2, *mythic-literal faith,* is contained in the stories and beliefs that symbolize one's community. Symbols are one-dimensional and literal, and there is a perception of belonging, of recognizing "those like us." Moral judgments are based on "instrumental hedonism," that is, behavior that will increase pleasure or avoid pain. In Stage 3, *synthetic-conventional faith,* the authority of the particular group or class to which one belongs underlies the symbolic universe. Conformity to the group and a sense of law and order dominate moral judgment. Stage 4, *individuating-reflexive faith,* corresponds with what Erikson has called the "ideological stage."[2] At this point the individual comes to realize polar tensions in human existence between the self and the community, subjectivity and objectivity, self-fulfillment and service to others, and the like. Resolution of those tensions may take place through commitment to a simplified but comprehensive organization of reality—an ideology. Stage 5, *paradoxical-consolidative faith,* adds to the loyalties developed in Stage 4 an understanding of the choices taken and appreciation of the alternatives that have been eliminated in that process. Ideally in Stage 5 one understands that taking up particular values and beliefs requires some risk, involving a potential loss of lesser loyalties. Stage 6, *universal-*

izing faith, is rare, perhaps the style of the saint, who in Fowler's words "dwells *in* the world as a transforming presence, but is not *of* the world."

While Fowler attaches certain age levels to these stages, he notes that any stage may be delayed. There is, however, an assumption that one must pass through each stage at some time if a later one is to be reached. Ideally, Stage 1 is reached in the preschool years and Stage 2 in early childhood. Stage 3 would ordinarily be expected to coincide with the elementary school years, Stage 4 with adolescence and youth. Later stages, if reached, are the product of adult life experiences. One of the assumptions behind the stage theory is that the nature of faith changes with the boundaries of the group in which one is identified, each stage making it possible for one to feel loyalty and kinship with a broader segment of humankind. This would parallel, then, the movement of the child from the nuclear family out into the extended family or church congregation, then to larger units of schoolmates, etc. An orderly faith development, like the more specific moral development it supports, requires at each of these stages certain social foundations which may not always be present, but which may be expected to come from the family, the religious institution, or the school.

It behooves us, then, to look at the structure of American education, both to note its relation to individual development and to trace its relation to other structures of the society, particularly the institution of religion.

In primitive society the most consciously formal instruction tended to be reserved for the transmission of rites, formulas, and mythic tales attached to the religion. As society became more specialized, formal learning was highly concentrated in the priestly strata. One of the great thrusts of the Reformation was the impetus toward universal education brought on by a theology that stressed the "priesthood of all believers" and a consequent need for open access to the sacred writings. The relationship between religion and education has always been direct and strong.

Yet a second thread can be followed in the historic relationship between education and religion. While the priests have sought and transmitted knowledge, they have also maintained power by keeping it to themselves. The Protestant emphasis has often been related to the growth of science, but even in Protestantism there has remained a strong suspicion that too much knowledge might undermine one's faith. Religious institutions have long been involved with education; they have always preferred to control it. We must examine the American scene with this in mind.

Several contrasting sources may be found for the present institutional forms of religious and secular education in the United States. Without doubt the most prominent source is the New England settlement, where a Calvinistic commitment to universal education (of believers and potential believers, at any rate) was given form in the local school. Religion was the focus, but reading was a necessity for the type of religion being fostered. Skills in the "3 Rs" were expected to improve the quality of Christian life, which included one's daily occupation. There is little doubt that the relative prosperity of the Yankee Puritans can be traced primarily to their open access to skills provided through formal schooling.

Meanwhile, a different pattern was developing in the southern colonies, which were largely Anglican at first. The Church of England, more Catholic than Puritan in its theology, had less interest in pushing universal literacy. In these areas, schools were in many cases less focused on religion, and instead were maintained as training grounds for the elite who needed an education in order to do a better job of governing the masses. It was from this tradition that the private school developed.

The Great Awakening and its aftermath combined the Calvinist theology with a strain of pietism imported mostly from continental Europe through America's Middle Colonies, to some extent taking as the mark of the "priesthood of all believers" a spiritual sanctification or conversion rather than the more rational literary search of the Scriptures. Much of the popular Protestantism carried into the South and West was less supportive of education as necessary to salvation than had been the case in New England. Perhaps for this very reason, along with the more settled state of society in the Northeast, New England publishing houses came to dominate the textbook market for over a century, setting much of the mold of public education for the nation.

If from the earliest settlers we received traditions of public and private schools, it remained for later immigrants to bring to important proportions the parochial school as we know it. The name implies a school based on a geographic unity which makes up a religious parish. As such it could be applied to the village schools of New England. But in America the meaning of the term "parochial school" has come to include a pluralistic view of the society. A parochial school to Americans is a church-run school that is an alternative to existing public and/or private systems available in the area and may indeed be diocesan or related to some other church unit than the parish. Because the public and private systems are generally assumed to have been around longer, the parochial school in America has been expected to reflect cultural backgrounds at least somewhat different from that of the locality.

Though seldom articulated in this way, parochial schools in American society are expected to be formed by minority groups, and they bear the stigma of being somewhat outside the "American tradition." Yet they have in reality become an important part of that tradition and have provided a solid base for the continuing diversity and pluralism of American culture.

The American emphasis on the separation of church and state has resulted over time in a constant increase in the secularity of the schools' teachings. At the same time, the rate of this change has been erratic and has shown great regional variation. It is quite probable that the separation of church and state would not long remain a firm plank in the public platform of any denomination if it were assured that it would always be able to dominate the government. Yet in most cases violations of the separation, particularly those concerning the public schools, have occurred not because of deliberate church action, but rather because people in a locality where one religious form has dominated have taken it for granted that religious activities in the school were simply normal American ways of doing things.

The secular character of the government-operated public school has generally been assumed ever since the official disestablishment of religion in the separate states. (This, however, was not completed until 1821.) Churches have recognized that schools are secular by establishing special educational activities within the local church to supplement the schools. Although Robert Raike's original Sunday schools in England were both religious and grammar schools for children who worked all week in industry, the Sunday school in America became the churches' way of adding specific religious content to the formal training of their children. The concentration on religion in those schools has been gradual and has varied from church to church. For example, it was reported in 1900 that many Sunday school libraries contained a high proportion of books that were essentially secular.[3] In many cases, the content of Sunday school lessons was specifically denominational, but one of the first cooperative activities of Protestants was the establishment of the American Sunday School Union, later the International Sunday School Union. The organization became strong enough to send out its own missionaries, who organized denominationally independent Sunday schools in many parts of the country. Since 1872 the organization has distributed Sunday school lessons which have provided basic Bible instruction for generations of American Protestants.

Eventually the independence of the Sunday school movement proved troublesome for some denominations. The nonsectarian materials provided were fairly conservative theologically, tied to an evangelical emphasis and a literal interpretation of the Bible. In many cases the local congregations, trained in the Sunday school tradition, found their ministers' college-based theology unacceptably liberal or bearing unfamiliar emphases. The ministers and others in denominational leadership began to push more strongly for church-oriented materials that would reflect the theology of the denomination, so that the perspectives would be similar in the classroom and the pulpit. This effort was decried by some as an exercise in denominational narrowness and by others as bowing to "modernism." Standardized Sunday school lessons came to be more often used in churches that characterized themselves as "evangelical." Denominations known to be more "liberal" provided their own church school material, more and more often cooperatively as a part of the ecumenical movement. Many in recent years have shifted to providing a range of choices from which local congregations may select materials, rather than a single approved curriculum. Even then, many local congregations choose to ignore denominationally sponsored teaching materials in favor of those more like the old Sunday School Union variety.

The early thrust of the Sunday School Union was closely tied to the missionary movement, and its lessons were created to provide an acquaintance with the scriptural base of the Christian faith. Denominations that were more churchlike in orientation, such as the Lutheran, tended to view Sunday school as training for members rather than evangelistic mission and consequently did more teaching from their own tradition with their own materials. The exchange of materials from the Sunday School Union for those provided by the denomination in other churches may be taken as an indicator of movement from sectlike to churchlike orientation.

Most Jewish groups in the United States have made a similar adjustment to public schooling, providing "Hebrew schools," Saturday (or Sabbath) schools, Sunday schools, or a combination of these, separate from and additional to the public school—although some Hebrew schools are comprehensive "parochial" schools. Since they have been in the minority in practically every locality where they have settled, Jewish groups have been vociferous in the defense of a full separation of church and state. At the same time, since their value system tends to give the educated person particular honor, they have been among the strongest supporters of the public school system.

Catholics, who brought a churchlike form of organization when they came to America, have preferred to provide religious education along with the secular in parochial schools. The tradition of the Catholic church, of course, has not been strongly in favor of a separation of church and state, and in America there are reasons why Catholics frequently align themselves with opponents of such separation. Probably one of the main reasons why Catholic schools constitute the only major church-related system lies in their tradition of religious teaching orders. Much of the extra cost of parochial education has been absorbed by "contributed work" from those orders. In recent years, however, the drop in number of teachers in religious orders and consequent increase in lay teachers has led to serious budgetary problems in many schools. All citizens are required to pay taxes that support the public schools. Those who wish to have their children educated elsewhere must pay additional funds for the privilege. Schools established by most denominations that do not have such sources of low-salaried trained personnel must charge tuition so high they cannot serve a broad clientele. They become simply private schools that provide some religious training from a particular tradition. Catholic schools appear to be moving in this direction, and those who pay their increasing tuitions seek relief from the double burden of that tuition and taxation.

Most Protestant denominations have strongly supported public schools, maintaining that secular education is best obtained in institutions provided by the secular state. Yet one of the reasons it was easy for them to do so was that these "secular" schools have reflected much of the Protestant culture of the community. Only with the diversification of communities have people come to realize that some practices in the school have been sectarian or have served to disadvantage some sects. Over time, the national climate has changed. Compulsory-attendance laws have been instituted in nearly all localities and have been more rigidly enforced as time goes on. Also, accreditation of schools has come to require teacher preparation and curricular offerings that make it more difficult for small local groups to maintain qualified schools for their children. As a result, children from religious sects that formerly maintained separate schools or provided only informal education now have been required to attend public schools whose teachers do not share their religious assumptions.

There have been a number of conflicts over compulsory-education laws between school districts and states and religious groups such as the Amish. While they have been able to maintain their separateness from the rest of the society by sending a few selected members out for teacher training that would qualify them for certification, this has been effective only at the elementary school level. Increased age requirements for compulsory attendance and curriculum requirements for secondary school accreditation have resulted in civil suits against Amish communities that refused to send their children to high school outside the community. At the moment, at least, the Amish have won the battle and have been allowed to keep their children out of the secular high schools. It is under such circumstances that the strain between some religious practices and common public assumptions becomes visible.

One of the first problems involved religious groups whose teachings considered pledges of allegiance or salutes to the flag of a nation as idolatry for those whose allegiance was to God alone. The reaction to this phenomenon was ambivalent, since patriotism was considered a prime virtue by most people and yet freedom of religion was one of the central expressed values of the national creed. The ambivalence was reflected in the actions of the Supreme Court itself. While in 1940, in the case of *Minersville School District* v. *Gobitis,* the court had ruled that public schools had the right to demand of students that they salute the flag, that decision was reversed in 1943 in the case of *West Virginia Board of Education* v. *Barnette.* In this case the Court ruled that the state did not have the right to force public school students to salute the flag if it was against their beliefs to do so.[4]

Other issues that have been brought to the Supreme Court have included various attempts by supporters of parochial schools to receive some relief from the double tax burden mentioned above. Suits have been brought concerning the right to transportation to school, to school lunches and textbooks, and the like. Often it has been ruled that benefits to students, not to the schools as institutions, would be allowable. But the court battles continue, and each specific issue continues to be contested without setting a general policy upon which the schools and their supporters could depend.

Perhaps the most controversial area of change in governmental control of the public schools, however, has come from Court decisions involving the incorporation of religious teachings, programs, or practices in the public schools themselves. This has involved two areas, one of distinct and formal religious teaching, the other that of more informal, taken-for-granted practices.

During the upswing of religious interest that followed World War II, churches generally began to note that the combination of the secular public school and the church-sponsored Sunday school simply was not providing as strong a grounding in the faith as they felt necessary. As their students became more heterogeneous religiously and their teacher-training more devoted to a secular scientific orientation, the schools in many places dropped much of the moral teaching once provided almost unconsciously as part of a common religious background. One answer to the situation was to incorporate religious teachings in the school curriculum through a policy of "released time," where different religious groups could provide explicit religious training for their own children as part of the regular school curriculum. Children could attend the "class of their choice" much as on weekends the families could attend the "church of their choice." This practice was attacked as divisive and particularly unfair to those church groups that could not or would not provide instructors and materials for the program, as well as to the children who belonged to no religious group. In the *McCollum* case of 1948 the Supreme Court ruled against the use of school buildings for the program, as insufficient separation of church and state. The action was praised by the Baptists, the Unitarians, and most Jewish groups, as well as by such periodicals as *Christian Century*. Evangelical Protestants and Catholics joined in deploring the Court's action. This case was followed by the *Zorach* case, in which the Court approved released-time religious teaching if it occurred off the school grounds. Opposition to this decision began within the Court itself, with Justice Frankfurter summing up his reasons for dissent as follows:

> There is all the difference in the world between letting the children out of school and letting some out of school into religious classes. . . . [T]he pith of the case is that formalized religious instruction is substituted for other school activities which those who do not participate in the released time program are compelled to attend.[5]

Currently, instead of official released-time activities, some religious groups offer instruction to their youth in the early morning hours, or in the evening, where no conflict with the school system will arise.

Later, controversy arose around the subject of prayer in the public schools. It finally came to the Supreme Court after the New York Board of Regents, responding to complaints about the use of prayers that seem too sectarian, attempted to compose an all-purpose, nonsectarian prayer which could be used in the opening exercises of schools in the state. The Court ruled this unconstitutional, saying that "it is no part of the business of government to compose official prayers for any group of the American people to recite as part of a religious program carried on by government."[6]

While the ruling was specific to the providing of state-written prayers to be used in the schools, it overlay a general understanding that prayers of any specific group would be in even greater violation of the separation of church and state. Consequently, public opinion simplified the decision to state that no prayer could be made in the public schools, and evangelical Christians in particular were incensed at the thought of a totally godless school. Specifically, they reacted against the Supreme

Court, and the animosity developed out of this issue has colored the reaction to later decisions unrelated to schools or religion. Meanwhile, a number of states have passed laws instituting a period of silent meditation in the schools, which to date has not provoked suits claiming the violation of the separation of church and state.

Reaction against the Supreme Court grew after the *Schempp* case in 1963, when the Court ruled that states could not require Bible reading in the public schools. The Court in its decision stated that the First Amendment is violated if either the purpose or the primary effect of the law is the advancement or inhibition of religion. Considerable public pressure has built up in some areas, as some citizens fear that familiar religious teachings are being replaced in the public schools by a "gospel of secularism," which actually competes against religious teachings.

The schools, caught in the midst of this controversy, have responded with three kinds of policy and practice, often overlapping and confused. In some areas they still schedule planned religious activities, especially such things as Christmas pageants and the like in which the children are expected to participate. Usually this pattern is found in places where one faith is dominant and the population fairly homogeneous. Other schools try desperately to avoid religious subjects and activities entirely. This practice, as might be expected, is most common in communities that are religiously heterogeneous. In some schools, especially where a strong school administration has been able to push the program, a factual study of religion has been made part of the general curriculum, nearly always as an elective course. This practice was specifically suggested in the Supreme Court ruling and has been recommended by the American Council on Education.[6]

However, such courses—or indeed any consideration of religion—have continued to stir up controversy. One reason some religious groups had supported the removal of religious practices from the schools was that they did not consider adequate the sort of bland civil religion those practices represented, and they wanted to be sure that any teaching the students received was not of that kind. Yet they could not agree on the nature of a more explicit kind of teaching, and some opposed the sort of objective examination of the religious tradition offered in courses such as "The Bible as Literature" in the hands of nonbelieving teachers. As the public schools responded to legal pressure to mix the races by instituting busing of students into neighborhoods outside their residential areas, the cultural mix in the schools became more complex and with it the number of religious traditions represented. Faced with the problem of dealing with so many points of view, most school administrators simply removed all forms of religious teaching from the schools and instructed teachers not to use religious language in dealing with morals or values.

In recent years there has been a move to institute programs of "values clarification," in which students are urged to think through the system of values each of them may espouse, with no effort to make judgments among them. However, if one accepts the stage theory of faith development posited by Fowler or those of Kohlberg and Piaget on moral development, such an attitude of freedom of choice among meaning systems is inappropriate before adolescence. At the elementary school level there is a need to develop a single coherent system in conjunction with a sense of belonging to a group. It is assumed that this function cannot be provided by the school but must center in the family and the religious community. Yet the proportion of time spent in school and with schoolmates is so much greater than that spent in church or even in the family that it seems logical to question that assumption. This is even clearer when seen in the context of evidence that many families are too small and too fragmented to offer any sense of being moral communities, and many children have little if any contact with religious groups in that kind of communal setting.

Because of the lack of a common culture, the schools have had increasing problems with enlisting students in their tasks with any sense of a common enterprise. Teachers complain that they are reduced simply to keeping order and trying to impart disjointed facts without any way to tell students why they should learn those facts. Disorder, violence, and vandalism have led to the institution in many schools of guards in the halls, some of them armed. Parents with strong commitments to public education have ruefully removed their children from public schools to place them in private institutions which are free to inculcate specific value systems. Parents who cannot afford this option protest to school boards and city officials, but few know of solutions to the problems. Teachers caught in such systems receive few of the traditional gratifications of their profession in the way of witnessing the development of students they have learned to care for. Instead, they seek monetary compensation (some even ask for "combat pay"), form unions through which to deal with the growing bureaucracy of the school administration, and more and more frequently express their alienation from the process by closing down the schools with strikes for higher pay and better working conditions.

Under such circumstances it is not difficult to understand the growth in number and importance of schools sponsored by particular religious groups. Roman Catholic parochial schools, once almost exclusively devoted to educating the children of local parish members, have been besieged by parents of other districts and other faiths seeking to enroll their children. Thus, while they have lost many of the personnel who kept their education inexpensive and have lost some of the authoritarian hold over members who in earlier days felt a religious obligation to keep children safe within the bounds of an exclusively Catholic education, they are not disappearing from the American scene. There has been a significant decline in the number of and attendance at Catholic elementary schools in the United States, but not in the central city where these problems are most evident.[7]

While Catholic schools may impart a sense of order both in the classroom and in the perception students have of the nature of human existence, it has been shown that their ability to impart lasting values is closely linked to their relationship to the home environment. In 1963 Greeley and Rossi found a kind of "multiplier effect" in the factors of a religious Catholic home and the Catholic school which showed a much stronger effect from the combination of the two than would be predicted from their effects taken separately.[8] In a follow-up study, Greeley et al. found that ten years later the relationship still held in matters of public values and private piety, though no longer for corporate ritual behavior or sexual orthodoxy. They found that the importance of continuing Catholic education (over ten years in Catholic schools) had increased in the decade between the two studies.[9] In other words, the formation of lasting values was dependent upon consistency over time as well as across major institutional loyalties.

This was also reinforced by their findings that Catholics educated in secular schools who received religious training through the Confraternity of Christian Doctrine (CCD) program, which approximates the organization of most Protestant religious education, showed little effect of the religious training in their adult values. There seems little reason not to assume that the need for cross-institutional consistency applies to young people outside the Catholic tradition as well.

Some other religious groups have traditionally maintained their own schools, particularly the Missouri Synod Lutherans and the Seventh Day Adventists. The Yeshiva schools of Orthodox Judaism also fit this pattern. However, in the past decade or more there has been a significant rise in the number of church-related schools sponsored by religious groups once devoted to the support of public education. In most cases these have arisen among people whose experience of public education had been in communities that unconsciously reflected a conservative Protestant culture which has now been threatened by a secular and pluralist society.

The first major development of such "Christian day schools" occurred in California, where the post-World War II population contained such a wide variety of internal migrants that secular pluralism became a necessity and yet where a large percentage of those migrants had come from the small towns of the South and the Midwest where conservative Protestantism infused the culture. The next major movement for such church-related schools came as a reaction to forced racial integration of the public schools of the South in the form of the so-called segregation academies. Since that time the movement has spread along with the rise of militantly evangelical or fundamentalist churches as a protest against the growing secularity of the culture and a perception of the inability of public education to inculcate values important to these families.

Recently an executive of the Association of Christian Schools International, based in Whittier, California, estimated that there are some five thousand such schools scattered about the country, with an enrollment of about a million pupils. While a government official was quoted as saying he thought that too large an estimate, he also admitted that it was hard to tell, because these schools are not inclined to be in contact with government agencies.[10]

These schools are once again beginning to test the relationship between church and state, refusing to submit to state guidelines on curricula in the name of freedom of religion. The particular issue in most cases has been the requirement of science texts that take for granted the Darwinian theory of evolution, in conflict with their interpretation of Scripture, and that of teaching sex education in the schools. In a clear reversal of trends since the 1928 Scopes trial, conservatives in California have managed to make it a state law that science courses present the "creationist" as well as the evolutionary understanding of the origin of the human species.

While scholars may scoff at the simplistic ideology represented in such movements, the issues at stake are less one-sided. What is seen by protesters against modern secular education is that the teaching of cultural relativity and the concept of humankind as simply a further development in the animal world have not been able to inculcate in the young a sufficient sense of personal worth and social responsibility to maintain the public order. Insofar as their charges are true, it will be difficult for the political system—that guarantor of order—to ignore their protests.

Problems at the elementary school level seem only complicated at the secondary school level. Where the issue in faith and moral development in prepubescent years revolves around providing a consistent environment in which the child may develop a sense of identity-in-community, the adolescent years are assumed to be the time for questioning, for individuating the self from the closed communities of childhood. Usually this occurs through some attachment to an ideology that expands the loyalty of youth beyond the narrow confines of childhood belonging.

As we have seen, one of the immediate problems with that pattern as a model for personal development in modern society is that many young people have never experienced the kind of closed, bounded community assumed here, and so they have no need to break out of one. Rather, if the theory is correct, we may assume that a significant number of young people are still trying to achieve the grounded belongingness of Stage 3.

It is these young people in particular that the evangelical youth organizations, particularly those with "discipling" or other small group study, prayer, and training programs, seem most able to serve. Their conversionist programs, requiring a distinct commitment to a fairly specific and simply defined faith, meet the adolescent need for an ideology through which they can organize choices forced upon them that would otherwise be chaotic. In the small groups they are given the sense of a place in a community with specific moral guidelines. Thus it is not just in traditionally conservative parts of the country, but also in the large high schools and universities of urban areas that such groups as Young Life, Campus Crusade, Intervarsity Christian Fellowship, and the Navigators find a significant clientele. Some of the revivals of Hasidic Judaism among the young, particularly those tied to communal living arrangements, fit this model also, providing both community and the firm bounds of Orthodox Jewish practice. Similar groups exist among Catholics, perhaps the best example being the St. Ignatius Institute at the University of San Francisco, an elite cadre of conservative students in a special program of the university who also tend to form their own closed community on campus.

The Protestant groups seem to be the most highly organized. Each has its own distinct organization, its own particular emphasis and style. All are national or international in scope, with considerable centralization of control. Intervarsity Christian Fellowship (IVCF) allows the greatest amount of local control, in line with a basic ideology that includes a belief that God has placed Christians on each campus who are called to serve in that place, and IVCF is simply there to assist them. They tend to be particularly adept at organizing small groups in college dormitories and in providing such large-group experiences as retreats and camps.

Campus Crusade for Christ is much more highly centralized and is focused more on direct personal evangelism. Their approach is based on the "Four Spiritual Laws":

1. God *loves* you and has a wonderful *plan* for your life.
2. Man is *sinful* and *separated* from God, thus he cannot know and experience God's love and plan for his life.
3. Jesus Christ is God's *only* provision for man's sin. Through Him you can know and experience God's love and plan for your life.
4. We must individually *receive* Jesus Christ as Savior and Lord: then we can know and experience God's love and plan for our lives.[11]

Their primary goal is to get others to recognize the reality of those laws and commit their lives to God in this manner. It is then assumed that they will join in the task of presenting the laws to others. Full-time workers in this organization are expected to find enough people interested in carrying on the work to pledge all the money needed for their support. That money, however, is not given directly to the workers but is funneled through the central organization, which takes care to see that there are no distinctions in salary between those who know many rich backers and those who can barely scrape together enough support to prove that they have the ability to win the commitment of others. The process also, of course, increases the power of the central organization over its workers. This is evident in the amount of uniformity in Campus Crusade programs and approaches across wide areas of geographical space and types of clientele.

The Navigators have a similar program, with a strong emphasis on small groups and Bible study. As the name suggests, this organization began as a mission to seamen, then spread to college campuses, then to young married couples. Here also workers are expected to find financial supporters for their work, but the Navigators claim to keep nearly all their funds in the local area, sending only a portion back to the central headquarters. The type of organization, however, is explicit and hierarchical.

Young Life is concentrated on high school campuses and tends to mix friendly sociability with traditional biblical and moral teaching. Usually a Young Life Club will have two levels of membership, one more social and one a committed cadre of core members. Again, Young Life has a quite centralized organization, though it also depends a good deal on the work of volunteer adult leaders. Young Life offers itself as an alternative to youth programs in local parishes, in that its focus is the school rather than any particular church. It sees the school as the primary focus of the lives of young people, and it meets them on their "turf" as missionaries would go into foreign lands. Indeed, in some areas, the school as a whole is seen in relation to the Young Life Club as traditional theology has seen the "world" in relation to the "church." At the same time, there is a definite attempt to recruit into the Young Life program those young people who are school leaders, to show that Christianity is worthy of student interest.

There are a number of other similar organizations for which these may stand as examples, some of them national, many local. The most distinctive feature about this type of organization is its separateness from the churches. Nearly all the groups encourage young people in their organization to attend local churches with a compatible theology, and many such churches help to support their workers. But they are organizationally separate, and there is some resentment even in churches that support them, because of the competition they offer for the time and the loyalty of the young.

It is primarily in this way that these groups differ from the older international organization, the Christian Endeavor Society. This movement was organized in the early part of this century in order to give young people a more intense style of Christianity than that which was available to them in many local churches. The style and appeal of this organization paralleled the old Sunday School Union, and through its young people made common cause across denominational lines within the boundaries of evangelical Protestantism. In most cases, however, the local society was sponsored directly by the congregation of which its members were a part, with added donations to the international organization.[12]

Another program for youth devoted to community maintenance, but with much less explicit religiosity at its beginning stages, has been the Catholic Youth Organization (CYO). Known mostly in the past for its athletic programs, the CYO has in recent years become more visible in programs for retreats, camps, and workshops. In pre-Vatican II days this organization existed primarily as a vehicle for keeping youth within the bounds of their own religious community, helping to shape identity and religious loyalty. All these endeavors, as well as communicants' classes, may be seen primarily as contributors to Stage 3 of Fowler's schema of faith development.

Since the Vatican Council, however, CYO has become much more involved in dealing with the questioning and experimentalism of youth, at least in some areas, thus moving their programs more into Stage 4 activities. But for many religious organizations Fowler's Stage 3 is a legitimate final goal in the religious training of members. This achieves institutional loyalty and an understanding of the symbolic structure and moral teaching of the church sufficient to produce a life lived in harmony with religious ideals. It also gives the individual a secure sense of identity and an understanding of the purpose of one's life consonant with that of the group. To move to Fowler's later stages of questioning and reintegration can be seen as an invitation to heresy, disloyalty, or personal psychological strain, not to be encouraged by the religious community.

This, however, is not generally considered sufficient in religious organizations whose theology is more "liberal," one more predicated on growth and progress. Neither do the more orthodox patterns fit well the life experience of those people in society who are highly—and successfully—socially mobile. To achieve genuine mobility one must be able to move both physically and psychologically beyond the bounds of the local community and its particular religious expression. The function of the later stages of faith development is to provide religious grounding for the person who must separate him- or herself from local tradition —a way in which to allow one to identify with a larger whole which can include that tradition but not be limited by it.

Liberal churches have tended to see this as an important need to be met by religious programs aimed particularly at youth, whether in the local church or on college campuses. Such programs have generally fostered at least three forms of expansive learning: (1) a willingness to question the religious symbol system and come to terms with more sophisticated or more experiential understandings of the symbols; (2) an experience of a wider fellowship of people who may share a commitment to central religious symbols, but whose traditions are very different; and (3) an involvement in programs of service or action toward social change motivated by their faith and ideals of a righteous society that proceed from it.

At the high school level these programs have encouraged young people to engage in discussions of personal or social morality which do not always take for granted the givens of the local religious community but seek within the faith reasons to accept or modify them. Experientially they may provide opportunity to engage in service projects or trips to areas where social problems are evident or life-styles are clearly different. They may engage in ecumenical activities or in specific interfaith dialogue. There may be a tendency to avoid the kind of ideological oversimplification Erikson says is necessary at this stage of development, because of liberal values that decry the kind of psychological coercion that may accompany the presentation of an ideology. If ideology is made visible in these groups, it usually is in the form of attachment to some current movement toward social change—welfare reform, ecological responsibility, peace, or other such causes, often somewhat removed from the daily life of most of the young people involved.

Youth programs of this type are usually provided in the local church by persons specifically hired as youth ministers, by volunteer adult leaders, or (usually) by both. They generally are also supported to some extent by district organizations of the denomination, which may include the services of youth specialists. In the 1950s and early 1960s this was a common pattern. Budgetary problems in the early and mid 1970s reduced the number of denominational specialists, to be replaced by a form of decentralization that often put one local minister in the position of heading up youth programs for a cluster of nearby churches of the denomination. By the latter half of the 1970s, district specialists were beginning to reappear where they had been dropped.

The pattern has been somewhat different in liberal programs for college youth, if only because many of them leave the local parish to attend college. Patterns of campus ministry have gone through many alterations over the years. Many church-related and private colleges provided their own religious programs and hired chaplains as part of their regular staff. Many still do, although the old compulsory chapel service is a thing of the past on all but the most conservative campuses. Again, this was an expression of a bounded community now generally considered inappropriate at the college level. Even those campuses with their own chaplains tend to have a student body so heterogeneous that representatives of several denominations or faiths are added to the chaplains' staff to minister to the various student constituencies.

On state university campuses, considerations of the separation of church and state have kept the chaplaincy from being part of the college staff. In most cases state university students were first served by local congregations near the campus. When this became too great a burden, denominations stepped in with salary money for extra staff, perhaps a "student minister" on the church staff. But often the disparate needs of the student constituency and the local parish led to a separation, and the campus ministry came to be centered in a house near the campus where the students could find a "home away from home," with social activities, study groups, coordination of service projects, and the like.

These tended at first to be denominationally identified. The inter-denominational movement that paralleled this and often preceded it was that of the YMCA and the YWCA, which frequently also provided housing, activities, projects, and a Christian environment for students. The Ys, though often highly favored by the churches, were separate organizations with their own funding and no particular denominational loyalties. In that way they were like the evangelical organizations mentioned earlier. But their theology was much more liberal, and in time they have become quite thoroughly secularized, often qualifying for government programs not available to more sectarian groups. They have dropped their Bible studies and prayer groups and are engaged more in community organizing and group therapy than identifiable religious activities. They also continue the programs of physical fitness and practical skills that made them famous. In all this, they are no longer an adjunct to religious programming per se.

Another liberal transdenominational collegiate activity was the Student Christian Movement, which provided contacts and a united voice for college youth interested in issues of peace, justice, and the like. During the campus movements of the 1960s the SCM was overwhelmed by activist groups and almost disappeared, but in some areas by the late 1970s it was again becoming visible.

During the 1950s and 1960s campus programs of the liberal churches moved into cooperative, ecumenical activities. Campus ministries, inclined toward social change and activist causes, had always had some problems with local congregations and their emphasis on providing a moral community. Their expansive world view often seemed threatening to institutional loyalties which congregations by their nature are committed to upholding. Thus, campus ministries came to rely on denominational support at the regional or national level, and with the growth of the ecumenical movement among the denominations a transdenominational organization, United Ministries in Higher Education (UMHE), was formed. That organization, with assistance from local boards representing local churches of the cooperating denominations, hired campus ministers who would be responsible to them rather than directly to their denominations or local congregations. Thus they were more free to pursue a course consonant with their view of the place of campus ministry.

In the 1960s, the views of campus ministers tended strongly in the direction of supporting student antiwar activity, including counseling conscientious objectors and draft resisters. Many campus ministers were also quite supportive of the kind of cultural protest embodied in the so-called counterculture, the flower children of the late 1960s. They had earlier been involved in much of the civil rights protest and, like many of the youth they counseled, were alienated from the society because of its slowness to respond to this protest or to deal with questions of the legitimacy of the war that was dealing havoc in the young lives to whom they ministered. Like the young, they felt the need for cultural alternatives. Campus ministry centers were often used as crash pads for drifting young hippies. Their mimeograph machines became presses for revolutionary literature, their chapels sanctuaries for war resisters.

But as the war wound down and the radicals moved further to the fringes of an antireligious New Left, many liberal campus ministers found themselves without a student constituency and so alienated from supporting denominations that it was easy for the churches to deal with growing budgetary problems by cutting off campus ministry funds. UMHE was cut back and began to go out of business. By the late 1970s, the campus ministers were beginning to rebuild bridges to supporting denominations and to find new programs with which to reach the students.[13]

But all this activity was only one part of one of four functions usually considered appropriate to campus ministry. These functions, as spelled out in the "Danforth Report" of 1967,[14] which has become something of a standard for campus ministry, are the *pastoral,* the *priestly, prophetic inquiry,* and *governance.* The activity of liberal campus ministers in the 1960s was defined by them as prophetic, but directed to the area of governance. That is, they were speaking against activities within the governing structure of the society that they considered violations of the divine order of justice.

Campus ministries that were basically priestly have had a somewhat different history. This mode of ministry seems most within Fowler's Stage 3, involving the maintenance of tradition, particularly in its sacramental and liturgical aspects. A definition of youth as a time for questioning tradition raises problems for priestly activities in campus ministry, and indeed during the 1960s most liberal Protestant campus ministers had almost entirely abandoned liturgical services—partly because the students had also abandoned such activities. Going through the old forms while agitating for massive social change seemed irrelevant, if not hypocritical.

After the period of activism, it became evident, particularly with the rise of new religions on the campuses, that young people deprived of traditional liturgy had found it in new places—the rock concerts, drug trips, or meditation practices of the counterculture. By the late 1970s liturgy had come to occupy a considerably more important place in the liberal Protestant campus ministry, and the rebuilding of bridges to supporting denominations also brought a renewed appreciation of specific traditions.

The priestly activities of Catholic campus ministry were always more central. Catholics were involved in ministry on secular campuses early, as well as with an extensive network of church-related colleges. The Newman Clubs were devised to maintain a Catholic milieu on the secular campus, in which students of that faith could stay within the bounded community of the church, socializing primarily with one another, under the kindly supervision of the Newman priest. After the reforms of Vatican II, less emphasis was laid on keeping students safely within the bounds of the faith, but the definition of youth as a time of questioning and experimentation was turned at least in part to participation in experimental liturgies and greater lay participation in worship. Thus, when greater emphasis on liturgy and celebration emerged in the youth culture, Catholic campus ministers were in a position to provide it. Their growing openness to other denominations and students' traditional looseness about specific traditions allowed them to be the providers of worship for many Protestants during that period, as well as for their own constituencies.

Chaplains on private and church-related college campuses have always had certain priestly functions, if only to preside at official occasions such as convocations and baccalaureate services. However, their priestly activities have gradually been downplayed in favor of such pastoral roles as individual counseling. Few campuses are so homogeneous in modern society that communal celebrations for the entire student body have much meaning except on those very important moments of celebration noted above.

Counseling has also been a primary pastoral role of other campus ministers on nearly all campuses. One of the purposes for which the church has placed ministers on campus was to provide a "presence" there, by which to make it evident that the church cares for students and the world they live in. That presence includes comfort for the homesick, consolation for the distressed, and guidance for the troubled at a time in life when all those problems are likely to arise. With the growth of counseling as a profession and of mental health centers on campus devoted to psychological counseling, not to mention career-guidance clinics, pastoral counseling has been adjusted on campus as elsewhere. Many campus ministers have received specific clinical training in order to provide counseling of a quality equal to that of the psychologist or at least in order to know when someone should be referred to specialists. They hold on, however, to the idea that it is appropriate for someone who has a problem he or she considers religious to come to a minister for religious counseling. They also see the value of a religious group, whether a church congregation or a campus organization, to serve as a therapeutic community for persons in need of support. The overall framework of meaning and purpose provided by religion becomes part of their counseling package in ways not available to the usual psychological counselor. The pastoral role tends to relate one to a community and to one's roots more directly also and so continues to serve important functions on campus.

The area of prophetic inquiry is one of particular interest to many campus ministers, because it involves the actual processes of education to which the campus is dedicated. In simple terms, prophetic inquiry involves the attempt to inject religious values into the academic process. Part of this has to do with subject matter itself. Campus ministers in a number of studies have indicated that college teaching would be a valued alternative to their present work, and many do find ways to offer courses in the regular curriculum of the schools they serve. This may well be one of the duties of the chaplain employed by a college; it may also be a task sought after by the denominational campus minister, who sometimes volunteers to co-teach a course with an established faculty member if other channels to the classroom are not open. Often these courses are in the field of ethics, where a campus minister, for example, might team up with a biologist to present a course on the ethics of biological experimentation.

The interpenetration of religion and higher education in the area of prophetic inquiry may also be focused in the opposite direction, where the tools of scholarship are applied to the study of religion in an attempt to come to a better understanding of the faith. There has been a trend in recent years to institute programs of religious studies on secular campuses. Often campus ministers serve as advisors when such programs are undertaken; they may be organizers of pressure groups fighting for their adoption.

Campus ministers, of course, are not the only voices of the church on all campuses. Theological schools are also institutions of higher education, and many of them are closely attached to or actually a part of larger university systems. A significant proportion of their graduates receive scholarly degrees and go on to teach in religious studies departments. Their work assists the scholarly critique of the religion. In many respects these scholars are even less tied to the church—at least to the church defined as local congregations—than the campus ministers, since they depend upon the university rather than the church for both financial and professional support.

Campus ministers tend to be interested in programs beyond those explicitly devoted to religious studies. They may join forces across a number of interest groups and all major faiths to promote programs that are in the realm of their religious values. Programs of peace research, or those linking social or political science with service in depressed areas, for example, have been given strong support by campus ministers. It is in areas of prophetic inquiry and governance that they have worked out many of the closest patterns of cooperation across the boundaries of major faiths in campus ministry. Judaism, with its traditional emphasis on learning and on social justice, is a willing partner with Catholicism and Protestantism on such programs. Jewish Hillel programs have offered on many campuses the kinds of ministry mentioned earlier as well, but they are particularly evident in those ministries involving learning or social justice.

Campus ministry is not just ministry to students. Rather, the campus minister perceives himself or herself to have a mission to the entire campus. Either in the mode of pastor or of prophetic inquiry they may call faculty to attend to their own basic values, encouraging them to keep in mind both the consequences of their research and the human dimensions of their teaching.

It is perhaps in the area of governance that campus ministers also address the universities on subjects of the human dimensions of campus life or the overall objects and methods of the educational system. And it is here that some of the basic conflict arises between religion and education. Much of the basis of modern education was laid in the Enlightenment period of Western history, when the search for truth was often hampered by institutional constraints imposed by religious institutions. There is built into much modern scholarship an unexamined assumption that religion, if not the enemy of learning, is at least part of the primitive past that education is attempting to overcome. Thus the presence of official representatives of the churches on college campuses is not welcomed by all members of the faculties and administrations of those institutions. At best it is assumed that they can help with counseling those students who insist that their psychological problems are religious. Few faculties or administrations admit the legitimacy of prophetic inquiry or governance as functions of campus ministry.[15]

In general, the effect of higher education has been to erode commitment to religious institutions.[16] There is considerable evidence that the norms of scholarship offer a competing world view to that of the churches. Some of the effect of college on church attendance and the like, of course, may be laid to the age of most students and to competing activities. Even among nonstudents, church involvement tends to be low during late adolescence and early adulthood. But the effects seem more lasting than that; many people who commit themselves to a life of scholarship withdraw entirely from the religious institution.

Yet campus ministers are in a particularly good place to measure, if not to deal with, the extent of the dysfunction within the educational institution that arises from the lack of a coherent set of values binding the many facets of higher education into a meaningful whole. They may be resented by many on the campus, but they raise questions that will probably have to be dealt with if the educational system is to contribute meaningfully to an ordered society. If indeed youth is a period when some sort of ideology is needed to pull one into a meaningful future, the separate and somewhat self-centered academic disciplines represented on a campus may not be able to provide that kind of focused motivation. What we have seen in the past two decades could be interpreted as evidence that (1) those disciplines have *not* served as ideologies for a significant number of students, and (2) students then have been prey to a number of ideological fads that have not always proven consistent with their learning or constructive for their own lives or for the society. Campus ministers and other representatives of the religious institution on campuses attempt to offer an alternative to those fads, although they may also get caught up in them if institutional ties are too weak.

In many cases the alternative offered by religious leaders on campus has been relatively radical in relation to given social patterns of the time. The college campus has traditionally been somewhat separate from the rest of the society, offering space for a kind of moratorium in which the young could question and experiment without the serious consequences such action might engender elsewhere. Similarly, the campus ministry has been a place where the church could allow experimentation that might lead to renewal, without destroying its ongoing program in the process.[17]

Changes in the nature of higher education are requiring changes in campus ministry. Campuses are becoming less isolated. With the growth of the community college and a commuting student body, students no longer leave their local parish to go to college. Students may be in school only part-time and be involved in jobs and family life at the same time. They may be of any age, rather than primarily the young. Yet education continues to open new vistas to allow people to change self-concepts as well as their occupations and associations. This may put the commuter student under more strain than the one at a residential campus, because all these new attitudes and ideas are emerging in the context of families and friends who may not understand the changes. The particular kinds of integration offered by campus ministry may be most needful, yet religious belonging, if it exists at all, is most likely to remain in the local parish. In a sense, every minister becomes a campus minister. One of the chief functions of the professional campus minister of the future may be to train local clergy to respond to that situation.

The penetration of higher education into the local community in this way may be one of the most significant changes in the relation of religion to education at this stage of American history. It is forcing the church to rethink its adult education programs, and it is also forcing the educational institution into greater community responsibility than has been its role in the past. It remains to be seen whether the churches will have any impact on the way in which that role is defined, just as it remains to be seen whether the colleges will take over more of the functions in the community traditionally provided by the churches or change significantly the way in which religious practice and symbol systems are related to the ongoing life of the community.

Notes and References

1. The following discussion of stages of faith development is taken from James Fowler, "Faith Development Theory and the Aims of Religious Socialization," in *Emerging Issues in Religious Education,* ed. by Gloria Durka and Joan Marie Smith (New York: Paulist Press, 1976), pp. 187–208.
2. Erik Erikson, *Identity: Youth and Crisis* (New York: Norton, 1968), pp. 128–135
3. Herbert R. Adams, *The Church and Popular Education* (Baltimore: Johns Hopkins Press, 1900), pp. 17–18.
4. The following discussion is based on the AASA (American Association of School Administrators) monograph *Religion in the Public Schools* (New York: Harper & Row, 1964).
5. Quoted in ibid, pp. 17–18.
6. Quoted in ibid., p. 19.
7. Andrew Greeley, William McCready, and Kathleen McCourt, *Catholic Schools in a Declining Church* (Kansas City, Mo.: Sheed & Ward, 1976), pp. 9–10.
8. Andrew Greeley and Peter Rossi, *The Education of Catholic Americans* (Chicago: Aldine, 1966).
9. Greeley, et al., op. cit. (1976), Chapter 6.
10. *New York Times,* April 28, 1978.
11. "Have You Heard of the Four Spiritual Laws?," tract produced by Campus Crusade for Christ, Inc., 1965.
12. For more information on the Christian Endeavor Society, see Francis E. Clark, *The Christian Endeavor Manual* (Boston: United Society for Christian Endeavor, 1925).
13. See Barbara Hargrove, "Church Student Ministries and the New Consciousness," in *The New Religious Consciousness,* ed. by Charles Glock and Robert Bellah (Berkeley: University of California Press, 1976), pp. 205–226
14. Kenneth Underwood, ed., *The Church, the University, and Social Policy* (Middletown, Conn.: Wesleyan University Press, 1967).
15. See Parker Palmer, "Selections from Review of Danforth Campus Ministry Fellowships," *CSCW Report* 32, no. 2 (March 1974).
16. David Caplovitz and Fred Sherrow, *The Religious Drop-outs: Apostasy Among College Students* (New York: Russell Sage, 1977) is a good review of this phenomenon.
17. See, for example, Phillip E. Hammond and Robert E. Mitchell, "Segmentation of Radicalism—the Case of the Protestant Campus Minister," *American Journal of Sociology* 71, no. 2 (September 1965): 133–143.

11

Politics and Government

There are two main ways in which the interrelationship of religious and political institutions in modern society may be traced. The first, which we have mentioned in connection with folk or civil religion, lies in the area of religion's function in stating, justifying, and reinforcing the values of the society. These values then are translated into political behavior, as well as attitudes toward the laws that govern the society, its goals, and its self-image. Political behavior includes not only voting and participating in political campaigns in a democracy, but also any form of behavior that relates the individual to the government—obedience or disobedience to the law, the formation of groups and coalitions to promote special interests, payment or nonpayment of taxes, voicing support or protest, and the like.

The second way in which religion is related to politics is as an institution that serves as an interest group, exerting its powers of persuasion in the decision-making process. There are many ideological battles within religious organizations as to the relative merit of direct institutional action in politics and the occasions when it is appropriate, but the facts are clear that such action does exist.

The action, direct or indirect, that religious groups take in the political life of the society is based upon two factors: the ideology of the religion and the objective circumstances of its adherents. In turn, these factors affect one another. A religious group that is otherworldly in its focus is likely to affect political life through the passivity and noninvolvement of its members. If this kind of religion is dominant in a society, then a small group of leaders may be expected to be in power—and to remain there. At the same time, this kind of religion is most likely to occur among those who have little hope of exercising political power. In fact, as we have seen earlier, religious sects have arisen most often among the deprived, including those deprived of political and economic power. It has been common in history that under such conditions of deprivation, people who have reason to believe they can exert power in the political area will form political organizations. It is those who do not have such a hope who turn to religious sects—and often otherworldly religions—as a solace. In these cases the condition of powerlessness results in religious behavior that makes the condition more tolerable psychologically while increasing it sociologically.

The kind of sect that Weber called inner-worldly is less likely to withdraw from the political scene. In fact, in the tradition of the ethical prophet, members of such sects may see themselves as instruments in the hand of God, charged with setting right those things in the political realm that do not meet their approval or are opposed to their goals.

Much of what we see in the religiopolitical realm, however, is better understood as churchlike rather than sectlike behavior. This is a particularly confusing sort of designation in the context of American political life, because the established pattern of religion (so in that sense the established religion) is composed of a large number of competing and cooperating groups, many of which were originally sects. If it is assumed, as it usually is, that the religion of a society reflects the nature and self-image of that society, then it may be appropriate that American religion is so clearly pluralistic. At the same time, religion's focus upon ultimate values causes each group to have certain feelings about being the one right religious form, so that competition does continue, and this again may help to reinforce basic American assumptions about the competitive nature of human existence.

The type and amount of political activity to be found in any of these religious groups varies according to at least three kinds of characteristics: social characteristics, historical experience, and ideology.[1] First, different religious groups often vary greatly as to their social characteristics—socioeconomic, ethnic, or geographic. The types of services and ways of looking at the world offered by different religious groups tend to attract people of similar background, and this is reinforced by the interaction people find in their religious group. Many religious groups had their origin in the home country of immigrants, and they tend to reinforce ethnic cultural distinctions. Geographic differences in the United States are based on these and historic factors; and the fact that there are definite areas of concentration of particular religious groups becomes important in political decision making in those areas and in the country at large. Traditionally, areas of particular concentration have included:

1. Mormons in Utah and some counties of neighboring states, where a clear majority is held by members of this one group.[2]

2. Lutherans in two-thirds of North Dakota's counties, as well as Nebraska and South Dakota. In Minnesota and Wisconsin every county is predominantly Lutheran or Catholic.
3. Baptists in the South. Even when black Baptists are not counted because of their different stance on many political issues, this denomination still prevails in most Southern states.
4. Catholics in Louisiana, the valley of Texas, most of New Mexico, Arizona, California, and most New England states.[3] (This designation in New Mexico, Arizona, and California is undergoing considerable dilution with the massive population increase brought about by internal migration to the "sun belt.")

The interaction of local needs and assumptions with the patterns of religious thought and action produces pluralistic results even within religious denominations. The political stance of New England urban Catholics is not likely to be the same as that of Spanish-speaking Catholics in the Southwest on every issue, regardless of any Protestant fears of the monolithic power of Rome.

A second factor of variability is that of historical experience. Religious groups which, from their social characteristics or ideology, would be expected to behave similarly in the political arena may have become accustomed to different sorts of actions. Any religious group that is locally dominant is likely to find itself thrust into political activity, and few make the choice taken by Pennsylvania's early Quakers to remove themselves from politics rather than compromise their ideals. At the opposite pole, groups whose tradition is churchlike, such as Catholics, Lutherans, or Episcopalians, may find themselves taking sectlike positions in political action because of their local status as minority groups. Members of that numerous and typically American denomination, the Methodists, respond like persecuted sectarians in the small towns of Utah where Mormon power is overwhelming.

Finally, then, the particular ideology of the group determines its action toward politics. Traditionally such denominations as Baptists and Methodists have felt called into action in the political life of the community or the nation to fight against such alleged evils as liquor and gambling. Catholics, in turn, have been moved to action particularly against divorce or birth control and, more recently, abortion. The appropriate moment and subject for political action is governed by the specific religious values of the group.

In large measure, however, the political influence of a religious group is felt not so much through specific directives as through the associations formed within the group. The bonds of religious fellowship influence people to vote for their coreligionists and so support their platforms. The value orientations taught in church schools and from the pulpit are applied to the political decision-making process just as they are applied to individual moral and ethical decisions. The specific teachings of the church are reinforced by close associates in the church fellowship.[4] Lenski, in *The Religious Factor,* saw religion influencing subcultures that he called socioreligious groups and in turn membership in the subculture influencing political behavior.

An example of these forces in operation has been shown by Fenton, who in one study discussed the effect of Catholic church membership in particular parishes of Louisiana as a factor in black voter registration. Northern Louisiana, largely Protestant, showed a far lower percentage of blacks registered than did southern counties, which were predominantly Catholic. These differences remained significant even when the amount of urbanization of the area and the percentage of blacks in the local population were held constant. One direct reason given for this difference was that although Catholics in Louisiana were not eager supporters of integration, their bishop had denounced segregation as a sin. Consequently, some moral conflict existed among Catholics on the issue which was probably not reinforced in this way by the Protestant churches of that time and place. Ideologically, then, the church may have had some effect. Its previous activities also may have had a good deal to bear on the situation, since black Catholics had been attending parochial schools probably more geared to preparing them for political (and social) participation than black public schools. In this case, giving blacks greater political power probably was conceived as less a threat in the predominantly Catholic counties. This also, then, was a church-related phenomenon. At the same time, other factors totally unrelated to religion were in operation. Chief of these was the fact that the economy of the northern counties was predicated on a high rate of farm tenancy, a sort of plantation economy which could not be maintained unless the blacks were "kept in their place." In spite of such economic factors, however, there seemed to be clear evidence that religion did influence the attitudes and actions of Louisianans in regard to black civil rights.[5]

There appear to be many confusing results in studies seeking the effect of religion on political attitudes and behavior. Lipset sees one cause of this confusion in the fact that religion serves more than one function for its adherents. The religious group is a source of beliefs, including political beliefs. It is also a determinant of social status and may be adhered to as a sign of social standing. For example, many blue-collar members of such denominations as the Congregational, Episcopal, or Presbyterian express voting preferences more in line with their church preference than their current socioeconomic position. When the working-class vote is inclined to be classified as "liberal," these church members may vote "conservative." Yet many members of reasonably high status churches, whose social and economic positions would indicate a vote for the status quo, may support liberal changes in the society. This may be because their high standards of qualification for leadership expose them to ministers trained in large and prestigious universities, where liberal humanism provides the motivation for working in favor of change.[6]

Benton Johnson has documented the fact that, particularly in denominations large enough to be diverse, it is theology rather than denomination that is a predictor of political preference. In a study of Protestant clergy, he found a strong relationship between fundamentalist and conservative theology and Republican party preference, with liberal and neo-orthodox pastors tending to be Democrats, particularly among the young clergy.[7] This difference held when tested for attitudes on particular public issues, to the point that Johnson suggested that the liberal-conservative split in theology denotes two separate religious subcultures.[8]

In comparing lay responses to public issues in two sections of the country, Johnson was also able to demonstrate the effect of cross-pressures from social class and religion. Thus he reasoned that religion was one force shaping political attitude, to be reckoned along with several others.[9] It becomes clear that it is much too simplistic to assume that voting behavior can be predicted on the basis of denomination alone or even on the theological tendencies of the local congregation. Except in cases where the subject of political action is one specifically and strongly tied to the ideology of the group, there is little possibility of predicting the vote of a specific religious group. Most studies show patterns similar to that noted by Kohut and Stookey in a survey on opinions about the Viet Nam war. They said that while some effect of religious affiliation could be noted here and there, in general, differences in opinion about the war were more closely related to other demographic variables—education, race, geographic region, and the like—than to religion.[10]

Hoge has noted that church members may be influenced by religious values, but only when they do not conflict with the "Big Three"—their primary commitments to family, career, and life-style (with health as a fourth where it is a problem).[11] Only those groups that have been able to inspire among their members a *primary* commitment to religious values—and they tend to be few and small—can expect adherence to those values contrary to the people's own good as measured by the Big

Three. Even the greater commitment of black church members to political action can be seen in this light.

While church leaders seldom can "deliver the vote" of their members, they are not without effect in the political scene. America's "establishment" of a diversity of voluntary religious associations lives in a "friendly alliance" with the state. There are at least four specific ways in which this is written into the structure of the society. The first of these is the tax exemption allowed church property, as well as the right of citizens to deduct contributions to the church from their income tax returns. Opponents of civil religion see this as an indication of the churches' bondage to the state, since the assumption underlying such exemptions must be that the church is providing something of worth to the state. This, say the critics, limits the freedom of the church to fulfill a prophetic role by speaking out against the state if it is violating religious principles.[12] In recent years a number of churches have begun making direct payments to local governments "in lieu of taxes," partly to relieve this anxiety and also in recognition of services they receive, such as fire protection, at the expense of taxpayers.

The second and third forms of alliance between church and state reinforce the suspicions of those who reject such cooperation. They are the exemption from military service of clergy, seminarians, and conscientious objectors on the one hand and the provision by churches of chaplains for such governmental installations as prisons and military units on the other. Critics see the latter as a payoff for the former, where the churches in essence sanction the government's various arms in return for particular favors. Again, Pfeffer says that individuals are free to say that God is not on our side (or anyone's), but the church under such circumstances is not that free.[13]

Finally, the church is allied with the state through tax-supported financial assistance of church-sponsored social agencies. Here the services rendered seem both a public good and free from undue government coercion, but even here governmental rules may limit the use to which the funds may be put and so influence the actions of the churches.[14] As we shall see later, such programs have also pulled church people into heavier involvement with the political process than they might even wish, as they engage in lobbying for increases of funding or improvement of programs.

The controversy over church-state cooperation points up what Yinger has referred to as "the dilemma of the churches." Particularly in relation to political institutions, churches often find themselves caught between their religious teachings on the one hand and powerful interests of their clientele on the other. They are forced to choose between maintaining an ideologically pure point of view, and losing their adherents in the process, or compromising their ideal while trying to move the society a little closer to it. The social background of the members is usually the key to the decision between these two paths. To remain pure means to withdraw from active participation in the social structure and is really open only to those who are not in positions of responsibility in the society. It is a sectarian response. The churchlike response is to compromise and retain influence, and a group whose members tend to be influential usually chooses this route.[15]

Yet in America even this picture is clouded by the sectarian history of many church groups and the pluralistic influence they have. The compromise often occurs only within part of the ideology of the group, while certain emphasized areas are dealt with in pure form. Thus each group may act as a pressure group for its particular interest, while maintaining a more neutral point of view in other areas. In this way the American model of separation of church and state sets up the conditions for church influence on the government. By contrast, in Europe, where separation of church and state generally took the route of disestablishment of some particular church, the result frequently has been an alienation that has been blamed for permitting the rise of totalitarian government unchecked by religious counter-pressures.[16]

The American experience has produced five recognizably different, though not mutually exclusive, approaches to church-state relations: one whose background is rooted in the Lutheran tradition, a second stemming from the Anabaptist-Mennonite experience, a third from the Quakers, and finally two more general approaches, the separationist and the transformist.

In the Lutheran concept of church and state, both orders signify God's activity in the world. It is the function of the church to offer salvation to people who are sinful in their present state. It is up to the state to control and restrain the unregenerate. Christians who participate in the political order do so out of love, in service to their fellows. Given this view of the functions of government, it becomes possible to sanction war as a necessary evil which will help rulers carry out their divine commission of providing a proper, stable framework of order for the people. At the same time, civil disorder is not condoned because it strikes at the roots of that framework. Christians under an unjust ruler should accept their suffering and wait for God to punish the ruler. Yet the church does have a role to play over against the state. It must make sure that the state does not interfere with spiritual authorities, and it must admonish the unjust ruler out of love for humankind. Resistance to injustice, however, must be passive and nonviolent. While this view has had some strong criticism, especially in view of the response of the German churches to Nazi atrocities, this kind of orientation has prevailed in a significant segment of the American population and is not limited to members of formal Lutheran bodies.

The Anabaptist-Mennonite tradition is a near opposite, based as it is on total separation of church and state. This is the classic sectlike approach, with a theology that sees the church as a fellowship of the redeemed, separated out from the corrupt society. The genius of this group is its distinctive style of life, which is reinforced by many boundary-maintaining activities such as distinctive modes of dress, speech, or behavior. Church members in this tradition may refuse to take an oath or swear allegiance, since the Bible states that Christians should not swear by anything, and their allegiance is only to God. They will not hold office because the duties of such a role might force one to compromise religious ideals. They will not fight in wars, for they deny the state's right to exercise powers of life and death over anyone. Only God is to have that right. They will, however, pay taxes and pray for those in office, recognizing that secular government maintains the surroundings in which they can practice their style of life. In the face of persecution they offer nonresistance. Perhaps the most noticeable effect of this tradition has been in the area of conscientious objection to the military service. In World War I there was little public tolerance of those who refused to answer the draft call. But since a high proportion of people in the Mennonite tradition have settled in agricultural areas, and farmers in that war were generally excused from military service, many were not faced with the problem. The same was true to a lesser extent in World War II, but during that conflict nearly ten thousand Mennonites were called. Variations among groups in their adherence to the tradition show clearly in their response to the draft call. Overall, 46.2 percent performed various kinds of alternate service, and 53.8 percent served in the armed forces. However, 100 percent of the Old Order Mennonites and 93.5 percent of the Old Order Amish registered conscientious objection. These groups will register for the draft but will not support war even by service in the medical corps or the Red Cross. Their stand was legitimated by the government during World War II to the extent that they were allowed to set up their own Civilian Public Service program —at a cost of over three million dollars to the churches. Recently the Mennonite position has undergone some change as pressures have arisen to become involved in politics in order to serve humankind. As we shall see in more detail later, Mennonite groups have worked with other pacifist organizations on behalf of conscientious objectors. Yet Sanders found that, at least in the eastern portion of the country, Mennonites were becoming less involved, more opposed to voting or other political participation. In general, their emphasis has been on doing justice rather than seeking it, and they choose to do it personally more often than through the structures of government.

The other view of church and state that is linked to a specific tradition is that of the Quakers. This tradition has gone through a number of radical changes, from a belief in a theocratic government dominated by the religion to a period of quietism and withdrawal not unlike that of the Mennonites to a policy of involvement in a limited area. At the present time, the political influence of the Quakers is greater than their numbers would warrant, mostly because they do concentrate their efforts in areas of particular value of their ideology. The principal focus of Quaker activity in this century has been in the areas of peace and civil liberties. They hold to philosophical principles shared by liberals in many other denominations: that people are not totally ruled by self-interest and are amenable to appeals to their better nature, and that moral individuals can indeed influence national policy. In keeping with these principles, they have organized two agencies that have political influence, the American Friends Service Committee and the Friends Committee on National Legislation. The latter is more directly related to political action, serving as an interest group primarily in the area of the treatment of conscientious objectors to the draft. The AFSC has since its inception in 1917 served as a center for information and action in matters of worldwide relief for persons suffering from military and social injustice. It has run afoul of the American government more than once, in such activities as shipping medicine and first aid supplies to North Vietnam during that conflict. In fact, Sanders found that the Quakers' major contribution has been this continued loyalty to a truly Protestant style, where for religious reasons they may feel that both God and the state are best served by disobedience or resistance.

The two more general views of church-state relations, separationists and transformationists, are named from categories outlined by H. R. Niebuhr.[17] The separationism in this category differs from the radical separateness of the Mennonites in being based more on political or pragmatic than theological reasons. Sanders found three sources of this view. The first, the millenarian, expects the imminent return of Christ and the establishment of the Kingdom of God on earth. Followers of this view are involved in banding together in small groups which may proliferate into a growing segment of the society actively preparing to reign in the new order. They have no call to participate in the present, doomed order. In addition to those sectarian groups usually put in this category, such as the Jehovah's Witnesses, it may be noted that those strains of fundamentalism that stress a "premillenial" doctrine of the end times are pushed in this direction, and that those segments of the Jesus movement that are most attuned to this type of apocalypticism clearly fit the model. In addition, a number of other groups arising out of the counterculture whose ideology is not Christian but rather politically anarchist seem to fit this category. A second separationist stance comes form the tradition begun in this country by Roger Williams, in which it is understood that the duty of government toward religion is simply to provide a situation in which all religious forms may be freely practiced. No interference or interaction between the two institutions is to be countenanced. A third separationist stance is particularly prominent among evangelical Protestants, whose focus is on individual religious experience freely expressed, but this type has its proponents among most groups in certain areas of the country. It is mirrored to some extent, also, in those secular groups that have become substitutes for religion for some people, and it is expressed in the political programs of those who advocate no government interference with the use of drugs for the purposes of attaining what is described as a religious high. Traditionally, controversies over the separation of church and state have arisen over such subjects as nuns teaching in public schools, Sunday closing laws, the censorship of books and movies by religious groups, Bible reading and prayers in the public schools, laws forbidding the distribution of birth control or abortion information, and a number of other issues. A strong focus for political activity in the cause of the separation has been Protestants and Other Americans United for the Separation of the Church and State (POAU), which has engaged in lobbying and other political activity. This group in the past tended to be strongly anti-Catholic, fearful that the nondemocratic tradition of Catholicism could provide an irresistible pressure group promoting Catholic values. However, over time it has become less Protestant and more favorable to "other Americans," so that the attraction it has for evangelicals has not resulted in consistent pressure for their particular causes.

Many of the court cases involving religion have been within the separationist model. The record of the courts, including the Supreme Court, on these matters has not always been consistent. We have seen this in the area of public education, where within three years the Supreme Court reversed itself on the right of public schools to demand that students say the pledge to the flag (the *Gobitis* and *Barnette* cases). A similar lack of clarity can be found in early cases dealing with the Mormons. In 1870, in *Reynolds* v. *the United States,* the Court unanimously ruled that while Mormons were free to *believe* anything they wanted to about the propriety of plural marriage, their *actions* must stay within the laws of the state. The principle on which the ruling was based was that of action rather than belief. In *Davis* v. *Beason,* however, when a Mormon challenged an Idaho law requiring that in order to vote a person must swear he or she was not a member of a group that teaches, counsels, or encourages polygamy, the Court used the *Reynolds* case as a precedent to uphold the discriminatory law, even though no action of polygamous marriage was indicated.[18] One may question whether the Court was ruled more by strict legal considerations or by a widespread revulsion in the society of that time to the Mormon practice of plural marriage. Certainly news stories and novels of the period indicate that the popular conception of Mormons was a picture of licentious old men carrying off young virgins to a life of white slavery under the guise of religious principle. Inaccurate as this picture was, it may well have been the context within which the Court decisions were made.

The same sort of criticism has been leveled at the Supreme Court for its stand on Sunday closing laws. It admits that such laws were originally promulgated for religious reasons but says they now serve secular purposes. The appeals of those who for religious reasons are enjoined from working on a day other than Sunday, and who must consequently compete in a five-day week with Christians who work a six-day week, are not heeded. The states are left free to pass Sunday closing laws if they choose to do so. In much of the country secularization has resulted in ignoring or revoking Sunday closing laws, but in many states they remain on the books, to be invoked on occasion against unpopular groups or businesses—and to be upheld by the courts.[19]

A clear example of judicial action that breaches the wall of separation between church and state is the ruling of the Supreme Court on the disposition of St. Nicholas Cathedral in New York. In 1948, in response to pleas from local churches of Russian Orthodox background, the state of New York set up the legal machinery whereby these churches could organize into a denomination separate from the authority of the patriarchate in Moscow, much as the Russian church had done earlier in breaking off from Constantinople. The Orthodox Church in North America then placed a bishop in St. Nicholas Cathedral, whose right to be there was contested by the bishop appointed by Moscow. The Supreme Court, taking as its precedent an 1821 Presbyterian case in which it was ruled that the higher judicatory had precedence, ruled in favor of the Russian synod and patriarchate.[20]

It may have been the controversy aroused by this decision in the field of church authority that caused the Supreme Court to refuse to hear a few years later a Presbyterian case that would appear to fall directly under that 1821 precedent. In this case, local congregations in Georgia sought to leave their denomination, taking with them the church properties that under Presbyterian law belonged to the denomination. The local jury, strongly influenced by the congregational polity of the Baptist denomination that dominates that area, awarded the land to the dissident congregations, in spite of the claims held by higher judicatories. By refusing to hear the issue, the Supreme Court avoided the possibility of reversing the lower court's decision, which the 1821 precedent probably would have required.

Clearly, the record of separation of church and state, whether in legislation or in the courts, is fraught with inconsistencies. Public opinion seems particularly potent in decision making in this area, probably because it tends to be one that is delicate and emotion laden. Whenever possible, potentially religious questions are treated under the rubric of other factors in the case, so that decisions about religion need not be made. The Jehovah's Witnesses, for example, have been taken into court a number of times because of their proselyting methods. Their distribution and sale of books and handbills, and such activities as the operation of a sound truck, have been supported by the Supreme Court under the rubric of freedom of speech and of the press, rather than that of religious liberty.[21] At the present time, similar issues are being raised by a number of the new religious groups, who have been taken to court for public soliciting of funds, usually on the basis that they have not made it clear what group they serve. A more serious test of the judicial system seems to be in the making at the present time, as recruitment methods of some of the new groups are being accused of being "brainwashing" and countermethods of "deprogrammers" also attacked as forms of coercion. In these cases, as in the older ones, the fact that these groups are taken to courts of law at all indicates that stated religious freedom for all religious sects does not eliminate social harrassment of those that are unpopular. The separation of church and state, with its guarantees of religious liberty, simply puts legal limits on the amount of social pressure that can be applied to deviant religions. These limits, in many cases, are not clear and absolute but could best be described as ameliorating forces that check the potential excesses of religiosocial conflict.

The final Protestant form of church-state relations is transformationist—what religionists often refer to as the "prophetic ministry of the church." In this view of the matter, state influence on the church is expected to be minimal, so that the church may be free to take a critical stand against the state in the name of the higher values it claims. Based on Calvinist views of the nature of the state, this approach is most recognizable in its involvement in politics on behalf of reform or the improvement of the society.

Much of this kind of action can be encountered in local affairs throughout the history of American churches. Ministers have often taken the lead in causes of community betterment, whether these have involved the prohibition of saloons and bawdyhouses, clean-up/paint-up/fix-up campaigns, social gatherings aimed at fostering goodwill, or the rights and needs of the poor and downtrodden. It is from this tradition that the Social Gospel developed and that more recent activities in the area of civil rights and peace arose. It is this tradition that developed the idea of churches as political pressure groups. Separationists may involve themselves in politics as "self-interest interest groups" (a phrase of Leo Pfeffer's) in insuring the continued separation of church and state and the maintenance of church strength; transformationists become political primarily as ideological or reform groups. The size of this task and its smaller degree of relationship to individual denominational concerns has led to an ecumenical, cooperative inclination among transformation-minded groups. The organization of the Federal Council of Churches and its later development into the National Council of Churches, with membership in the World Council of Churches and other broad-based organizations, are examples of formal cooperation in the cause of transforming the society. Local councils of churches and informal alliances may also be noted.

The ideological base of transformationist action has been well delineated by Bennett in a statement of the "Biblical basis for Christian citizenship." Points in this base include (1) a faith in God as Lord of history; (2) recognition of the commandment of love as a call to act to improve the conditions of life for others; (3) a call to repentance—to transform what can be changed for one's neighbors' sake; (4) a Christian understanding of sin which recognizes that anyone will pursue personal or in-group interests unless those interests are countered by others—that no person can be trusted to run the society for the benefit of all; and (5) a recognition of one's neighbor as a whole person in the context of the community, so that action will be taken in this broader frame of reference.[22]

Transformationist principles have resulted in lobbying activities by some church groups that are in direct opposition to the kind of church-related lobbying carried on by groups such as POAU. Within the strictures surrounding church-state separation there have been a number of loopholes, probably the greatest being that groups seeking simply to provide information or education to Congress or other governmental agencies have not been required to register as lobbyists. Under this rubric a strong church lobby has been allowed to develop without much public recognition, one that covers a rather wide spectrum of religious groups. In 1970 Adams identified nine permanent and relatively powerful church groups engaged in lobbying in Washington: the United Methodists, whose General Board of Christian Concerns continued a presence begun in early work against alcoholic beverages; the National Council of Churches, which represents mainstream American Protestantism; the National Association of Evangelicals, who recognize that some sins in the nation have to be dealt with at the legislative level; the United Presbyterian Church in the U.S.A., with a history of political involvement; the Lutheran Council, representing major Lutheran bodies in the U.S.; the Church of the Brethren, whose concern for peace has inspired consistent lobbying; Reform Jews, represented by the Union of American Hebrew Congregations and the Central Conference of American Rabbis; the Unitarian-Universalists; and the U.S. Catholic Conference.[23] He failed to name those black denominations, perhaps most particularly the AME Zion churches, that have also maintained consistent lobbies. Other groups less tied to specific church bodies that have been active in the past two decades in the name of religion have included the Southern Christian Leadership Conference, first headed by Martin Luther King and active in civil rights matters; and Clergy and Laity Concerned, a title originally completed with the words, "About the Viet Nam War."

Church political activity peaked in the 1960s with at least three issues on which a majority of transformationist groups could agree and act in concord. The first of these was the civil rights movement, where the moral dimensions of discrimination and segregation became religious issues. Church groups became visible both in lobbying on this matter and also through their participation in sit-ins, freedom rides, voter registration drives, marches, and demonstrations. Joint involvement in these endeavors served two functions at least: (1) in some cases these demonstrations of religious concern in segments of the society usually respected by politicians proved persuasive, and thus were effective; and (2) sharing both the efforts and the new sense of power across lines of denomination, region, and race gave an experience of religious unity to the participants that had lasting effects on interchurch—and interfaith —relations.

The second major issue of the 1960s was the War on Poverty. In this case not only did the moral fervor of the civil rights struggle extend to cover this area, but it also held out the opportunity of church-related agencies to be conduits of public money to the poverty stricken. The Office of Economic Opportunity was designed to bypass existing political channels, which were perceived to have been self-serving vehicles for people in power and unlikely to be responsive to the powerless poor.

While laws called for "maximum feasible participation" of the poor in programs for their rehabilitation, the lack of political skill and powerful contacts that plagues the poor made it necessary—or so it seemed—for them to be assisted by people of higher status but of proven goodwill. Who else but the churches? They had the organizations, the buildings, and the contacts. In many cases church groups not only formed and administered poverty agencies but also served as informants to the national officials about violations of civil rights or misdirection of poverty funds on the part of local officials. A more detailed survey of some of these activities will be undertaken in the following chapter. Here it will suffice to say that the War on Poverty helped to involve churches in the political system both at the level of influencing the government to take action against poverty and as indirect recipients of governmental funding for antipoverty action. One of the dangers of such action was pointed out by Adams at the end of that decade:

> The prevailing attitude that if government has money which the church can use, then damn the theology and the constitution and full speed ahead, is a religious shortcut with long-run implications. The idiom of Utopia is not the language of the church. And church leaders should be wary of politicians espousing noble but unrealizable goals. Confusing the Great Society with the millenium was both poor theology and poor politics.[24]

The third issue of the 1960s, of course, was the Viet Nam war, and again both lobbying and participating in public demonstrations became common activities in some church groups. While this became a source of serious internal friction in the churches, it is usually conceded that religious groups helped to increase the unpopularity of that war.

By the end of the decade, political activity at upper levels of church bureaucracies had brought about considerable disaffection among those members for whom the changes being promoted were most likely to threaten the "Big Three" of career, family, and life-style. When the 1968 election went to a Republican administration that began systematically to dismantle the War on Poverty, transformationist religion could not muster the power to prevent it. And when eventually the unpopular war in Viet Nam was "wound down," that unifying cause ceased to exist. Instead, the transformationist causes of the 1970s have been issues upon which the primary forces of the 1960s religious lobby were not in clear agreement: issues such as abortion, Gay rights, the Equal Rights Amendment, capital punishment, selective boycotts against certain manufacturers or employers. Here again the "Big Three" may be seen as an issue, since the first three could be understood to be a threat to the family and the last three a potential threat to a middle-class life-style.

Nonetheless, long-term political activity continues to go on, including lobbying in the nation's capitol and in those of the various states. Methods frequently used include helping to draft platforms on those rare occasions when their interests are considered salient enough that they should be consulted. More regularly, they watch legislation in order to alert their constituencies when action involving their interests is imminent, make friends in Congress, assist in drafting legislation, furnish information to legislators, and work with congressional committees. They keep records of legislators' attitudes and votes, apply pressure directly or indirectly on legislators, work with administrators of programs that are set up to reach goals they endorse, and, when possible, make direct contact with the White House staff. They also cooperatively provide educational programs, conferences, and quantities of publications. They have lobbied for benefits to particular groups whose causes have seemed worthwhile, working in such areas as fair labor standards and employment practices, health, housing, social security, the immigration of displaced persons, and the abolition of the poll tax. Broader measures such as liquor advertising, child research, compulsory military training, trade agreements with other nations, and foreign aid have been addressed by these lobbies.[25]

While the five styles of relating to government discussed above were applied primarily to Protestant traditions, their overlap with Catholic action has also become evident. At the same time, it may be useful to examine in some detail the particular contribution American Catholicism has made to church-state relations. In general, Catholic attitudes toward the relationship of church and state are similar to the transformationist stance. Essentially, this is a churchlike position and so one natural to Catholicism's historic style. Catholic theory of church and state is based upon three principles: the primacy of spiritual over temporal affairs, the necessary freedom of the church, and the need for cooperation between church and state.[26] Catholic orientations toward church-state cooperation have brought reactions from rigid separationists that include explicit anti-Catholic biases. Criticism of Catholic political action by such organizations as POAU follow about the same format as that laid down by Blanshard in his influential book *American Freedom and Catholic Power.*[27] In it he stated that the structure of the Catholic church was authoritarian and antidemocratic, and that it tried to force its will on the American public by requiring Catholic parents to send their children to parochial rather than public schools and by working for laws that would enforce their view of birth control, marriage, and medicine (particularly concerning abortion and obstetrics). He also accused the Catholic church of limiting American rights of free speech through the censorship of books and movies.[28]

The actual behavior of the Catholic church in American political issues is, as we have seen, more nearly like that of the transformationist Protestants, and frequently cooperative with them. Though their ideology may allow greater cooperation between church and state than that of most Protestant churches, their position as one denomination among many in American society results in typical American churchlike behavior from Catholic leaders. If there is any qualitative difference in effect, it is based on politicians' perception of Catholic unity more than the specific activities of the denomination. The hierarchical organization of the Catholic church and the greater opportunities for Catholic socialization in parochial schools, as well as the manifest ethnic unity of some Catholic groups, has led to the assumption that the hierarchy can indeed speak for Catholic voters and "deliver the vote." However, this impression is diminishing as, since Vatican II, audible dissent within the church is a recognized phenomenon.

Ebersole found three factors relevant to the analysis of Catholic lobbying. The first was the length of time a consistent Catholic presence had been felt in Washington. Two main Catholic agencies, the National Catholic Welfare Conference and the Catholic Action Studies Department, had been there since 1910 and 1917 respectively, and the result had been to give Catholic lobbyists contacts of long standing. A second factor was the presence of Catholic lay people in government. Given the greater clarity of Catholic positions on some issues, Catholic legislators might be expected to work for Catholic goals as part of their political values, with greater unanimity than could be expected of Protestants with the same level of commitment to their religion but less clarity as to its relevance to the issue at hand. The third factor concerned the great involvement of Catholic lobbyists with administrative agencies and their push to have Catholic representation on boards and advisory councils.[29] There is some division among observers of these phenomena as to whether Catholic emphasis on participation in such areas is based on a churchlike desire to dominate the society or the sectlike assertiveness of a minority group that feels pressed to make its interest heard against the threat of a dominant majority.

Certainly such explicit efforts to be heard in the various channels of government may be seen as efforts to counter the kind of informal influence felt in the face of such occurrences as the close relationship between Richard Nixon and evangelist Billy Graham, the explicitness of Jimmy Carter's Southern Baptist background, or the participation of presidents and legislators in prayer breakfasts that are part of an evangelical religious style even when they encourage the participation of those whose background is quite different.

Jewish participation in American politics is in some ways even more defensive. Jews have been prominent as one group of "other Americans" in POAU working to keep government out of religious affairs. Probably the most active Jewish group in this field is the Anti-Defamation League of B'nai B'rith, which is most concerned with educating the public against anti-Semitism. Jewish influence in politics is generally liberal and international in viewpoint. Ideologically, Judaism tends to be less otherworldly than some of Christianity, and the emphasis on learning and justice in Judaism inclines its adherents' political values toward transformationism. At the same time, the minority status of Judaism affects a strong separationist view of church and state in a predominantly Christian society.

In recent years the relation of American Judaism to the "Israel lobby" has been of particular interest. The status of Jewish people as patriotic American citizens does not prevent their attachment to Israel as their homeland. There are dissenting voices in the Jewish community, but most are strongly supportive of economic and military aid to Israel and any other form of favorable contact between the two countries. The international aspects of Judaism are behind much of the cooperation between its adherents and Christian transformationists in the sphere of world affairs. Though issues involving the military defense of Israel have clouded some of the traditional cooperation between Jews and international religious pacifist organizations, they have also been involved in educational programs and lobbies whose concerns are for the relief of hunger, disease, displacement, and the like as well as international justice and human rights. Representatives of the World Council of Churches and from the Vatican also work with the United Nations Food and Agriculture Organization, offering the skills and values of the religious community to its work. Such organizations serve as disinterested agencies in making policy decisions.[30]

Not all religious involvement in foreign affairs has been disinterested, however. In general terms, religion has often served as a source of loyalty and hence as a sanction for political and national loyalties. It may offer sources and sanctions for conflict, but also channels of reconciliation or escape. In more specific ways, religion often becomes involved in foreign affairs because of the foreign interests of the churches. As mentioned above, Zionism in the American Jewish community is a powerful influence in the activities of the United States vis-à-vis Israel. Christian missionaries have become involved at times through direct participation in the work of the American diplomatic corps and have recently been revealed as occasional informants for the CIA as well. Often special treaties have been drawn up that specifically protect missionaries, and always in the case of civil strife or the outbreak of war missionaries are among the American nationals who must be protected or evacuated. Activities of American missionaries have effects on public opinion at home and abroad. For a considerable segment of the populace, reports from missionaries serve as their most direct link with foreign areas, so that missionary education is a fairly strong source of opinion on foreign relations. Perceptions of persons of other nationalities as hostile pagans, childlike converts, or fellow Christians lie behind many political opinions. Overseas, missionary activity in many areas has encouraged the new nationalism, either by providing the education that results in national self-awareness or by serving as symbols of paternalism and colonialism against which nationalist sentiment could be mobilized. In some cases they seem to have done both. Information through religious channels is often the only form of contact between persecuted minorities in some countries and the outside world, and many of the international campaigns for human rights depend on church channels for information as well as zeal for the cause of the oppressed.

Few church lobbies are as strong as the membership of the churches would indicate. Particularly in the case of the Protestant churches, lawmakers recognize the existence of an "opinion gap" between church leaders and many of their lay members. American Protestants, to a large extent, have become a suburban people in an urban society and have removed themselves from the problems and influences that affect those in decision-making centers. Individualistic emphases in much of Protestant theology reinforce this sort of isolation. While the churches provide massive educational programs to make up for this "gap," they are only partially successful in mobilizing lay opinion behind the leadership. They have been somewhat successful in reaching ministerial students, where seminary curricula may include courses in political thought, foreign policy, and the like. However, one consequence of this method of appeal is an increase in the differences of attitude and perceptions of ministers and their congregations. Activities such as ministerial participation in civil rights marches and other "radical" behavior left many lay people confused and alienated; and indeed the number of clergy so involved has never been particularly high.

The efforts of transformationist churches to mobilize lay opinion have also been hampered by Protestant sectarian leaders for the political right who see the whole program as a Communist plot. Theological positions maintained by these leaders are not unlike those of more liberal churches a generation or two ago; to the isolated they may sound more orthodox. So while organizations such as Clergy and Laity Concerned were sponsoring peace rallies, clergymen such as Carl McIntire were organizing "Victory Marches" to protest any slowdown in hostilities. It becomes obvious that American Protestantism does not speak with a united voice. The disunity is within denominations as well as between them and not only in Protestantism but in all religious groups large enough to have moved out of the designation of sect.

Another and probably more important source of the lack of unanimity in the voice of the churches is the gap between what the church as an organization is promoting and the extent of that promotion on the local scene. In most congregations, political views are put forth lamely, if at all, within the formal church structure. While a large number of church members belong to denominations that would be ranked on any scale as transformationist, their attitudes and behavior speak loudly of separationist views. And while ministers in denominational meetings may speak and vote for transformational positions, at home in the pulpit they most generally cater to their perception of their congregations as unwilling to be pushed into any particular position.

In a 1968 survey of Protestant ministers, Stark found 38 percent reporting never having taken a stand from the pulpit on any political issue, and 25 percent never having given a sermon that dealt mainly with any controversial social or political topic in the past year—although it was a year of many controversies upon which church leaders had been vocal.[31] Since separatism is commonly related to theological positions generally defined as orthodox in Protestantism, it is not surprising to find a negative correlation between orthodoxy and political expressions from the pulpit. But there was also a low degree of sermonizing on political issues by ministers in such known transformational bodies as the United Church of Christ (where 20 percent said they had preached on controversial social or political issues eight or more times in the past year), Methodists (17 percent), Episcopalians (19 percent), and Presbyterians (10 percent).[32] In a 1969 study in North Carolina, Earle, Knudsen, and Shriver found few of the ministers interested in opting for a "prophetic" role, except in the black community.[33]

The explanation of such behaviors appears to lie in the dynamics of the minister's interaction with his or her congregation. While it seems obvious that for a person who chooses the ministry for a vocation religion has a great amount of salience, it may be expected to be somewhat less salient for the average lay person. Recent studies have shown that the effects of an individual's religious orientation on political activism are governed at least to some extent by the salience of religion in his or her life.[34] Lay people may belong to transformationist churches and still favor their own brand of separationism—a compartmentalizing of religion in their own lives that militates against applying its standards to other "nonreligious" compartments. Much of the comparison between lay and clergy attitudes in Hadden's *The Gathering Storm in the Churches* reinforces this view. For example, he reported that in a national sample 50 percent of the respondents from Catholic and Protestant churches agreed with the statement "Clergy should stick to religion and not concern themselves with social, economic, and political issues," with the percentage of those agreeing increasing as the frequency of church attendance decreased.[35] This attitude seems quite common among the laity; in Earle, Knudsen, and Shriver's study few white lay respondents approved clergy action in situations they labeled "prophetic," with exception of one involving working for a traffic light to provide a safe crossing for children.[36]

Faced with this attitude in their congregations, ministers whose attitudes are transformationist may take three courses of action: They may speak out on political issues in spite of their congregations, in the name of the prophetic function of religion; they may speak obliquely rather than directly to the issues, in order not to arouse resentments; or they may remain silent.[37] The consequences of the first course of action may involve being rejected as minister. In churches of congregational or presbyterian polity, this may mean the actual loss of the position in that congregation if it revokes its "call" or contract. In denominations where ministers are placed by the hierarchy, the rejection may simply come through infrequent attendance or ignoring what the minister is saying. It may mean leaving a congregation for one where the sermons will be more congenial. In nearly all cases, dissatisfied laity are likely to withdraw financial support from the church, often particularly from programs most directly related to political causes.

It is small wonder that the response of ministers to the North Carolina study mentioned above tended to be as conservative—or as cautious—as the response of their laity. Few found it necessary to take a prophetic role except in the case of a direct outgrowth of pastoral concerns, such as the safety of children.[38] Those who feel obliged to speak out about broader social issues tend at least to take the soft methods of the second alternative style: They speak in generalities that they hope their congregations will apply to the particular political issue at hand, without making applications themselves. Such nuances are generally picked up and appreciated by members of the congregation who are already activated politically, but they are seldom clear enough to break down the walls of compartmentalization built up in those who are not accustomed to applying religious values to the political arena.

Many ministers, even those vitally concerned with political issues, assume that the pulpit is not an effective place to witness to their political views. For those who take a separationist view this is no problem. Those who are transformationist in their orientation may find outlet for their frustration in the pulpit by working with other similarly situated ministers in denominational or secular political activities. Many express the hope that they may influence their congregations by their example in this way; others simply get involved as a personal response to the situation. The latter are probably more realistic. According to most studies, laity in congregations do not view political activities by the church very favorably.

In more recent research, however, Hoge has shown that many conclusions about lay reluctance to mix religion and politics are not particularly accurate. While the rhetoric may include many statements about keeping the two separate, lay respondents to Hoge's study were quite willing to take political stands on religious grounds on certain issues. In general, the crucial point was not political activity but the theological interpretation of its relevance, as well as whether that activity would enhance or threaten their life-styles, careers, or families—the "Big Three."[39]

Most of the ministers who have been particularly active in transformationist causes have not been parish ministers. They have been those involved in campus ministry or specialized staff positions, where their identification is most likely with the church as an institution rather than with a particular congregation. In this case, one may raise the question from Hoge's work about whether becoming a "prophetic voice" for the society in such positions may enhance careers, and so for these people contribute to rather than threaten the "Big Three."

It must be remembered, however, that such a cynical view can never account for the great personal cost paid by many religious leaders who have attempted to gain political influence. It is impossible to say that there were no sacrifices of career, family, or life-style among such persons as Martin Luther King, Philip and Daniel Berrigan, A. J. Muste, Dorothy Day, or the many other prophetic leaders who have indeed made a difference in the society. Such individuals will probably never compose a statistically significant portion of any population; it is the fact that their behavior flies in the face of statistical norms that makes them influential.

On the whole, then, much of the political action of the churches that can be called genuinely transformational applies to a segment of church professionals plus a relatively small core of laity for whom religion is both salient and interpreted as concerned with political issues. Since salience tends to be positively related to an orthodoxy that is negatively related to this kind of political activism, that core of laity is comparatively minute.

While the political action of committed church people probably has more import on the political scene than their numbers would indicate, it seems fairly clear that the greatest impact of religion on the thinking of the laity lies in the boundary definitions provided by religious groups to various socioreligious communities. Input from concerned members of such communities can conceivably raise the awareness of religious values in relation to various political activities. But religion is seldom central enough in such communities that the application will be made, unless the issue is one that threatens the community boundary maintenance. In most cases the ministers themselves do not make it—at least not in public.

The crosscurrents of religious values influence political life, but in multidimensional ways. American "civil religion" may be an expression of a noncontroversial common denominator of religious images which provide some unity without either denying or accepting in any meaningful way the conflicting interpretations of different religious groups. A pluralistic pattern prevents open polarization on political issues, leaving the churches to act as interest groups or to attempt to apply religious principles indirectly to individual political action. It is probable that for the majority of church members neither of these approaches carries much conscious weight. Religion remains "privatized," and politics involves public action. The two are seldom seen as relevant to one another, unless the public action has direct bearing on the private lives of church members.

Notes and References

1. A full discussion of these may be found in S. M. Lipset, "Religion and Politics in the American Past and Present," in *Religion and Social Conflict,* ed. by Robert Lee and Martin Marty (New York: Oxford University Press, 1964), pp. 71–126.
2. For an example of the importance of Mormon influence in these areas, see James T. Richardson and Sandie Wightman Fox, "Religious Affiliation as a Predictor of Voting Behavior in Abortion Reform Legislation," *Journal for the Scientific Study of Religion* 11 (1972): 347–359.
3. Franklin H. Littel, *The Church and the Body Politic* (New York: Seabury, 1969), pp. 27–28, carries a more complete list of these areas.
4. John H. Fenton, *The Catholic Vote* (New Orleans: Hauser, 1960), p. 35.

5. Ibid., pp. 41–44.

6. Lipset, op. cit., pp. 100–102.

7. Benton Johnson, "Theology and Party Preference Among Protestant Clergymen," *American Sociological Review* 32, no. 2 (April 1966): 200–208.

8. Benton Johnson, "Theology and the Position of Pastors on Public Issues," *American Sociological Review* 32, no. 3 (June 1967): 433–442.

9. Benton Johnson, "Ascetic Protestantism and Political Preference in the Deep South," *American Journal of Sociology* 69, no. 4 (Jan., 1964): 359–366.

10. Andrew Kohut and Lawrence H. Stookey, "Religious Affiliation and Attitude Toward Viet Nam," *Theology Today* 26 (Jan., 1970): 470.

11. Dean Hoge, *Division in the Protestant House* (Philadelphia: Westminster, 1976), pp. 99–102.

12. A full statement of this point of view may be found in Leo Pfeffer, *Creeds in Competition* (New York: Harper, 1961).

13. As presented in a panel on "Caesar and His Godly Friends" at the meeting of the Society for the Scientific Study of Religion, New York, Oct. 22, 1970.

14. Robert F. Drinan, *Religion, the Courts, and Public Policy* (New York: McGraw-Hill, 1963), pp. 7–31

15. J. Milton Yinger, *Religion in the Struggle for Power* (New York: Russell & Russell, 1961). Also, an excellent description of this process may be found in Sidney Mead, *The Lively Experiment* (New York: Harper & Row, 1963).

16. The following discussion is largely based on Thomas G. Sanders, *Protestant Concepts of Church and State* (New York: Holt, 1964).

17. H. Richard Niebuhr, *Christ and Culture* (New York: Harper & Row, 1951). These are two of several categories on which this work is based.

18. Philip B. Kurland, *Religion and the Law* (Chicago: Aldine, 1961), pp. 21–25.

19. Ibid., pp. 97–106.

20. Ibid., pp. 91–96.

21. Ibid., pp. 50–74.

22. John C. Bennett, *The Christian as Citizen* (New York: Association Press, 1955), pp. 20–21.

23. James L. Adams, *The Growing Church Lobby in Washington* (Grand Rapids, Mich.: Eerdmans, 1970), pp. 245–276.

24. Ibid., p. 87.

25. Luke E. Ebersole, *Church Lobbying in the Nation's Capitol* (New York: Macmillan, 1951), pp. 74–153.

26. Jerome J. Kerwin, *The Catholic Viewpoint on Church and State* (Garden City, N.Y.: Doubleday, 1960), pp. 99–100.

27. Paul Blanshard, *American Freedom and Catholic Power* (Boston: Beacon, 1958).

28. A good summary of his views may be found in Blanshard's portion of the Harvard Law School Forum presentation, *The Catholic Church and Politics* (Cambridge, Mass.: 1950), which also contains a Catholic reply.

29. Ebersole, op. cit., pp. 106–113.

30. Alan F. Geyer, *Piety and Politics* (Atlanta: John Knox Press, 1963), pp. 123–125.

31. The data covered the period between the spring of 1967 and the spring of 1968, during which time there were many severe riots in major cities, the Kerner report on urban violence was issued, the Biafran conflict was at its peak, and Martin Luther King was assassinated. There was growing unrest about the Viet Nam war, and a number of particularly salient local issues developed, about which denominational groups had taken firm stands.

32. For a full report of this study, see Rodney Stark, Bruce Foster, Charles Glock, and Harold Quinley, *Wayward Shepherds* (New York: Harper & Row, 1971).
33. John Earle, Dean Knudsen, and Donald Shriver, *Spindles and Spires* (Atlanta: John Knox Press, 1976), Chapter 4.
34. For example, significant effects of salience on the generally negative relationship between orthodoxy and activism is reported in Howard Bahr, Lewis Bartel, and Bruce Chadwick, "Orthodoxy, Activism, and the Salience of Religion," *Journal for the Scientific Study of Religion* 10, no. 2 (Summer 1971): 69–75.
35. Jeffrey K. Hadden, *The Gathering Storm in the Churches* (Garden City, N.Y.: Doubleday, 1961), pp. 133–134.
36. Earle, Knudsen, and Shriver, op. cit., pp. 153–155.
37. The application of such behavior to specific situations may be found in Thomas Pettigrew and Earnest Campbell, "Racial and Moral Crisis: The Role of the Little Rock Ministers," *American Journal of Sociology* 64 (March 1959): 509–516.
38. Earle, Knudsen, and Schriver, op. cit., pp. 154–158.
39. For example, see Rodney Stark and Charles Glock, *American Piety* (Berkeley: University of California Press, 1968), particularly Chapter 9.

12

Economics and Development

The relation of religion to the economic structure of the modern world finds its base in ancient linkages between virtue and group survival. As was mentioned earlier, all societies have tended to choose as divine figures symbols of their primary subsistence or of persons most successful at providing sustenance or both. Thus, in hunting tribes the primary object of the hunt may be venerated or the gods defined as great hunters. Agricultural peoples may have corn goddesses or other fertility symbols at the center of their worship. Human fertility, in the form of a mother goddess or a phallic symbol, has also been central. Similarly, the epitome of virtuous behavior has generally been that which insured the survival of the tribe and its culture: the successful hunter, the tiller of the most fertile field, the most fertile parent. As technology has improved and made mere physical survival less an immediate concern, the gods and their virtuous subjects have become more concerned with the defense of what has been gained, materially or culturally, by which the tribe or society defines its nature. Survival thus has come to be defined in more than economic terms, but it has never lost its economic base.

Historic religion, as noted in Chapter 7, has been primarily tied to relatively settled civilizations with societies organized into a number of fixed castes or classes. One of the primary factors of early modern religion was its ability to provide grounding for a more open system with greater social mobility and hence to support an economy based on rapidly expanding technology and resource development. This religious type, tied to what has come to be known as the "Protestant ethic," even when it is divorced from Protestant Christianity, is still significant in the modern world.

While the Protestant ethic has already been discussed in relation to early modern religion and to social class, it may be worthwhile to look at it once more, this time in the context of the relation of religion to the economic structure. As Weber described the relation of the Protestant ethic to the rise of capitalism, he showed ways in which Reformation Protestantism provided the moral basis for voluntary restraint in the personal use of economic surplus, so that it could be plowed back into the means of production made available through the Industrial Revolution. Here an inner-worldly asceticism defined all productive occupations as potential Christian vocations, if they were performed with diligence and their rewards were not spent in riotous living. In an expanding economy, diligent work is likely to result in an excess of reward, and this ethic defined as appropriate the employment of that excess in capital investment. Thus the successful capitalist became the ideal of virtuous behavior, since all benefited from the expansion of the economy made possible by that investment.

Similarly, the ideal worker came to be seen as the industrious, mobile individual who would be willing to move into new occupations opened up by the expanding economy, without allowing the restraints of tradition, family, or local community to impede that progress. Evangelical Protestantism, in particular, emphasized the individual's relationship with God and provided in its small sectarian churches the kind of emotional support once expected of the extended family but no longer available to the mobile worker. Hard work, clean living, and individual religiosity provided the kind of workers most needed in an industrial economy. The churches supported the goals and styles of both owners and workers and implicitly equated industrial development with the building of the Kingdom of God on earth.

Clearly, the broad strokes of such a picture ignore the many details in which the model proved far less ideal than this, but for the past four hundred years, and particularly in areas where Protestant Christianity and economically underdeveloped geographical areas have coincided, at least some of these elements of the Protestant ethic have prevailed. The effects of the western frontier, the immigrant experience, and a culture built on that ethic have served to create a similar pattern in American Catholicism, especially those portions derived from Irish and German roots. The constraints of a community-oriented ethnicity are still evident in many of the other subcommunities of Catholic America, just as they exist for some Protestants. Thus, modern tests of Weber's thesis tend to have negative results, with Catholic-Protestant differences in economic attitude less important than other variables.

On a worldwide scale, the influence of Western missionaries has often been so entangled with the exportation of Western industrial technology that the ties between Christianity and economic development seem even closer than on the American frontier. Whether intended or not, there has been a consistent mutuality between the attempts of missionaries to convert individuals to a Christianity opposed to indigenous communal religions and the attempts of industrialists and mine owners to entice workers away from local subsistence economic activities to centers of resource exploitation and industrial development. It would be too expensive for company towns to accommodate extended families of workers; those too old or too young are better left back in the home village. In many cases, colonial governments have imposed taxes on local tribes which could be paid only in money earned by the exportation of a number of their members to mines or factories. Often these political strictures have been reinforced by missionary conversions that required the breakup of polygamous families or other cultural associations not amenable to Western morality—or economics.

In a more positive fashion, Christian missionaries have provided schools for previously illiterate peoples, giving them skills to read the Scriptures and to improve the local economy but also to move beyond that local economy into industrial occupations. Many mission schools have, in fact, sent their graduates to European or American secondary schools, colleges, and universities, from which they have returned to become educational and political leaders.

It must be noted that what is involved in the world view introduced by Western training is far more broad than simply a religious symbol system or organization. As Berger et al. have made clear, we are dealing here with a whole transformation of consciousness. Their description of the kind of consciousness necessary for modernization contains a number of significant elements. It requires one to accept a definition of human order based on a hierarchy of specialties, in which the individual is primarily known by the specific tasks he or she can accomplish. The mind-set in dealing with those tasks is mechanistic, based on the reproducibility of any work process, its interdependence with other such processes, and the assumption of a sequence of production in a large organization. Like tasks in the organization, different portions of one's life are compartmentalized, and the relation of means to ends is diminished. Because one is known primarily by one's task, social relations tend to be anonymous, emotions managed, and private life segregated from the work place.[1]

In theory, nothing could be further from the pristine Protestant ethic, with its emphasis on economic activity as religious vocation, its stress on the ultimate value of each person, and the close relationship of fellow believers within the religious group. Yet the individualism of that definition of personal worth and the instrumentalism of the vocational drive can be seen as factors in the development of this modern mind-set. One of the factors that must be recognized as well is that the central values of the Protestant ethic were most appropriate to the individual entrepreneur, the developer, rather than to those workers who were needed to carry out the tasks of the industrial organization. Calvinism, which Weber took as the epitome of this form of religious ethic, began with a firm sense of the division between the elect and the damned which tended over time to be translated into the division between "creative" economic leadership—ownership and management—and the masses who could not be expected to be self-motivated but rather must always be controlled by the goad of poverty.

In the international setting, this division of elect elite and trainable masses was transposed to a division between "native savages" and "civilized whites" whose task in bringing them into a modern culture was paternalistic—the "white man's burden."

It must be understood that this interlocking of Christianity and industrial development is not confined to Western Protestantism. Weber, in tracing the historic effects of the Reformation, was not positing a continued division between Catholicism and Protestantism on this matter, but rather was showing how the European world view was opened to individual mobility and capital investment by the new forms of Christianity. In many areas of the Third World, the Roman Catholic missionary influence has been almost identical to the Protestant in providing a cultural base for economic development. In some areas, however, notably much of South America, geographic dispersion and a shortage of trained leadership have resulted in a localized folk Catholicism loosely tied to an aristocratic ecclesiastical hierarchy. Here the Roman Catholic church has in the past been closely identified with a primarily agricultural society much like that of feudal Europe. Protestantism has tended to be limited to the small sectarian organizations of the disinherited.

In recent years that picture has changed radically, primarily through movements within the Roman Catholic church. A significant number of priests, along with some bishops, have become involved in movements for land reform and other economic changes in the name of Christian liberation. South America has been the source of much of the "liberation theology" that has affected the thinking of many church people on political and economic issues.

There has been constant discussion as to the applicability of Weber's "Protestant ethic" thesis to societies whose primary religious tradition is not Christian. Just as Bellah found the Protestant Reformation the only unambiguous model of early modern religion, other scholars in the area have found both similarities and differences in the relation of other religious traditions to economic modernization. It seems most useful to take as Weber's primary point the importance of religious legitimation for certain forms of economic activity, rather than the exact way in which that has occurred. Two of the primary aspects of modernization are the expectation of rational, goal-ordered choices, and a structure of specialized roles created to reach those goals. In western Europe and America the choices legitimated by the Protestant Reformation tended to be those of the individual entrepreneur and the voluntarily mobile worker. By contrast, both Bellah and Geertz have shown that in the East modernization has more often been accompanied by communal or governmental decisions to move into economic development, but that religious legitimation for such activity has nonetheless been important.

While many students of Japanese society could find no evidence of the presence of any "Protestant ethic" to accompany the modernization of that culture, Bellah has made a good case for the importance of a kind of imperial religion that gave legitimacy to the Meiji reforms that began that process. While merchant classes may have promoted an ethic more similar to Protestant economic individualism, the critical group in Japan was that of the samurai officials. Their ethic included articles demanding an orientation toward expansion, success, hard work, and devotion to the national interest. Rather than beginning as individual entrepreneurs later organized into a bureaucracy, they began with a traditional bureaucracy which they turned into an instrument of modernization.[2]

Wertheim, in discussing the importance of state action in the modernization of the East, still found religious legitimation an important factor. In fact, even in the case of so-called secular Marxism he noted the importance of spiritual forces in creating the conditions of modernization:

> Over against the theoretical Marxists who sustained the thesis that the spirit of those administrators who foster economic growth is nothing but a reflection of existing economic forces, I hazard to put forth the thesis that the practice in countries under Marxist domination has demonstrated the spiritual strength dormant in an ideology. Without their Spartan sobriety and their strict devotion to their cause, the builders of modern industrial states in the East would never have been able to build a counterpart of the imposing edifice of British eighteenth-century industrial society, which, according to Max Weber, was based on the Protestant ethic.[3]

Even traditionalist religions tend to become more open to the kind of organizational forms that foster a world view supportive of modernization if they are placed in a position of defending the faith against such development. Geertz has described this process in Java, where he shows that modernist movements in Javanese Islam forced traditionalists into providing meeting styles and educational forms consistent with a modern world view in order to present their case.[4] Such organizational elements have proven highly significant in the development of American denominations, as we shall see in the next chapter. It will suffice here to point out that while religious legitimation of the economic structure appears crucial for the successful functioning of a society, that economic structure also has important effects on the forms of the religion.

This interaction of economy and religion is also apparent in regional differences in the United States. In the broad bifurcation of American religion between "main-line" and "evangelical," the evangelicals appear to adhere more closely to the individualism of the Protestant ethic and its celebration of an entrepreneurial ideal. While there are, as we have seen, class-based differences in religious ideology and organization, we find here also that the areas of greatest evangelical strength are those parts of the country still characterized by economic growth—primarily the "sun belt" of the South and the Southwest—where population increase and industrial development are the norm. It is in the older urban areas, where the economy has stabilized or begun to decline, that liberalism, otherworldly sectarianism, and religions stressing ethnic community are more dominant. It is these areas that provide the background for most religious critiques of current forms of capitalism, as well as theologies dealing with forming a religious ethic for a "postindustrial age."

The churches have always been involved in dealing with some of the negative consequences of the economic order. Early church actions in this realm, which still continue, were in the area of welfare programs, and a constant source of disagreement within religious circles is the relative merit of action taken to relieve suffering caused by the economic system or that aimed at changing the system in order to alleviate such suffering.

Most religions make some provision for the care of the poor through alms, tithes, or charitable acts. In Western society under Christendom, the church has provided a number of welfare functions which have been gradually transferred to secular governments. The giving of alms was expected, with special types of gifts to the poor at some seasons. Convents and monasteries sheltered the homeless and gave food to the indigent. In fact, the young person who did not fit into the occupational niches provided by the society for one of his or her station had the alternative of choosing a religious vocation, where one could be housed and clothed by the order as well as trained by them to do work within their bounds. All this activity, however, took place within the membership of the church, since in Christendom nearly everyone was a member.

As established religion has faded into the background and the church has emerged as a voluntary association, Christians have been faced with the problem of whether their charity should remain a process of caring for their own or should reach out to the unchurched or those with different denominational ties. In America, where circumstances and history have tended to produce an attitude of local autonomy regardless of the denomination, many people have rather taken it for granted that people not in their local congregation are unchurched. Since most of the poor have not joined the congregations of the more affluent, the decision to provide for the poor was resolved in the direction of reaching out beyond the religious fellowship. The doctrine of hard work and an appreciation of riches was tempered by the understanding that riches should be shared with the less fortunate. Since their poverty was often seen as something of a moral lapse, it seemed normal that the poor should remain outside the church of their benefactors. Yet evangelistic beliefs led to the feeling that the poor too should be converted. What resulted was the establishment of missions in the poor part of town—or in poor sections of the country—which dispensed cast-off clothing and simple food, along with evangelistic sermons and songs and polemics against such vices as drink and gambling, which were understood to be the sources of much of their poverty.

A growing awareness of social sources of poverty and distress led to what has been called the Social Gospel. Under such leaders as Washington Gladden and later Walter Rauschenbusch, churches began to bend their efforts to serve the poor by altering the social conditions that created their poverty. Churches began to establish settlement houses in inner-city areas, with programs designed to teach basic skills, provide recreation for young people in the slums, and in other ways have a more lasting effect upon the lives of the poor than the earlier "handouts" had provided.

An interest in dealing with those in power on behalf of the downtrodden also began to develop. In some cases this required the church to speak out against its own members, as when Washington Gladden opposed acceptance of a $10,000 gift from John D. Rockefeller because of the practices by which he had obtained the money. Gladden denounced the existence of social classes, particularly the one composed of persons who had acquired great wealth in a short period of time. He insisted that the very existence of fortunes of this sort proved that there was social injustice, for there was no way in which a single person could in one lifetime provide the society with benefits worth hundreds of millions of dollars. He also pointed out the dangers of such inequalities to democracy, and he said that men like Rockefeller should be considered enemies of the society.[5]

An interchurch report sponsored by the Federal Council of Churches, forerunner of today's National Council of Churches of Christ in America, provided American churchgoers a new glimpse of the working conditions that led to the steel strike of 1919 and set the stage for popular action against the twelve-hour day and other oppressive practices. However, this was probably the most influential church action ever taken in the cause of the workers in America.[6] The influence of the Social Gospel waned during the public reaction in favor of business "normalcy" in the 1920s. It is probable that it had considerably less grip on the common lay members, particularly outside the urban industrial centers of the country, than has been thought. The Social Gospel, in many cases, may be taken as a sort of sectarian response of church leaders suffering from ethical deprivation in a business-oriented society. During this period the leadership of the church diminished in influence, and probably in quality, as secular interests and higher salaries siphoned the more creative young men into fields other than the ministry.

The thrust of the churches in dealing with economic and social class differences fell back to the mission and settlement house until the civil rights and poverty emphases of the 1950s and 1960s. Once again, clergy became involved with trying to change the society in ways that might relieve the lot of the poor and oppressed, but generally they were not highly effective in mobilizing support in their congregations. The consequential dimension of Christianity and Judaism in America has never approached the sort of self-sacrifice urged by Richard T. Ely, economist proponent of the Social Gospel, who wrote in 1896:

> Our resources of every sort, time, strength of body and mind, and our economic resources, are all limited, and however great they may be, love will show us how we can use all to the last minute of time and the last farthing of money for the promotion of the welfare of humanity.[7]

Alongside activities within the churches aimed at benefiting the poor, there have been some organizations of a political nature, often with international ties, advocating Christian socialism. In Europe this movement has been institutionalized into political parties that are generally supportive of industrial capitalism as it exists but also demand state control over some basic resources and a program of economic support for individuals generally in the nature of the "welfare state." They would mitigate the primary problems of a capitalist economy—unemployment, dislocation, lack of security in old age or illness, and the like —through governmental programs. The relation of such party platforms to what Americans define as political liberalism is clear. The relation to liberal religion may be traced through programs of social service within the Social Gospel movement.

The actual promotion of Christian socialism in America has had a checkered career, tied largely to the development of socialist movements in Europe. In the late nineteenth and early twentieth centuries, explicit socialism was promoted by organizations such as the Christian Socialist Society and the Christian Socialist Fellowship. These had disappeared by 1918. It is probably no coincidence that the date coincides with the institution of a Marxist government in Russia, which claimed both an international tie to socialist and communist movements and a militant atheism. While Christian socialism began as a protest against both the unsocial aspects of Christianity and the unchristian aspects of socialism, these latter put them in the position of being painted with the same brush whenever they became dominant in world affairs.[8]

However, as we have seen, international politics could not destroy the uneasiness felt by many Christian leaders in the face of evident human consequences of industrialization legitimated by an individualist Protestant ethic, and by the time of the Great Depression there was a resurgence of interest in Christian socialism. Often tied to the rising neo-orthodoxy of that period, Christian socialism tended to accept Marxist analyses of social problems but to posit a transcendent referent for an ethic by which to deal with the problems defined by that analysis.

Because Christian socialists could not identify with Marxist states that denied the value of religion, nor yet with economic structures traditionally identified with Christianity but now seen by them to be perversions of the faith, they tended to speak abstractly more often than to organize for political action. Their statements were more in the nature of theological principles than political rallying cries. For example, Paul Tillich wrote:

> The ethic of religious socialism, like its entire outlook, is dynamic. It does not recognize an abstract system of values that is universally valid, but, rather, it discerns as an attribute of being itself a demand that changes according to the nature of the encounter between man and another entity. This demand can be fulfilled or it can be neglected; it is always concrete. Abstract value systems are exposed as the ideologies of ruling groups who instinctively want to give eternal sanction to their power by ascribing an eternal and transcen-

dent character to their ethic. In place of this religious socialism posits devotion to the dynamic meaning and its demands that are inherent in things and situations.[9]

While this pragmatic approach and openness to change reinforced the criticisms of contemporary religion, it provided little basis for the political mobilization of people around a specific cause. Political calls to action are difficult when the concept of the diety is primarily immanentist—that is, that God dwells within persons and events. Yet these theologians were particularly aware of the dangers of identifying human systems with some transcendent diety. Reinhold Niebuhr made clear his separation from a religion of this kind when he said that

> if religion is no longer the recognition of the sacred in the developing purpose of history, if it is no longer the gospel of the Kingdom, it is wholly of the decadence, it is world-denial, delusion, and the cult of death, "the opium of the people."
>
> It may well be that the time has come for religion to dissolve like an insubstantial dream and leave not a wrack behind, dying to be born again as the Holy Spirit of a righteous social order.[10]

The idea of the Kingdom of God, and of the call for Christians to build a society as nearly like the perfect human community denoted by that term, has been a consistent factor in Christian criticisms of modern industrial capitalism. They find their roots in the stress on social justice in the Old Testament, as well as the example of the early church, where believers were reported to have sold all their possessions and held everything in common. The first of these emphases points to political solutions of economic injustices, but the only model of democratic state intervention has been that of the welfare state, a pattern that has not always proven adequate to the task.

During World War II Christian socialism once again faded into the background. The exigencies of war and the economic stimulus it brought made economic problems seem relatively unimportant, and in the Cold War period that followed all leftist ideologies were suspect. But with the leftist movements of the 1960s once again this stream of Christianity found its voice. The mood of the 1960s was strongly anti-institutional, so those church people who accepted a Marxist analysis of the society were not inclined to form themselves into Christian socialist societies, but rather worked with others in particular situations or one of the many ad hoc organizations of the period. Most of the activity during that period tended to be focused upon political rather than economic issues, but there was also a pattern of coherence between this branch of Christianity and the counterculture that emerged out of that period—one with a foundation far older than that recent movement.

While the so-called Protestant ethic has encouraged individualism and industrial development, Christianity has always carried, even in Protestantism, a strain of communalism, as well as a tendency to devalue economic gain. Voluntary poverty has had a long and honorable history, especially when teamed with a dedication to improving the lot of the poor. Some religious orders within the Catholic church and some Protestant sects, such as the Salvation Army, have been organized around this principle, and other sects, such as the Amish, have made resistance to the technological and social changes brought about by the Industrial Revolution their primary focus. It must be noted, however, that this form of religiosity has always been a minority movement, though often more influential than its numbers would indicate. A good example is the Catholic Worker movement, begun by Dorothy Day as a protest against both the irreligious nature of the socialist groups she had been working for and the lack of concern for the plight of the workers she found within the church she loved. In partnership with Peter Maurin, a French priest, Dorothy Day founded the *Catholic Worker,* a newspaper of the Christian left, published by a group of people whose work was communal and largely volunteer. The movement also set up a number of communal farms, attempting to provide an alternative to the assembly line and a wage economy. People in the movement participated in strikes and demonstrations, always in the name of more humane conditions for workers. It has been active for over fifty years and has throughout that time maintained a strong religious style.

Movements such as this have provided models for two kinds of action in relation to an industrial economy. The first involves the development of new forms of a Christian life-style, involving minimal use of resources, cooperative or communal living arrangements, and an attempt to recover a more holistic understanding of the nature of human existence. Liberal churches have taken up the twin causes of ecology and hunger, and they have been promoting new approaches to these causes through study groups and the like.[11] More radical changes in life-style have been advocated not only within the ranks of those whose theology is liberal, but also among those classified by Quebedeaux as the "radical evangelicals." Groups such as the Peoples' Christian Coalition in Washington, D.C., and Berkeley's Christian Coalition practice communal styles of living. Publications from these two groups (*Sojourners* magazine by the former, *Radix* by the latter) are joined by others such as *The Other*

Side, put out by a radical evangelical group in Philadelphia, in spreading the word of the Christian basis for new life-styles.[12] In all these cases a movement appears to be developing that would reverse the process of modernization of the consciousness as defined by Berger and his associates.

On the other hand, direct political action has come to be a part of the attempt to restructure the economy. We have already seen how churches cooperated with governmental programs in the War on Poverty, many of which were designed to challenge local power structures that kept the poor "in their place." They also have taken direct and aggressive action in community organization, making use of tactics developed by Saul Alinski to empower the poor and the dispossessed. Ecumenical cooperation in such ventures has been the rule, but the concentration of Catholics in many urban areas most amenable to such tactics has led to some dominance of that church in this style of action. As with Protestants, this kind of activity has been the role of a small minority within the church and has not gone unchallenged by other segments of the organization. But even in rural areas such as Appalachia, the Catholic influence has been evident in action on behalf of the poor. For example, through the efforts of community organizers a document was developed and formalized as a pastoral letter from the bishops of the area, thus designed to be read from all its pulpits. Titled "This Land Is Home to Me," the letter offers a view of the problems of the people of Appalachia in the context of Christianity and with a real sense of their dignity and worth. It shows one example of the kind of Christian criticism of the modern industrial system, for example, when speaking of

a different kind of powerlessness,
one common to the rest of our society—
the powerlessness of isolated little people
in the face of the most powerful corporate giants
on this earth.

The way of life
which these corporate giants create
is called by some
"technological rationalization."
Its forces contain the promise
of a world where
—poverty is eliminated
—health cared for
—education available for all
—dignity guaranteed
—and old age secure.

Too often, however,
its forces become perverted,
hostile to the dignity of the earth
and of its people.

Its destructive growth patterns

—pollute the air
—foul the water
—rape the land.

The driving force
behind this perversion is
"Maximization of Profit,"
a principle which too often converts itself
into an idolatrous power.

This power overwhelms the good intentions
of noble people.
It forces them to compete brutally
with one another.

It pushes people into
"conspicuous consumption"
and "planned obsolescence."
It delivers up control
to a tiny minority
whose values then shape
our social structures.

Of course technological rationalization
and the profit principle
have served important functions
in human development.
It is not they themselves
that form an idol,
but the idol is formed
when they become absolutes
and fail to yield,
when the time has come,
to other principles.

Neither do we believe
that our people
or the people of the nation
have totally fallen prey
to the power of this idol.
But even without that happening,
"maximization of profit"
in today's world,
has become a crazy death wish,
every day using up more and more
of the earth's riches

and our own dignity.
Like those who write spy thrillers,
its process is fascinated
with everything that can
"self-destruct,"
even if it is ourselves.

Without judging anyone,
it has become clear to us
that the present economic order
does not care for its people.
In fact,
profit and people frequently are contradictory.
Profit over people
is an idol.
and it is not a new idol,
for Jesus long ago warned us,
No one can be the slave of two masters:
either he will hate the first
and love the second,
or treat the first with respect
and the second with scorn.
You cannot be the slave
of both God and money.
(Matthew 6: 24)
This is not a problem
only for mountain folk;
it is everybody's problem.[13]

While this document came out as a pastoral letter from Roman Catholic bishops, its perspective is not limited to that church. It was created in cooperation with the Commission on Religion in Appalachia, an organization defining itself as "17 denominations united, in the name of Jesus Christ, to meet the pressing human needs of the Appalachian people." The issues are viewed as much too large for sectarian identification. A similar situation has existed in the religious support of union organizing among migrant farm workers. Cesar Chavez, the leader of the United Farm Workers movement, is a devout Catholic and has been able to mobilize many supporters from that church. (Dorothy Day's latest brush with the law, in fact, occurred when that elderly lady was forcibly removed from a UFW picket line and jailed.) But many Protestants and Jews as well have aided in demonstrations and in consumer boycotts of grapes and lettuce which helped strengthen Chavez's hand.

In the Third World also, Christians have been active in movements against the dehumanizing effects of modern industrial development. The Catholic church in South America has been the scene of movements and counter-movements with an economic focus. The traditional identification of church leadership with the rich and powerful has been challenged not only by local priests but by some bishops who have advocated land reform and economic redistribution. The challenge may be found in the higher councils of the Latin American church, where political maneuvering has reached a high level. The dominance of Roman Catholicism in that area has led to an identification with those currently in power, but also to a sense of responsibility for the powerless.

In the past, that responsibility has most often been taken in a paternalistic manner, and the effects of the church have been felt more in its urgings to private philanthropy aimed at alleviating the most severe effects of poverty. But new theological perspectives, particularly those of the theology of liberation, have tended to place the focus of divine action among the poor and the powerless. Traditions of the exodus of Hebrew slaves from Egypt, the writings of Old Testament prophets on social justice, and the founding of the early church among the poor by a messiah who was himself from a lowly family have been called into play as justification for locating the Kingdom of God among the poor and the oppressed. In this way, Christianity is defined as the religion of revolution rather than that of the powerful.

It is ironic that the churches within which this type of theology has gained the greatest acceptance are those that are themselves powerful. As social institutions with a large clientele composed more often of the well-to-do than of the disadvantaged, churches have in the past been important political and social forces. In addition, all the larger denominations are corporate structures with a significant amount of investment capital. Not only do churches own property of great worth, often in choice areas of major cities, but they also have accumulated large endowments. In many cases individual congregations have been able to maintain their programs almost entirely with the income from investments—a situation that has often reduced members' sense of responsibility for those programs, but which has also allowed them to serve the community in ways far beyond the ability of the present membership. Similarly, the denominations have acquired large endowments and in addition handle such other money as pension funds and long-term grants. A criticism of corporate behavior must of necessity extend to the way in which religious bodies handle their investments.

This is no new problem. Early in this century such ecclesiastical landlords as Trinity Church in Manhattan were being taken to court by tenants who accused them of being among the worst of slumlords.[14] But it has in recent years become a particular focus of discontent and attempted action by those within the churches who are concerned with economic justice.

In this context, the position of the churches vis-à-vis the "younger churches" founded by missionaries has been severely criticized. In many cases Third World churches have demanded freedom from oversight by their parent denominations as part of general nationalistic movements. But even when that freedom has been granted politically, Western churches, like most Western corporations, have retained power over them through their economic holdings. When Western churches hold properties or fund important programs, they withhold legitimation of indigenous expressions of the faith. Bernard Quick, a former Presbyterian missionary to Egypt, writes:

> One of the most powerful ways that the United Presbyterian Church is using to perpetuate its concept of what it means to be the church in the world is through leadership training. Because most of the overseas churches are oriented toward the West in terms of theology, policy and practice, it has been the policy of these churches and mission groups working with them to assume that the leaders of these churches should receive their advance training in the West and usually in the United States.
>
> Most of the leaders of the overseas churches do their postgraduate study at seminaries in the United States. Of course, these seminaries are geared to the American scene. Many of the men and women who receive degrees from these institutions tend to be alienated from their home churches overseas. It is either because the theological education is more "liberal" than the theological position of these Third World churches or the leaders expect positions and salaries commensurate with those in America who have the same level of education.[15]

Western sectarian groups may come nearer to sharing the poverty of the people to whom they send missionaries and so escape the dilemma of the larger denominations. But the more explicit rendering of religious beliefs and practices in sects leads to a devaluation of native cultures as "pagan," so that it becomes difficult to deal with converts within an indigenous context. Rather, they are taught Western ways as part of the religion, with results similar to those of the more liberal programs. Their other effect is to provide a sectarian model that has led to the breaking away and establishment of a number of indigenous churches proudly separate from Western Christianity.

Church involvement in the Third World and in the structures of local and international economics is not limited to direct action of religious bodies. Much of the investment capital of the churches rests in other large corporations in which they hold shares. One of the movements of the 1970s in which the churches have participated is the revolt of shareholders who have begun to demand certain forms of social responsibility of the corporations. The basic assumption of corporate management has always been that their responsibility to shareholders is to increase profit; if other considerations about public consequences of their activities were to be taken into account, it was assumed that the shareholders would have to be placated, since it was not in their interest. Thus a movement on the part of shareholders to demand an accounting of employment practices, environmental impact, or long-range consequences has been a relatively new thing. Where church groups own a significant block of stock, there is some possibility of their being heard on such issues. And while this movement, like most of the church-related activism of the 1960s, is particularly salient to denominational officials and staff personnel, in most cases it appears less threatening to rank and file church members, many of whom have no conception of the economic resources of their denomination or of their disposition.

Some churches are not only dealing in this way with their own investments but are also attempting to educate members who may themselves own shares in corporations subject to such pressures. For example, a flier produced for insertion in the Sunday bulletins of American Baptist churches makes the following statement:

> Investments are more than a matter of ensuring sufficient income, they carry a responsibility of stewardship and Christian commitment. As shareholders, we share in the decisions of corporations which affect the kind of world in which we live. The development and use of investments must be consistent with Christian standards of stewardship and justice.[16]

Cooperation among religious groups is particularly useful in challenging corporate policy, and much of the action is currently coordinated through the Interfaith Center on Corporate Responsibility, an arm of the National Council of Churches that claims as members fourteen Protestant churches and some 150 Roman Catholic orders. Particular issues addressed through this agency have included the use of church funds for companies manufacturing military hardware, the environmental impact of strip-mining planned by some companies, equal-opportunity employment practices, contracts with the South African government that support its program of racial apartheid, illegal campaign contributions, advertising practices that contribute to infant malnutrition in the Third World, other Third World investments that contribute to world poverty and hunger, violence on television, and various issues of labor practices and company unions. In the beginning such issues were simply raised at annual meetings and seldom carried enough voting power to do more than bring the subject to light. In recent years the style of approach has become more sophisticated. Background information has been gathered, and contacts have been made with corporate officials. Open letters and public hearings often bring political pressure to bear on management, and in some cases study guides or other publications have assisted churches in becoming public forums on certain issues. If information is refused, companies are sued. Proxy resolutions are often tendered before annual meetings, and issues are negotiated before they come to a vote. In an era of corporate power, some churches as corporate bodies are attempting to provide the kind of moral and ethical guidelines religion once gave to individuals. While churches can scarcely hold over the head of a corporation the promise of heaven or the threat of hell, insofar as they retain their image as moral guides of the society they can embarrass or praise economic organizations for their actions. Insofar as they control some of the wealth of the society, religious institutions can offer some material backing to that praise or blame. But their stewardship of those resources is likely to come under harsh scrutiny in the process, the results of which may be definitive for the position of moral leadership they assume. It is a very narrow path the churches have open to them in this arena of corporate action.

Notes and References

1. Peter Berger, Brigitte Berger, and Hansfried Kellner, *The Homeless Mind* (New York: Random House, 1973), Chapter 1.
2. Robert Bellah, *Tokugawa Religion* (New York: Free Press, 1957). See also a discussion of this work and others in W. F. Wertheim, "Religion, Bureaucracy, and Economic Growth," in *The Protestant Ethic and Modernization,* ed. by S. N. Eisenstadt (New York: Basic Books, 1968).
3. Wertheim, op. cit., p. 269.
4. Clifford Geertz, "Religious Belief and Economic Behavior in a Central Javanese Town," in Eisenstadt, op. cit., pp. 327–328.
5. Washington Gladden, "Shall Ill-Gotten Gains Be Sought for Christian Purposes?" in *The Social Gospel in America, 1870–1940,* ed. by Robert T. Handy (New York: Oxford University Press, 1966), p. 128.
6. Paul Allen Carter, *The Decline and Revival of the Social Gospel: Social and Political Liberalism in the Churches, 1920–1940* (Ithaca, N.Y.: Cornell University Press, 1956), pp. 21–22.
7. Richard T. Ely, *The Social Law of Service,* Chapter 4, as quoted in Handy, op. cit., p. 232.
8. For further information on these movements, see Richard B. Dressner, *Christian Socialism: A Response to Industrial America in the Progressive Era* (Ph.D. dissertation,

Cornell University, 1972); James Dombrowski, *The Early Days of Christian Socialism in America* (New York: Columbia University Press, 1936); and Handy, op. cit.

9. Paul Tillich, "Religious Socialism," in *Political Expectations* (New York: Harper & Row, 1971), p. 50 (first published in Germany in 1930).

10. Reinhold Niebuhr, "Christian Politics and Communist Religion," in *Christianity and the Social Revolution,* ed. by John Lewis, Karl Polanyi, and Donald Kitchin (London: Gollancz, 1935), p. 504.

11. See, for example, Thomas Sieger Derr, *Ecology and Human Need* (Philadelphia: Westminster, 1975), promoted as a study guide by the World Council of Churches and its cooperating denominations.

12. Richard Quebedeaux, *The Worldly Evangelicals* (New York: Harper & Row, 1978), pp. 151–152.

13. This pastoral letter is widely available and not copyrighted. It may be obtained directly from the Catholic Committee of Appalachia, 31A South 3rd Avenue, Prestonburg, KY 41653.

14. Ray Stannard Baker, *The Spiritual Unrest* (New York: Stokes, 1910), pp. 1–48.

15. Bernard E. Quick, *He Who Pays the Piper. . . .* (privately published, 1975), p. 82.

16. From "Christian Responsibility in Investments," published by the Social and Ethical Responsibility Program, National Ministries, American Baptist Church, USA, Valley Forge, PA 19481. No date.

Earle, John; Knudsen, Dean; and Shriver, Donald. *Spindles and Spires.* Atlanta: John Knox, 1976.

Glazer, Nathan. *American Judaism.* 2nd ed. Chicago: University of Chicago Press, 1972.

Glock, Charles Y., ed. *Religion in Sociological Perspective.* Belmont, Calif.: Wadsworth, 1973.

Greeley, Andrew; McCready, William; and McCourt, Kathleen. *Catholic Schools in a Declining Church.* Kansas City, Mo.: Sheed & Ward, 1976.

Hoge, Dean. *Division in the Protestant House.* Philadelphia: Westminster, 1976.

Niebuhr, H. Richard. *The Social Sources of Denominationalism.* New York: Meridian Age, 1957.

Pope, Liston. *Millhands and Preachers.* New Haven: Yale University Press, 1942.

Powers, Charles W. *Social Responsibility and Investments.* Nashville: Abingdon, 1971.

Stark, Rodney, and Glock, Charles Y. *American Piety: The Nature of Religious Commitment.* Berkeley: University of California Press, 1968.

Vallier, Ivan. *Catholicism, Social Control, and Modernization in Latin America.* Englewood Cliffs, N.J.: Prentice-Hall, 1970.

Part IV

RELIGION AS STRUCTURE AND MOVEMENT

One of the assumptions of sociologists of religion before the 1970s was that the process of secularization was direct and inevitable, with religion occupying a smaller and smaller portion of the life of the society. In this most recent decade that has proven to be an oversimplification.

Organized religion has followed the pattern defined by Weber as the "routinization of charisma" to the point of becoming a number of large interlocked bureaucracies with their own motivation for survival scarcely tied to the religious character of their charter. In addition, new movements have emerged, each offering an alternative world view with a religious base. It is possible to see this proliferation of religions as the beginning of the end, where like the gingham dog and the calico cat they eat each other up. But it is also possible that the result will be not the elimination of religion but a realignment of its structure and functions in the society.

Robert Wuthnow has posited a future of a "diversified society" in which the various religions will continue to function without destroying one another, held in the society less by institutional structures than by a number of processes. The first of these, *commercialization,* ties the religions together into a common marketplace in which they vie for the support of potential adherents. Joining a religious group under such circumstances becomes more a trivial choice than a permanent commitment, and it is unlikely to create conflict. The second, *privatization,* keeps religion in the private sphere of life, where different styles and different choices will not result in social disruption. The third process, *ritualization,* isolates religious activity into particular compartmentalized periods of time where it will not interfere with other aspects of the life of the society. Finally, *isolation* refers to spatial aspects of the separation of religion from the rest of life.[1]

The churches, though they have in many ways contributed to these processes, are unlikely to welcome such a future. Already there is evidence of need for some consistent source of public values such as the churches have provided in the past, both in the loss of confidence in public figures whose primary values seem to be based on expediency and in the search for a common universe of moral discourse in which to socialize the young. In Wuthnow's diversified society there would be little corrective force against the imposition on the rest of the society of the special interests of the economically or politically powerful. Also, there is evidence that it is psychologically unsatisfying for individuals to have all their commitments defined as trivial.[2]

Whether within the compartmentalized framework or not, recent statistics indicate several areas of increased religious impact on American society. After nearly two decades of steady decline, a 1976 Gallup poll has shown increases in church attendance. Gallup has also indicated a jump from 14 percent to 44 percent of the population who perceived the influence of religion to be increasing between the years 1970 and 1976. Church membership, however, has not increased significantly, but there has been some shift from liberal to conservative denominations. While interest in ecumenical cooperation at the upper levels of church organizations appears to be diminishing, local interdenominational contact seems to be expanding. Some of that contact is occuring in charismatic groups that tend to ignore denominational affiliation in the rush of religious enthusiasm. Evangelical religion appears to be on the rise, showing some militancy in political affairs and also harboring new movements that seek to link evangelical fervor with social activism. Various forms of mysticism, Eastern religions, and occult practices are on the rise as well.[3] Internationally, the rise of militant Islamic groups has assumed great political and economic importance.

In other words, if religion is disappearing into secularism, it is going out with a bang, not a whimper. This is a period of tremendous religious activity, and it is to this arena that we now turn our attention.

Notes and References

1. Robert Wuthnow, *The Consciousness Reformation* (Berkeley: University of California Press, 1976), Chapter 7.
2. It is difficult to avoid this interpretation of Wuthnow's account, when he writes of commercialization, "It soon becomes evident that which one is chosen actually makes little difference . . ." (p. 206); and of privatization, that it allows experimentation to be

limited to "activities that individuals can participate in without affecting the organizational structure of society" (p. 208).

3. For a summary of these and other trends, see Peggy Shriver, *What's Happening to Churches Today?* (New York: Office of Research, Evaluation and Planning, National Council of the Churches of Christ in the U.S.A., November 1977).

13

The Nature of the Organized Church

In recent years new perspectives have emerged in the sociology of religion that reflect both a greater recognition of the organizational nature of religious institutions and a growing sophistication of the discipline in the study of organizations of all kinds. Questions have been raised concerning the utility of such complex and relatively static concepts as those of "church," "sect," and "cult." Instead, some developments have begun that would bring into the sociology of religion insights from other areas, particularly those that would study religious organizations on the basis of "open-systems" models. In a comprehensive review of this approach, James Beckford has noted four important aspects of religious organizations as systems: their social environment, resources, processes, and structures.[1]

Reviewing the literature on the relationship of religious organizations to their environment, Beckford has drawn these generalizations:

1. The influence of environmental factors is felt most strongly by those religious organizations that have either a poorly articulated or an indistinct collective outlook.
2. The precise effects of environmental influence are mediated for religious organizations by their leaders, and the outcome depends to a large extent on the nature of the leaders' position in the organizational structure.
3. Religious groups that make strenuous attempts to maximize their recruitment or to produce major changes in the outside world are highly susceptible to environmental influence.
4. Changes in environmental conditions may occasion changes in the internal structure and the external products of religious organizations.[2]

Resources, he says, involve ideas, people, and materials; and religious organizations may be studied on the basis of ways they acquire and use each of these. Particular processes he notes include those of teaching, recruitment, and control; and he indicates that the structures studied may be those of specialization, formalization, centralization, or the distribution of authority.

One of the primary strengths of this approach is that the researcher may deal with each of these elements separately when studying any religious organization, rather than—as has frequently been the case—classifying the group as church or sect on the basis of its most striking characteristics, even though others may not fit the pattern.

Clearly it is particularly germane to sociologists that the organizational nature of the church be a primary focus, although it may run counter to some deeply ingrained stereotypes of people who are actively involved in it as well as those outside. The picture of the church as a large corporation given in the last chapter is foreign to many—probably most—members of those denominations to which it applies. Even in the large denominations most congregations have a membership of less than two hundred, so that the actual experience of many church members still fits patterns that have come down from an earlier, less urban time.

The common stereotype of the church in American society comes from its rural past—a picture of "the little brown (or white, or brick) church in the wildwood." Urban Americans tend to hold an idealized view of the rural past, of a society typical of the *Gemeinschaft,* where everyone shared in a local community, born of common experiences. The central focus of these shared values and experiences was the community church. In the stereotype the church is more closely related to the community than to any denominational structure; regardless of its name it is more congregational than not in polity. Services of worship in such a church are the expression of an already experienced sense of community. The church reinforces rather than creates the bonds of fellowship among its members. Frequently such a church serves as a community center where groups may gather, wedding and baby showers are held, and dinners, bazaars, and ice cream socials provide much of the social life of the community. Members are baptized, taught the faith, married, and buried from this one center.

Such is the stereotype; and its real counterparts do exist, though seldom in pure form and in decreasing numbers. What has happened to that sort of church depends, as Beckford would say, on its environment, on what has happened to the small town or rural area it once served. In the vast areas of the Great Plains and in scattered pockets of other rural areas, the effect of urbanization in the nation has been population loss. As improved technology has allowed fewer people to farm larger acreages, many farm families have sold their land to neighbors and moved to the city. Even more evident has been the loss of young people who have gone to the cities to pursue different occupations because they are no longer needed to keep the family farm going. Businesses in local villages have felt the loss of markets as fewer people are left to buy their goods and services, and better transportation has permitted shopping in larger, more distant centers. Many local business and service people have closed down their shops and joined the move to the city, following their customers. The same thing has happened in areas not devoted to large farming, such as the coal mining sections of Appalachia, where mining technology has put a high percentage of the people out of work.

The effect of this population loss in the local church is at least in part obvious. Its members dwindle, and with them much of its financial support. The congregation, losing its young people at a faster rate than that of any other group, becomes increasingly old in composition. The life of the community becomes less rich and varied. People begin to worry that it is usually the brightest and most ambitious of their young people who leave, so that an aura of apathy overtakes those who stay behind. Farmers who remain and buy more land tend to identify with Big Business and to have interests in areas much larger than the local community, so that the common life expressed in the local church is less real to them and their families. The pull of churches in larger, more distant centers may be strong for these families. Yet they are the very ones most capable of providing leadership and financial support for the struggling little church at home, which is having more and more trouble maintaining a minister and a program. As differences in life-styles grow, well-to-do commercial farmers may find it less and less satisfying to contribute to a congregation whose tastes in ministers and programs varies greatly from theirs; yet they are likely to be a minority in such congregations and so subject to those tastes. Sooner or later the little church is likely to reach the point where it can no longer maintain a full-time minister. It may share a minister with a nearby church that is in similar straits. It may eventually close down or be taken over by some sectarian group that has a program that does not rely on a trained ministry or a funded program.

This process is not a new one in American society. By the beginning of the century people were noting the decline of the country church. A good example of the situation can be found in a book by Gill and Pinchot published in 1919, called *Six Thousand Country Churches*.[3] This was a careful analysis of country churches in the state of Ohio, and it showed a high proportion unable to maintain a resident minister, and many no longer in operation. Many congregations still extant were too small to take any reasonable action in their communities. What was the case then is even more widespread now and has moved from the "old" Midwest into the wider regions of the center of the country.

One of the chief solutions to the problems of the rural church attempted by the denominations has been the effort to provide appropriately trained leaders for rural churches. This is partially taken up as a concentration in ministerial education, which in itself is no easy task. It takes a particularly gifted and well-trained person to provide ministerial leadership in a rural area with a declining population and resources. The rural church is most likely to lose many of its able lay leaders as they pursue economic—and social—opportunity elsewhere. The minister may be called upon both to provide solace to those left at home and to spark interest in an increasingly apathetic group. Financial problems plague churches in such circumstances, so it is clear that the job will not be a remunerative one. Neither is it likely to be inspiring to the seminary student to specialize in a field in which one may expect to work with a congregation whose proportion of young adults is dwindling, leaving perhaps a majority of older citizens who have neither the resources nor the inclination to try new ways of expressing their faith. While religious principles may encourage a decision to serve people in adverse circumstances, other religious principles may cause a minister to wish to expand the area of his or her influence, rather than to see it contract. Yet in such communities the minister may be one of the few remaining people who can offer professional leadership. He or she may be called upon to do so with little support from anyone whose role is similar.

In spite of such a gloomy picture, a fair number of seminary graduates are recruited into such areas. One source of hope for churches seeking recruits is the recent movement of women and older men seeking second careers into training for the ministry. In some cases their wider experience makes them better able to cope with the rural situation, and they may be less in need of the high salaries demanded by the younger ministers who may be supporting growing families. A less positive aspect of this selective recruitment applies primarily to the women, who often encounter prejudice in their efforts to obtain pastoral positions but are hired by churches that "cannot afford anything better." The result may either be a particularly happy discovery that women do well in such situations or a severe problem for the woman minister who finds herself isolated in a community that has no understanding of the professional woman, and has no one with whom to share the problems she has encountered.

A number of programs have been developed to deal with the problems faced by all rural ministers. In many states land-grant colleges have offered special training programs for town and country pastors already in the field, concentrating on bringing them up to date on the latest sociological, economic, and psychological insights into rural areas and people. Seminaries also offer forms of in-service training, including doctoral programs that are largely field based. Denominational and interdenominational agencies supply materials and programs, which sometimes at least provide channels of contact among rural ministers so that they may share ideas and encouragement. Denominational specialists tour the country in an attempt to meet with ministers and lay leaders and talk with them about programs and problems.

Denominational or cooperative assistance is not always met with open arms, however. The stereotypical rural or village church as an expression of the life of the people brings with it a degree of suspicion about "outside experts" and their programs. Many rural churches are the embodiment of a sort of ethnocentrism that is suspicious of training, materials, or programs that originate at denominational headquarters in the "wicked city." Not only are they morally suspect, they are bound to cost too much and require skills not present in the local congregation. Thus we see that some of the isolation of the rural church is self-imposed and self-perpetuating.

Many rural churches maintain programs only through grants from denominational sources, and one of the less pleasant tasks of area denominational officials is that of assessing the value of maintaining a faltering program for a few people in some distant spot with funds badly needed in areas where more people would be served. Sooner or later they may have to close down a church, but this action is always a cause of bitterness. People who have closely identified with a local church do not accept happily a decision to close it down that is made by some distant agency or meeting.

Other alternatives have been tried, with varying success. One is the "larger parish" plan, where several churches within traveling distance of one another elect representatives to a common board, which by pooling the resources of all the churches may be able to hire a staff ministry and recruit sufficient lay leadership to provide an adequate program for them all. For example, half a dozen churches may pool their budgets to hire a senior and an assistant minister and a director of religious education, who could each supply specialized services to the congregations. In such a way each congregation has the advantage of the specialized skills of a staff ministry, but under local direction. This arrangement is weakened when there are many differences between congregations such as relative size, community rivalries, traditional emphases, and competition for the time of the staff.

In towns where several churches of different denominations have been struggling to survive, the federated church has sometimes proven a viable alternative. Under this arrangement, the congregations may meet together, elect a common board, hire a minister, run a common Sunday school, and combine other organizations as a single church. Yet they maintain their denominational affiliations. New members may choose the denomination they join, and money sent to denominational centers is prorated according to some agreed plan. Ministers are often chosen from each denomination in rotation, although this method of hiring ministers is probably the biggest weakness of this type of church. In denominational districts ministers tend to be rotated among churches formally or informally. The minister who serves a federated church and is replaced by someone from another denomination may find that he or she has lost out in this game of "musical chairs." Also, one may hesitate to take a parish where programs built up would not be maintained by a successor from another tradition.[4] Sometimes federated churches also have difficulty because of different expectations arising from the separate traditions represented. In many cases, however, community identification is stronger than denominational traditions, and such difficulties may be overcome rather easily.

In particularly isolated areas, mobile ministers have carried on the tradition of the frontier circuit riders and the early "Sunday school missionaries," traveling from place to place with educational materials and encouragement, preaching, baptizing, marrying, burying—serving in any way they can a widely scattered flock. In some cases mobile ministers have attempted to organize their far-flung congregations, having them elect members of a board that meets occasionally to make program decisions. Sometimes they try to gather them all together three or four times a year to experience worship in a larger fellowship and gain a broader sense of belonging.

Rural black churches offer a particularly vivid example of the isolation, problems, and adaptations of the rural church. Here we find a pronounced lack of clerical leadership. Most rural black churches are controlled by the laity, with ministers traveling in to preach once or twice a month. Sunday schools tend to be strictly lay projects, with no minister in attendance. In a study of rural black churches in selected counties of Arkansas, Tennessee, Mississippi, Florida, North Carolina, Alabama, Georgia, and Virginia, Felton found only one-third of the rural ministers he contacted serving a single parish. Over one-third served two churches, and nearly 30 percent served three or more. Less than one-fourth of the ministers lived within five miles of the church they served. The average pastor spent two days a month in the parish, other than the Sundays he preached there. Nearly one-third were never in their parishes except on Sunday. Yet, for all their prominence, lay leaders received little training. Less than 10 percent of the churches studied had any kind of training for Sunday school teachers; less than 3 percent had classes to prepare people for the responsibilities of church membership. Ministers, likewise, had little training. Over half had not gone beyond high school; less than 4 percent had full college and seminary training. About two-thirds, however, were participating in some kind of in-service training—institutes, night schools, extension classes, correspondence courses, and the like. Such training was often found in colleges with departments of rural religion.[5]

The lack of training is partly based on lack of opportunity for such training. It is reinforced by the charismatic nature of the services, which may be important as a psychological release mechanism for many rural blacks. Between these two forces a cycle is set up that makes charismatic emphasis almost inevitable. The services in these churches tend to be emotional, aimed at "getting people ready for glory." Hymns used are usually spirituals, a tendency strengthened by the shortage of hymnals in almost all the churches studied by Felton. Yet even in rural areas there is a growing trend toward less emotionalism and a more rational style.[6]

In rural black churches the organization with the most members has often been the burial society. The otherworldly emphasis of rural black religion makes funerals more important than they are in the typical white congregation, a fact that often results in a severe financial burden on families. For a small monthly fee the burial society guarantees a decent funeral for its members. Sometimes these societies are totally within the organizational structure of the congregation; sometimes they are fully secular and operated by a funeral director. Usually they are a bit of both, with the burial society also serving as a community social club within the church.

The most prevalent organization in rural black churches is the missionary society, which tends to involve much more local charity than its white counterpart. Usher boards are also common and are organized groups with fairly wide responsibilities. In these as well as other organizations, women tend to be considerably more active than men. Much of the activity of the rural black church involves money raising—a serious occupation since only 18 percent of their ministers are fully supported by their congregations.[7]

Many of these rural patterns have been transferred almost unchanged to cities in which there are heavy concentrations of recent black migrants. However, urban black religious forms are as varied as those of whites and in many cases are not appreciably different.

Rural churches, black or white, have often been valuable centers of service to their area. Though they do not always have the personnel to deal with some local problems, they may sponsor and serve as staging areas for service projects in the larger area in which they are located. Head Start and other OEO programs were established through some rural churches, and summer work programs for student volunteers or VISTA workers have been centered there.[8] Churches have long been, and still remain, centers for supplementary education, as well as for distribution of food and clothing to the needy.

But much of the churchly service to rural America has not come from local rural churches, which so often seem to be struggling simply to maintain themselves. For example, programs for migrant agricultural laborers nearly all have been financed by and directed out of urban areas. Often, in fact, they have met resentment from local rural churches whose members are the employers of these migrants and who find themselves cast as villains by the rhetoric of the programs. Similar resistance was found in rural churches in areas of civil rights or other programs by the church for blacks in the South. Local white churches rarely cooperated and frequently condemned the activities.

This pattern has held true in Catholic as well as Protestant churches. In Texas and California efforts to unionize agricultural workers who are predominantly Mexican-American and Roman Catholic have created problems for local priests. Since they serve both workers and landowners, the priests are caught in the conflict of interests and often are either immobilized or choose to favor their more influential parishioners, even while continuing to preach the social teachings of the church. As a consequence, it has been priests from other dioceses and Protestant ministers who have assisted with picketing and care for the strikers, along with members of certain religious communities and lay people who could be recruited. The priests who first participated in the action ran into trouble with both civil and ecclesiastical authorities, but a result of the controversy was the appointment of a priest as chaplain to the workers, a separate mission paralleling Protestant migrant ministries.[9]

Local churches are unequipped to handle changes of this proportion. While motivation for social change may be traced to religious sources, it seldom comes from the kind of folk religion typical of the isolated rural church. A religion experienced as the celebration of the common life of a community is threatened by major change, regardless of its formal doctrines.

Not all rural churches, however, fit the pattern of dwindling population and growing isolation. Many, located fairly near to centers of urbanization, are faced with an entirely different set of problems. Rather than a declining population, they deal with an expanding one; but the growth comes from new people with new interests and outlooks. People who work in urban centers go out into nearby rural areas to settle for a number of reasons. They may be seeking open space, cleaner air, quieter living conditions. They may be looking for cheap land, low taxes, and freedom from stringent zoning regulations. Some who move into these areas are trying to return to an idealized rural past. They buy a small tract of land on which to garden and raise a few chickens and a calf or two. They look forward to participating in a rural community and attending a rural church. At a time when local residents are becoming part-time workers in the city and trying to come to terms with urban life, these new residents may try to lead the congregation back into its past. Their support and leadership are needed, however, and when they seek out the local rural church they are usually welcomed—at least at first.

The other "new people" may pose more of a problem. Many may have a low opinion of "local yokels," and if they are church oriented enough to do so may set in motion plans for organizing a congregation of their own, one likely to gain not only their support but also that of local residents who for one reason or another are becoming more urban in their outlook. This is most likely to happen, however, in areas that are really losing their rural character, and this may be seen as the extension of a suburban pattern. More often in areas that retain at least some of their rural character, urban people who come there are not organized but fairly isolated. They may drive back into the city on Sunday to attend a familiar church there. More often, they simply lose touch. In that case, local church people are left with the decision as to whether they should try to serve them in any way. In some cases, the answer is no, and the country church continues to celebrate a sense of community and a life-style in which the "new people" have no part. Sometimes, at least in denominations that have decision-making and policy-forming functions at broader levels than the local congregation, there are many pressures to try to reach out to the new neighbors. Evangelism in one form or another is common to the church, and the new people may be seen as proper targets for evangelistic action. If the new residents are poorer than the older ones, they may be seen as objects for charity drives; if they are richer, they may be courted as needed financial supporters. In most cases the perceptions of new residents and any action taken toward them are likely to be structured by the minister. In most rural communities ministers are expected to take a leadership role, and in most denominations they are trained to understand some of the social forces in action in such processes as this. There are many reasons why people enter the ministry, but usually they include some sort of commitment to make religion as they understand it central to their lives. The minister, then, is more likely than anyone else in the congregation to view worship as an expression of a common faith in something above and beyond daily life, rather than as an expression of a common life-style. Since this orientation is likely to be vital if a congregation is to expand to include a heterogeneous group, it may well be up to the minister to educate the congregation to this point of view. The first skirmishes may be theological and liturgical. The church service may have to incorporate elements foreign to local tradition, whether these are new hymns, new sermon topics, a slightly different style of worship, or such adjuncts as a coffee hour before or after the service where people may become acquainted. These may seem minor changes to the casual observer, but many pitched battles have been fought over new hymnals, changes in the order of worship, the use of written prayers and creeds, and other such details of congregational life.

At times such as this the church's education program becomes vital. Adult education through the Sunday school is more a norm for the rural Protestant church than its urban counterpart, if only because parents driving their children several miles are not likely to return home for the hour before church service, and a small congregation can hardly afford to have its teaching staff absent from services to hold classes during the worship hour. Traditional Sunday school lessons have not always been windows to the outside world, but denominational lessons of many churches today attempt to make them so. Adult education through women's groups may have been most successful along this line, since even the most traditional women's groups have been interested in missions. Most important, however, is the education of children, who may learn in the church school to isolate themselves from the outside world or to identify with it. The inclusion of new residents in the church program may make it easier to provide this wider social identification. To some members that may be a point against such inclusion, rather than for it, since they are suspicious of urban culture. But most rural children are likely to leave the country at least for a part of their lives, and the church that provides them with a religious basis for that life away from the home environment is more likely to be valued by those going through the process.

One of the basic characteristics of urban life is its mobility, not only in receiving people out of rural areas but also in redistributing those already in metropolitan districts. In many urban areas one may exchange a high proportion of one's neighbors in a single year. For example, Rossi found that in relatively stable urban areas 14 to 16 percent of the households had been in residence less than twenty-three months; in less stable areas the percentage was between 30 and 41.[10] Clearly such communities cannot rely on a long-lasting network of personal relations, nor can their churches. Rather, they must build the sort of organizational framework in which one person may easily substitute for another, giving at least some semblance of permanence to the congregation as a whole. The framework must be strong enough to outlast the people who occupy it. One criticism of the urban church is that the organization seems to be more important than the people, but it may have to be for the church to be there at all.

Rossi has distinguished between *client-oriented* and *member-oriented* organizations, saying that churches tend to be the member-oriented variety. Member-oriented organizations are more strongly affected by mobility than client-oriented ones because of the large number of interrelationships that must be broken when someone moves. In contrast, client-oriented organizations can shift fairly simply from one client to another, only altering the service slightly as they change.[11]

Winter has stated that Roman Catholic churches tend to be more client-oriented, Protestant churches more member-oriented, so that Protestant churches are more highly affected by mobility.[12] As a comparative measure this may be true, but such accounts as Fichter's *Social Relations in an Urban Parish* make it clear that parish life does suffer from mobility across parish lines by members of that denomination as well. Fichter assumes that full participation in Catholic life involves two dimensions, religious practice and integration into the life of the parish. His studies show that mobility does not affect the former so much as the latter.[13]

Yet Catholics, like Protestants, have built up a wide range of organizations aimed at maintaining parish life in the face of high rates of change in personnel. The geographic parish as a social unit is supplemented by interest groups, some of which exist on a supraparochial level. These include the Third Orders—lay adjuncts to monastic orders —as well as retreat leagues, interracial councils, cursillo groups, Cana conferences, and the like. Other groups are formed on the basis of occupation and again often gain membership by crossing parish boundaries. Within the local parish there are many of the same organizations found in the Protestant churches—scouts, youth organizations, women's societies devoted to service within the church or in its name to the world outside, men's groups, and the like. The nomenclature varies, but the number and range of specialized voluntary associations within the local parish structure is characteristic of the metropolitan church regardless of its denomination and whether Christian or Jewish.[14]

Winter has posed some interesting questions regarding the phenomenon of the organizational church. He notes that in order to have a structure that can survive a rapid turnover of members, relations must be kept impersonal to some degree. The result is what Winter calls an attempt to "fabricate a community through activity." Because of this he questions its religious significance as well as the basis of loyalty aroused by organizational activity. Winter suggests that the solidarity of the group is increased through fund raising, cooperative work, and contributions to activities, much as in primitive societies it is done through the exchange of gifts. Church work may provide an outlet for energies and a chance to achieve status. The duller tasks, he says, may take the place in Protestant churches of the Catholic sacrament of penance. Thus in the organizational church Winter sees the creation of a religious group based on celebrating organizational unity and relieving feelings of guilt, which can survive the changing population patterns of the metropolitan community.[15]

Naturally, not all members of a church are drawn into this organizational activity. Winter reports that studies of Protestant churches show that approximately two-thirds of their members are caught up in the organizational whirl in some way or another. A recent study of Presbyterians in a Southern community indicates that the proportion would be just a little over half for that sample. By contrast, although Fichter discusses a great variety of parish associations, he also states that less than 4 percent of the members of Catholic churches over the age of fourteen are involved in them.[16] This tends to support Winter's contention that the Catholic church is more client-oriented; certainly organizations play a far greater part in the religious life of the constituency of the member-oriented Protestant churches.

While a variety of voluntary associations is characteristic of the metropolitan church, the nature and comparative importance of such groups vary with the location and the theological orientation of the congregation. The primary difference between liberal and conservative congregations is not the style of internal activities, though these do vary, but rather what they consider appropriate public action. Sociologists have commonly held the view that liberal religiosity is associated with public action and conservative with an emphasis on the private nature of religion. However, Hoge has documented the fact that both theological forms support public action. Conservatives, however, see social aspects of religion in terms of evangelism, where liberals are more attuned to programs that will affect social change.[17]

Most studies comparing theologically liberal with conservative churches have been made at the denominational level, but there has always been significant variation on this subject among congregations within denominations. Hoge has documented this both historically and in contemporary society, with a primary focus on the United Presbyterian Church. He found strong differences among members of this denomination that were significantly related only to their theological position and a psychological factor he defined as a sense of "social threat."[18] One may question whether the range of social class identification within that denomination is sufficient to test all the assumptions of the effects of class on religious perspectives, but it is difficult to ignore his documentation of the two "parties" within Presbyterianism. It would also seem inappropriate to assume that condition to apply only within that denomination, since there is abundant evidence to the contrary.

Regional and national assemblies of most major denominations have been the scene of heated controversy arising from these theological positions. In some cases funds have been withheld from particular programs, and many denominations have been forced to reduce staffs and curtail activities because of such actions.

Another way in which these parties are evident is through the channels of communication they use, which are outside ordinary denominational structures. In seeking out materials for their educational programs, for example, many congregations in liberal denominations ignore the products of their own publishing houses in favor of those from nondenominational, often fundamentalist sources such as Gospel Light, David C. Cook, or Scripture Press. Conservative journals such as *Christianity Today* may vie for the attention of church members, in competition with denominational publications. Conservative radio and television programs attract a wide audience from within the liberal denominations as well as the more conservative ones. Liberals within more conservative denominations are more likely simply to change denomination than to involve themselves in other webs of communication, but this is not always the case. Certainly there is a wide readership for such publications as the *National Catholic Reporter* among liberal Catholics from dioceses far more conservative. Interdenominational meetings and well-known speakers draw audiences more on the basis of their theological stance than their denominational affiliation, and people who come to such affairs get to know one another across lines of parish and denomination.

There appear to be close parallels between sentiments in favor of the autonomy of local congregations and theological conservatism. This was not evident in the more hierarchically organized and more liturgical denominations until recent years, when organizational decisions to introduce significant changes in liturgy, creed, or moral guidelines have met with firm resistance from local congregations. In many instances the result has been a significant weakening of the power of the church hierarchy. There are some indications of a conservative move in some denominations to infiltrate if not take over the denominational hierarchy, including its professional staff. The very act of doing so, however, may change the consciousness of those who attempt it to the point that they become like those they would replace. Professionalism appears to have its own style, which overlays particular theological perspectives.

There are three major forms of denominational organization, or polity. The "episcopal" form, found not only in denominations carrying that title in their name but also in the Roman Catholic and Eastern Orthodox churches, is a centralized pattern in which it is assumed that the divine charisma flows out from the center through authorized channels. Local congregations are served by priests whose first loyalty is to the hierarchy, and who serve their congregations in its name. They are placed in parishes by bishops and serve at their sufferance rather than at the behest of the congregation. In this tradition there is considerable emphasis upon the priestly role, and on the idea of "apostolic succession," the commissioning of priests in a direct line back to the original apostles.

In "presbyterian" polity the model is that of representative government in which equal weight is given to clergy and to laity. Local congregations are part of larger "judicatories" which have certain powers over them, often including the ownership of church property. Ministers are members of the judicatory rather than of the congregation they serve, and are expected to represent the interests of the wider church. However, they are "called" and dismissed by the local congregation (under the eye of judicatory committees), so are clearly responsible to the local body. This lay power over the clergy is somewhat mitigated by the representational processes to higher judicatories, where ministers are often permanent members while lay representatives are rotated.

"Congregational" polity is typical of such denominations as the Baptists and the United Church of Christ, as well as most Jewish traditions. In this form, at least theoretically, local congregations exercise final authority, and any organization beyond that is only a cooperative federation of autonomous congregations. Ministers are called and dismissed by the congregation and are members of the congregations they serve.

In actual practice these differences are far less evident. In the first place, many denominations have a style that has from the beginning been a mixture of these types—the Lutherans and Methodists, for example. Secondly, the realities of financial support in American religious institutions tend to undermine the episcopal type. Since there is no established religion that can depend upon tax funds for support, priests tend to be dependent upon decisions of the local vestry for their own support as well as that of programs they hope to maintain. They also, of course, live in the communities they serve and tend to understand their problems more clearly than those of the hierarchy. For many priests this creates considerable role conflict, since advancement in the church is likely to require identifying oneself with the hierarchy, but doing a good job in one's present position may require greater sensitivity to local issues. Priests caught in such a dilemma may form lay councils to give the appearance of listening more to the congregation but hold them in powerless advisory roles; or they may delegate to such groups power more consistent with a presbyterian polity.

By far the most significant influence modifying denominational polity, however, is the nature of modern bureaucratic society, with its expectation of professional expertise, and the increase in size of the denominations. Early cooperative efforts in missionary work and religious education made the churches aware of the value of centralized structures for such activities. Even the most congregationally oriented have seen the value of having denominational publishing houses and seminaries which will train ministers according to their traditions. It becomes essential then to have governing boards over these kinds of operations and political structures through which such boards can be made responsive to the membership. In turn, board actions may require educational programs among the membership in order to gain support, and the trained ministers or educational specialists resulting from such programs have loyalties both to the larger body and to the congregations they serve. In the long run, the denomination becomes an organization not far removed in structure from any other modern bureaucracy.[19]

There is a tendency for boards and agencies to proliferate and to become more important in the workings of the denomination. Historically, the bureaucratization of the churches has been linked to liberal theology and the progressive movement. Church leaders caught up in cultural enthusiasm for efficiency and modern business methods adopted those methods both because they thought they would contribute to the organizational health of the churches and because their pride demanded modernization of the church to keep up with that of other social institutions. To implement the programs of the Social Gospel they needed efficient organizations capable of dealing with the large-scale bureaucracies of the commercial and governmental worlds.

However, modern business practices have not been shunned by more conservative bodies, either. Rather, they have been tied to evangelistic campaigns or to the espousal of political causes consistent with conservative views. Primer has cited the example of the Baptist General Convention of Texas, which hired a Jewish-owned advertising agency to plan an evangelistic campaign, a move supported not only by denominational executives but by local pastors as well.[20] Such drives as Bill Bright's "Here's Life, America" (the "I've Found It!" campaign) used all the commercial tricks of the trade, with organizational sophistication equal to any commercial bureaucracy.

In the churches, then, as in other institutions of the society, there has been a tendency for traditional political structures to become overlaid with specialized bureaucracies of professional staff. Many of the staff people define the church as that organization rather than as the voluntary association perceived by most lay members. To staff members, local parish ministers are often seen as the outermost limits of the church, rather like the local sales personnel of a large corporation. To rank-and-file laity, however, the center of the church is the local congregation, with bureaucratic staff serving as consultants or coordinators of special projects. In many cases, parish ministers are the buffers between those two views of the church, with the task of interpreting each to the other.

This task may create a considerable sense of alienation from the laity on the part of parish ministers. In addition, they may also be alienated from their work because of role expectations they may neither have learned nor desired. Much of the recruiting process for ministers militates against attracting people who are "management material," yet today's organizational church requires that the minister be an administrator of a large and diverse enterprise.

Fichter has listed nine functional roles the parish priest is expected to play: the *communal* role, in which he is expected to relate to his parishioners as individuals and as a community; the *administrative* role, as coordinator of the many groups and activities of the parish; the *businessman* role of being responsible for soliciting contributions and making financial reports; the *civic* role as an influential person in the community and the official representative of the parish; the *recreational* role of working with boys' clubs and athletic leagues and the like; the *ameliorative* role of supervising and performing acts of mercy; the *educational* role of supervising the parochial school as well as teaching from the pulpit and in counseling situations; the *sociospiritual* role of supervising organizations of a spiritual or liturgical nature; and the *liturgical* role of presiding at services.[21] While changes in the church since Fichter's study have made it easier for the priest to share many of these duties, in many parishes he still carries the responsibility of seeing to it that all these things are done. Similar lists have been made for roles of Protestant clergy, with perhaps more definite characterization of the preaching and counseling role than Fichter makes and the dropping of such items as parochial school supervision.[22] Rabbis, particularly in Conservative and Reform congregations, also find themselves caught up in the web of organizational leadership.[23]

The situation of the modern minister involves a series of important role conflicts. Blizzard lists a number of the most frequent. He says a minister is expected to be above all a person of belief, yet if one wants to keep the church strong and well supported, he or she will express those beliefs only at certain times and under certain circumstances. As head of a large organization that according to American cultural standards needs to be doing things, one is expected to be a person of action, and yet as a person devoted to declaring the Word of God, one must be a scholar. He or she plays a very private role as pastor and counselor, yet in the public role as preacher may be expected to speak to the problems that were confided in private. One is expected to serve as a teacher for the people, yet to have time and talent for managing organizations. One is expected to be a generalist, able to apply religious insights to all of life, yet one is treated as a specialist who concentrates on religion. One's training and status are those of a professional, yet there is seldom the leisure or the opportunity to arrange one's own schedule that are expected of such persons.[24] The simple service of God and one's fellows becomes a complex executive position. The minister of a large church who has several colleagues may be able to share with them some of the conflicts inherent in the position; however, if one is senior minister, there may be the added burden of coordination and supervision of the work of the staff.

The staffs of local churches, like those of denominations, are becoming more specialized. Even lay volunteers are likely to find themselves on boards of particular projects rather than simply offering undifferentiated service. Often their activities within the church are extensions of their secular careers: bankers may serve on the finance committee, schoolteachers staff the educational program, professional musicians form the choir, recreation specialists help with the youth group, and so on. Many people who seek a sense of wholeness and a broad-based experience of community in the church find it no different than any other organization in which they work and perhaps less satisfying in this way than recreational clubs. The connection to the broader functions of the church is so indirect that they feel little involvement in it.

Similarly, outside observers of the churches find little that is distinctive in their activities, but rather see other organizations functioning more efficiently to meet the needs of individuals and the society. The question is whether some of those needs are explicitly religious, and so are not being met elsewhere. Theologian Hans Küng has suggested that this is the case and furthermore that repression of innate religious drives in a secular society may have consequences more serious than those Freud traced to the repression of sexual drives in his culture.[25] He found one evidence of this in the many religious movements that are sweeping the modern world, and it is to these that we now must turn.

Notes and References

1. James Beckford, *Religious Organization,* published as volume 21, no. 2 of *Current Sociology* (1973): 34–92.
2. Ibid., p. 50.
3. Charles Gill and Gifford Pinchot, *Six Thousand Country Churches* (New York: Macmillan, 1919).
4. Rockwell C. Smith, *The Church in Our Town* (Nashville: Abingdon-Cokesbury, 1945), pp. 191–192.
5. Ralph A. Felton, *These My Brethren* (Madison, N.J.: Department of the Rural Church, Drew Theological Seminary, 1950), pp. 43–73.
6. Ruby Funchess Johnston, *The Religion of Negro Protestants* (New York: Philosophy Library, 1956), pp. 124–127.
7. Felton, op. cit., pp. 52–67.
8. Lyle Schaller, *The Churches' War on Poverty* (Nashville: Abingdon, 1967), pp. 43–76.
9. Patrick H. McNamara, "Social Action Priests in the Mexican American Community," *Sociological Analysis* 29 (Winter 1968): 181–185.
10. Peter Rossi, *Why Families Move* (New York: Free Press, 1955), p. 23.
11. Ibid., pp. 59–60.
12. Gibson Winter, *The Suburban Captivity of the Churches* (Garden City, N.Y.: Doubleday, 1961), pp. 89–90.
13. Joseph Fichter, *Social Relations in an Urban Parish* (Chicago: University of Chicago Press, 1954), Chapter 8.
14. Ibid., Chapters 11 and 12.
15. Winter, op. cit., pp. 91–98.
16. Fichter, op. cit., p. 157.
17. Dean Hoge, *Division in the Protestant House* (Philadelphia: Westminster, 1976), pp. 86–91.
18. Ibid., Chapter 2.
19. The classic description of this process may be found in Paul Harrison, *Authority and Power in a Free Church Tradition* (Carbondale: Southern Illinois University Press, 1971).

20. Ben Primer, *The Bureaucratization of the Church: Protestant Response to Modern Large-Scale Organization, 1929–1976* (Ph.D. dissertation, Johns Hopkins University, 1977), pp. 302–303.
21. Fichter, op. cit., pp. 127–137.
22. See, for example, David O. Moberg, *The Church as a Social Institution* (Englewood Cliffs, N.J.: Prentice-Hall, 1962), pp. 487–492.
23. Norman Miller, "Changing Patterns of Leadership in the Jewish Community," *Jewish Social Studies* 17 (July 1955): 13–15.
24. Samuel W. Blizzard, "Role Conflicts of the Urban Minister," *The City Church* (September–October 1956), pp. 13–15.
25. In the Terry Lectures at Yale, April 1978, as he applied some of Jung's insights to the current situation.

14

New Religious Movements I: The Response of the Alienated

Confusion as to the nature and function of the religious institution is only one of many indications that there is something of a crisis of confidence in modern Western culture that affects and is affected by religion. In each of the chapters of Part III we have raised questions, not just from the point of view of religion but from that of the larger society, concerning ways in which major social institutions are being judged dysfunctional for reaching goals defined by the culture. Robert Merton has posited a number of responses that can be manifested by persons for whom there is a discrepancy between cultural goals and the institutional means provided for reaching them. Beginning with a state of "conformity," in which both the cultural goals and the prescribed means of reaching them are possible to the individual and accepted by him or her, he posits a response of "innovation," in which the person accepts the goals as appropriate, but blocked by circumstances or personal ideology from using the accepted means, devises new ways of reaching those goals. In "ritualization," the person, well socialized into the institutional patterns of goal attainment, continues with such behavior even though it is impossible in this case to reach the goals by that means. "Retreatism" signifies the giving up of both goals and means and simply opting out of the process. "Rebellion" rejects both but goes on to posit new goals and new means to reach them, guiding further action in the basis of the new position.[1]

This model can be used to explain religious behavior in two ways. First, it may describe deviation of religious activity within the religious institution. Second, in the context of the wider society it may describe religious behavior, institutionalized or innovative, as a means for reaching culturally prescribed goals or for compensating for the inability to reach such goals or for creating new ones. Conventional religious behavior may help a person to "get ahead." Expressive religions may provide psychological compensation for failure to do so. Some isolated religious communities may be places of retreat for those who reject both goals and means. Religious activity learned in childhood as the "right way to behave" may be continued long after it has lost meaning in terms of either proximate or ultimate ends. And religion may become the source of new ways of looking at the world, new goals, and a new moral order based on those goals.

This last form, fitting Merton's category of "rebellion," is a type of religion Wallace has categorized as a "revitalization movement." In his discussion of the functions of ritual, Wallace notes that ritual often is involved with providing experiential confirmation for an image of self or a sense of identity, often with some sort of mystical experience. In a similar way, entire communities may on occasion suffer crises of identity, and it is at such crises that rituals of revitalization become necessary. Traditional rituals for individual salvation are no longer effective, or are overburdened because problems have become too widespread. The system can no longer provide a comfortable identity for enough of its people. The result may be a revitalization movement.

However, such a movement does not spring up overnight. Rather, Wallace finds several stages of cultural change necessary before such a movement can arise. Beginning with a "steady state," in which change is not occurring so rapidly as to cause difficulty for more than a small minority of the people, a sociocultural system moves into a phase when it is sufficiently out of balance to cause a sharp increase in the amount of stress on the individual. The situation is still usually viewed as a fluctuation in the steady state, but there is widespread disillusionment and anomie, accompanied by a rise in crime rates and illnesses, a defection from the norms of kinship systems, and similar symptoms of disorganization. In Wallace's next stage, that of cultural distortion, asocial behavior that was previously idiosyncratic now becomes common to a group and is institutionalized as an effort to circumvent what is perceived as an increasingly venal "establishment" or "system." Because these efforts are not well coordinated, their result is usually further disorganization of the society. After this stage has been reached, it is almost impossible for a culture to regain the steady state without completing the process of revitalization.

The actual revitalization movement involves the formulation of a code—some blueprint of the ideal society, or *goal culture,* and a *transfer culture* which provides a system for reaching that ideal. Often the code or ideal is arrived at mystically, by a person in the role of shaman or prophet. The code must then attract converts, who gradually form into an organization which can adapt the new insights of the code to the realities of the society. These adaptations may transform the society, if they can be made without destroying the economic base of the social order or requiring destructive levels of coercion. The resulting institutionalization is likely to resemble the transfer culture more than the goal culture, but definite changes will have occurred. A new steady state may now have been achieved, with at least a slightly different cultural base.[2]

Certainly there are overwhelming indications that Western culture has moved beyond any kind of steady state. The data are available in the newspaper headlines, in the content of successful theatrical or cinematic productions, in the titles on the best-seller lists, in the most popular music, and more and more in ordinary conversations. Crime and divorce rates testify to the sort of personal disorganization mentioned by Wallace. The remarkable increase in the number of patients in mental hospitals and of such stress-induced conditions as ulcers and heart disease also indicates the strain people encounter in living in modern urban society. The young have been the most vociferous in expressing their disenchantment with the "system," but even in the homes of the comfortable and the mature a sort of unease is expressed. That we have reached the stage of cultural distortion seems evident when we realize that many of the symptoms of stress are appearing among those who, according to cultural definitions, have attained success and well-being.

Attacks on the culture that have arisen under these conditions strike deeply, often at the very root of the world view that has sustained Western civilization for centuries. While earlier unrest was often caused by groups denied access to the cultural mainstream, much of today's unrest appears to emanate from the cultural center, taking a form well expressed in the title of the recent show, "Stop the World, I Want to Get Off." Since the beginning of the modern age, Western culture has been dedicated to an objective, scientific view of the world and to the development of material technology to meet its problems. Basic to most of the assumptions upon which the social order has been based are a manipulative attitude toward our natural surroundings and a linear view of the process of history. Both these views are supported by the Judeo-Christian heritage. The creation myth, for example, includes the injunction to humankind to take dominion over the earth and subdue it. The entire Judeo-Christian world view is that of a progressive history in which a transcendent God is working out his will, and which will in the end result in the culmination of a divine plan. The optimistic, progress-oriented pragmatism of American culture has been firmly planted in these traditions. Essentially, we have assumed that by the grace of God we will learn more and more about how to dominate our environment, so that we can glorify God by making that environment a glorious setting for the development of the highest potential of humankind. Over time, references to a transcendent divinity have appeared less necessary in the scheme of things. Science gave insights into natural laws that could be manipulated without the interference of any *deus ex machina*. It seemed that if there were any god, it must be his will that we come of age and be no longer dependent upon a divine parent figure. And the social sciences had shown rather clearly how we create our own gods out of our experiences and needs.[3] Modern people felt they had the tools to control the universe so that they could live without fear or anxiety. Religious people felt that the Kingdom of God could be brought about by the efforts of people of goodwill.

In the past generation the fear has grown that the very tools we have developed are proving unmanageable and threatening. While some Cassandras have long complained of this, it was probably the development of the atomic bomb that brought the point home to rank-and-file members of the society. Yet that fact alone did not bring on the present apocalyptic mood. It was lost for some time in the political efforts to control this new tool of destruction—the United Nations and then the machinations of the Cold War.

Another important ingredient of the present malaise is the apparent inability of our technical sophistication to bring about culmination of human happiness. The wheels of progress have come to demand an increase in the consumption of the products of technology. This is true both in the relationships of richer nations to poorer ones and of the rich to the poor within the nation. To keep production going the easiest method of maintaining a market is to increase the sense of need of the products among those who can pay for more. So planned obsolescence, status striving through the amassing of material possessions, and a constant state of dissatisfaction with present acquisitions are encouraged. Those who benefit most from the technology have little time to relax and enjoy it. They are too busy seeking the wherewithal to buy more, or simply maintaining what they already possess. They are not happy because they are not allowed to feel a sense of fulfillment, yet they are envied and often hated by those who, subject to advertisements aimed at raising the level of need, find no way to maintain even the minimum level of what we have defined as civilized culture.

The deprivations that are felt are not just those of time, effort, and material need, however, or even the feeling that we have been imprisoned by the rhythm of the assembly line. The rise of modern psychology has put the stamp of science on a more personal sort of malaise. People are beginning to be aware that somehow they are treated as objects rather than persons, and that this deprives them of important satisfactions. The world view of the scientist can be that of the disinterested observer who treats self and others as objects of study; because of this the scientist is less a hero than formerly. The findings of science support the perception of a need for persons to be reunited with themselves as subjects involved in experience. Psychology itself has evolved into several branches, not always appreciating one another's views. While some psychologists remain distant and objective, the branch that speaks more directly to the needs mentioned above is that developed by Harry Stack Sullivan, Abraham Masow, Carl Rogers, and such mavericks as R. D. Laing. All emphasize the need for the individual to be allowed to develop his or her full potential in conditions of openness and positive response. Laing's work testifies to the idea that modern consciousness, with its objectification of the self, requires people to be schizophrenic.[4]

Added to the personal disorganization affirmed in this point of view is the growing awareness of the environmental consequences of expanding technology. Not only does technology appear to be getting physically in the way of human happiness by making people too busy with acquisitions to enjoy life and by alienating them from themselves by using them as objects, it also is setting up environmental conditions that may make life intolerable, if not impossible. Increasingly, people are beginning to picture themselves as coming to the point where the world will be one foul garbage heap, on which we must engage in a constant—and losing—battle even to find food, air, and water that are not so contaminated as to poison us. The manipulation of nature appears to have become the destruction of nature, and hence a violation of our nature also.

In summary, there is a growing awareness in modern society that the basic assumptions of technical progress and scientific knowledge may be leading not to Utopia but to a loss of humanity, if not total destruction. Not only is this so, but that awareness is compounded by the feeling that the technological machine cannot be stopped, that we are caught in an ever-descending spiral of our own making from which there is no escape.

While not everyone in the society shares this perception, the disaffection seems to be growing. News of corruption in high places only reinforces the feeling that the best one can do is to pursue individual and immediate gain before anything more goes wrong. In religion as well as in other areas of life, individual salvation becomes the most one can expect to achieve.

Yet one of the perceptions of the present situation involves a loss of confidence in the traditional methods of achieving salvation, whether individual or corporate. According to Bellah, when change has under-mined common assumptions, there is danger to the commitment people have to any system of faith, for many of the structures upon which they have rested their faith are changing or disappearing. The result of this may be one of three responses: people may sink into a condition of "permanent undercommitment" or loss of faith, becoming alienated from any faith system; they may create changes in the symbol system which make it responsive to a changed environment, either through limited reform or through charismatic revolution; or they may react by forming an overcommitment to the present system.[5]

Loss of commitment to standard religious forms may take the form of various kinds of secularism. For individuals pursuing a private form of salvation, but not satisfied with an existence approaching autism, many of the practices based on forms of humanistic psychology have come to be the secular alternative to religious faith. In general, this type of psychology builds on a scientific framework that has often been perceived as antithetical to traditional religious world views. Positivistic science has often been posited as the successor to religion, the latter being interpreted as the set of inadequate explanatory systems devel-oped out of a sense of awe at the mystery of the unknown, which was gradually being replaced by rational responses as science pushed back the frontiers of knowledge and provided the context for responsible action.[6] At the same time, humanistic psychology represents a break with the rational world view of science, in that it takes seriously the emotional and expressive needs of the individual and sets up methods by which people are freed from any religious, moral, or rational system that prevents the meeting of those needs.

This quest for secular personal salvation through the methods of humanistic psychology has come to be known as the "human potential movement." It had its beginnings in the late 1940s in the National Training Laboratory in Bethel, Maine, in what were known as T-groups. At the beginning there was a close resemblance of such groups to forms of group therapy used by clinical psychologists. The therapeutic em-phasis fits well into models of the processes of social change that hold that initial reactions generally locate any problems with the individual, who is seen as needing help in adjusting of functioning properly. T-groups and "encounter groups," which was the term that came into general use next, were used as tools for sparking creativity and more harmonious relations in large organizations, as methods of dealing with such social ills as racism, sexism, and classism by allowing oppressors and oppressed to confront one another directly, as ways to induce "honest relationships" in marriages, and as new ways to induce the primary relationships deemed necessary for a sense of community in religious groups. But the largest percentage of people who subscribed to some form of the human potential movement soon came to be those secular seekers who desired some form of individual salvation.[7]

Centers for personal growth have appeared everywhere, some with national reputations such as Esalen or *est*, others with a local clientele under the rubric of self-help, marriage or sex therapy, consciousness raising, assertiveness training, or countless other emphases. Some are the result of leadership formed through a recognized training program; some are led by people whose primary source of information has been one or more popular books on the subject; some are led by charlatans who have discovered that an affluent society provides princely rewards to those who promise to mitigate its negative effects.

The structured training-type program has penetrated most major institutions of the society, including its churches. Clergy or lay leaders are often subsidized in obtaining training, and they then form the staff of some conference of retreat center or the leadership of occasional evening or weekend group sessions or the facilitators of ongoing groups in the church. Particularly in liberal churches where religion has tended to stress rationality over emotion, this form of activity has managed to return some emotional content to the interaction of members without giving in to stereotypical emotional religion. In churches that have become impersonal and client oriented, the forms of intimate sharing and physical contact encouraged by these groups may result in feelings of knowing and being known seldom, if ever, experienced elsewhere by the participants.[8]

While churches may interpret such responses as intimations of the grace of God, there is no necessity in the basic structure of the human potential movement for any religious ideology to be present. Rather, the image of humankind that is presented is that of the autonomous, responsive individual whose capabilities are infinite and simply need to be freed and nourished. The divine image most compatible with this ideology is one of immanence: God dwells within us, only waiting to be recognized and celebrated.

The image of society in the human potential movement comes close to that which Berger has described as typical of *alienation.* That is, the structures of the society are experienced not as human creations or projections of the self, but as external and alien forces impinging on the development of the self.[9] The human potential movement expresses this alienation not by attempting to change the culture to prevent such effects, but by finding ways of escaping those effects through the stimulation of a certain form of consciousness. This being the case, it offers little threat to the society and can be subscribed to by many who are in favored positions in the social structure. In 1970 Carl Rogers estimated that three-quarters of a million Americans were involved in encounter groups in that year alone.[10]

The self-help type of human potential activity is best attested to by the number of best-selling books on the subject in recent years. Such titles as *Self Creation, Looking Out for #1, Pulling Your Own Strings, Games People Play, I'm OK—You're OK, Winning through Intimidation, Breaking Free,* and a host of others provide ideas and methods for persons to use in the pursuit of self-realization. Closely allied with these are the current celebrations of physical fitness as a form of new consciousness, represented in such books as *Running and Being.*

Assistance in the pursuit of secular salvation is also provided by those who have made it a business venture. An early form of this was the Dale Carnegie Success Course, in which the typical "loser" is taught the social skills to become a "winner." A more recent and more full-blown example is Werner Erhardt's *est.* Erhardt, who among other things is a former Carnegie course instructor, makes no apologies for having combined techniques taught there with aspects of encounter groups, Zen, Scientology, Gestalt therapy, Transcendental Meditation, and a number of other sources. He has packaged the result of his synthesis into seminars that are run by well-trained leaders according to a highly explicit format. Participants pay for the experience (at latest report, $250 each, though inflation may be affecting *est* as it is everything else). According to Stone, some 30,000 persons had been involved in *est* by 1974, from its beginning in 1971, and at that time it was only beginning to attain national recognition. Similar groups that offer a synthesis of methods of an essentially secular enlightenment are Arica (Stone estimates 20,000 involved in this movement between 1970 and 1974) and Psychosynthesis (1,000). Two other groups that are similar but have more explicit membership requirements are Transcendental Meditation (TM) and Silva Mind Control, estimated by Stone to have involved between them over a million people by 1975.[11] Similarly, Dianetics, later to become Scientology, at first offered a form of secular salvation by way of self-improvement provided through an organization that asked remuneration. Its later stages will be dealt with in the following chapter.

As we begin to consider such movements we have begun to breach the boundary between Bellah's categories of loss of faith and of developing new symbol systems or reforming old ones. The pure type of his "faithless" response may not be represented here at all, but it is assumed that ideologies that leave the individual to be his or her only source of meaning come close. When one begins to pin one's hopes on the methods or programs provided by another, we seem at least to be approaching what Campbell has called the "cultic milieu," a sort of underground of ideas and movements from which cults arise.[12] We may, indeed, be beginning to deal with movements that could be defined as cults.

It may be worthwhile here to look briefly at the way in which Wallis has defined cults in this context, for one of the problems of sociological concepts is that they are in continual need of readjustment to fit the realities of the specific social structure to which they are applied. In looking at the current plethora of religious and parareligious groups, Wallis defines a cult in relation to other religious forms—the church, the denomination, and the sect—on the basis of their comparative respectability and their claim to be the exclusive source of salvation, thus:

A Typology of Ideological Collectives[13]

	Respectable	Deviant
Uniquely legitimate	Church	Sect
Pluralistically legitimate	Denomination	Cult

In other words, a denomination differs from the classic concept of the church in that it is at one and the same time the accepted religious form in the society and recognized internally and externally as only one segment of that legitimate religion. Other denominations are also considered legitimate religious options, although members of each may have reasons for thinking theirs is the best—at least for them. Similarly, among groups defined by themselves and/or others as deviant from the institutional pattern, sects claim exclusiveness. To be a sect a group must have some form of strict boundary maintenance around the organization; it must be able to define heresy so as to maintain boundaries around the dogma. Cults, on the other hand, may be sought out by persons who have no intention of restricting their ideology or their membership to a single group. Transcendental Meditation, for example, has been quite explicit about not competing with other religious loyalties people may have, but rather enhancing their ability to participate in them.

In times of cultural stress cults tend to proliferate, each building on some aspect of the culture in a manner unlike more normative interpretations. At the present time, for example, in addition to the traditional esoteric approaches of occultism, divining, spiritualism, and astrology, which have long been part of the "spiritual underground," new mythologies are being built around UFOs and space travel, the magic of primitive shamans such as Castenada's "Don Juan," various forms of parapsychology, and the ability of pseudoscientific gadgets or radiation to diagnose, heal, or transport the believer. Truly, there is reason to liken modern society to that heady period in the Hellenistic world that became a "cultic hothouse."[14]

Because of their lack of clear boundary maintenance, Wallis characterizes cults by "doctrinal precariousness," noting that there is little to distinguish the ideology of the cult from its background, the cultic milieu. People may move from one to the other with scarcely any recognition of having left or entered. They also face problems of authority, described by Wallis in this way:

> First, their membership is predominantly composed of seekers who see a variety of paths to the truth or salvation and who regard it as their right to select those ideas and practices which will lead towards this goal. Second, cults are typically service-oriented, purveying an experience, knowledge or technique through teachers and practitioners. Hence charisma tends to be dispersed towards the lower echelons. Membership (or clientele) loyalties are often centred on the local teacher or practitioner rather than on the movement as a whole. There is therefore a perennial threat of schism and secession as local teachers or practitioners assert their autonomy. Third, cults tend to face a problem of commitment. They are viewed as one among a range of paths to truth or salvation rather than a unique path. They typically dispense commodities of a limited and specific kind. The involvement of the membership tends, therefore, to be occasional, temporary, and segmentary. Retaining, institutionalizing, and enhancing membership commitment therefore presents a problem to cults which, if unresolved, may lead to passive and limited involvement, apathy, and declining adherence.[15]

Where there is a relatively unlimited market for the ideological or methodological offerings of the cult, these problems of boundary maintenance are negligible. No business need worry about customer loyalty so long as there are as many customers waiting as the organization can handle. However, all this business language should not cloud the fact that many of those who lead groups or offer services to clients who participate in cults are themselves sincere "true believers" who assume that they are in touch with a unique revelation others should find important.

Part of the modern cultic milieu in Western society are many religious forms legitimate to Eastern cultures. A significant number of Americans are involved in one form or another of Buddhism, with Zen, Nicheran Soshu, and Tibetan versions probably the most common. Indian religions are evident not only in the commercialized version of TM, but among followers of various gurus and practitioners of many sorts of Yoga. Many—perhaps most—Eastern religious forms have been adapted and reshaped by American adherents, often combining more than one in the process. An example is the 3HO—the Happy, Healthy,

Holy Organization, followers of the Yogi Bhajan. In the practices of this group may be found elements of Yoga (particularly in its kundalini and tantric forms) and Sikhism—elements not commonly combined in this fashion in their native India.[16]

Similarly, the Divine Light Mission, the followers of the young Maharaj Ji, combine traditional Hindu mythology with many other elements, as do the followers of Meher Baba. A common element in these groups is their basic monism—their understanding of the unity of all things, including the divine. Thus cultic rather than sectarian forms are more natural to these ideologies.

While the exclusiveness of traditional Islam (fully a "church" on its own soil) makes it an unlikely candidate for cultic option, there has been considerable involvement of Westerners in Sufism, the mystical, experiential branch of Islam, in a cultic manner.

One of Wallis's primary contributions to the study of cults is found in his discussion of the process by which cults become sects. He traces the ways in which responses by the leadership of a cult to problems of the precariousness of doctrinal boundaries and authority result in new ideological and organizational forms that begin to claim a uniqueness to the revelation through definitions of heresy or organizational defection.[17] However, he has been criticized by Richardson for ignoring factors implicit in the ideology, the culture, and the particular needs of members.[18] As noted above, a religion with a monistic ideology is much more open to being treated as a cult than one that posits a dualistic universe, where there is a clear division between good and evil, and thus the need to classify ideologies as one or the other. Also, cultic milieus are much more likely to expand at points in the history of a society when the culture is under some strain, so that it is appropriate to seek out new versions rather than accept the institutional formulations. Finally, Wallis's studies of the development of Scientology as a sect out of its cultic phase of Dianetics deals with an organization that has a clear leadership pattern, where the founder has a good deal to lose if the movement is dissolved. Thus Richardson, looking at the process more from the point of view of members than of the leadership, posits the following:

A Generalized Model of Major Factors Involved in the Change of a Cult to a Sect[19]

Group factors
1. Need for leadership to guide group
2. Need for "boundaries" (both doctrinal *and* behavioral) to define the group

3. Need for commitment from participants

Individual factors
1. Need for an "order" and an ethic by participants
2. Predispositions of participants
3. More recent experiences of participants

Similarities or "bridges" between cultic milieu and sect perspective and life-style
1. Ideological bridges
2. Experiential bridges
3. Behavioral bridges
4. Affective ties

External factors
1. Pressures from the society to give up certain elements of the counterculture cultic milieu
2. Encouragements from society to adopt a more acceptable perspective and life-style
3. "Movement" on the part of the greater society that makes it easier to become an "acceptable" sect

As we shall see later, Richardson's assumptions about the potential acceptability of the sect are similarly based on unique characteristics of the group he studied, whose Christian ideology was more in line with institutional religion in the West than some cultic forms that may turn into sects while retaining a clear separation from normative cultural patterns. What is really involved here is a pair of contrasting definitions of the term "cult." Wallace, focusing on social organization, limits his definition to the loose boundary maintenance of the cult and the individualism of its clients; while Richardson and a number of others add a third qualification, that the ideology be deviant from institutional forms—for example, in the Western world, something other than a variant of the Judeo-Christian tradition. In modern society, where a considerable proportion of the people have had a basically secular background, it would seem that Wallis is on safer ground with his definition. For many people modern culture is genuinely pluralistic; there is no one normative ideology by which cults could be distinguished from sects.

However, an individualistic emphasis by itself is insufficient as a definition of a cult. The third response to change mentioned by Bellah is an increased commitment to the present system. While the culture is still in a state of increased individual stress, increased commitment to the system may mean a voluntary renunciation of individual response, an accession to institutional authority. But in American society, one element of institutional religion has been the individually oriented strain of Protestant evangelicalism. In this context, the current "rise of the evangelicals" can be seen as a type of the overcommitted response at this stage.

A good deal of the apparent increase of evangelical Christianity is in reality an increase in media and scholarly *interest* in the evangelicals.[20] For example, a 1976 Gallup poll showed 34 percent of the American population claiming to have had a "born again" experience.[21] However, the poll is not particularly useful for ascertaining trends, since it was only in that year that the question had seemed worth asking. A significant percentage of those claiming the experience were older people who might be expected to have been converted many years ago. There is, however, little doubt about an increase in public awareness of evangelical Christianity and in its respectability. That in itself could be considered a new movement.

In a way, the phenomenon of the rise of this religious form is like the discovery in the 1970s that secularization was not a straight-line trend. Modern science and scholarship were expected to make a literalist Christianity impossible for all but a few marginal persons for whom its offer of salvation could make life more tolerable. Instead, as the rational, liberal churches have shown declining membership and participation rates, evangelical churches are bulging at the seams, largely with relatively affluent participants.[22]

Evangelical Christianity shows a great deal of variation but in general can be counted on to stress three basic theological principles. These, as stated by Richard Quebedeaux, are:

1. The full authority of Scriptures in matters of faith and practice;
2. The necessity of personal faith in Jesus Christ as Savior and Lord (conversion); and
3. The urgency of seeking the conversion of sinful men and women to Christ (evangelism).[23]

On this basis, the Gallup poll shows that 18 percent of those polled would fully qualify as evangelicals, with many others subscribing to at least two of the three points.[24] This is a sufficiently high percentage to be considered more than a marginal minority as has been done in the past. In fact, Quebedeaux goes so far as to say that evangelicalism is really the main-line form of American Christianity.[25]

At the same time, the rising respectability of the evangelicals has allowed their public image to be separated from that of hard-core fundamentalism, which really is a marginal movement. Quebedeaux earlier distinguished five types of evangelical Christianity: separatist fundamentalism, open fundamentalism, establishment evangelicalism, the new evangelicalism, and charismatic renewal.[26] Perhaps with the exception of the charismatics, these may be seen as degrees of the sort of commitment to past forms noted by Bellah, with the separatist fundamentalists the most extremely overcommitted. Evangelicalism as a whole, and fundamentalism in particular, can be perceived as a "nativistic movement," which Ralph Linton has described as "any conscious, organized attempt on the part of a society's members to revive or perpetuate selected aspects of the culture."[27] While Linton sees this phenomenon arising out of contact between two dissimilar cultures, a good case can be made that under conditions of massive change this kind of dissimilarity exists between generations or between various portions of a society unequally affected by change. The primary source of such conscious, organized efforts to hold on to a culture is the awareness that the culture is threatened. And while nativistic movements conceivably could be built around nonreligious aspects of a culture, serious ones nearly always incorporate elements of the basic value system that are related to religious interpretations. If the myth of a society is the ground for the culture, then the preservation or recovery of the myth is seen as essential. In the same way, the ritual and organizational forms that embody the myth are among the most likely elements of the culture to be singled out for emphasis in a nativistic movement.

Linton distinguishes two dimensions for classification of nativistic movements. The first dimension is found in the distinction between *revivalistic* and *perpetuative* nativism. That is, some nativistic movements seek to revive elements of the culture that have been lost; others seek to perpetuate elements that appear in danger of being lost but are still present in the society. The other dimension is concerned with the orientation toward the object of the movement. While there are elements of unreality in all nativistic movements, some are relatively *rational* in their approach, while others are heavily *magical* or supernatural.[28] Elements of both dimensions can be found in the reaction against change in religious institutions of modern society.

Basic to the negative reaction to change is the sense of the sacred in religious institutions. While it is quite possible to legitimate change as an attempt to do the will of a transcendent of God, it is equally if not more possible to oppose change as an attack on sacred values and beliefs. Since such an attack threatens the world view of the adherents of the religion, and consequently the foundations of their identity, reaction is likely to be particularly strong.

Fundamentalism developed as a countermovement to the liberal "modernist" trends in the churches, which seemed to be casting aside any distinctions between Christianity and the sinful world. The beginnings of fundamentalism go back to the preaching of such great evangelists as Dwight L. Moody for their style. To the basic emphasis on a simple, upright life and the acceptance of Jesus as one's personal savior the fundamentalists add dogmatic assertions about the literal inerrancy of the Scriptures, the Virgin Birth, and certain eschatological beliefs. True fundamentalists concentrate on a "premillenial" view of the future which expects Jesus to defeat the Antichrist in battle and reign for a thousand years of peace on earth before the Last Judgment. Faithful Christians, however, will be "raptured" before the awful days of the final battle. They reject all other interpretations of the "final events" as unbiblical.[29] Since they assume everything must continue to get worse until the end, they have little reason to take action to ameliorate any social ills.

Another building block of fundamentalism has been a way of interpreting the Scriptures known as "dispensationalism." This view sees in the sacred history seven "dispensations" (for example, ancient Israel was under the dispensation of the Law; the Christian is under the dispensation of Grace; the Last Judgment will bring about the final dispensation). Dispensationalism was communicated chiefly through the "Scofield Reference Bible," an issue of the King James Version with notes by Dr. C. E. Scofield, which also carries the more ancient dating of Bishop Ussher, who through biblical study set the date of the creation of the world as 4004 B.C.

Both the idea of scriptural inerrancy and the notions of judgment bespeak a closed view of the world. The Truth is understood to involve a set of God-given absolutes. Thus doctrinal change is anathema; social change is wrong. The right view of the world comes from recollections of a more simple rural America and a familiarity with the culture of biblical times.

Closed fundamentalism seems to fit this description best, particularly in the way in which it has come to be linked with political movements of the far right. Organizations such as Carl McIntyre's American Council of Christian Churches and Billy James Hargis's Christian Crusade have managed to keep alive the Cold War rhetoric of Christian capitalism versus atheistic Communism/Socialism, excoriating the supposed Communist influence in the major denominations.

Open fundamentalism, according to Quebedeaux, is particularly distinguished from the closed variety on this matter of conservative politics. It is much more apolitical, more open to different life-styles as found in the Jesus movement, so long as theological orthodoxy is maintained.[30]

Establishment evangelicalism is the primary locus of the increase in numbers and influence of evangelicals in the 1970s. Its reaction against change is not the deep and bitter type of the fundamentalists, many of whom have had personal experiences of the loss of small businesses or farms to larger corporations, the devaluation of their occupations, or— in the case of some open fundamentalists—the alienation of the counterculture. That portion of establishment evangelicalism that reacts in this way is less likely born of personal experience than it is a perception of the urban society from the safety of the suburbs or small towns to which it escaped. The simpler moral universe of a more rural America is celebrated in opposition to the ambiguities of a pluralist urban society. Establishment evangelicalism is centered in such denominations as the Southern Baptist and Lutheran Church–Missouri Synod, in the National Association of Evangelicals, and in a number of internal movements within the liberal denominations. Leaders include such well-known evangelists as Billy Graham and, since his election to the presidency, Jimmy Carter. This form of evangelicalism tends to be supportive of a middle-class way of life and, according to Quebedeaux, is in danger of losing its distinctiveness from the general culture.[31] Quebedeaux's category of "New Evangelicals" may fit better into the discussion in the following chapter.

The primary way in which all evangelicalism can be seen as a response to a culture that is perceived to be at a point somewhere between a period of increased individual stress and one of cultural distortion is its emphasis on the individual and on individual salvation. No matter how bad things may be in the society, the evangelical Christian may have the "blessed assurance" of eternal salvation. He or she is not dependent upon the social order for a sense of purpose and value, although in American society this kind of individualism has deep cultural roots.

Quebedeaux's final category of charismatics deserves special attention, particularly because it can be seen as a bridge between the type of religious movements considered in this chapter and those discussed in the next. The charismatic movement as treated here has some ties to, but is separate from, old-line Protestant Pentecostalism as contained in such denominations as the Church of God and the Four Square Gospel churches. It is, rather, a middle-class phenomenon, found primarily within main-line Protestant and Catholic churches. Theologically, charismatics may be distinguished from other Christians by their insistence upon the experience of the "baptism of the Holy Spirit," expressed in particular religious gifts—charisms—such as prophecy, healing, and, most particularly, the gift of tongues, or glossolalia, through which the believer may pray to God in ways beyond expressing in one's own language. This gift, understood primarily through the story of the founding of the church on the day of Pentecost when each listener heard the Gospel in his or her own language (Acts 2), is no longer expected by most to be a known language, but rather a way of speaking to God alone and explicit evidence of the presence of the Holy Spirit. In the early days of this movement and for many current participants, this experience of the divine cut across all barriers of doctrine and life-style, uniting Catholic and Protestant, young and old, men and women, black and white in a common fellowship of praise. While the worship was communal, the experience came individually to each believer, and each recognized his or her primary loyalty to God alone as experienced in his spirit, and to one another through that spirit.

However, the literal experience of gifts mentioned in the Bible, and the need to interpret their enthusiasm in those terms to scoffing outsiders, led to an increasing dependence upon a literal interpretation of Scripture and hence to boundary maintenance around dogma previously considered unnecessary. Similarly, attempts to recreate the New Testament church have led, particularly among Roman Catholic Pentecostals, to new forms of authority more appropriate for next chapter's consideration. It appears to be a classic case of Weber's concept of the "routinization of charisma," where the strength of the charismatic experience has evolved a particularly strong, authoritarian religious style.

Before turning to that, it is necessary to note that the charismatics represent a theme common to nearly all the movements considered in this chapter, as well as such others as the rise of Hasidic Judaism, and that is a focus on individual religious *experience*. In a society where cultural change has undermined the faith of people in social institutions to the point where they may be alienated from them, they are likely to feel that they are dependent upon themselves alone to provide meaning and order for their lives. To accept such a responsibility, many people need the assurance that can be supplied through a religion that gives them some direct experience of the divine—the ultimate source of meaning. Whether through getting in contact with one's essential self as the divine spark we all possess or through the immanent divinity of Eastern religion, or the contact with Jesus of the evangelicals, or the baptism of the Holy Spirit of the charismatics, these seekers have found in their own lives the experience of the divine that gives them confidence in the meaning of their existence.[32] With this to stand on, they are able to face the uncertain future of a changing society.

Notes and References

1. Robert Merton, *Social Theory and Social Structure,* enl. ed. (New York: Free Press, 1968), pp. 185–248.
2. Anthony F. C. Wallace, *Religion: An Anthropological View* (New York: Random House, 1966), pp. 157–164.
3. See Franklin L. Baumer, *Religion and the Rise of Skepticism* (New York: Harcourt, 1960), particularly the introduction and Chapter 4. An appropriate sequel to Baumer's work is Colin Campbell, "The Secret Religion of the Educated Classes," *Sociological Analysis* 39, no. 2 (1978): 146–156.
4. See, for example, R. D. Laing, *The Politics of Experience* (New York: Pantheon, 1967).
5. Robert N. Bellah, *Beyond Belief: Essays on Religion in a Post-Traditional World* (New York: Harper & Row, 1970), p. 284.
6. For an impassioned statement of the anti-Christian bias of psychology, particularly humanistic psychology, see Paul C. Vitz, *Psychology As Religion: The Cult of Self-Worship* (Grand Rapids, Mich.: Eerdmans, 1972).
7. A detailed account of the development of this approach from a scientifically based technology to a social movement may be found in Kurt W. Bach, *Beyond Words: The Story of Sensitivity Training and the Encounter Movement* (New York: Russell Sage, 1972).
8. For a more detailed and sympathetic description of the churches' use of the human potential movement, see Gerald J. Jud and Elizabeth Jud, *Training in the Art of Loving* (Philadelphia: Pilgrim, 1972).
9. Peter L. Berger, *The Sacred Canopy* (Garden City, N.Y.: Doubleday, 1967), Chapter 4.
10. As quoted in Vitz, op. cit., p. 29.
11. Donald Stone, "The Human Potential Movement," in *The New Religious Consciousness,* ed. by Charles Glock and Robert Bellah (Berkeley: University of California Press, 1976), p. 100.
12. Colin Campbell, "The Cult, the Cultic Milieu, and Secularization," in *A Sociological Yearbook of Religion in Britain 5,* ed. by Michael Hill (London: SCM Press, 1976), p. 122.
13. Roy Wallis, *The Road to Total Freedom: A Sociological Analysis of Scientology* (New York: Columbia University Press, 1977), p. 13.
14. Theodore Roszak, *The Making of a Counterculture* (Garden City, N.Y.: Doubleday, 1969), p. 141.
15. Wallis, op. cit., p. 16.
16. For further information on this group, see Alan Tobey, "Summer Solstice of the Happy-Healthy-Holy Organization," in Glock and Bellah, eds., op. cit., pp. 5–30.
17. Wallis, op. cit., pp. 16–18.
18. James T. Richardson, "From Cult to Sect: Creative Eclecticism in New Religious Movements," *Pacific Sociological Review,* forthcoming, pp. 2–5.
19. Ibid., p. 20.
20. For an assessment of this, see Gary Wills, "What Religious Revival?" *Psychology Today* 11, no. 11 (1978): 74–81.
21. "Half U.S. Protestants Are 'Born Again' Christians," *The Gallup Poll,* September 26, 1976.

22. See Dean Kelly, *Why Conservative Churches Are Growing* (San Francisco: Harper & Row, 1977).

23. Richard Quebedeaux, *The Worldly Evangelicals* (New York: Harper & Row, 1978), p. 7.

24. Ibid., p. 4.

25. Ibid., p. 132

26. Richard Quebedeaux, *The Young Evangelicals* (New York: Harper & Row, 1974), pp. 18–45.

27. Ralph Linton, "Nativistic Movements," *American Anthropologist* 45 (1943): 230.

28. Ibid., pp. 231–233.

29. Erling Jorstad, *The Politics of Doomsday* (Nashville: Abingdon, 1970), pp. 20–33.

30. Quebedeaux, *Young Evangelicals*, op. cit., pp. 22–28.

31. Quebedeaux, *Worldly Evangelicals*, op. cit., p. 79.

32. For a valuable comparison of the more secular responses with the charismatic groups in the light of Durkheim's predictions concerning the rise of a "cult of man" in industrialized society, see Frances Westley, " 'The Cult of Man': Durkheim's Predictions and New Religious Movements," *Sociological Analysis* 39, no. 2 (1978): 135–145.

15

New Religious Movements II: Anomie and the Sectarian Response

While alienation arises from a perception that the institutions of one's society are foreign, external forces impinging upon and misshaping the self, *anomie* arises from the feeling that there is not enough coherent shape in the social environment for the individual to be able to find a place, a goal, or a style of life that receives any social support. The idea of everyone doing his or her "own thing" may be particularly liberating to those who know what their "thing" is, but to those who do not it may bespeak chaos and induce panic. A person may feel betrayed by a society that offers no guidance or support.[1]

David Loye has tied the tendency to one or the other of these responses to social-psychological distinctions between the liberal and the conservative personality and to patterns of child rearing.[2] The liberal personality, he says, is generally nourished in a family that encourages independent action and experimentation and is primarily growth oriented. The child is consistently rewarded for behavior that shows development of initiative; life is seen as a process, and progress is a prime value. In times of social change, where innovation frequently appears called for, persons of this type become impatient with what they perceive as outmoded elements of the culture and succumb to alienation from the "system." If their alienation is not too great and they have access to movements within the religious institution, they may become advocates of ecclesiastical reform and choose among current theological options some form of liberation theology or the like. If they are more alienated from the religious institution but still recognize personal religious needs, they may opt for one of the cultic religious forms mentioned in the previous chapter, seeking innovative religious practices for themselves.

To the conservative person, however, such behavior only results in deepening social chaos. This individual, says Loye, is generally the product of childhood training in which the greatest rewards were given for learning well the rules of appropriate behavior and following them. Anomie is the response to the kind of frustration felt when the "rules of the game" are unclear. If one's primary goal is to live a properly disciplined life according to the standards of the society, it becomes impossible to reach that goal when the standards are in flux. A person with this type of orientation may cling desperately to his or her religion as one steady anchor in a changing world. If changes are introduced in the form of the religion—in doctrine, liturgy, or organization—it may seem as if the last prop has been pulled out from under the beseiged individual. In the wake of, for example, post–Vatican II changes in the Roman Catholic church, liberal Protestant and Catholic denominational support of radical social change movements in recent years, Episcopal votes on the ordination of women, the apparent weakening of doctrines of the inerrancy of Scripture in the Lutheran Church–Missouri Synod and other conservative bodies, countermovements have arisen that threaten denominational schism. For those whose involvement in institutional religion has been marginal or nonexistent, one solution to anomie may be involvement in some religious group that maintains a clear boundary between itself and the chaotic society, provides a well-defined creed, and enforces strict and clear roles among its members. This, according to most definitions, constitutes a sect.

In the past there has been a close relationship between sectarian involvement and lower-class status. The pattern of childhood rearing noted above has frequently been class linked, with members of the more affluent classes expected to exhibit "leadership potential" in independent, creative behavior, while children of the working classes learned that their best tactic was to "keep their noses clean," abiding by the rules and staying out of trouble. Life for the poor, nearer the edge of survival, was more likely to be chaotic and productive of anomie. One particularly interesting facet of the new sectarianism is the breaking down of this pattern.

While it is important to keep in mind the influence of family training and of the region, neighborhood, and class milieu on the personality type and consequent action of persons, in modern society these are no longer definitive. The exposure to events and conditions in the wider society provided to individuals and communities through the media, the centralization of institutions of education, and the geographic mobility of many families have combined to dilute the effects of the home and neighborhood environment. In an affluent culture dependent on a high rate of consumerism, the children of workers as well as of the more affluent are encouraged to try new things and hope for new places in the living of their lives. The movements of the 1960s were largely those of the alienated, and they were not confined to upper- and upper-middle-class people, though they were dominated by them. In Wallace's terms, one might say that they were responding to individual stress and that in many cases that response helped to lead to a sense of cultural distortion within the society as a whole.

Many of today's youth are the little brothers and sisters—literally or figuratively—of the activists of the 1960s. They were too young to have understood the rhetoric of liberation that accompanied those movements. Instead, what they saw was the suffering of families disorganized in the process, drug-wasted or brutality-marred lives of those older brothers and sisters, burning cities on the television, and increased levels of hatred and exclusion. Most had little idea why students were protesting at Kent State; most know that some of them were shot and killed. Many are old enough to know something of the Watergate and other scandals—at least enough to have a firsthand perception of the venality of public officials mentioned by Wallace as characteristic of such a period.[3] Most are products of public education since the system has come to refuse to teach values lest they breach the wall of separation between church and state. Many have had no contact with institutional religion or have participated in it as a voluntary association competitive with others for their time and interest rather than as the locus of ultimate values. For many, mobility has meant the loss of all primary groups, instilling a desire to keep associations shallow and commitments to others low, so as not to be hurt when the next break in relationships occurs. Divorce has made this often the case within families as well as in other associations. Age segregation in residence patterns as well as in associations has given them no sense of what life will be like as they grow older, although medical science assures them they will have a long life span. Such a life experience seems a formula for anomie.

It is not only the young who are likely to perceive cultural distortion in such times. Parents whose children left home to join some movement and, if they returned at all, came back strangers, are likely candidates for anomie. The elderly, often separated physically from the young and psychologically from their world, are subject to anxiety about the kind of people in whose hands they must place the future, as well as for their own safety as they continue to hear of juvenile violence against the aged. Workers find their jobs becoming obsolete or their salaries eaten up by taxes and inflation and see no way that they can reach goals of respectability and financial security. Women caught between demands for liberation that denigrate the role of the housewife, and their love for and desire to serve their families in traditional ways, suffer role conflict, vacillating between the extremes of the "Total Woman" and assertiveness training. Blacks, given hope by new social legislation, find their way blocked once again by movements against "reverse discrimination" and taxpayer revolts that decimate public programs for training and placement. Homeowners find taxes rising to the point at which they can no longer afford to keep their property. Political leaders find people so caught in the assumption that they must represent the vested interest of their own groups that they are unable to make compromises for the good of the whole. All these and many more are the building blocks of the cultural malaise of anomie. Small wonder, then, that the scientific study of religion in our time should pay particular attention to the rise of sectarian forms of religion.

We have noted in the last chapter Wallis's and Richardson's definitions of the process of development of a religious group from cult to sect. Their differences give rise to the notion that there may be several root causes of this process, among which are (1) members' sense of the precariousness of the organization in relation to their needs for organizational and doctrinal specificity to assuage their anomie; (2) the need for leaders to maintain direction and control over an organization threated with cultic anarchy; and (3) the need to respond to a threatening environment which defines the group as deviant and dangerous.

Some developments in the charismatic movement provide an excellent example of the first type. Much of the strength of contemporary Pentecostalism has come from denominations with a tradition of quite fixed liturgical practices—for example, the Roman Catholic and the Episcopal. The expressive freedom of charismatic worship can be seen as a particularly liberating movement for people whose background is in these traditions, as well as those that stress a rational, sermon-oriented style. This, indeed, was the emphasis at the beginning of the movement, and it remains so in many of the groups that have formed out of it. Their experience has led to new openness and an expansive attitude in organizational style, membership, and doctrine.[4]

However, a number of groups give evidence of having reached a point where that openness threatens the need for order of persons reacting to the threat of an anomic society. These have come to develop a structure that is clearly sectarian. Rather than depending upon the vagaries of uncontrolled divine inspiration, they have developed "Life in the Spirit Seminars" which serve at least two functions. First, they provide specific behavioral guides for potential members, by which they may achieve contact with the Holy Spirit. Secondly, they serve as a sort of catechesis, through which everyone must pass before becoming a core member of the community. There is a strong emphasis on the gift of tongues as evidence of the baptism of the Holy Spirit, so that in essence speaking in tongues becomes a necessary part of the initiatory rite. Thus boundary maintenance is set up and, according to Ford, is sometimes reinforced by keeping a guard at the door who will only allow fully confirmed core members to attend meetings, lest their effectiveness be diluted.[5]

Membership requirements are only part of what has become a necessity to this portion of the movement, a clearly recognizable community. In some cases core members are expected to become part of a residential community in which income, expenses, meals, and much of the rest of their lives are shared. Even where this is not the case, a clear discipline is exercised, and those who will not submit to the authority of leaders are banned. Leadership is hierarchical, based on New Testament definitions of the family, with the idea of God at the top, then male heads of "families"—communities—as his representatives, then various subgroups exercising particular "gifts" within the community. Part of a member's religious duty is submission to the leaders, as to God.[6]

What seems evident here is a reaction to the early liberating force of the charismatic experience on the part of people whose previous training in religion had contained strong elements of organizational and doctrinal authority. The charismatic experience had freed them from the authority of priests, bishops, and creeds, making them feel that they were directly in contact with the source of that authority, the spirit of God himself. Yet for many that freedom could become chaos unless it was put into some clear system, and they tended to turn to the New Testament and its indications of the response of the early church to its pentecostal origin, emulating here the pattern of old-line Pentecostalism.

Ford traces the similarities of this process to the "radical Reformation" of the early Anabaptists, and indirectly accuses those Catholics who are involved in this type of charismatic groups of Protestant schism.[7] At the present time there has been no clear break of this sort, but a number of priests and bishops who have been supportive of the charismatic renewal have expressed concern over these developments. It is of interest to the sociologist that in Weber's theoretical discussions of the charismatic origins of new forms of religion, he always attached the charisma to a leader—a shaman or a prophet—who could then form a group so loyal to his or her authority that they could institute a new world view. Unfocused charisma—charisma that does not have a particular person upon whom it appears to rest—may not in the history of religion have proved to possess the societal power to have made an impact. It will be of great interest to watch developments in this current movement with that in mind.

While some charismatics have been inspired by the experience to become more deeply involved in traditional structures, others have found it the source of an entirely new self-image and style of life. For them, it may not be too extreme to predict some sort of organizational schism. The very possibility awakens fears of conservatives within the church, who then tend to respond with greater rigidity to their activities. This, of course, can have the effect of pushing more charismatics into the sectarian type of organization. Moderate Catholic leaders, caught between liberalizing forces released by the Second Vatican Council and conservative backlash from those who find change threatening, do not find their troubles lightened by such movements. Many bishops have attempted to set up specific liaison between the charismatic groups and their offices, but in some cases there is a distinct problem as to the relative authority of traditional church structure and that of a perceived direct experience of the God whom the church claims to serve.

Charismatics may also be found in other major denominations than the Roman Catholic. The issues they raise are dealt with in styles consistent with the denominations involved. Episcopalians, long tolerant of diversity, after hostile reactions to some early and well-publicized charismatic groups, have attempted to keep them within the fold and have given considerable legitimacy to certain types of healing services and the like which are favored by charismatics. Presbyterians appointed a study group which reported back to their General Assembly a balanced statement of the pros and cons of the movement. On the local level, such movements are dealt with according to the tastes and concerns of local pastors and congregations. This is, as one would expect, true of those churches more congregationally oriented as well.

In the case of most charismatics of this type, we find the strange paradox of a movement that has defied authority binding itself into a more authoritarian structure than the one it left behind. Other movements appear to be moving into sectlike structures more because of the need of the leaders for a dependable clientele than of the members for explicit structure—although such statements must always be taken with the caveat that it is very difficult for a leader to lead people in a direction they have no disposition to follow. This is the kind of situation upon which Wallis based his theory of the development of a cult into a sect. The method of Dianetics as first developed by L. Ron Hubbard offered a new combination of techniques through which a number of clients found themselves able to function better in their everyday lives. While for some the process resulted in an entirely new self-image, others found it a useful tool to be added to other disciplines or views. A number of leaders of local groups formed around this basically cultic response experimented with additions or combinations that were not part of the original "package." This threatened Hubbard's leadership of the group, and while Wallis does not take note of this, it undoubtedly also affected the security of those who had found a new identity in Dianetics.

Hubbard's response was to tighten up the doctrinal and organizational structure of his followers, renaming the movement Scientology, and in effect excommunicating those who differed from him. He maintained firm control over any new theory or technique, only passing information on to those who remained in good standing. Wallis finds the organization of Scientology a pure type of bureaucracy as defined by Weber, with hierarchical order, carefully delimited positions at each rank, extensive use of written files, elaborate rules, and easy substitutability of lower-level functionaries.[8] Thus authority is centralized and the boundaries made clear.

One of the limitations of American law and the public opinion that supports it is that anything related to religion comes out of a background of Christendom. One result is that it is taken for granted that a religious institution, at least in the long run, should be nonprofitable. Given the service orientation of the cult, and its relation to its adherents as casual clients, profit taking can be seen as appropriate to that form of religious organization. Thus Werner Erhardt makes no apologies for the fact that *est* is a money-making venture. And while we have here defined it as a religion because it appears to meet religious needs of clients, Erhardt does not claim status as a religion or the kind of tax exemption that goes with it. However, when such a cult becomes more sectlike, as happened in the case of the transition from Dianetics to Scientology, problems begin to rise. When Hubbard changed the name of his organization to the Church of Scientology, sociologists may say that he was accurately describing the movement as a religion, but critics claimed that he was just trying to escape paying taxes. Perhaps more serious is the underlying suspicion that while anyone may have the right to waste their money on the idle offerings of those who may be charlatans, when this is done within the intense relationships of the sect it smacks of manipulation and the undermining of individual religious freedom. Hubbard is only one of many leaders of recent movements who have been hauled into court on one or both these accounts. In fact, Wallis suggests that this kind of pressure, and the drop in clientele that followed it, were important factors in the rigidification of doctrine and structure in Scientology.

Tightening up of the organization often comes not from the very top, but from slightly lower levels of leadership of the group. Weber's model of the "routinization of charisma" allows a distinction to be made between the prophet who has the revelation that begins the movement and those successors who set up the organization. In like manner, Sophia Collier has documented changes in the Divine Light Mission, the followers of the young Maharaj Ji, being brought about by lieutenants who desired to have the organization run by modern business methods. Collier's autobiographical account makes clear the kind of cult-client self-definition with which she joined the movement, as well as her dismay at the actions of those who would attach broad metaphysical import to every saying of the leader or those who would rationalize the structure.[9] Her story is a distinct protest against a process by which the cult to which she had attached herself was turning into a sect.

As in the case of Scientology, the process of moving from sect to cult began after the initial enthusiasm of the group had diminished, public pressure had been put on the group concerning its use of money, and the limits of membership growth appeared to be much narrower than had earlier been supposed. The development of a sectlike form of organization is often at least partially a response to pressure from a hostile social environment that makes tighter boundaries seem essential for survival.

We have noted some similarity to cultlike organizations within groups identified with religious denominations and traced the ways in which sects may become denominations. Recent events also remind us that, under certain circumstances, a denominational religion may move in the direction of the sect. The murder of outsiders and mass suicide by members of James Jones's People's Temple give evidence of the extremes of sectarian organization—centralized and authoritarian leadership, high levels of commitment, rigid boundary maintenance—and yet, even at the time of this terrible dénouement, the group was a recognized congregation of a mainline denomination, the Christian Church (Disciples of Christ).

One reason such an event could have happened lies in the low level of boundary maintenance typical of the denominational form of religious organization. The Christian Church (Disciples of Christ) has been particularly loath to set qualifications for affiliated congregations, since the historical origin of that denomination and its continuing emphasis have been an effort to do away with interdenominational rivalry and conflict and to establish a singie Christian church open to all.[10]

But other factors were also in operation in this case, particularly those forces of outside hostility—real and perceived—that push groups toward sectarianism, as well as social-psychological conditions that tend to give rise to authoritarian social movements. In San Francisco, the People's Temple was one of a very small number of religious groups that continued social action programs many mainline denominations undertook during the previous decade. Thus the organization provided meaningful involvement for middle-class people who continued to seek social change through religious organizations.[11] At the same time, the People's Temple appeared less hypocritical than many churches in that it not only served the poor and disadvantaged, but also admitted them to active membership. Thus in terms of Glock's categories of deprivation, the People's Temple apparently attracted all the types: the economically deprived, those deprived of status, the psychically deprived (anomic), the organismically deprived (to whom Jones offered faith healing), and the ethically deprived, who were seeking social change. The group attained considerable political power, as Jones demonstrated to San Francisco politicians his ability to mobilize block votes.

However, positive relationships with the outside world began to deteriorate in a number of ways, as the generally conservative trends of the 1970s resulted in a cutback of public programs with which the People's Temple had cooperated and the group was thrown back on its own resources to meet rising demands in the area it served. Members with a background of economic and status deprivation faced frustration of rising expectations, thus becoming susceptible to authoritarian direction. Jones, always a charismatic leader, undoubtedly found himself turned to by more and more people in ways that increased his power over them. The temptation to exercise that kind of power is hard for anyone to resist, and there is no evidence Jones tried to resist it. However, the internal dynamics of a movement which is becoming more authoritarian tend to alienate those members whose motivation for joining was ethical deprivation, who are more likely to suffer alienation than anomie as defined above. These members and others less in need of finding security in a powerful leader began to leave and to bring accusations from the outside concerning the increasing authoritarianism of the movement. Thus both political-economic developments and political-social pressure provided a sense of outside threat, which reinforced the stronger boundary definition required by the internal demand for a form of organization and leadership able to provide security in a hostile environment.

Finally, the move to a new environment in Guyana served both to put distance between the group and its hostile detractors and to increase dependency on the leader, while demanding the ultimate in bridge-burning acts of commitment by members pooling all their resources in Jones's hands and cutting off all outside ties. Under such circumstances, neither destroying a team of outside investigators defined as hostile forces nor joining Jones in a suicide pact could be defined as a sudden aberration. Rather, they were logical progressions in a course of events set in operation long before.

Given the pressures of urban society toward anomie and anonymous choice within religious pluralism, one might conclude that the surprising fact of the Jonestown deaths is not that they occurred, but that there have been so few similar occurrences. It is also clear that no society can tolerate groups this extreme in any number and hope to survive. Thus it is not surprising that movements opposing sectarian religion have become increasingly evident.

However, the presence of opposition groups does not by itself give evidence of returning stability with the religious institution. Rather, a particularly interesting phenomenon in the current situation is the near sectlike form of opposition to these movements. In recent years a number of groups have developed among parents of young people who have become involved in various new religious movements, along with some psychologists, pastors, and lawyers who have made it their concern, whose aim is to save young people from these alien influences. The first to gain national recognition was the FreeCOG group (an acronym based on "Free Our Children from the Children of God"), organized in 1971. By 1975 it had expanded its focus and evolved into the Citizens Freedom Foundation. Other well-known groups are Citizens Engaged in Reuniting Families, the International Foundation for Individual Freedom, Individual Freedom Foundation, and Citizens Engaged in Freeing Minds—this last a national federation of a number of the other groups, with fifty state chapters.[12]

These organizations have been active in seeking political restraints on groups that define themselves as religious but that the opposition contend are manipulating people for economic and political reasons. Some defectors from Jones's People's Temple and their affected families turned to these organizations for help in fighting for what they considered the liberation of members of that community. It was through these channels that Representative Leo Ryan received some of the information that led to his ill-fated investigatory trip to Guyana, where he was murdered by People's Temple adherents. Yet the opposition movement has gained a reputation in some circles for overreacting, so its involvement in decrying Jones's group may have been somewhat counterproductive among people for whom the whole issue of government intervention in the free practice of religion has been raised in the current controversy.

The inspiration for opposition groups appears to have come primarily from one man, Ted Patrick, a black evangelist who works on the conviction that recruitment to any of the new religious groups takes place through a process of brainwashing similar to that perpetrated upon U.S. prisoners of war by the Chinese during the Korean conflict.[13] They accuse the groups of recruiting with the use of such processes as enforced isolation (such as at weekend retreats or rural camps of the Unification Church), preventing them from sleeping, withholding food or providing food high in starch, such psychological manipulation as withholding friendship until the proper response has been made—or, on the other hand, "love bombing" with irresistible shows of affection— and forcing them to listen to long, meaningless lectures until they are psychologically confused. Recruits are described as "zombies," with a "thousand-mile stare." Psychiatrists supporting the deprogrammers have described recruits as lacking in creativity.

Patrick's cure for such a state is "deprogramming." That is, he attempts to reverse the process until the subjects are once again able to think for themselves. In some cases this has required the forcible abduction of religious devotees, holding them in some isolated place such as a motel, seeing to it that they are physically uncomfortable, and bombarding them with truths as understood in their original environment, until they give up the new world view to which they had been converted. Not all deprogramming is so violent, but all is intended to do violence to the new views the subjects had come to espouse. The process has resulted in a further service by the deprogrammers—rehabilitation centers where their clients can recover from the experiences in the religious groups and in the exit process.[14] Critics accuse deprogrammers of a profit motive; parents frequently pay high fees for the return of their children.

If one accepts the diagnosis of brainwashing, such strenuous deprogramming measures may indeed be called for if the subject is to be returned to a normal state. But the deprogramming movement raises a number of questions for the outside observer. There is no doubt that much of the activity arises out of genuine anguish on the part of parents who have nurtured their children in a culture they take for granted as the right way to live and then find them rejecting it for a world view they cannot understand and forsaking them for a new circle of intimates they do not know. Yet it is also hard to completely discount those cynics who say that Western Christianity has always assumed that experience to be appropriate to the families of converts of our missionaries and that we still applaud such alienation from the home environment for people who are poor or of foreign background. To the objective observer there is little to distinguish between what Patrick and his followers have called brainwashing and the classic pattern of religious conversion. Members of the new groups, met in their new environment, may show the typical excess of religious zeal found in new converts to most religions, but it is hard to define their behavior as zombie-like or their expressions as any unusual kind of stare. They appear rational within the limits of their new world view, although it is clear that they no longer base their thinking on the same premises as they had in the past.

It is here that the problem seems really to lie. Many of these religious converts, like many recruits to the counterculture a few years earlier, have rejected the cultural assumptions of their parents and have adopted an entirely different world view. Their aims in life have changed and often so have the symbol systems by which they organize reality. They have found a new reference group, a new set of "significant others" whose responses are now their primary guides for living. They raise the question of the rights of previous reference groups and significant others to their loyalty. What are the rights of the family in such cases?

Some families have simply assumed they had the right to save their children from forces they consider evil and arranged with deprogrammers to help them abduct them and straighten them out. In some cases this has proven effective, and the deprogrammed young people have not only returned home but also turned against the groups they had joined, affirming all the deprogrammers have claimed and adding their own horror stories. Some have joined with the deprogrammers seeking to rescue erstwhile fellow-believers. On the other hand, some have escaped, returned to their newfound faith, and in some cases instituted lawsuits against parents and deprogrammers. Faced with such legal response, particularly in the case of young people who are legally adult, many of the deprogramming groups have begun to seek out judges who will grant them conservatorships on the assumption that the devotees have been rendered legally incompetent by the psychological processes that recruited them to the group. Then they can legally remove the convert from his or her new group.

At the present time there has been considerable confusion in court rulings on such cases. There is little legal precedent on these issues. One of the most serious consequences of this activity has been that of putting judges in the position of setting precedents, of deciding between what is true religion and what is illegal psychological manipulation. The question has come to trouble many officials in main-line denominations, because establishing precedents in this area could result in a real breach of the separation of church and state, with the courts in essence establishing some religions while denying others the protection of the law. Given the recent history of governmental anger against church activists working for civil rights or against the Viet Nam war, many liberals see here the specter of political repression of expressions of religious conscience and have joined with some of the new religions in the courts, at least to the extent of filing "friend of the court" briefs in cases where they are accused of brainwashing. Conservative churches also have reason to be alarmed, since many of the deprogramming cases have involved the removal of converts from fundamentalist Christian or charismatic groups.

Thus the reaction of those opposed to new sectarian groups is also affecting the behavior of denominations. It may in some cases be almost the sole cause of the development of a cult as defined here into the kind of sectarian organization the movement deplores. If boundary maintenance is an important characteristic of the sect, a hostile society may be the maintainers of those barriers as well as the religious group itself. For example, the Hare Krishna movement tends to be more sectlike in Western culture than in its native India, where a pluralistic religious milieu has long been accepted. At the same time, people who abandon basic symbol systems of their own culture for those of a highly different one are probably already deeply disaffected. The type of bridge-burning act involved in shaving one's head and donning clothes recognizably foreign is a clear indicator of the recognition of boundaries on the part of the devotee as well as the outside society.[15]

Such recognition, at least in the initial stages, is not common in another sectarian organization against which the public has erected high barriers—the Unification Church of Sun Myung Moon. Recruitment methods of this organization are the epitome of the "soft sell." People —particularly young people—who appear to be lonely are invited to dinner with a group of friendly peers. Only after they have been made to feel comfortable and cared for are they told that the reason for the friendliness and care is the solicitude of the father of this "unified family," Reverend Moon. By then they may have agreed to go on a weekend or week-long retreat with the group, and after that they may be counted as members of the organization. There is no particular moment of commitment, and the only ritual near to a bridge-burning act is their repetition of a pledge on certain occasions.[16] In this case it may be primarily the strong public reaction against the group that has made the high barriers around it.

This does not mean that there are not high levels of commitment among members of the Unification Church. Indeed, their loyalty appears to be total, even to the point of allowing Moon to choose spouses for them and set the conditions of their married lives. They engage in heavy amounts of volunteer labor for the cause of the church and live simply, often defining themselves as a modern equivalent of a religious monastic order.

While the group frequently heads the lists of "cults" people are being warned against, and Lofland described it as a cult in an early study,[17] it has long since ceased to exhibit the attributes needed to fit the concept of "cult" as we have been defining it. Rather, these critics are using the word "cult" to define any religious group that appears foreign or strange to them—a definition hardly useful to the social scientist working out of a stance of cultural relativity which recognizes that what is strange to one group may be sacred tradition to another.

In the case of the Unification Church we have, it seems, classic sectarian characteristics. Members find their identity in the group, rather than taking from it just what they need to meet certain needs of a relatively well-defined self. Moon maintains strong central authority, and the level of commitment is intense.

Again, economic factors are clouded by differing assumptions concerning the nature of a religious group. While Moon is accused of using the labors of devotees to provide a luxurious life-style for himself—and indeed he does live well—members have a different interpretation. The form of the church is that of the oriental family. Moon claims to expend all his care and his energy on his "children," and they in return assume that the properties and businesses owned by the church are theirs, just as children assume family holdings to be theirs. The estate on which Moon lives is also a meeting center for church leaders, and the businesses provide both jobs and necessities for the members. It is, of course, doubtful that members have any legal rights to these holdings and benefits, but some also have reported that the church has paid off debts they brought with them when they joined, such as student loans.

An important characteristic of the Unification Church that distinguishes it from most of the newer sects involves its relationship to the political process. Most modern cults and sects offer their followers the means either to escape the vicissitudes of modern life or to so manipulate it that they personally may be successful. The Unification Church is an explicitly messianic movement, intended to establish the Kingdom of God on earth, and for all people. Unlike other apocalyptic groups that await the Second Coming or some other divine event to put down evil and raise up good, the followers of Moon speak of the "Lord of the Second Advent," who will come (or, perhaps, has come) to lead people to set up the new order in the here and now. Consequently, their accumulation of economic holdings is the beginning of a process of redeeming the world's economy by getting it into the hands of those who will use it justly. It also becomes important to have their influence felt in the centers of political power. In Korea, where the movement began, Moon has been a supporter of the autocratic Park regime, a fact that has caused him some grief in the United States where investigations into Korean influence peddling have touched on possible connections with the Unification Church.

There are elements in Moon's thought that are reminiscent of the sort of holy commonwealth envisioned by early Calvinists. There appears to be an assumption that God's plan is for the entire world to be a theocratic state, in which all aspects of life are governed by the divine principle. One is reminded of some of the attempts of Communist states to assume that all art and literature, all expressions of the people should reflect the political ideology. However, Moon's movement is militantly anti-Communist. Moon himself was imprisoned at one time in North Korea, and the movement reflects the ideological militance of that divided country. They equate Communists with the children of Cain, who according to their theology was the offspring of Eve and Satan. Given the age of most members, at least in the United States, and the militance of their views, the movement tends to remind one of medieval Children's Crusades. Unlike most Eastern religious imports, this movement contains a highly specific and explicit dualism. The unity it seeks is not the simple monism that assumes all things to be infused with the divine.

Yet within the realm of positive forces there is a strong impetus for overcoming the fragmentation of modern life. Moon's ideas about the unification of all things also extend to the realm of scholarship. His "International Conferences on the Unity of Science" have attempted to bring together scientists in all fields from around the world to share findings with one another. Participants report that the conferences are extremely well run, and leading scientists have participated. However, many have refused to participate after discovering the sponsorship of the conferences, fearing that their presence will help to legitimate a movement they do not approve.

Unification theology has certain parallels with Mormonism in that it is based on a further revelation beyond the Old and New Testaments. One could hypothesize that if events led to it and they could find a new wilderness like the Mormons' Utah, they might well settle there and establish a religious organization fitting the sociological concept of "church" as the Mormons have done. In the meantime, there is evidence that they are attempting to achieve public acceptance as a denomination, rather than as a sect. They have made every effort to have their seminary accredited through New York State channels as well as by the

304 RELIGION AS STRUCTURE AND MOVEMENT

Association of Theological Schools. They frequently invite theologians from recognized seminaries to conferences and discussions of their theology. Graduates from their seminary have been accepted for further study at some of the major universities in the country. Yet their theological position of having a further revelation (or being part of a later dispensation) makes main-line Christianity as nervous as claims by the Jews for Jesus to be "completed Jews" make main-line Judaism. In each case, the reality appears to be conversion to a competing religion, one that defines the existing one as inadequate.

Jews for Jesus is one portion of the wider Jesus movement that emerged from the counterculture as a new religious movement within Christianity. This movement combined the biblical literalism of the evangelicals with the life-style of the counterculture, often adding a form of apocalyptism and/or communal living. Quebedeaux placed most Jesus-movement groups in his category of "open fundamentalism," and indeed that openness has allowed many to be absorbed into more traditional evangelical churches. For many young people in the counterculture, the Jesus movement provided an entry back into the "straight" world.[18]

However, some groups that were equated with the Jesus movement at the beginning have maintained their separation from main-line Christianity in true sectarian fashion. One of these, as mentioned before, is Jews for Jesus, and with it other messianic Jewish groups. As with some of the groups mentioned before, one reason for their sectarian separation is pressure from the outside. Main-line Judaism takes their rhetoric of "completion" as Jews to be a dishonest cover-up of what is in reality a conversion to Christianity. To them it is an insidious raid on their future, since as an ethnic group they only replace themselves through their children. Jews for Jesus and other messianic Jews are seen as a serious threat, as is Moon's Unification Church, in which members of Jewish background are greatly overrepresented.[19]

Another sectarian group often identified with the Jesus movement, but treated as heretical by most evangelical Christians, is the Children of God. This group evolved out of a highly literalistic and apocalyptic treatment of Scripture, a sectarian separation from the evil world, and a pattern of communal living. They were the object of a considerable amount of harassment in the United States, and so moved much of their central organization to Europe. In 1971 Davis and Richardson found evidence that they were moving toward becoming a denomination rather than maintaining their sectarian separation, even to the point of having contact with the World Council of Churches.[20] However, they continue to receive negative publicity, especially concerning sexual practices.

It is a common feature of the public response to new religious movements that they are accused of sexual irregularities, and often this is a false claim. For example, most critics of the Unification Church say that the cause of Moon's imprisonment in North Korea was a charge of bigamy or some similar morals charge. Whether or not this is true, the Unification Church at the present time enforces a very rigid moral code, far more demanding than ordinary American standards, much less practices. However, literature distributed by the Children of God seems to support some of the claims of their critics in this regard. For example, a tract written in June 1977 by Moses David, leader of the group, titled "Mortal Sin? Or Salvation," is a discussion of Jesus as "a man who loved everybody," in which statements are made about the need to satisfy people's bodies as well as their spirits, as agents of Jesus. It is very difficult to interpret some of the statements as anything other than an explicit justification for behavior best described as "sacred prostitution." While today's sexual ethics hardly provide the basis for outrage at the thought, it is unusual to have such behavior grounded in a literal advocacy of Christian Scripture. It clearly separates the Children of God from evangelical Christians, whose sexual ethic may not always be followed but is still clearly expressed as "sex within marriage only."

Far more significant to the society, it would seem, are those sectarian successors of the Jesus movement who compose the radical communal groups that are part of what Quebedeaux has termed the "New Evangelicals."[21] Not all new evangelicals are part of these radical groups, just as not all members came out of the Jesus movement, but the sects articulate most clearly their distinctive thrust. They offer a distinctive combination of traditional evangelical theology with radical social concern. The reason for communal living is not only social support, as in many communal groups, but to demonstrate a life-style consistent with their concern about waste, ecological destruction, and the need to share surplus with the needy rather than escaping consumption among the affluent. They criticize main-line liberal churches for their theological diffuseness, and evangelical churches for their indifference to social injustice and need. Unlike many evangelicals, they are willing to take seriously the work of biblical scholars, but unlike many liberals they insist on taking the Bible very seriously as a guide for their lives and that of the society. They are not so sectarian as to cut themselves off from other churches, but they are eager to send speakers to explain what they are about. They spread their influence through such publications as *Sojourners, Radix,* and *The Other Side.* Their numbers are small, and are likely to remain so, given the radical commitment they expect of members. However, their influence is likely to be greater than the numbers would indicate, since the ideology and the action they embody speak to values given lip service by both evangelicals and liberals.

The question of social influence becomes particularly important if we return to the context in which this discussion of new religious movements was begun. If sectarian organization and ideology are responses to anomie because the society has reached a period of cultural distortion, then it is appropriate to analyze these groups in terms of their potential as revitalization movements out of which the society may be renewed. If none have that possibility, we may then consider whether the society has indeed reached a state where such a movement is called for, or where else one might look for revitalization to arise, or whether social disintegration is inevitable because it would be impossible for any movement to reunite people into any common purpose or world view.

Groups such as Scientology, whose movement from cultic to sectarian organization is largely based on the need for leaders to maintain control, seem unlikely candidates for broad transformative functions. They still tend to operate on the general cultic assumptions of helping persons cope with or manipulate to their own ends the social order in which they find themselves. If one searches these movements for a "goal culture" or a "transfer culture," one finds only the desire for greater personal health, happiness, and power. The attractiveness of such goals should not be discounted, but the methods of achieving them seem more curative than preventive. That is, adverse effects of the current culture are taken for granted, and the program of the group is to help the individual overcome them. This, then, is a response appropriate to Wallace's period of increased individual stress and has not taken on the features of a revitalization movement.

Borderline Christian groups such as the Children of God, similarly, appear either caught up in individual transformation or the kind of apocalyptic separation that assumes that members of the group may be able to escape the general doom of the society if they keep their barriers high enough. They have no hope for those outside their fellowship. If one can trust all that Ford says about those Catholic Pentecostals she labels Type I (and it is necessary to weigh her clear prejudice against a movement that expelled her against the hard evidence she has marshaled), these groups may also be removing themselves from the social order rather than speaking to it.[22] One receives the impression that they consider their groups both the transfer culture and the goal culture, and that only by joining the movement on their terms could people revitalize the society. Yet theirs is an incomplete culture, dependent primarily upon the outside society for economic foundations and many other features of their lives. One may here agree with Fichter's definition of Catholic Pentecostalism as a "cult," not because of its form of organization but because its primary focus is a reaction to given forms of Catholic structure and worship rather than having an independent base.[23]

By contrast, there can be little doubt that Moon's Unification Church has an explicit goal culture in mind and is busy building a fully operational transfer culture within which to operate in the meantime. They have their own family structure, appear to be developing their own educational institutions, are developing a political base, and have a clearly articulated pattern of governance and a mythological structure that supports all these. This movement is at a point of development where the question to be raised is not whether they posit a goal culture, but rather whether that goal is one consistent with the values of the questioner. For many, their ideal seems far too authoritarian to be acceptable in the modern West, but for others it offers order in a life now perceived as chaotic.

The radical evangelicals are also fairly clear about a goal culture, and some have begun living in what could be defined as an appropriate transfer culture. Their closer ties to institutional Christianity offer possibilities both of instituting transformation through existing structures and of being reabsorbed without significant influence. It may be that the influence of a more militant evangelicalism on more liberal churches, coupled with the willingness of radical evangelicals to deal with liberals, may spark a moderate form of revitalization through existing institutions, enough to return the society to a relatively steady state. It may be that this is insufficient for the present situation. The scientific observer is far too close to this situation to be able to trace all the influences necessary to predict the outcome; only time can provide us with sufficient distance.

Notes and References

1. For further discussion on the nature of anomie, see Peter L. Berger, *The Sacred Canopy* (Garden City, N.Y.: Doubleday, 1967), Chapter 4.
2. David Loye, *The Leadership Passion: A Psychology of Ideology* (San Francisco: Jossey-Bass, 1977), pp. 164–181.
3. Anthony F. C. Wallace, *Religion: An Anthropological View* (New York: Random House, 1966), pp. 157–263.
4. These have been designated "Type II" by J. Massyngberde Ford in *Which Way for Catholic Pentecostals?* (New York: Harper & Row, 1977), Chapter 5.

5. Ibid., p. 48.
6. See ibid., Chapter 1; also a series of six articles, "Whither Charismatics?" by Rick Casey in the *National Catholic Reporter,* August 15 and 29, September 5, 12, 19, and 29, 1975. Further discussion on the idea of the religious community as a family with this pattern of authority may be found in Larry Christenson, *The Christian Family* (Minneapolis: Bethany Fellowship, 1970). This last is apparently a source frequently used in charismatic groups of this type.
7. Ford, op. cit., Chapter 4.
8. Roy Wallis, *The Road to Total Freedom* (New York: Columbia University Press, 1977), pp. 132–134.
9. Sophia Collier, *Soul Rush: The Odyssey of a Young Woman of the '70s* (New York: Morrow, 1978).
10. Sydney E. Ahlstrom, *A Religious History of the American People* (New Haven: Yale, 1972), pp. 447–452.
11. At the time of writing, most information on this group has been available only through media sources. Primary printed sources for this discussion have been *The New York Times* issues from November 25, 1978, to December 3, 1978, and an article written by Ronald Major of the Pacific News Service entitled "Why Did Blacks Follow Jim Jones?", appearing in the *Boston Globe,* December 24, 1978.
12. *Deprogramming: Documenting the Issue,* prepared for the American Civil Liberties Union Conference on Religious Deprogramming. New York, February 5, 1977.
13. See Ted Patrick, *Let Our Children Go!* (New York: Dutton, 1976).
14. See Anson D. Shupe, Roger Spielmann, and Sam Stigall, "Deprogramming: The New Exorcism," *American Behavioral Scientist* 20, no. 6 (August 1977): 941–956. Also, by the same authors, "Deprogramming and the Emerging Anti-Cult Movement," a paper presented to the Society for the Scientific Study of Religion, October 1977.
15. For further discussion of the importance of "bridge-burning" in the process of conversion to deviant groups, see Luther P. Gerlack and Virginia H. Hine, *People, Power, Change* (Indianapolis: Bobbs-Merrill, 1970), pp. 119–135.
16. For a description and analysis of this process, see John Lofland, " 'Becoming a World-Saver' Revisited," *American Behavioral Scientist* 20, no. 6 (August 1977): 805–818.
17. The original description could be found in John Lofland, *Doomsday Cult* (Englewood Cliffs, N.J.: Prentice-Hall, 1966). With increased public attention to the Unification Church, Lofland has now written a revision of this work, which is a thinly disguised study of that group (New York: Irvington, 1978). Particularly in his epilogue to the second work, he updates both his observation and analysis.
18. See D. W. Peterson and Armand Mauss, "The Cross and the Commune: An Interpretation of the Jesus People," in *Religion in Sociological Perspective,* ed. by Charles Y. Glock (Belmont, Calif.: Wadsworth, 1973). For more on the Jesus movement, see also Ronald Enroth, Edward Erickson, and C. B. Peters, *The Jesus People* (Grand Rapids, Mich.: Eerdmans, 1972), and James T. Richardson, M. Stewart, and R. B. Simonds, *Organized Miracles: A Sociological Study of a Jesus Movement Organization* (New Brunswick, N.J.: Transaction, 1978).
19. Marcia Rudin, "The New Religious Cults and the Jewish Community," *Religious Education* 73, no. 3 (May-June 1978): 350–360.
20. Rex Davis and James T. Richardson, "The Organization and Functioning of the Children of God," *Sociological Analysis* 37, no. 4 (1975): 321–340.
21. See Richard Quebedeaux, *The Young Evangelicals* (New York: Harper & Row, 1974), pp. 37–41; also, by the same author, *The Worldly Evangelicals* (New York: Harper & Row, 1978), pp. 147–152.

22. In addition to Ford, see Meredith McGuire, "Toward a Sociological Interpretation of the 'Catholic Pentecostal' Movement," *Review of Religious Research* 16, no. 2 (1975): 94–104.

23. Joseph Fichter, *The Catholic Cult of the Paraclete* (New York: Sheed & Ward, 1975), Chapter 2. Fichter, however, makes clear that he is speaking primarily of those charismatics Ford has labeled Type II, since at the time of his writing the more sectarian groups were only beginning to gain prominence. See, e.g., p. 148.

16

Epilogue: Where Do We Go from Here?

A few years ago, when secularization was the taken-for-granted direction of social evolution, sociologists of religion tended to be regarded either as dilettantes playing around with exotic fringe activities or as religious hacks using their sociological skill to help churches predict membership trends or consequences of new programs or policies. The current interest among sociologists in new religious movements might seem to reinforce the first of those impressions. However, many of those movements—and the responses to them—have served to build an awareness that even in modern society religious behavior has important consequences for other social institutions.

New religious practices have called into question many patterns of legal protection for freedom of religion. Sociologists are being consulted as to definitions of religion on matters as diverse as tax exemptions for church property (what constitutes ritual use of a building, for example), definitions of ministry (who is entitled to draft deferment, or to special visas?), and definitions of conversion (is this brainwashing?).

Religious institutions are asking questions: Is this a legitimate option for our young people? Should we allow these groups to participate in our councils of churches or chaplaincy programs? Should we invite them for discussions or find ways of destroying them? And more importantly, they may ask what they have done wrong, what needs—personal or societal—are being met by the new religions that they should have met. Sometimes they come to sociologists for such information as they can provide on the functions of religion and how they are provided.

People whose hopes for the renewal of the society were pinned on rational technological advancement seek help in understanding the rejection of those hopes represented in the new movements. They puzzle over the sneaking suspicion they have that Jimmy Carter was elected president not *in spite of* the fact that he was an active Southern Baptist, but *because* he was one, with all the stereotypes of the nature of Southern Baptist religion in operation. It seems clear that a significant proportion of the people are turning to religion for assistance in coping with some part of their lives and that the movement has become too large to be treated as mere individual psychological aberration. And so they seek answers from those who, like them, rely on the scientific method.

Unfortunately, like the urban sociologists who were sought out for answers to the social unrest of the 1960s, sociologists of religion may not be very well prepared to serve as the seers or the sages of the 1970s. Many of the concepts upon which the discipline has been built have come out of Western culture alone and are having to be radically altered to deal with religious movements from the East. Definitions of church, sect, and cult have assumed a Christendom that is no longer clearly evident. Assumptions about human nature and the meaning of history out of which sociology has grown are themselves thrown into question by some of the new religions.[1]

Some sociologists of religion, particularly in Europe, have long worked out of the assumption that the field is a part of the larger study of the sociology of knowledge. That is, what is peculiarly at stake is the way in which we learn to structure the world of meaning, and its relationship to religious formulations concerning ultimate patterns and goals. Current movements may be pushing American sociologists of religion in this direction as well.

An example of this may be found in the relation of cultural assumptions about the nature of the universe to patterns of religious organizations commonly defined as "sect" and "cult." Eastern religions as a whole tend to affirm some sort of monism—some idea of the ultimate goal of life being an absorption into the unity of all things. If all things are really a basic unity, then any divine manifestation is bound to be only partial—though true—and dividing lines between one religious form and another would be evidence of "false consciousness."[2]

This kind of orientation allows the acceptance of a genuinely pluralistic society. It also tends to support a cyclical view of history. If all things are one, then the ultimate is already present. There need be no frantic race for improvement, mobility, or progress. Rather, one's efforts are likely to be spent on enlightenment, perception, coping. Religious forms are, in Wallis's terms, "pluralistically legitimate"—the cult or the denomination.[3]

In Western society the opposite has held true. Though there have been wide variations in the latitude given the idea of "one way," there

has been a basic assumption of transcendent monotheistic religion—
that there is a single center of value that is above the common experiences of daily life or beyond the horizon of a linear history. Thus
progress, striving, and change are endemic, based on the assumption
that there is a goal to be reached. This, then, allows a further assumption
of a dualistic rather than a monistic universe. Whatever serves to aid in
the achievement of ultimate ends is good; whatever interferes with that
goal is evil.

In such a world view, pluralism is at best a compromise, an admission
that no group has yet found the fully correct method of perceiving or
upholding the central values. The ideal state for religious groups, however, is to be "uniquely legitimate"—to be able to offer *the* truth. Thus
religious organization tends to be the church or the sect.

Modern society shows a growing mixture of dualistic and monistic
tendencies, and this is reflected in the growth of both cults and sects.
Social scientific assumptions have served to strengthen monistic tendencies, taking as they do an attitude of cultural relativism. However,
the results are ambiguous, because science as a whole tends more toward
the dualistic assumptions of progress in knowledge and in control.
Nonetheless, even as it was in Troeltsch's time, the conditions of cultic
development seem most evident among the educated.[4] This may, then,
indicate a trend as higher levels of education become more universal.

Evidence of growing pluralism and the acceptance of cultic forms of
religion can be found in many places. One example among many is the
membership of the Berkeley Area Interfaith Council, successor to the
Council of Churches of Berkeley, California. The following organizations were listed as contributors to the council in 1977:[5]

Baha'i Faith
Berkeley First Baptist
  Church
Berkeley Zendo
Nyingma Institute
University Christian
  Church
Church Women United
Canterbury Foundation
St. Mark's Episcopal
  Church
Berkeley Friends Meeting
Graduate Theological
  Union Guild

First United Presbyterian
  Church
St. John's Presbyterian
  Church
Subud International
Berkeley Fellowship of
  Unitarians
First Unitarian Church
Universal Yoga Church
First Church of Universal Life
Blue Mt. Center of Meditation
Church of Divine Man
New Education
  Development

Krishna Temple	New Age Metaphysical Research
Trinity United Methodist	Calif. Christian Committee
Church	for Israel

In practice as well as in organization such pluralism is evident. Harvey Cox has made an interesting case for taking up Eastern-style meditation as a substitute for the Jewish custom of the Sabbath, where modern men and women could take short periods of contemplation out of schedules far too complicated to allow an entire day of rest.[6] Many church groups are indeed encouraging some forms of meditation, Yoga, t'ai chi, or the like.

On the other hand, sectarian organizations and such movements as increased legitimacy for evangelical religion provide ample indication that there is a strong following for a monotheistic and dualistic under-standing of the universe. In some cases the attitude is direct and uncompromising: playing around with alien religions is idolatry, forbidden by the Scriptures. Others are concerned that Western-style political demo-cracies have only been able to function because of the shared value base of most of their citizenry. Our acquaintance with monistic, pluralistic cultures has been limited to countries under some kind of traditional autocratic or colonial rule, or in recent times suffering from political instability. Some observers question the possibility of Western democ-racy in societies that are genuinely pluralistic.

Reactions against the new groups give evidence of both kinds of assumptions. Some people excoriate them as dangerous heresies, evil subversions of Western values and Christian faith. Others seem most concerned with the sectarian exclusiveness they engender, showing that their primary value is in the openness of individual religious choice characteristic of a pluralistic pattern.

In all these areas genuine "hard-nosed" sociological study is needed. Is it necessary that each world view carry with it political and religious styles generally observed? Are there exceptions, and if so, what are their consequences? Are the forms of organization and the functions of reli-gion we have found in Western culture universal enough for us to make generalizations, or must all our concepts and theories be changed as we take seriously new forms of religion in modern society?

The field of the sociology of religion has been broken open by such questions, and by the renewed relevance of their answers. It is a time for creative and responsible scholarship, a time of challenge and renewal in the field. The growth in membership of such professional organiza-tions as the Society for the Scientific Study of Religion, the Religious

Research Association, and the Association for the Sociology of Religion attest to the fact that the challenge has revived interest and participation in the field of the sociology of religion.

Notes and References

1. Evidence of the increased interest in this area and the range of subjects involved may be found in both the article and its bibliography by Thomas Robbins, Dick Anthony, and James Richardson, "Theory and Research on Today's 'New Religions,' " *Sociological Analysis* 39, no. 2 (1978): 95–122.
2. Much recent work in the area of monistic and dualistic religion has been done by Thomas Robbins and Dick Anthony. See, for example, Dick Anthony and Thomas Robbins, "A Typology of Non-Traditional Religious Movements in Contemporary America," *Journal of Social Issues*, forthcoming, as well as the article cited immediately above.
3. Roy Wallis, *The Road to Total Freedom* (New York: Columbia University Press, 1977), p. 13. He also gives credit for the concept, used in a slightly different manner, to Roland Robertson, in *The Sociological Interpretation of Religion* (Oxford: Blackwell, 1970), p. 123; and to David Martin in the appendix to his *Pacifism* (London: Routledge & Kegan Paul, 1965).
4. Ernst Troeltsch, *The Social Teaching of the Christian Churches*, trans. by Olive Wyon (New York: Macmillan, 1931), p. 738.
5. *BAIC News/Notes*, February 16, 1978.
6. Harvey Cox, *Turning East* (New York: Simon & Schuster, 1978), Chapter 5.

James Beckford. *Religious Organization.* Published as vol. 21, no. 2 of *Current Sociology* (1973) by Mouton, the Hague, 1974.

Harvey Cox. *Turning East: The Promise and Peril of the New Orientalism.* New York: Simon & Schuster, 1977.

Joseph Fichter. *The Catholic Cult of the Paraclete.* New York: Sheed & Ward, 1975.

Charles Glock and Robert Bellah, eds. *The New Religious Consciousness.* Berkeley: University of California Press, 1976.

Richard Quebedeaux. *The Worldly Evangelicals.* New York: Harper & Row, 1978.

Anthony F. C. Wallace. "Revitalization Movements." *American Anthropologist* 58 (April 1956): 264–281.

Selected Bibliography

Adams, Herbert R. *The Church and Popular Education.* Baltimore: Johns Hopkins Press, 1900.

Adams, James L. *The Growing Church Lobby in Washington.* Grand Rapids, Mich.: Eerdmans, 1970.

Ahlstrom, Sidney. *A Religious History of the American People.* New Haven: Yale University Press, 1972.

American Association of School Administrators. *Religion in the Public Schools.* New York: Harper & Row, 1964.

Back, Kurt W. *Beyond Words: The Story of Sensitivity Training and the Encounter Movement.* New York: Russell Sage, 1972.

Bahr, Howard; Bartel, Lewis; and Chadwick, Bruce. "Orthodoxy, Activism, and the Salience of Religion." *Journal for the Scientific Study of Religion* 10, no. 2 (Summer 1971): 69–75.

Baker, Ray Stannard. *The Spiritual Unrest.* New York: Stokes, 1910.

Barowitz, Eugene R. "Jewish Theology Faces the 1970s." *Annals of the American Academy of Political and Social Science* 387 (January 1970): 22–29.

Baumer, Franklin L. *Religion and the Rise of Skepticism.* New York: Harcourt, 1960.

Becker, Howard. "Current Sacred-Secular Theory." In *Modern Sociological Theory in Continuity and Change,* ed. by Howard Becker and Alvin Boskoff. New York: Dryden, 1957.

Beckford, James. *Religious Organization.* Published as vol. 21, no. 2 of *Current Sociology,* by Mouton, the Hague, 1974.

Bellah, Robert N. *Beyond Belief: Essays on Religion in a Post-Traditional World.* New York: Harper & Row, 1970.

———. *The Broken Covenant.* New York: Seabury, 1975.

———. "Civil Religion in America." *Daedalus* 96, no. 1 (Winter 1967): 1–20.

———. "Religious Evolution." *American Sociological Review* 29, no. 3 (June 1964): 358–374.

———. *Tokugawa Religion.* New York: Free Press, 1957.

Bellah, Robert N. (ed.). *Religion and Progress in Modern Asia.* New York: Free Press, 1965.

Bendix, Reinhold. *Max Weber: An Intellectual Portrait.* Garden City, N.Y.: Doubleday, 1960.

Bennett, John C. *The Christian As Citizen.* New York: Association Press, 1955.

Benz, Ernst. *The Eastern Orthodox Church: Its Thought and Life.* Trans. by Richard Winston and Clara Winston. Chicago: Aldine, 1963.

Berger, Peter L. *The Noise of Solemn Assemblies.* Garden City, N.Y.: Doubleday, 1961.

————. *The Precarious Vision: A Sociologist Looks at Social Fictions and the Christian Faith.* Garden City, N.Y.: Doubleday, 1961.

————. "Religious Institutions." In *Sociology: An Introduction,* ed. by Neil Smelser. New York: Wiley, 1967.

————. *A Rumor of Angels: Modern Society and the Rediscovery of the Supernatural.* Garden City, N.Y.: Doubleday, 1968.

————. *The Sacred Canopy.* Garden City, N.Y.: Doubleday, 1967.

Berger, Peter; Berger, Brigette; and Kellner, Hansfried. *The Homeless Mind: Modernization and Consciousness.* New York: Random House, 1973.

Bianchi, Eugene C. "Resistance in the Church." *Commonweal* 90, no. 9 (May 16, 1969): 257–260.

Blanshard, Paul. *American Freedom and Catholic Power.* Rev. ed. Boston: Beacon, 1958.

Blizzard, Samuel W. "Role Conflicts of the Urban Minister." *The City Church* (September–October 1956), pp. 13–15.

Bloesch, Donald G. *The Reform of the Church.* Grand Rapids, Mich.: Eerdmans, 1970.

Boaz, Franz, ed. *General Anthropology.* Washington, D.C.: U.S. War Dept., 1944.

Bonhoeffer, Dietrich. *Life Together.* Trans. by John W. Doberstein. New York: Harper & Row, 1954.

Bonino, José Miguez. "Catholic-Protestant Relations in Latin America." In *The Religious Situation, 1969,* ed. by Donald R. Cutler. Boston: Beacon, 1969, pp. 134–145.

Boorstin, Daniel. *The Genius of American Politics.* Chicago: University of Chicago Press, 1953.

Braden, Charles S. *These Also Believe: A Study of Modern American Cults and Minority Religious Movements.* New York: Macmillan, 1944.

Braiterman, Marvin. *Religion and the Public Schools.* New York: Commission on Social Action of Reform Judaism, Union of American Hebrew Congregations, 1958.

Brothers, Joan, ed. *Readings in the Sociology of Religion.* Oxford: Pergammon, 1967.

Brown, Robert McAfee, and Weigle, Gustave, S. J., *An American Dialogue.* Garden City, N.Y.: Doubleday, 1960.

Brunner, Edmund deS. *The Country Church in the New World Order.* New York: Association Press, 1919.

Campbell, Colin. "The Cult, the Cultic Milieu, and Secularization." In *A Sociological Yearbook of Religion in Britain 5,* ed. by Michael Hill. London: SCM Press, 1976.

―――. "The Secret Religion of the Educated Classes." *Sociological Analysis* 39, no. 2 (1978): 146–156.

Campbell, Joseph. *The Hero with a Thousand Faces.* New York: Pantheon, 1949.

Caplovitz, David, and Sherrow, Fred. *The Religious Dropouts: Apostasy among College Students.* New York: Russell Sage, 1977.

Cardwell, Jerry. "The Relationship between Religious Commitment and Premarital Sexual Permissiveness: A Five Dimensional Analysis." *Sociological Analysis* 30, no. 2 (Summer 1969): 72–80.

Carothers, J. Edward. *Keepers of the Poor.* New York: Board of Missions of the Methodist Church, 1966.

Carter, Paul Allen. *The Decline and Revival of the Social Gospel: Social and Political Liberalism in American Protestant Churches, 1920–1940.* Ithaca, N.Y.: Cornell University Press, 1956.

Chandler, Russell. "Fanning the Charismatic Fire." *Christianity Today* 12 (November 24, 1967), pp. 39–40.

Childress, James F., and Harned, David B. (eds.). *Secularization and the Protestant Prospect.* Philadelphia: Westminster, 1970.

The Church and the Public Schools. New York: Board of Christian Education, Presbyterian Church of the U.S.A., June 1957.

Clark, Francis E. *The Christian Endeavor Manual.* Boston: United Society for Christian Endeavor, 1925.

Clark, Walter H. *Chemical Ecstasy.* Mission, Kans.: Sheed, Andrews & McMeel, 1962.

Cleage, Albert B., Jr. *The Black Messiah.* New York: Sheed & Ward, 1968.

Clear, Val B. "The Urbanization of a Holiness Body." *The City Church,* July–August 1958, pp. 2–4.

Coats, William. *God in Public: Political Theology Beyond Niebuhr.* Grand Rapids, Mich: Eerdmans, 1974.

Colaianni, James. *The Catholic Left: The Crisis of Radicalism Within the Church.* Philadelphia: Chilton, 1969.

Collier, Sophia. *Soul Rush: The Odyssey of a Young Woman of the '70s.* New York: Morrow, 1978.

Cone, James H. *Black Theology and Black Power.* New York: Seabury, 1969.

Conway, Russell. *Acres of Diamonds.* Edited for contemporary readers by William R. Webb. Kansas City: Hallmark, 1968.

Cox, Harvey. *Feast of Fools: A Theological Essay on Festivity and Fantasy.* Cambridge, Mass.: Harvard University Press, 1969.

―――. *The Secular City.* New York: Macmillan, 1965.

―――. *Turning East: The Promise and Peril of the New Orientalism.* New York: Simon & Schuster, 1977.

Cross, Robert D., ed. *The Church and the City.* Indianapolis: Bobbs-Merrill, 1967.

Cullman, Oscar. *Jesus and the Revolutionaries.* Trans. by Gareth Putnam. New York: Harper & Row, 1970.

Cutler, Donald Y., ed. *The Religious Situation, 1969.* Boston: Beacon, 1969.

Daly, Mary. *After God the Father.* Boston: Beacon, 1973.

————. *The Church and the Second Sex.* New York: Harper & Row, 1968.

Davis, Kingsley. *Human Society.* New York: Macmillan, 1949.

Davis, Rex, and Richardson, James T. "The Organization and Functioning of the Children of God." *Sociological Analysis* 37, no. 4 (1975): 321–340.

DeGrazia, Sebastian. *The Political Community: A Study of Anomie.* Chicago: University of Chicago Press, 1948.

Demarath, N. J. III. *Social Class in American Protestantism.* Chicago: Rand McNally, 1965.

"Deprogramming: Documenting the Issue." Prepared for the American Civil Liberties Union Conference on Religious Deprogramming, New York, 1977.

Derr, Thomas Sieger. *Ecology and Human Need.* Philadelphia: Westminster, 1975.

Derrick, Christopher. *Trimming the Ark: Catholic Attitudes and the Cult of Change.* London: Hutchison, 1967.

Dobler, Walter E. "The Church's Teaching Ministry and the Modern Family." *Social Action* 28 (September 1961): 17–25.

Dombrowski, James. *The Early Days of Christian Socialism in America.* New York: Columbia University Press, 1936.

Douglas, Mary. *Purity and Danger: An Analysis of Concepts of Pollution and Taboo.* London: Routledge & Kegan Paul, 1966.

Dressner, Richard B. "Christian Socialism: A Response to Industrial America in the Progressive Era." Ph.D. dissertation, Cornell University, 1972.

Drinan, Robert F., S.J. *Religion, the Courts, and Public Policy.* New York: McGraw-Hill, 1963.

Dunlap, Knight. *Religion: Its Functions in Human Life.* New York: McGraw-Hill, 1946.

Durka, Gloria, and Smith, Joan Marie, eds. *Emerging Issues in Religious Education.* New York: Paulist Press, 1976.

Durkheim, Emile. *The Division of Labor in Society.* Trans. by George Simpson. New York: Free Press, 1947.

————. *The Elementary Forms of the Religious Life.* Trans. by Joseph Ward Swain. New York: Free Press, 1965.

Earle, John R.; Knudsen, Dean D.; and Shriver, Donald W., Jr. *Spindles and Spires.* Atlanta: John Knox Press, 1976.

Ebersole, Luke E. *Church Lobbying in the Nation's Capitol.* New York: Macmillan, 1951.

Eisenstadt, S. N., ed. *The Protestant Ethic and Modernization.* New York: Basic Books, 1968.

Eister, Allan W. *Drawing Room Conversion.* Durham, N.C.: Duke University Press, 1950.

————. "An Outline of A Structural Theory of Cults." *Journal for the Scientific Study of Religion* 11 (December 1972): 319–334.

Eliade, Mircea. *Myth and Reality.* Trans. by Willard R. Trask. New York: Harper & Row, 1963.

————. *The Sacred and the Profane: The Nature of Religion.* Trans. by Willard R. Trask. New York: Harcourt, 1959.

Ellul, Jacques. *The New Demons.* Trans. by C. Edward Hopkin. New York: Seabury, 1975.

———. *The Technological Society.* Trans. by John Wilkinson. New York: Knopf, 1964.

Ellwood, Robert S., Jr. *One Way: The Jesus Movement and Its Meaning.* Englewood Cliffs, N.J.: Prentice-Hall, 1973.

———. *Religious and Spiritual Groups in Modern America.* Englewood Cliffs, N.J.: Prentice-Hall, 1972.

Ennis, Phillip H. "Ecstasy and Everyday Life." *Journal for the Scientific Study of Religion* 6, no. 1 (Spring 1967): 40–48.

Enroth, Ronald M.; Ericson, E. E., Jr.; and Peters, C. *The Jesus People: Old-Time Religion in the Age of Aquarius.* Grand Rapids: Wm. B. Eerdmans, 1972.

Erikson, Erik. *Identity: Youth and Crisis.* New York: Norton, 1968.

Felton, Ralph A. *These My Brethren.* Madison, N.J.: Dept. of the Rural Church, Drew Theological Seminary, 1950.

Fenton, John G. *The Catholic Vote.* New Orleans: Hauser, 1960.

Fichter, Joseph. *The Catholic Cult of the Paraclete.* New York: Sheed & Ward, 1975.

———. *Social Relations in the Urban Parish.* Chicago: University of Chicago Press, 1954.

Firth, Raymond. *Tikopia Ritual and Belief.* Boston: Beacon, 1967.

Fisher, Desmond. *The Church in Transition.* Notre Dame, Ind.: Fides, 1967.

Frazier, E. Franklin. *Black Bourgeoisie.* New York: Free Press, 1957.

Ford, J. Massyngberde. *Which Way for Catholic Pentecostals?* New York: Harper & Row, 1977.

Freud, Sigmund. *The Future of An Illusion.* London: Hogarth, 1934.

Fromm, Erich, *The Dogma of Christ and Other Essays on Religion, Psychology and Culture.* New York: Holt, 1963.

Fukiuama, Yoshio. "The Major Dimensions of Church Membership." *Review of Religious Research* 2 (1961): 159.

The Function of the Public Schools in Dealing with Religion. A report on the exploratory study made by the Committee on Religion and Education, American Council on Education, Washington, D.C., 1953.

Fustel, Numa Denis de Coulanges. *The Ancient City.* Garden City, N.Y.: Doubleday, 1956.

Garmann, W. C. H. *Communist Infiltration in the Churches.* Corrected and revised, 3rd ed. Tulsa: Christian Crusade, n.d.

Gerlach, Luther P., and Hine, Virginia H. *People, Power, Change: Movements of Social Transformation.* Indianapolis: Bobbs-Merrill, 1970.

Geyer, Alan F. *Piety and Politics: American Protestants in the World Arena.* Richmond, Va.: John Knox Press, 1963.

Gibbs, Mark, and Morton, Thomas. *God's Frozen People: A Book for and about Christian Laymen.* Philadelphia: Westminster, 1965.

Gill, Charles Otis, and Pinchot, Gifford. *Six Thousand Country Churches.* New York: Macmillan, 1919.

Glazer, Nathan. *American Judaism.* 2nd. ed. Chicago: University of Chicago Press, 1972.

Glock, Charles Y., and Stark, Rodney. *Christian Beliefs and Anti-Semitism.* New York: Harper & Row, 1966.

Glock, Charles Y.; Ringer, Benjamin B.; and Babbie, Earl R. *To Comfort and to Challenge: A Dilemma of the Contemporary Church.* Berkeley: University of California Press, 1967.

Glock, Charles, and Bellah, Robert, eds. *The New Religious Consciousness.* Berkeley: University of California Press, 1976.

Glock, Charles Y., and Stark, Rodney. *Religion and Society in Tension.* Chicago: Rand McNally, 1965.

Glock, Charles Y., ed. *Religion in Sociological Perspective.* Belmont, Calif.: Wadsworth, 1973.

Glock, Charles Y., and Wuthnow, Robert. "The Religious Dimension: A Report on Its Status in a Cosmopolitan American Community." Paper presented at the International Symposium on Belief, Baden bei/Wien, Austria, 1975.

Goldenweiser, Alexander. "Religion and Society: A Critique of Emile Durkheim's Theory of the Origin and Nature of Religion." *Journal of Philosophy, Psychology, and Scientific Methods* 14 (1917): 113–124.

Goldmann, Alfred A. *The Common Ground in Family Life Education.* New York: American Social Hygiene Association, 1950.

Goode, William J. *Religion Among the Primitives.* New York: Free Press, 1951.

Goodman, Grace Ann. *Rocking the Ark: Nine Case Studies of Traditional Churches in the Process of Change.* Division of Evangelism, Board of National Missions, United Presbyterian Church in the USA, 1968.

Gordon, James S. "Who Is Mad? Who Is Sane? The Radical Psychiatry of R. D. Laing." *Atlantic* 227 (January 1971): 50–66.

Greeley, Andrew; McCready, William; and McCourt, Kathleen. *Catholic Schools in a Declining Church.* Kansas City: Sheed & Ward, 1976.

Greeley, Andrew M., and Rossi, Peter H. *The Education of Catholic Americans.* Chicago: Aldine, 1966.

Grey, Francine duPlessix. *Divine Disobedience: Profiles in Catholic Radicalism.* New York: Knopf, 1970.

Gustafson, James M. *Treasure in Earthen Vessels: The Church as a Human Community.* New York: Harper, 1961.

Hadden, Jeffrey K. *The Gathering Storm in the Churches.* Garden City, N.Y.: Doubleday, 1969.

Hammond, Phillip E., and Mitchell, Robert E. "Segmentation of Radicalism— The Case of the Protestant Campus Minister." *American Journal of Sociology* 71, no. 2 (1965): 133–143.

Handy, Robert T., ed. *The Social Gospel in America: 1870–1920.* New York: Oxford University Press, 1966.

Harder, Mary. "Sex Roles in the Jesus Movement." *Social Compass* 21 (1974): 345–353.

Hargrove, Barbara W. "Local Congregations and Social Change." *Sociological Analysis* 30, no. 1 (Spring 1969): 13–22.

———. "Church Student Ministries and the New Consciousness." In *The New Religious Consciousness,* ed. by Charles Glock and Robert Bellah. Berkeley: University of California Press, 1976.

Harrison, Paul M. *Authority and Power in the Free Church Tradition.* Carbondale: Southern Illinois University Press, 1971.

Hartt, Julian. "Secularity and the Transcendence of God." In *Secularization and the Protestant Prospect,* ed. by James F. Childress and David B. Harned. Philadelphia: Westminster, 1970.

Harvard Law School Forum. "The Catholic Church and Politics." Cambridge, Mass.: Harvard Law School, 1950.

Herberg, Will. *Protestant-Catholic-Jew.* Garden City, N.Y.: Doubleday, 1955.

———. "Protestantism in A Post-Protestant America." *Christianity and Crisis* 22 (February 5, 1962): 5–6.

Hill, Samuel S., Jr. *Southern Churches in Crisis.* New York: Holt, 1966.

Hoebel, E. Adamson. *Man in the Primitive World.* 2nd ed. New York: McGraw-Hill, 1958.

Hoekendijk, J. C. *The Church Inside Out.* Ed. by L. A. Hoedmaker and Peter Tijmes, trans. by Isaac C. Rottenburg. Philadelphia: Westminster, 1966.

Hoge, Dean. *Division in the Protestant House.* Philadelphia: Westminster, 1977.

Homans, George C. *The Human Group.* New York: Harcourt, 1950.

———. "Anxiety and Ritual: The Theories of Malinowski and Radcliffe-Brown." *American Anthropologist* 43 (April–June 1941): 164–172.

Hori, Ochiro. *Folk Religion in Japan.* Ed. by Joseph M. Kitagawa and Alan L. Miller. Chicago: University of Chicago Press, 1968.

Howells, William. *The Heathens: Primitive Man and His Religions.* Garden City, N.Y.: Doubleday, 1948.

Illich, Ivan. *The Church, Change, and Development.* Chicago: Urban Training Center Press, 1970.

James, E. O. *Sacrifice and Sacrament.* London: Thames & Hudson, 1962.

———. *The Nature and Function of the Priesthood.* London: Thames & Hudson, 1955.

James, William. *The Varieties of Religious Experience.* New York: Modern Library, 1902.

Johnson, Benton. "Ascetic Protestantism and Political Preference." *Public Opinion Quarterly* 26 (Spring 1962): 35–46.

———. "Ascetic Protestantism and Political Preference in the Deep South." *American Journal of Sociology* 69 (January 1964): 359–366.

———. "Do Holiness Sects Socialize in Dominant Values?" *Social Forces* 39 (1961): 309–316.

———. "Theology and Party Preference Among Protestant Clergymen." *American Sociological Review* 31, no. 2 (April 1966): 200–208.

———. "Theology and the Position of Pastors on Public Issues." *American Sociological Review* 32 (June 1967): 433–442.

Johnston, Roby Funchess. *The Religion of Negro Protestants: Changing Religious Attitudes and Practices.* New York: Philosophical Library, 1956.

Jones, Lawrence. "Black Churches in Historical Perspective." *Christianity & Crisis* 30, no. 18 (November 2 & 16, 1970): 226–228.

Jones, William. *Is God a White Racist?* Garden City, N.Y.: Doubleday, 1973.

Jorstad, Erling. *The Politics of Doomsday.* Nashville: Abingdon, 1970.

Judah, Stillson. *Hare Krishna and the Counterculture.* San Francisco: Jossey-Bass, 1974.

Keen, Sam. *To a Dancing God.* New York: Harper & Row, 1970.

Kelley, Dean. *Why Conservative Churches Are Growing.* New York: Harper & Row, 1972.

Kelsey, George D. *Racism and the Christian Understanding of Man.* New York: Scribner's, 1965.

Kerwin, Jerome J. *Catholic Viewpoint on Church and State.* Garden City, N.Y.: Doubleday, 1966.

King, Winston L. "Eastern Religions: A New Interest and Influence." *Annals of the American Academy of Political and Social Science* 387 (January 1970): 66–76.

Kluckhohn, Clyde. "Myths and Rituals: A General Theory." *Harvard Theological Review* 35 (January 1942): 45–79.

Kohut, Andrew, and Stookey, Laurence H. "Religious Affiliation and Attitudes toward Viet Nam." *Theology Today* 26, no. 4 (January 1970): 464–470.

Krebs, A. V., Jr. "A Church of Silence." *Commonweal* 80 (July 10, 1964): 467–476.

Kroeber, A. L. *Anthropology.* New ed., rev. New York: Harcourt, 1948.

Kurland, Philip B. *Religion and the Law: Of Church and State and the Supreme Court.* Chicago: Aldine, 1962.

Laing, R. D. *The Politics of Experience.* London: Penguin, 1967.

Lecky, Robert S., and Wright, H. Elliott. *Can These Bones Live? The Failure of Church Renewal.* New York: Sheed & Ward, 1969.

Lee, Robert, ed. *Cities and Churches: Reading on the Urban Church.* Philadelphia: Westminster, 1962.

Lee, Robert, and Marty, Martin, eds. *Religion and Social Conflict.* New York: Oxford University Press, 1964.

Lenski, Gerhard. *The Religious Factor: A Sociological Study of Religion's Impact on Politics, Economics, and Family Life.* Garden City, N.Y.: Doubleday, 1961.

Lessa, William A., and Vogt, Evon Z., eds. *Reader in Comparative Religion: An Anthropological Approach.* 2nd ed. New York: Harper & Row, 1965.

Lewis, John; Polyani, Karl; and Kitchin, Donald, eds. *Christianity and the Social Revolution.* London: Gollancz, 1935.

Lincoln, C. Eric. *The Black Muslims in America.* Boston: Beacon, 1961.

Linder, Staffan Burenstam. *The Harried Leisure Class.* New York: Columbia University Press, 1970.

Linton, Ralph. "Nativistic Movements." *The American Anthropologist* 45 (1943): 230–240.

Littel, Franklin H. *The Church and the Body Politic.* New York: Seabury, 1969.

Liu, William T., and Pallone, Nathaniel J., eds. *Catholics/USA: Perspectives in Social Change.* New York: Wiley, 1970.

Lofland, John. " 'Becoming A World-Saver' Revisited." *American Behavioral Scientist* 20, no. 6 (August 1977): 805–818.

————. *Doomsday Cult.* Rev. ed. New York: Irvington, 1978.

Lowie, Robert H. *Primitive Religion.* New York: Grosset & Dunlap, 1952.

Loye, David. *The Leadership Passion: A Psychology of Ideology.* San Francisco: Jossey-Bass, 1977.

Luckmann, Thomas. *The Invisible Religion.* New York: Macmillan, 1967.

McClain, William B. "The Genius of the Black Church." *Christianity & Crisis* 30 (November 2 & 16, 1970): 250–252.

McGuire, Meredith. "Toward A Sociological Interpretation of the 'Catholic Pentecostal' Movement." *Review of Religious Research* 16, no. 2 (1975): 94–104.

McNamara, Patrick, ed. *Religion American Style.* New York: Harper & Row, 1974.

————. "Social Action Priests in the Mexican-American Community." *Sociological Analysis* 29, no. 4 (Winter 1968): 177–185.

Malinowski, Bronislaw. *Magic, Science, and Religion, and Other Essays.* Garden City, N.Y.: Doubleday, 1948.

Manglopus, Raul S. "Philippine Culture and Modernization." In *Religion and Progress in Modern Asia,* ed. by Robert N. Bellah. New York: Free Press, 1965.

Marett, R. R. *Head, Heart, and Hands in Human Evolution.* New York: Holt, n.d.

————. *The Threshold of Religion.* 4th ed. London: Methuen, 1929.

Martin, David A. *The Dilemmas of Contemporary Religion.* New York: St. Martin's, 1978.

Marty, Martin E. *The New Shape of American Religion.* New York: Harper & Row, 1959.

————. *A Nation of Behavers.* Chicago: University of Chicago Press, 1976.

————. *Righteous Empire: The Protestant Experience in America.* New York: Dial, 1970.

————. "The Spirit's Holy Errand: The Search for A Spiritual Style in Secular America." *Daedalus* 96 (Winter 1967): 99–115.

Marx, Gary T. "Religion: Opiate or Inspiration of Civil Rights Militancy among Negroes?" *American Sociological Review* 32 (February 1967): 64–72.

Mead, Margaret. *Culture and Commitment: A Study of the Generation Gap.* Garden City, N.Y.: Doubleday, 1970.

Mead, Sidney. *The Lively Experiment.* New York: Harper & Row, 1963.

Mehl, Roger. *The Sociology of Protestantism.* Trans. by James H. Farley. Philadelphia: Westminster, 1970.

Merton, Robert K. *Social Theory and Social Structure.* Rev. and enl. ed. New York: Free Press, 1968.

Michaelson, Robert. " 'Common Religion' in California's Public Schools." *Bulletin of the Council on the Study of Religion* 1, no. 2 (October 1970).

Miller, David L. *The New Polytheism: Rebirth of the Gods and Goddesses.* New York: Harper & Row, 1974.

Miller, Norman. "Changing Patterns of Leadership in the Jewish Community." *Jewish Social Studies* 17 (July 1955): 179–182.

Miyakawa, T. Scott. *Protestants and Pioneers: Individualism and Conformity on the American Frontier.* Chicago: University of Chicago Press, 1964.

Moberg, David O. *The Church as a Social Institution.* Englewood Cliffs, N.J.: Prentice-Hall, 1962.

———. *The Great Reversal: Evangelism Versus Social Concern.* Philadelphia: Lippincott, 1972.

Moltmann, Jürgen. *The Church in the Power of the Spirit.* Trans. by Margaret Kohl. New York: Harper & Row, 1977.

Murray, Gilbert. *Five Stages of Greek Religion.* New York: Columbia University Press, 1925.

Nadel, S. R. "A Study of Shaminism in the Nuba Mountains." *Journal of the Royal Anthropological Institute* 76 (1946): 25–37.

Neal, Sister Marie Augusta. *Values and Interests in Social Change.* Englewood Cliffs, N.J.: Prentice-Hall, 1965.

Needleman, Jacob. *The New Religions.* Garden City, N.Y.: Doubleday, 1970.

———. *A Sense of the Cosmos: The Encounter of Modern Science and Ancient Truth.* New York: Dutton, 1976.

Needleman, Jacob, and Baker, George, eds. *Understanding the New Religions.* New York: Seabury, 1978.

Newbigin, Leslie. "The Quest of Unity through Religion." *Journal of Religion* 35 (1955): 17–33.

Niebuhr, H. Richard. *Christ and Culture.* Harper & Row, 1951.

———. *Radical Monotheism and Western Culture.* New York: Harper & Row, 1943.

———. *The Social Sources of Denominationalism.* New York: Holt, 1929.

Nilsson, Martin P. *Greek Popular Religions.* New York: Columbia University Press, 1940.

Norbeck, Edward. *Religion in Primitive Society.* New York: Harper & Row, 1961.

Obenhaus, Victor. *The Church and Faith in Mid-America.* Philadelphia: Westminster, 1963.

O'Brien, David J. *American Catholics and Social Reform: The New Deal Years.* New York: Oxford University Press, 1968.

O'Conner, Elizabeth. *Call to Commitment: The Story of the Church of the Savior in Washington, D.C.* New York: Harper, 1963.

Orr, John B., and Nichelson, F. Patrick. *The Radical Suburb.* Philadelphia: Westminster, 1970.

Osborne, William A. "Religious and Ecclesiastical Reform: The Contemporary Catholic Experience in the United States." *Journal for the Scientific Study of Religion* 7, no. 1 (Spring 1968): 78–86.

Otto, Rudolf. *The Idea of the Holy.* Trans. by John W. Harvey. London: Oxford University Press, 1936.

Palmer, Parker. "Selection from A Review of Danforth Campus Ministry Fellowships." *CSCW Report* 32, no. 2 (March 1974).

Parsons, Talcott. *The Social System.* New York: Free Press, 1951.

Parsons, Talcott; Shils, Edward; Naegele, Kaspar D.; and Pitts, Jesse R., eds. *Theories of Society: Foundations of Modern Sociological Theory.* New York: Free Press, 1961.

Parsons, Talcott, and Shils, Edward A., eds. *Toward a General Theory of Action.* Cambridge, Mass.: Harvard University Press, 1951.

Patrick, Ted (with Tom Dulack). *Let Our Children Go!* New York: Dutton, 1977.

Paul, Leslie. *The Death and Resurrection of the Church.* London: Hodder & Stoughton, 1968.

————. *The Deployment and Payment of the Clergy.* Church Information Office, Westminster, London, SW 1, 1964.

Pelikan, Jaroslav Jan; Pollard, William G.; Eisendrath, Maurice, N.; and Wittenberg, Alexander. *Religion and the University.* Toronto: University of Toronto Press, 1964 (published for York University).

Peterson, D. W., and Mauss, Armand. "The Cross and the Commune: An Interpretation of the Jesus People." In *Religion in Sociological Perspective,* ed. by Charles Y. Glock. Belmont, Calif.: Wadsworth, 1973.

Pettigrew, Thomas F., and Campbell, Ernest. "Racial and Moral Crisis: the Role of the Little Rock Ministers." *American Journal of Sociology* 64 (March 1959): 509–516.

Pfeffer, Leo. *Creeds in Competition: A Creative Force in American Culture.* New York: Harper, 1958.

Pope, Liston. *Millhands and Preachers.* New Haven: Yale University Press, 1942.

Powers, Charles W. *Social Responsibility and Investments.* Nashville: Abingdon, 1961.

Primer, Ben. "The Bureaucratization of the Church: Protestant Response to Modern Large-Scale Organization, 1876–1929." Ph.D. dissertation. The Johns Hopkins University, 1977.

Quebedeaux, Richard. *The New Charismatics.* Garden City, N.Y.: Doubleday, 1976.

————. *The Worldly Evangelicals.* New York: Harper & Row, 1978.

————. *The Young Evangelicals.* New York: Harper & Row, 1974.

Quick, Bernard. *He Who Pays the Piper. . . .* Privately published, 1975.

Radcliffe-Brown, A. R. "Religion and Society." *Journal of the Royal Anthropological Institute of Great Britain & Ireland* 75, no. 5:33–43.

————. "The Sociological Theory of Totemism." *Proceedings of the Fourth Pacific Science Conference, Java, 1929.* Batavia, 1930.

————. *Taboo: The Frazier Lecture, 1939.* London: Cambridge University Press, 1939.

Radin, Paul. *Primitive Religion: Its Nature and Its Origin.* New York: Dover, 1957.

Raines, Robert A. *The Secular Congregation.* New York: Harper & Row, 1968.

Ranaghan, Kevin, and Ranaghan, Dorothy. *Catholic Pentecostals.* New York: Paulist Press Deus Books, 1969.

Redfield, Robert. *The Little Community: Peasant Society and Culture.* Chicago: University of Chicago Press, 1960.

———. *The Primitive World and Its Transformations.* Ithaca, N.Y.: Cornell University Press, 1957.

Reich, Charles A. *The Greening of America.* New York: Random House, 1970.

Reiterman, Carl. "Birth Control and Catholics." *Journal for the Scientific Study of Religion* 4, no. 2 (Spring 1965): 213–236.

Reitz, Rüdiger. *The Church in Experiment.* Nashville: Abingdon, 1969.

Rhodes, A. Lewis, and Nam, Charles B. "The Religious Context of Educational Expectations." *American Sociological Review* 35, no. 2 (April 1970): 253–261.

Richardson, Herbert. *Nun, Witch and Playmate: The Americanization of Sex.* New York: Harper & Row, 1971.

Richardson, James T. "From Cult to Sect: Creative Eclecticism in New Religious Movements." *Pacific Sociological Review,* forthcoming.

Richardson, James T., and Fox, Sandie Wightman. "Religious Affiliation as a Predictor of Voting in Abortion Reform Legislation." *Journal for the Scientific Study of Religion* 11 (1972): 347–359.

Richardson, James T.; Harder, Mary; and Simonds, R. B. *Organized Miracles: a Sociological Study of a Jesus Movement Organization.* New Brunswick, N.J.: Transaction Books, 1978.

Richey, Russell E., and Jones, Donald G., eds. *American Civil Religion.* New York: Harper & Row, 1974.

Robbins, Thomas; Anthony, Dick; and Richardson, James. "Theory and Research on Today's 'New Religions.'" *Sociological Analysis* 39, no. 2 (1978): 95–122.

Roberts, J. Deotis. *A Black Political Theology.* Philadelphia: Westminster, 1974.

Robinson, John A. T. *Honest to God.* Philadelphia: Westminster, 1963.

Rokeach, Milton. *Beliefs, Attitudes, and Values.* San Francisco: Jossey-Bass, 1968.

Rosen, Bernard Carl. *Adolescence and Religion: The Jewish Teen Ager in American Society.* Cambridge, Mass.: Schenkman, 1965.

Rosenberg, Milton, J.; Hovland, Carl I.; McGuire, William J.; Abelson, Robert P.; and Brehm, Jack W. *Attitude, Organization and Change.* New Haven: Yale University Press, 1960.

Rossi, Peter H. *Why Families Move.* New York: Free Press, 1955.

Roszak, Theodore. *The Making of a Counter Culture.* Garden City, N.Y.: Doubleday, 1969.

———. *Where the Wasteland Ends.* Garden City, N.Y.: Doubleday, 1973.

Rudin, Marcia. "The New Religious Cults and the Jewish Community." *Religious Education* 73, no. 3 (May–June 1978): 350–360.

Russell, Letty Mandeville, ed. *The Liberating Word: A Guide to a Nonsexist Interpretation of the Bible.* Philadelphia: Westminster, 1976.

Ryder, Norman B., and Westoff, Charles F. "Use of Oral Contraception in the United States, 1965." *Science* 153:3741 (September 9, 1966): 1199–1205.

Sandeen, Ernest R. "Fundamentalism and American Identity." *Annals of the American Academy of Political and Social Science* 387 (January 1970): 56–65.

Sanders, Thomas G. *Protestant Concepts of Church and State: Historical Approaches for the Future.* New York: Holt, 1964.

Schaller, Lyle E. *The Churches' War on Poverty.* Nashville: Abingdon, 1967.

Schneider, Herbert W. *Religion in 20th Century America.* Cambridge, Mass.: Harvard University Press, 1952.

Schneiderman, Leo. "Psychological Notes on the Nature of Mystical Experience." *Journal for the Scientific Study of Religion* 6, no. 1 (Spring 1967): 91–100.

Schroeder, W. Widwick, and Obenhaus, Victor. *Religion in American Culture: Unity and Diversity in a Midwestern County.* New York: Free Press, 1964.

Schuller, David S. *Emerging Shapes of the Church: Signs of Renewal in Response to Change.* St. Louis: Concordia, 1967.

Sheares, Reuben A., II. "Beyond White Theology." *Christianity & Crisis* 30 (November 2 & 16, 1970): 229–235.

Sherif, Carolyn W., and Sherif, Muzafer. *Attitude, Ego-Involvement and Change.* New York: Wiley, 1967.

Shiner, Larry. *The Secularization of History: An Introduction to the Theology of Friederich Gogarten.* Nashville: Abingdon, 1966.

Shupe, Anson; Spielman, Roger; and Stigall, Sam. "Deprogramming: The New Exorcism." *American Behavioral Scientist* 20, no. 6 (August 1977): 941–956.

———. "Deprogramming and the Emerging Anti-Cult Movement." Paper presented at the meetings of the Society for the Scientific Study of Religion, October 1977.

Sklare, Marshall. *Conservative Judaism: An American Religious Movement.* New York: Free Press, 1955.

Slater, Phillip E. *Microcosm: Structural, Functional, and Religious Evolution in Groups.* New York: Wiley, 1966.

———. *The Pursuit of Loneliness: American Culture at the Breaking Point.* Boston: Beacon, 1970.

Smelser, Neil J. *Theory of Collective Behavior.* New York: Free Press, 1963.

Smith, Rockwell C. *The Church in Our Town.* Nashville: Abingdon-Cokesbury, 1945.

Sontag, Frederick. *Sun Myung Moon and the Unification Church.* Nashville: Abingdon, 1977.

Stanner, W. E. H. "The Dreaming." In *Australian Signpost,* ed. by T. A. G. Hunderford, pp. 51–65. Melbourne: Cheshire, 1956.

Stark, Rodney, and Glock, Charles Y. *American Piety: The Nature of Religious Commitment.* Berkeley: University of California Press, 1968.

Stark, Rodney. "The Economics of Piety: Religion and Social Class." In *Issues in Social Inequality,* ed. by Gerald W. Theilbar and Saul D. Feldman. Boston: Little, Brown, 1971.

Stark, Rodney; Foster, Bruce; Glock, Charles; and Quinley, Harold. *Wayward Shepherds.* New York: Harper & Row, 1971.

Stark, Werner. *The Sociology of Religion: A Study of Christendom.* 4 vols. New York: Fordham University Press, 1967.

Stein, Maurice R. *The Eclipse of Community.* Princeton: Princeton University Press, 1960.

Stone, Donald. "The Human Potential Movement." In *The New Religious Consciousness,* ed. by Charles Glock and Robert Bellah, pp. 93–115. Berkeley: University of California Press, 1976.

Stylianopoulos, Theodore G. "The Orthodox Church in America." *Annals of the Academy of Political and Social Science* 387 (January 1970): 41–48.

Swanson, Guy E. *The Birth of the Gods.* Ann Arbor: University of Michigan Press, 1960.

Thomas, W. I., and Znaniecki, Florian. *The Polish Peasant in Europe and America.* New York: Knopf, 1927.

Tillich, Paul. *Political Expectations.* New York: Harper & Row, 1971.

Tönnies, Ferdinand. *Gemeinschaft und Gesellschaft.* Trans. by Charles A. Loomis. East Lansing: Michigan State University Press, 1957.

Tracy, Phil. "The Jesus Freaks: Life on Sunset Strip." *Commonweal* 93, no. 5 (October 30, 1970): 122–125.

Troeltsch, Ernst. *The Social Teaching of the Christian Churches.* Trans. by Olive Wyon. New York: Harper, 1960.

Turner, Victor W. *The Forest of Symbols: Aspects of Ndembu Ritual.* Ithaca, N.Y.: Cornell University Press, 1967.

Underwood, Kenneth. *The Church, the University, and Social Policy: The Danforth Study of Campus Ministries.* Middletown, Conn.: Wesleyan University Press, 1967.

Vallier, Ivan. *Catholicism, Social Control, and Modernization in Latin America.* Englewood Cliffs, N.J.: Prentice-Hall, 1970.

van der Leeuw, G. *Religion in Essence and Manifestation.* Trans. by J. E. Turner. London: Allen & Unwin, 1938.

Verdesi, Elizabeth Howell. *In But Still Out: Women in the Church.* Philadelphia: Westminster, 1976.

Vernon, Glenn M. *Sociology of Religion.* New York: McGraw-Hill, 1962.

Vitz, Paul C. *Psychology as Religion: The Cult of Self-Worship.* Grand Rapids, Mich.: Eerdmans, 1977.

Wach, Joachim. *The Sociology of Religion.* Chicago: University of Chicago Press, 1944.

Wallace, Anthony, F. C. *Religion: An Anthropological View.* New York: Random House, 1966.

Wallis, Roy. *The Road to Total Freedom: A Sociological Analysis of Scientology.* New York: Columbia University Press, 1977.

Washington, Joseph R., Jr. *Black Religion.* Boston: Beacon, 1964.

———. *The Politics of God.* Boston: Beacon, 1967.

Watts, Alan W. *Myth and Ritual in Christianity.* Boston: Beacon, 1968.

Weber, Max. *Ancient Judaism.* Trans. and ed. by Hans Gerth and Don Martindale. New York: Free Press, 1952.

———. *From Max Weber: Essays in Sociology.* Trans. and ed. by Hans H. Gerth and C. Wright Mills. New York: Oxford University Press, 1946.

――――. *On Charisma and Institution Building.* Ed. by S. N. Eisenstadt. Chicago: University of Chicago Press, 1968.

――――. *The Religion of China.* Trans. by Hans Gerth. New York: Free Press, 1951.

――――. *The Religion of India.* Trans. and ed. by Hans Gerth and Don Martindale. New York: Free Press, 1958.

――――. *The Protestant Ethic and the Spirit of Capitalism.* Trans. by Talcott Parsons. London: Allen & Unwin, 1930.

――――. *The Sociology of Religion.* Trans. by Ephraim Fischoff. Boston: Beacon, 1963.

Westley, Frances. " 'The Cult of Man': Durkheim's Predictions and New Religious Movements." *Sociological Analysis* 39, no. 2 (1978): 135–145.

Wills, Gary. "What Religious Revival?" *Psychology Today* 11, no. 11 (1978): 74–81.

Wilson, Bryan, ed. *Patterns of Sectarianism.* London: Neinemann, 1967.

――――. *Religion in Secular Society.* Baltimore: Penguin, 1969.

Winter, Gibson. *The Suburban Captivity of the Churches.* Garden City, N.Y.: Doubleday, 1961.

Wood, Leland Foster. "Church Problems in Marriage Education." *Annals of the American Academy of Political and Social Science* 272 (November 1950): 171–178.

Woodson, Carter Godwin. *The History of the Negro Church.* Washington, D.C.: Associated Publishers, 1921.

Wuthnow, Robert. *The Consciousness Reformation.* Berkeley: University of California Press, 1976.

――――. *Experimentation in American Religion.* Berkeley: University of California Press, 1978.

Yinger, J. Milton. *Religion in the Struggle for Power.* New York: Russell & Russell, 1961.

――――. *The Scientific Study of Religion.* New York: Macmillan, 1970.

――――. *Sociology Looks at Religion.* New York: Macmillan, 1963.

Zaretsky, Irving I., and Leone, Mark P., eds. *Religious Movements in Contemporary America.* Princeton: Princeton University Press, 1974.

Index

Abortion, 163, 165
Adams, James L., 213, 215
Adaptive function, 33
Adjustive function, 33
Adult education, 260
Africa, 93–94
Alienation, 60, 276–277, 289, 297
Alinski, Saul, 237
American Council on Education, 185
American Friends Service
    Committee, 209
American way of life, 81–83
Amish, 182–183, 208
Anabaptist, 293
Anabaptist-Mennonite tradition,
    separation of church and state
    in, 208–209
Anglican Church, 146, 179
Anomie, 61, 289, 290, 292, 296–298
Anti-Defamation League of B'nai
    B'rith, 218
Antitherapy, 35
Anxiety, 32, 89
Apostolic succession, 264
Aquinas, Thomas, 99
Archaic religion, 66, 86–90, 95
    See also Primitive religion
Asceticism, inner-worldly, 108, 110,
    144, 227
Attitudes, 48
    See also Beliefs

Authoritarian leadership, 296–298
Autonomy of local congregations,
    264

Babbie, Earl, 162
Baptism, 159
Baptists, 114, 184, 213, 242
    black, 147
Becker, Howard, 54, 121, 122, 124,
    128, 131
Beckford, James, 251–253
Beliefs, 46–62, 138
    Type A (primitive, supported by
        full consensus), 47, 52, 54, 56,
        61
    Type B (primitive, with no
        consensual support), 47,
        50–51, 61
    Type C (authority), 47, 49, 51, 52,
        56, 59, 61
    Type D (derived), 47, 51, 52, 59,
        60
    Type E (inconsequential), 47,
        52–53, 60
Bellah, Robert, 43, 65, 80, 86, 88, 93,
    95, 96, 97, 105, 118, 121, 124,
    128, 229–230, 275, 277, 283
Bennett, John C., 213
Berger, Peter L., 18, 60, 82, 228,
    276

333

Passover, 77
Patrick, Ted, 299
Patterning, 5–6
Paul, St., 112
Pentecostalism, 285–286, 292, 306
People's Temple, 296–298
Permissiveness, sexual, 165–166
Perpetuative nativism, 283
Pfeffer, Leo, 206
Pinchot, Gifford, 253–254
Pluralism, 105, 118, 202, 312–313
Political activities by churches,
    213–223, 297
    See also Christian socialism; Social
        Gospel
Political behavior and attitudes,
    201–206
Political solutions, religious sectarian
    solution vs., 111–112
Poor, the, 231–233, 237, 296, 297
Practice, religious, 139
    See also Ritual
Presbyterian polity, 264
Presbyterians, 120, 211–212, 220,
    262, 263, 294
Prescriptive society, 122
Priests (priesthood), 76, 86–90,
    95–97, 100
    See also Clergy
Primer, Ben, 266
Primitive religion, 65, 69–71, 80, 86,
    105
    civil religion and, 81–84
    communal cults and, 69, 76–80
    individualistic cults and, 69, 70
    shamanic cults and, 69, 71–76
    See also Archaic religion
Principal society, 123
Privatization, 247
Profane, distinctions between the
    sacred and, 11, 14–18
    See also Secularization
Projection, 31–32
Prophetic inquiry, campus ministry
    and, 196–197
"Prophetic ministry of the church,"
    212–214, 220, 221

See also Transformationist view of
    church-state relations
Prophets, 105
    ethical, 152
    ethical vs. exemplary, 118
    Hebrew, 104, 108
Protestant ethic, 113–114, 226, 230
Protestant evangelicalism, 282–285
Protestantism (Protestant churches),
    43, 81–82, 92
    capitalism and, 143–144
    as early modern religion, 108–116
    institutionalization and, 123,
        124–125
    as member-oriented, 261–262
    political activity and, 219–223
    process orientation of, 123
    See also Calvinism; and specific
        denominations, churches, sects,
        and other topics
Protestant Reformation, 108–110,
    113, 123, 152, 153, 171, 178,
    228, 230
Protestants
    evangelical, 210, 282–285
    kin-group involvement of,
        161–162
Protestants and Other Americans
    United for the Separation of
    the Church and State (POAU),
    210
Psychology, 274
    developmental, 170–171
    humanistic, 275
Public schools, 179–188
    Bible reading in, 185
    factual study of religion in, 185
    prayer in, 184–185
    religious training in, 183–184
Puritans, 179

Quakers, 114, 147
    church-state relations and, 209
Quebedeaux, Richard, 236, 282–286,
    304
Quick, Bernard, 241

DATE DUE

4 Oct 81			
GAYLORD			PRINTED IN U.S.A.